MW01241367

Beloved Lover

The Priesthood in the Song of Songs

Gregory Cleveland, OMV

En Route Books and Media, LLC
Saint Louis, MO

Make the time

En Route Books and Media, LLC

5705 Rhodes Avenue

St. Louis, MO 63109

Contact us at **contact@enroutebooksandmedia.com**

Cover Credit: Julius Schnorr von Carolsfeld (1794-1872)

"The Wedding at Cana" (1819)

Copyright 2023 Gregory Cleveland, OMV

ISBN-13: 979-8-88870-088-4

Library of Congress Control Number: 2023945477

Table of Contents

Introduction

"Romance is the deepest thing in life; romance is deeper even than reality."[1] We know the power of a love story or a romantic film to evoke strong emotion, even to move us to tears. Every love story ever written is a faint version of the sacred romance of the ages, the divinely inspired Scriptures. God is the author of the most amazing romance ever told. His passionate imprint is inscribed into the tablet of every human heart. That is why, whether we realize it or not, it is the standard by which every love story should be measured. Romance traverses the epochs of human history. It never grows old or goes out of fashion. You and I were born into God's romance, drawn into the eternal circle of love of the Father, Son, and Spirit.

The love story of God and human beings begins in the first book of Scripture, Genesis with the creation of man and woman and his marriage covenant with them. The romance then progresses until the book of Revelation and the wedding feast of the Lamb with his bride, the Church. About halfway through the Bible, the Song of Songs describes, in lush tones, the beauty of the Lord's intimate relationship with his people. The author uses the image of the Lord as Bridegroom and of his people as bride. The bride desires to be pursued and loved by her Bridegroom, and her Bridegroom takes her as his chosen beloved. On the surface, the Song of Songs appears merely to be a passionate dialogue between these two lovers that intensifies their union and appreciation of one another. A deeper reading of the Song of Songs reveals the bride's transformation as she grows in awareness of the bridegroom, which parallels our growth in holiness.

---

[1] G. K. Chesterton, *Heretics*, XIV (New York, John Lane Company, 1919) Christian Classics Ethereal Library Website, http://www.gkc.org.uk/gkc/books/heretics/ch14.html

1

The rich literal meaning of the Song of Songs includes references to the Temple and Israel's love and worship of the Lord. Citing the Song of Songs, Brant Pitre notes that in the Jewish tradition, "the wedding of God and Israel is consummated through sacrifice and worship. ... Jesus himself will unite mankind to God through an act of sacrificial worship."[2] In Hosea 2:19, the Lord passionately declares to Israel: "And I will take you for my wife forever; I will take you for my wife in righteousness and in justice, in steadfast love, and in mercy." These passages clearly reveal the Lord as the divine Bridegroom who espouses Israel as his bride. The Song of Songs describes the nature of their love relationship.

In later New Testament Passages, Jesus calls himself the Bridegroom, fulfilling the figure of the lover of the Song. He said that while he, the Bridegroom, was with his disciples they should not fast, but that when he was taken away, they would fast (cf. Mk 2: 18-20). John the Baptist proclaimed of Jesus: "He who has the bride is the bridegroom" (Jn 3: 29). John considered himself the friend and herald of the bridegroom, who stands and hears him, rejoicing greatly at the bridegroom's voice. The role of the bridegroom in Israel was to bring the wine for the wedding feast. The Scriptures affirm that when the Messiah comes, the hills will flow with wine. At the wedding feast of Cana, Jesus, as Messiah and Bridegroom, fulfills this expectation by changing the water into wine in abundance. Paul notes that as Bridegroom "Christ also loved the church and gave Himself up for her, so that He might sanctify her, having cleansed her by the washing of water with the word, that He might present to Himself the church in all her glory, having no spot or wrinkle or any such thing; but that she would be holy and blameless" (Eph. 5: 25-27). Finally, in Revelation the marriage of the Lamb (Christ) comes and the bride (the Church)

---

[2] Brant Pitre, *Jesus the Bridegroom, The Greatest Love Story Ever Told* (New York, Image, 2014), 27.

makes herself ready to welcome him. Christ is the Lamb, and the Church is the bride, the New Jerusalem that has come down from heaven, adorned for her husband (cf. Rev. 20-21).

Jesus fulfills his role as bridegroom by giving his life in sacrifice for his bride. He washes her by water and the word, by Baptism and preaching, to make her holy and spotless. Jesus takes his bride to himself and makes her one body with him in the Church. He continues to save and sanctify his bride, to make her one with himself through his ministerial priests in the Church. When he washes the Apostles' feet, he tells them they must do to others as he has done to them. He also tells them that the things he does they will also do, and even greater things besides (cf. John 14:12). Whose sins they forgive, they are forgiven (cf. John 20:23). They are also to celebrate the Eucharistic mystery, to "do this in memory of me" (Lk. 22:19). As the priest acts *in persona Christi Capitis*, "in the person of Christ the Head" (of the Church), he acts as Christ the Bridegroom. St. John Paul II speaks of this mystery in the life of the priest:

> Hence Christ stands "before" the Church and "nourishes and cherishes her" (Eph. 5 :29), giving his life for her. The priest is called to be the living image of Jesus Christ, the spouse of the Church. Of course, he will always remain a member of the community as a believer alongside his other brothers and sisters who have been called by the Spirit, but in virtue of his configuration to Christ, the head and shepherd, the priest stands in this spousal relationship with regard to the community. Inasmuch as he represents Christ, the head, shepherd and spouse of the Church, the priest is placed not only in the Church but also in the forefront of the Church. In his spiritual life, therefore, he is called to live out Christ's spousal love toward the Church, his bride. Therefore, the priest's life ought to radiate this spousal character, which demands that he be a witness to Christ's spousal love and thus

be capable of loving people with a heart which is new, generous and pure—with genuine self-detachment, with full, constant, and faithful dedication and at the same time with a kind of "divine jealousy" (cf. 2 Cor. 11:2) and even with a kind of maternal tenderness, capable of bearing "the pangs of birth" until "Christ be formed" in the faithful (cf. Gal. 4:19).[3]

Much of this book's application of the Song of Songs to the life of priests will therefore be about the priest acting in the person of Christ as Bridegroom. Christ the Bridegroom kisses his bride with the Holy Spirit and his Word. He looks upon her with mercy, forgives her, and redeems her. He shepherds her and feeds her at his banquet table. "It is the Eucharist above all that expresses the redemptive act of Christ the Bridegroom towards the Church the Bride."[4] The Bridegroom is always present to his bride. He lays down his life in dying for her, to wash her by baptism and initiate her into his life. By his resurrection he establishes his kingship, governing his bride in love. He calls her first to be with him and then to go forth with him throughout the land to harvest the fruits of evangelization. He incorporates her into the Temple of his body where she worships. He forms her in communion with himself and others. The priest manifests this identity of Christ, the Bridegroom:

---

[3] St. John Paul II, *Pastores Dabo Vobis*, 22 (Vatican City, Libreria Editrice Vaticana, 1992), Vatican Website, https://www.vatican.va/content/john-paul-ii/en/apost_exhortations/documents/hf_jp-ii_exh_ 25031992_pastores-dabo-vobis.html

[4] St. John Paul II, *Mulieris Dignitatem*, 26 (Vatican Website, Libreria Editrice Vaticana, 1988), Vatican Website, https://www.vatican.va/content/john-paul-ii/en/apost_letters/1988/documents/hf_jp-ii_apl_19880815_mulieris-dignitatem.html

The priest finds the full truth of his identity in being a derivation, a specific participation in and continuation of Christ himself, the one high priest of the new and eternal covenant. The priest is a living and transparent image of Christ the priest. The priesthood of Christ, the expression of his absolute "newness" in salvation history, constitutes the one source and essential model of the priesthood shared by all Christians and the priest in particular.[5]

The essential key for discerning the reality of priesthood is through its orientation to Christ.

Priests are also members of the community of Christ's body. Priests act not only *in persona Christi*, but *in persona Ecclesia*— "in the person of the Church." As mediators, they manifest not only Christ to his Church, but the Church to Christ, and ultimately, the Father. "Through the ministry of the priests, the spiritual sacrifice of the faithful is made perfect in union with the sacrifice of Christ. He is the only mediator who in the name of the whole Church is offered sacramentally in the Eucharist and in an unbloody manner until the Lord himself comes."[6] Priests are disciples alongside the lay faithful and their brothers. While they are set apart for holiness of life and service, they are in no way separated from any of Christ's faithful. "They cannot be of service to men if they remain strangers to the life and conditions of men (Cf. 1 Cor 10:33). Their ministry itself, by a special title, forbids that they be conformed to this world (Jn 3:8.); yet at the same time it requires that they live in this world among men."[7]

---

[5] St. John Paul II, *Pastores Dabo Vobis*, 12.

[6] Vatican Council II, *Presbyterorem Ordinis*, 2 (Vatican City,Libreria Editrice Vaticana, 1965), Vatican Website, https://www.vatican.va/archive/hist_councils/ii_vatican_council/documents/vat-ii_decree_19651207_presbyterorum-ordinis_en.html

[7] Ibid., 3.

Given that the priest is member of the Church, he is also a spouse of Christ. He is already configured to Christ through baptism to be one in heart with him in the most profound way. Marital union is the best analogy we have for the union that we experience with Christ. Of course, all analogies limp, and the union we have with Christ through baptism is much greater than marital union. In considering Christ as Bridegroom, the priest also fulfills the spousal role of the bride in the Song of Songs. Though women more naturally image the bride's receptive love, men also participate in this bridal receptivity. Both the male and female members of the body of Christ participate in the Bridal nature of the Church: "in the Church every human being—male and female—is the 'Bride,' in that he or she accepts the love of Christ the Redeemer, and seeks to respond to it with the gift of his or her own person."[8] As the bride symbolizes the disciple of Christ, priests should also be aware of their intense spousal discipleship. They should cling to Christ by sharing their whole lives in friendship with him. They should live in holy, familiar, and attentive union with the Father, through Christ, in the Holy Spirit. Priests must also take the lead as disciples and members of the Church in seeking the things of Jesus Christ.[9]

The application of the Song of Songs to the life of priests will therefore acknowledge the priest as spouse and disciple of Christ the Bridegroom. The priest is evangelized by the Word and the kiss of the Holy Spirit. He is forgiven, redeemed, and purified in God's mercy. He is shepherded in the ways of the Lord and fed in his banquet hall. In daily prayer, he renews his commitment to Christ, his spouse, and grows in deep intimacy with the Lord. As bride, he is called to "arise and come," to leave everything to

---

[8] St. John Paul II, *Mulieris Dignitatem*, 25.

[9] See Vatican Council II, *Optatam Totius*, 12 (Libreria Editrice Vaticana, 1965), Vatican Website, https://www.vatican.va/archive/hist_councils/ii_vatican_council/documents/vat-ii_decree_19651028_optatam-totius_en.html

follow Christ. He receives the gift of salvation from the cross of Christ and shares in his sufferings. The priest is subject to the authority of Christ in his life of obedience. He goes forth with Christ in mission and, like the bride, bears Christ's very imprint or seal as his representative. Before he is ever a teacher, the priest is a disciple of the Lord. He is a man of communion in the Church as the bride of Christ, which is also Christ's body. The priest as spouse is truly "married to Christ" in a way that transcends natural marital union.

Within the fundamental images of priest as spouse of Christ and bridegroom of the Church, I will treat many other images of the priest that emerge from the Song of Songs in this book. The priest is preacher of God's word. He is the minister of mercy and healing. He is the shepherd who guides the flock. Like Jesus who dwelt among us, the priest is a constant presence to his people. The priest as father generates the new life of Christ in the hearts of the faithful through the power of word and sacrament. He is a fatherly provider of food to nourish his family. In imitation of Christ, the priest offers himself as sacrificial victim for his bride. The kingship and rule of the risen Christ is mediated through the priest. The priest as a man of communion brings the people into fellowship with God and one another. He is evangelizer and teacher in the ways of holiness. As leader of worship, he calls down the Holy Spirit as a consuming fire. In these and many other images and roles, the priest radiates the beauty of Christ the Bridegroom, and perfects the beauty of Christ's bride, the Church.

Chapter 1

Seek His Face

The Song of Songs, which is Solomon's.

> O that he would kiss me with the kisses of your mouth!
> For your love is better than wine,
> your anointing oils are fragrant,
> your name is oil poured out;
> therefore the maidens love you.
> Draw me after you, let us make haste.
> The king has brought me into his chambers.
> We will exult and rejoice in you;
> we will extol your love more than wine;
> rightly do they love you. (Sg 1:1-4)

I witnessed the glory of God in the third grade. I was at St. Patrick's elementary school in Largo, FL, and early morning classes had just begun. My teacher was Mrs. Gaudette, a stout and formidable woman with a quick temper. Though she was good and kind, our whole class was terrified of her when she would show anger. Her face would turn red, her eyes bulge, and she would raise her bellowing voice. One morning, in the middle of the first class of the day, a request came for altar servers for the daily mass that was about to happen at the Church, which was just a stone's throw away from our school. Mrs. Gaudette surveyed the class and asked the boys who would like to go? At the opportunity to get out of class, a flurry of hands went up, with the usual "ooh, ooh"—each desperate to be called upon to go. Mrs. Gaudette noticed that a couple boys did not have their hands up, I being one of them. She then queried, "Who here has never served mass before?" Sheepishly, I held my hand up. Get over there right now," she ordered. I jumped quickly and dutifully obeyed her command.

Pretty soon, I was in the sacristy and my classmate Craig was waiting for me to show me the ropes. I was fitted with a red cassock and white surplice. He gave me the easy job. "You can do patten," which meant holding the communion plate. When I got out into the sanctuary at the start of the holy Mass, I was completely awestruck. During the Eucharistic prayer I was kneeling to the side of the altar, looking up past the long curtains to the giant crucifix of our Lord. I felt a holy fear in God's presence and at the same time a deep longing in my heart for Jesus and his salvation. God seemed so other, so beyond, and yet so terrifyingly close, seizing my heart. Still trembling, the time came for Holy Communion. Who presented herself but my mother, who attended mass daily after she dropped us kids off at school. I perceived a look of delight on her face as she saw me approaching, holding the gold-colored plate under her chin as Father McCall gave her the sacred Host. When mass was over, Craig showed me around the sanctuary a bit more, and I continued to be fascinated by the holy objects and spaces. He flashed the tabernacle curtains open and closed and gasped "don't look in there!" I was at once fearful and curious about what was inside.

Seeing Beyond the Veil

The holiness of God at once attracts and repels us. We are fascinated and drawn by his beauty and glory, while, at the same time, overwhelmed by dread and fear. This is true of human beings throughout salvation history. The Jews longed to see the face of God, while believing that no one could see that face and live. Moses proved to be the exception. Moses first encountered the Lord in an indirect and sacramental way in the burning bush, when the Lord revealed his name, "I Am," to Moses. However, when

God led the Israelites into the desert, Moses encountered the Lord face to face in the meeting tent. There he spoke with the Lord, as one friend speaks to another (cf. Ex 33:11). When Moses descended from Mount Sinai with the tablets of the covenant, he was not aware that the skin of his face was shining from his speaking with God. Aaron and the Israelites were terribly frightened by his appearance. After Moses revealed the Commandments to them, he veiled his face. He would only remove the veil to go back into the tent to meet with the Lord. Again, he related what the Lord spoke to him and again he veiled his face because it was shining. (cf. Ex 4:29-35)

Moses prefigures Jesus, who is a new and greater Moses. Whereas Moses encountered God only indirectly, Jesus has the direct vision of the Father. Jesus beholds the Father's glory, and Jesus himself is glorified. His face is radiant as the fullness of the revelation of God. He is one with the Father and intercedes with the Father on our behalf. He does the Father's will and reveals the Father to us. Jesus forever gazes upon the Father and only desires to glorify him by the light, love, suffering, and purity of his soul. Jesus lives forever to intercede for us before his Father (cf. Heb 7:25). According to Archbishop Luis Maria Martinez of Mexico City:

> Begotten by the Father, in his holy image, bearing his divine physiognomy, constituting his glory, Jesus yearns unspeakably to attract and present all to his heavenly Father. ... The Incarnate Word, like a flower opening to the sun, has opened his entire being to receive the glory of the Father, to reflect it, pure and complete. Jesus receives not only the rays of the eternal sun but the Sun itself, with its glorious light, its infinite fire, and its eternal life.[1]

---

[1] Luiz Maria Martinez, *Only Jesus*, Tranl. Sr. Mary St. Daniel, B.V.M (Providence, RI, Cluny Media, 2020), 59.

With Jesus, the veil of the old covenant is set aside for the freedom of the Spirit. The Spirit now grants us a vision of the glory of the Lord, as though reflected in a mirror, and calls us to be transformed into Christ's image by increasing degrees of glory (cf. 2 Cor 3:7-17).

As intercessor before God on behalf of his people, and interlocutor from God to Israel, Moses was truly a priest (cf. Ps 99:6). Additionally, Moses appointed seventy elders to function as priests and to assist him in the task of governing the people. The Spirit descended upon them, and they prophesied. The firstborn sons of Israel had originally been chosen to be priests. When they failed to uphold God's law at Sinai, God took the priesthood away from them and gave it to the Levites, who had served him faithfully.

Intimacy with the Son

Moses models the essential intimacy that priests are to have with the Lord, encountering the Lord face to face, or, more accurately in the translation of the Hebrew, mouth to mouth, in the meeting tent. In the Song of Songs, the bride desires this same loving encounter with her Bridegroom, mouth to mouth, the very kiss of God. This indescribable kiss of God is the communication of the Holy Spirit in union and intimacy. According to St. Bernard, the Holy Spirit was communicated by the Savior to his Apostles in the form of breath (Jn 20:22), which was like a kiss from Him, so that we might comprehend that it proceeds from the Father and the Son, as a genuine shared kiss.[2] The love and intimacy of the Father and Son spirals forth in the third person of the Trinity, the Holy Spirit, who is the bond of

---

[2] See St. Bernard, *On the Song of Songs*, Sermon 8, no. 2, Patristic Bible Commentary Website, https://sites.google.com/site/aquinasstudybible/home/song-of-songs/st-bernard-on-the-song-of-songs

love between them. This same Spirit communicated to our human spirits brings the fullness of divine love and peace to our souls. According to the Spanish Jesuit Baltasar Gracian:

> The mouth is the desire; and God's Love is nothing but the joining of our desire with the desire of Christ, to want what Christ wants, to desire what He desires, to surrender our own will to the divine, and to be in peace with Him; for when it is pleasurable, sweet, and gentle and a gift, love is very properly signified by the mouth. And since the soul does not have it from her own resources…, she asks it from God….[3]

The Bridegroom's love draws the bride, and she will live by his Spirit. She will no longer live in herself, but in Jesus Christ who has drawn her. By this same love, the Lord reveals his holy inspirations to us and makes us fall deeply in love with him, transforming us into him, becoming one Spirit with him (cf. 1 Cor 6:17). Gazing upon the face of the Lord, we are transfigured from glory to glory (cf. 2 Cor 3:17). We are called to die to ourselves and to all that is not God, and to live only that which is God. The Lord takes upon himself our weaknesses and communicates to us the strength of his Spirit. According to St. Ambrose, it is this completely spiritual kiss by which the soul is united with the Word and through which "a transfusion of the Divine Spirit is brought about within her…just as those who give one another the kiss of peace not only join lips but pour forth

---

[3] Baltasar Gracian, S.J., in Father Juan G. Arintero, O.P., *The Song of Songs, A Mystical Exposition*, Transl. James Valender and Jose L. Morales (Rockford, IL, Tan Books and Publishers, 1992), 45.

their hearts and souls into those of the other."[4] Jesus pours out his Holy Spirit upon us to make us intimately one in Spirit with Him.

Jesus' entire Last Supper Discourse (Jn 14-17) is an expression of intimacy with his Father and of intimacy with his Apostle-priests,[5] with whom he wishes to share his love of the Father. Jesus saves his most tender and loving words for his priests as he nears the moment of his death. He goes to prepare a place for them, that where he is they may follow and be with him for all eternity (cf. Jn 14:2-4). If they ask for anything in his name, he will grant it to them (Jn 14:13-14). He leaves them the gift of peace so that their hearts will not be troubled. He promises to send the Holy Spirit as their Advocate and Counselor (cf. Jn 14:26-27). Jesus uses the rich imagery of a vine and its branches to illustrate that they are to abide in him as he abides in them (cf. Jn 15:1, 4). He has chosen them as friends who are to go and bear fruit (Jn 15:15-16). They are to love one another as he has loved them, even to the point of laying down their lives for him and one another (cf. Jn 15:12-13).

As practicing Jews, the Apostles understood the showbread of the temple (which would later be a figure of the holy Eucharist) as the symbol or face of God's presence. In an even more profound manner, the Lord draws us as priests into this blessed intimacy in the Sacrament of his Body and Blood, which is his real presence to us. "I am the bread of life ... Eat my flesh and drink my blood ... Whoever eats my flesh and drinks my blood lives in me and I in him" (Jn 6). Because of his incarnation, death, and resurrection, the face of Jesus' presence is real in the transubstantiated bread of the holy Eucharist. The greatest form of public prayer is the Holy

---

[4] St. Ambrose, *Concerning Virgins, To Marcellina, His Sister,* in *The Early Church Fathers and Other Works* (Edinborough: Eerdman's, 1867). Note: the kiss of peace was common among early Christians, but fell out of practice.

[5] Jesus offers this same intimacy with every Christian, but the Apostles were the first to experience it.

Sacrifice of the Mass in which Jesus communicates his very being to us. When I received Holy Communion at the mass of my ordination, I trembled in mystical awe of the Lord's presence to me. As I heard the choir sing Psalm 23 by composer John Rutter, I knew in the deepest part of who I am that The Lord would be my Shepherd. He would lead me and nourish me in green pastures. He would always be by my side as my intimate friend and guardian. I did not need to fear the evil valleys of the shadow of death. Together with him I would dwell in the house of the Lord as a priest all the days of my life.

The Church as the sacrament of Christ makes present and reveals the face of Christ to every person. She is the ongoing manifestation of the Incarnate Christ. The Church realizes her purpose of making Christ present when she performs her three-fold office of teaching, sanctifying, and governing, especially through the ministerial priesthood. The priest's mission is to mediate the presence of Christ and Christ's face." Human beings have the inalienable right to be able to see the face of the Lord in the face of the Church, in order that in her and through her they can see and contemplate him." [6] In her teaching office, she manifests the face of Christ the Teacher in his Word proclaimed in and by the Church. [7] It is Christ who speaks through the mouth of the Church. The Church also manifests the face of Christ the Priest in her office of sanctifying: "Christ is always present in his Church, especially in her liturgical celebrations. He is present in the sacrifice of the Mass, not only in the person of his minister, ... but especially in

---

[6] *The Face of Christ in the Face of the Church*, 2, Congregation for the Causes of Saints (Libreria Editrice Vaticana), 2002, Vatican Website, https://www.vatican.va/roman_curia/congregations/csaints/documents/rc_con_csaints_doc_20021210_martins-rosto-de-cristo_en.html

[7] See *Dei Verbum*, 10, *Lumen Gentium*, 24-25, *Sacrosanctum Concilium* 7 (Libreria Editrice Vaticana, 1965), https://www.vatican.va/archive/hist_councils/ii_vatican_council/index.htm

the Eucharistic species. By his power he is present in the sacraments, so that when a man baptizes, it is really Christ himself who baptizes."[8] Finally, the Church makes present the face of Christ the King in performing her office of governing. Priests participate in the bishop's office of governing the particular churches entrusted to them as "vicars of Christ"[9] in his name. The priest's mission is to bring every human person into a complete identification with Jesus, to become an ever-fuller reflection of his face. Each Christian is called to become another Christ, sharing in his life and mission.

We can contemplate the grace given to us in the Holy Eucharist to more profoundly internalize the mysteries of Christ and to practice them more assiduously. Christ lives his mysteries in us and desires that we participate in his very life, death, and resurrection. During my experience of the thirty-day Ignatian Spiritual Exercises, my heart was conformed to Jesus' heart in contemplating his mysteries. At the beginning, I experienced the mercy of God as I considered my life of sin, judgment, repentance, and forgiveness. The more I looked at my sin, the more I felt Jesus' mercy. The Lord purified me with the white-hot flame of love from his burning heart. My experience of forgiveness corresponded to the Penitential Rite of Mass with the exclamation, "Lord, have mercy!"

As the retreat progressed, I pondered the incarnation, hidden life, and public ministry of Jesus as a disciple. I felt awe at the Word made Flesh in the womb of Mary, heartfelt devotion at his birth and infancy, and humility at his hidden life. I experienced his compelling call to follow him closely by sharing his way of life and values. I was amazed at his miracles. Through my imagination, he enabled me to walk on the water toward him in the face of the storms of doubt produced by the enemy. I was also struck by

---

[8] *Sacrosanctum Concilium*, 7.
[9] See *Lumen Gentium*, 27.

the real humanity of Jesus, how he took our weakness upon himself, being tempted in every way that we are (cf. Heb 4:15). These contemplations corresponded to the Liturgy of the Word of the Mass and the memory of Christ's life and teaching proclaimed and interpreted. It also corresponded to the Body of Christ in the Liturgy of the Eucharist as "Christ in his servant state, distinguished by possibility, poverty, the Cross; the Word 'made flesh,' who worked sweated, suffered, prayed among us."[10]

In the final phase of the Spiritual Exercises, I was immersed into the passion, death, and resurrection of Jesus. Jesus hid his divinity and became vulnerable to the ravages of evil and suffering. He manifested his willingness to bear contempt and rejection by his own people. I came to realize he suffered all this for me personally, and I could in no way doubt his love. I felt anger at the injustice toward him and wanted to intervene to stop it. Realizing this had to be, I came to cherish his precious outpouring of love. His Resurrection brought me to a place of rejoicing with Jesus for his sake, for his vindication and glorification at the right hand of the Father. I realized his Resurrection meant his glorified presence to me in the Holy Eucharist, and in all the circumstances of my life. He was truly risen and able to manifest himself in and through all persons, places, events, and circumstances of my daily life. I would grow in my ability to perceive his presence, having spiritual eyes to see and spiritual ears to hear. My experience of Jesus' death and resurrection corresponded to the Liturgy of the Eucharist and especially the Lord's Blood poured out in death for our salvation. While his Body especially indicates his life, his Blood especially indicates his death: "Not any kind of death but a violent one, and in the language of the covenant, an expiatory death."[11] As we are washed in the blood of the

---

[10] Raniero Cantalamessa, *The Eucharist, Our Sanctification* (Collegeville, MN: Liturgical Press, 1995), 29.

[11] Ibid., 29.

Lamb, we are cleansed of our sins and our consciences are purified. His blood becomes the "medicine of [our] immortality."[12]

Drawing from this contemplation of the mysteries of the life, death, and resurrection of Jesus enriches our reception of the Body and Blood of Jesus in the Holy Eucharist. His love is discovered to be "better than wine" (cf. Sg 1:2). In contemplation, Jesus takes us into his inner rooms (cf. Sg 1:4) and pours his name (cf. Sg 1:3), his presence upon us. In the Holy Eucharist, we are well-disposed to live in him and he in us (cf. Jn 15:4).

Centered in the Eucharist

As a priest, I find the greatest form of abiding in Jesus to be in Eucharistic Adoration, where our Lord is most fully present to us, face to face and heart to heart, communicating the kiss of his Spirit (cf. Sg 1:2). Since being ordained, the Lord has shone his face upon me and sustained me with the kiss of his Spirit in daily Eucharistic ordination. Throughout my life, my most profound moments of prayer have been before the Blessed Sacrament in the monstrance, where Jesus is shown to us as the Bread of Life. My earliest memories of worship at St. Patrick's elementary school were making the Stations of the Cross combined with exposition of the Blessed Sacrament. The holiness of God was palpable, especially when we finished the ceremony with solemn Benediction, as the Divine Praises were sung by the priest. I felt at once both transcendent awe and profound intimacy with the Lord who had died so that he might become one with me in the Sacrament of Love.

Eucharist-centered prayer continued to be profoundly holy in my young adult years at churches of perpetual adoration. When I joined the

---

[12] St. Ignatius of Antioch, *Epistle to the Ephesians*, 20, 2 New Advent Website, https://www.newadvent.org/fathers/0104.htm

seminary, my deepest longings for the Lord were satisfied in time spent in adoration during our daily holy hour, which laid the foundation of prayer for my future priesthood. Ever since I was ordained, the Lord has shone his face upon me and sustained me with the kiss of his Spirit in daily Eucharistic adoration. It is during these moments that I experience the intimacy of friendship most deeply. In the Eucharist, the Lord calls me not only servant, but also friend. I can reveal the secrets of my heart and know that he understands with compassion. Sometimes, I reveal crushing hardships and become aware of his merciful presence strengthening me. At other times, I rejoice in the consolation of his presence and love. I also understand that he, in turn, desires my presence and love. I seek him because he has sought me, a poor and miserable sinner, delighting in me when I turn to him. I experience his personal call to be with him as his priest, often perceived as an inspiration to engage in certain apostolic activities. Often, I experience my own emptiness and surrender myself into his loving fullness.

The bride's desire for the kiss of her Bridegroom in the Song of Songs mirrors our desire for the Lord's kiss in the Holy Eucharist. This desire becomes all-consuming in us, such that nothing else will satisfy us. In receiving the Holy Eucharist, in adoring the Lord in the Blessed Sacrament, our spiritual hunger and thirst are satisfied. We hunger to be accepted for who we are. We crave relationships that break through our experience of loneliness. We need to feel valued by others, especially God. Jesus is the gratification of all these desires in his Eucharistic presence. He also fulfills our deep desire to have a mission to accomplish and grants the inspiration to carry it out. The bride is contented in receiving the presence and kiss of her Bridegroom.

As human beings we require a faith perspective and tenets of belief to follow. We need hope for our future well-being and that of others. Our hearts constantly desire to be fed with love, which most deeply satisfies our hungers. Finally, there is one yearning that undergirds all other desires—the yearning for eternal life. This is our desire for God himself, who came that we might have life, and have it to the full (cf. Jn 10:10). In the Holy Eucharist, Jesus gives us a foretaste of eternity. When we receive his body, blood, soul, and divinity, it is a sharing in his eternal life. Jesus himself says, "those who eat my flesh and drink my blood have eternal life, and I will raise them up on the last day" (Jn 6:54). Tasting his everlasting life makes us desire all the more to have this life forever.

Jesus draws us to his face and to his heart in the blessed Sacrament of the Eucharist. He draws us to love him in all things and above all things in this world. He draws us to experience eternal life with him, beginning even now and extending to everlasting life. The mystical theologian Pierre Teilhard de Chardin was once inspired by the stories of his friend who was a priest on the battlefields of France during World War I.[13] This priest carried the blessed Sacrament with him in a pyx at his heart and commented: "I suddenly realized just how extraordinary and how disappointing it was to be thus holding so close to oneself the wealth of the world, and the very source of life without being able to possess it inwardly, without being able to either penetrate it or to assimilate it." So, he "gave himself Holy Communion." He consumed the Body of Christ. And yet, his realization was unexpected. The sacred Host had become "flesh of my flesh of my flesh, nevertheless it remained outside of me." He piously gathered his thoughts, humbled himself, and sought only the Lord in a "vain yet blessed attempt!" The priest imagined the blessed Sacrament as always ahead of him, "further on in a greater permeability of my being to the divine influences." While he entered more profoundly into the mystery of the blessed Sacrament, its center was "receding from me as it drew me on."

---

[13] Pierre Teilhard de Chardin, "Christ in the World of Matter," *Hymn of the Universe*, trans. Simon Bartholomew (New York: Harper and Row, 1965), 42-58.

Given that the priest could not penetrate the inner dimension of the blessed Sacrament, he decided to gaze upon the surface. "But there a new infinity awaited me." When he attempted to grasp the surface of the blessed Sacrament, he found that it was "not the host at all but one or other of the thousand entities which make up our lives: a suffering, a joy, a task, a friend to love or to console…" The interior dimension of the blessed Sacrament escaped him and now the exterior of the Sacrament was similarly evading him, "leaving me at grips with the entire universe which had reconstituted itself and drawn itself forth from its sensible appearances." In putting on the mind of Christ (cf, Rom 13:14), he realized that both God and the universe were beyond his comprehension. He merely stated, "I will not dwell on the feeling of rapture produced in me by this revelation of the universe placed between Christ and myself like a magnificent prey." De Chardin was deeply moved to contemplation by the priest's testimony: "After listening to my friend, my heart began to burn within me and my mind awoke to a new and higher vision of things. I began to realize vaguely that the multiplicity of evolutions into which the world process seems to us to be split up is in fact fundamentally the working out of one single mystery…"

The Lord's presence in the Eucharist is a wonderfully captivating, yet elusive mystery. We are possessed by him and desire to capture him but are incapable of doing so. We experience his loving gaze and are invited into his merciful heart. We are changed interiorly by his presence and activity in and through us. If we have Christ, we have all things in their right order and proportion. The mysteries of the universe are present to us and are reduced to the one mystery of his death and resurrection. By his death he gives us his Body and Blood to eat and drink and so become one with him. We are also given the promise of resurrection and the principle by which we are raised on the last day. "Whoever eats my flesh and drinks by blood has eternal life" (Jn 6:54). De Chardin's priest friend is akin to the bride who desires the presence of her Bridegroom and then immediately finds him present (Sg 1:2). Like the bride, he is drawn to hurry to his chambers (Sg 1:4), to the depths of the heart of Christ.

Finding Christ in the Eucharist, and through the Eucharist, his dwelling in our hearts, we are able to discover him in the whole of life. Just as De Chardin's priest friend gained the whole universe in Jesus Christ, everything in the world is now able to lead us to Jesus. We love Christ in all things and above all things. We often think that our life and activities in the world distract us and take us away from God, sapping our divine energy. Far from that, our active life in the world is meant to be the very place of our encounter with God. According to Jean Pierre de Caussade, the Lord is present to us in all our life as surely as he is present to us in the blessed Sacrament.

> I should die of thirst rushing like this from one fountain to another, from one stream to another when there is a sea at hand, the waters of which encompass me on every side. All that happens to me therefore will be food for my nourishment, water for my cleansing, fire for my purification, and a channel of grace for all my needs. That which I might endeavor to find in other ways seeks me incessantly and gives itself to me through all creatures.[14]

God desires to communicate himself to me in every daily experience, and we can seek to encounter God in all persons, places, and events.

In order to find God in all things we must first find him within through contemplative prayer—face to face—just as Moses did in the Holy of

---

[14] Jean Pierre de Caussade, *Abandonment to Divine Providence* (Exeter, England: The Catholic Herald Press, 1921), 32, Internet Archive Website, http//archive.org/details/divineprovidence00causuoft.

Holies. Jesus revealed his name and his face to us in a new Holy of Holies, the Upper Room when he celebrated the Last Supper with his Apostles, giving them his body and blood in the Holy Eucharist. He made them priests through the ritual of washing of feet[15] (cf. Jn 13) and laying on of hands (cf. 1 Tim 4:14; 2 Tim 1:6). As he offered himself in his holy body and blood, he told them to "do this in memory of me" (Lk 22:19), establishing the memorial of his sacrifice to be offered by his priests. In the same Upper Room, he appeared to his Apostles, revealing his risen and glowing face, and his true divine nature, shining through his humanity. He breathed the Spirit upon them and gave them the mission to forgive sins in his name (cf. Jn 20:22). Jesus breathes the same Spirit upon his priests with the specific mission and power to forgive sins in the Sacrament of Penance. Finally, in the same Upper Room the Apostles gathered with Mary to pray and await the coming of the Holy Spirit (Acts 1:14). The Spirit came with a great force of wind and a burning fire of tongues to empower the Apostles to boldly proclaim the good news of Jesus' death and resurrection to the ends of the earth (Acts 2:1-21). The same Spirit is given in abundance to priests to proclaim the good news and confer the sacraments.

Every sanctuary of every church is an Upper Room, a Holy of Holies, in which the priest is renewed in these mysteries and renews them also in the hearts of the faithful. In the sanctuary, the priest is brought into the Bridegroom's chambers and encounters the face of Christ, reflecting that holy face to God's people. The name, the very essence and presence of Jesus is manifested and poured out as an oil in the Spirit to make us one with him and to act in the person of Christ the head of the body, his Church.

---

[15] The washing of feet was a ritual of ordination to priesthood in the Old Testament. Aaron and his sons had their feet washed on the night of their ordination to the priesthood (See Ex 40).

His anointing oils of the Spirit are fragrant and enticing, drawing others to follow Christ through the priest's preaching, teaching, and shepherding of God's people. The kiss of the Spirit is the Lord's presence given to us through the face, mouth, lips, and breath of the Incarnate Son of God. His kiss to us as priests is the face of his friendship, love, and peace that communicates his heart.

Questions for Reflection and Discussion

1. How have I experienced the divine kiss of the Holy Spirit from Jesus and the Father in prayer?
2. What is my experience of "being transfigured from glory to glory" in prayer and in life?
3. How do I experience the face and heart of Christ in Eucharistic adoration?
4. In what way have I felt myself to be the face and heart of Christ in my priestly office of teaching, sanctifying and governing the holy people of God?
5. How has contemplative prayer increased my ability to receive the Lord in the Eucharist in a fuller way?
6. As I find God in the Eucharist, to what degree am I able to find him communicating himself to me in all circumstances of my life?

Prayer Exercises

1. Read the Martinez quote and pray with Moses 33:7-11. Ask for the grace to speak to the Lord face to face, as one friend speaks to another.

2. Consider the St. Bernard quote and pray with Song 1:1-4. Ask for the grace to experience the divine kiss of the Holy Spirit from the Father and the Son.

3. Ponder the importance of being the face of Christ to God's people. Pray with 2 Cor 3:12–4:6 and ask for the grace to be transfigured into his image with ever increasing glory.

4. Reflect on the Teilhard de Chardin story. Pray with Jn 6:35-40 and ask for the grace to rejoice in the fullness of life in Christ in the holy Eucharist.

5. Consider the De Caussade quote. Pray with Eph 3:14-21 and ask for the grace to know the vastness of God's love in all experiences of your life.

Chapter 2

Announcing the Gospel of God

O that he would kiss me with the kisses of your mouth!
For your love is better than wine,
your anointing oils are fragrant,
your name is oil poured out;
therefore the maidens love you.
Draw me after you, let us make haste.
The king has brought me into his chambers.
We will exult and rejoice in you;
we will extol your love more than wine;
rightly do they love you. (Sg 1:2-4)

In 1999, I was heartbroken to learn that I was being transferred to Boston. Heartbroken because my transfer meant leaving my first assignment as a priest at St Andrew's parish in Avenel, New Jersey. At the same time, I was so grateful for the many people with whom I had grown so close, knowing that the support and wisdom they had shared with me would be a blessing in my next ministry as novice master for our Oblate seminarians. My gratitude and sadness increased as my former pastor and I made the trip northward to my new assignment. During our trip, I opened the cards and gifts collected at my farewell party. One card, in particular, from a faithful widow who still had a very active life, resonated deeply with me. She wrote "You don't know how many times I came into Sunday mass with a heavy heart from all my life's burdens and you had just the right words that spoke to my heart and helped me forge ahead. You helped me encounter Jesus." I was humbled, awed, and overjoyed to know that my homilies did not fall on deaf ears, but made an impact on someone's life. And now, the tables turned. Her words touched me in a profoundly personal way, touching my heavy heart and helping me forge ahead. Like many of my fellow priests, I was often not aware of the difference our preaching can make.

After surveying Catholic laity, a national opinion research center concluded that the strongest influence on church attendance and identification as Catholics was not the Church's stance on hot-button issues like sexuality, contraception, abortion, or women's ordination.[1] Instead the greatest influence on Catholic identity and behavior was the quality of the Sunday homily delivered in the interviewee's parish church. In another survey of young adults returning to the Church, the two most important factors were a personal relationship with the priest and the quality of preaching. Finally, in a third study of young adults coming home to the Church, the two most significant variables proved to be a pastoral relationship with one's priest and the quality of preaching.[2] It is notable that here in Denver, Archbishop Chaput would pack the Cathedral with young adults every Sunday evening because of his superb preaching and his pastoral presence. The people of God attest that they see preaching as the most important role of the priest.

Preaching an Encounter

Preaching is not just talking at people, but a real dialogue which evokes a response. It is a confrontation between the divine "I" and the human

---

[1] This is not to say these issues are unimportant or that we should not preach about them. Once we lead people to the encounter with Christ, they will be more ready to accept these more challenging teachings of Christ and his Church.

[2] Cardinal Sean O'Malley, Chrism Mass Homily, *We Are Anointed to Preach God's Word to the Poor*, Catholic Online Website, https://www.catholic.org/featured/headline.php?ID=868

"thou." The preacher is the instrument through which God speaks in a real communication of friendship with those who are open and respond to God with their assent and cooperation. The Spirit who is at work when we preach, opens the hearts of the listeners (cf. Acts 16:14).

For preaching to be effective, we must touch people where they are existentially situated, responding to their deepest needs and questioning. Dominican Father Peter John Cameron, in his book *Why Preach*, notes:

> Experience, then must be the starting point for preaching if it is to be effective. That is to say, the preacher must be aware of his own profound need for truth, beauty, love, goodness, justice, and happiness, and he must be attentive to this condition in his hearers. Recognizing and respecting this fact about the human heart is imperative for preaching. Any answer that a preacher intends to offer his people must be in response to a question. Giving the answer to a question that has never been asked is the perfect definition of boring. The answer might be brilliant, …but if I do not comprehend its relevance to my life, if I cannot grasp how it corresponds to what is urgent and important to me, then it is not worth listening to.[3]

As a priest, I am best prepared to preach when I consider people's desires, questions, concerns, and what answers they may be seeking. Their interests and desires emerge in my ministry to them in the parish, in conversations, during faith sharing in prayer groups, or at a gathering at the Knights of Columbus. All these opportunities provide a window into their thoughts and concerns about current events or issues within their families.

---

[3] Peter John Cameron, *Why Preach, Encountering Christ in God's Word* (San Francisco, Ignatius Press, 2009), 20.

Only then can I address their needs and deepest desires with the gospel and make my preaching relevant and effective.

Jesus is the answer to all the deepest desires of our hearts. People are longing for an encounter with Christ, his kisses which are the words that come from his mouth. The bride of the Song of Songs expresses a deep longing for the kiss of the Bridegroom. She has heard about him, waited for him, longed for his presence, just as Israel, the bride, waited and longed for the coming of the Messiah, the Bridegroom. Jesus, the Messiah, fulfills the figure of the Bridegroom. He is the anointed one, whose name is oil poured out (Sg 1:3). The Messiah as Bridegroom would make the hills flow with wine and the bride exclaims that his love is better than wine (Sg 1:2). Through the kisses of his mouth, his words, she finds him present and her desire is satisfied. She now speaks to him in the second person, shifting from "him" to "you." She now encounters the Lord as the answer to her deepest desires. "For your love is better than wine, your anointing oils are fragrant, your name is oil poured out" (Sg 1:2-3). She experiences the Lord as altogether wonderful, the fulfillment of all her expectations. Preaching is this same encounter with the Lord that meets peoples' expectations and inflames their deepest desires. It is not enough to know about Jesus. People desire a real encounter with him that ignites their hearts with love.

As preachers we sow seeds that touch peoples' deepest longings of the heart and encourage them to seek Jesus as their fulfillment. Preaching must address these divine longings in the hearts of believers. Spiritual longings are experienced as psychological needs that at their deepest level must be addressed spiritually. In addressing peoples' deepest longings, "the preacher has the wonderful but difficult task of joining loving hearts, the hearts of the Lord and his people."[4] The

---

[4] Pope Francis, *Evangelium Gaudium*, 143 (Libreria Editrice Vaticana, 2013), Vatican Website, https://www.vatican.va/content/francesco/en/apost_exhorta-

bride, like us, is longing for the one who can satisfy these deepest desires of her heart. She seeks communion with Christ the bridegroom who becomes manifest to her through the kisses of his word and in his very personal presence. She understands her identity as friend and bride in relation to him. She finds inspiration and fullness of life in his love, which is better than wine, and in the scent of his anointing oils. His name and presence are perfection as an oil poured out. As she exclaims "how right it is to love you" (1:4), she discovers true justice and the meaning of success in being his beloved disciple. The kisses of his mouth, his words, also evoke a response on the part of the bride. She exclaims "draw me after you, let us make haste" (1:3). Her desire is awakened, and she wants to quickly follow her Lover. The preacher's words are effective in evoking this same response to the Lord, as people feel drawn into the Lord's love and desire to be led.

Conformed to Christ

Jesus drew the Apostles into the depths of his heart in friendship and they followed him closely. At the Last Supper, he no longer called them servants, for the servants would not know what their master is doing, but he called them friends, for all that he heard from his Father he made known to them (cf. Jn. 15:15). Jesus shared his heart with his chosen ones, his love for them, and his desire that they share in his Sonship. He made known to them his values, his hopes and dreams for the kingdom, his desires to set the world ablaze with the Spirit of God, and his zeal for the

---

tions/documents/papa-francesco_esortazione-ap_20131124_evangelii-gaudium.html.

Father's will. Jesus invites us into this same friendship. He wants us to live in him as he lives in the Father. To be effective preachers of his word, we must be conformed to the heart of Christ. We must seek the face of the Lord in prayer and listen for his voice. Then our words will be Christ's words, not our own, and they will be efficacious in bringing about his saving power.

In New Testament times, when a king or some public ruler wished to proclaim to the people a significant message influencing their lives, he utilized a herald or town crier who would travel to a town, sound a trumpet, and declare at the top of his voice an authoritative communication from the governing powers. It was not the envoy who spoke; he was only an instrument for the voice of the ruler to reach the populace. The envoy did not speak of his own ideas, but was a spokesperson, or representative of the emperor. He had to proclaim a critical truth that would influence the lives of all his listeners. With this in mind, we can see how the Apostles understood themselves to be chosen heralds to announce an urgent message from God himself that would affect the destiny of all mankind. This message of salvation had to be made known to everyone. The Lord infused the power of the Holy Spirit into their minds and commanded them to "Go into all the world and preach the gospel to the whole creation (Mk. 16:15). Their preaching renewed the face of the earth, converting listeners' hearts from sin to faith, hope, love, and all virtue.

Conformed to Christ as preachers we become his ambassadors (cf. 2 Cor. 5:20). What does it mean to be an ambassador? Like the Apostles, we priests become ambassadors for Christ, especially through our preaching his words. The Lord continues to preserve and increase the faith of his people by preaching and so it is a matter of greatest urgency. St. Paul asks "how are they to call on one in whom they have not believed? And how are they to believe in one of whom they have never heard? And how are they to hear without someone to proclaim him? ... So, faith comes from what is heard, and what is heard comes by the preaching of Christ" (Rom. 10:14, 17). The apostles considered preaching so important that they chose deacons to minister to the poor so that they might have more time for prayer and the *ministry of the word* (cf. Acts 6:4). That is why the *primum officium* or primary duty of priests is the proclamation of the Gospel of the Lord to all.[5]

We are to preach Christ and to do so we must immerse ourselves in him. According to biblical scholar Jerome Murphy O'Connor "Christ will not be present if the word of his minister is not God's word, nor will he be present if God's word is not also his minister's."[6] The preacher can freely cooperate with God's grace by remaining constant in his charity and resolve. In his weakness and sin, the preacher could become an obstacle to God's grace. He can resist this grace and twist or misrepresent God's word into mere opinion and not the salvific message. Beyond preaching true doctrine, the preacher must put on Christ (Rom. 13:14) or else the Lord's presence in his message will be lacking. The preacher should invest as much of himself into Jesus as possible, into his ideas, into his complete devotion, into the adoration he offers the Father—until he can really say, along with St. Paul, "Christ lives in me" (Gal 2:20). The word of the Lord ought to change the preacher into the very image of Jesus, to become "another Christ," who extends his reign. To ensure that his proclamation is not mere human words he must reflect and radiate Christ and his saving message. Ven. Bruno Lanteri, founder of the Oblates of the Virgin Mary, wrote:

---

[5] See Vatican II, *Decree on Life and Ministry of Priests*, 4, Libreria Editrice Vaticana, 1994, Vatican Website, https://www.vatican.va/roman_curia/congregations/cclergy/documents/rc_con_cclergy_doc_31011994_directory_en.html

[6] Jerome Murphy O'Connor, *Paul on Preaching* (New York, Sheed and Ward, 1964), 300.

In every action, then, they will have Jesus Christ before their eyes, taking Him as their companion and model and seeking to imitate Him in the most perfect way. ... To this end, indeed, they will make constant efforts to keep the memory from dissipation, tranquilly fixed in Jesus, accustoming the mind to see and judge everything according to Jesus and keeping the will ever peacefully united to Jesus, conversing with Jesus, ever united with Jesus in their intentions and actions and becoming a living copy of Jesus. Jesus is the sole treasure of their hearts; Jesus lives in their hearts and they live in the heart of Jesus.[7]

For the preacher, there is an enormous difference between great rhetorical skills and the holiness of knowing Christ. Once there was a large event with a full banquet hall of distinguished guests. A famous orator had been hired to speak. At the end of the meal, he dazzled the audience with his grandiloquent skills, delivering segments of renowned speeches and exquisite poetry. Toward the end of the evening, he offered to deliver a favorite piece from a speech or poem that anyone would like to hear. An elderly priest waved and politely asked if the orator would please proclaim Psalm 23. The orator agreed and asked a favor in return—that the elderly priest would also proclaim it. The priest agreed. The orator eloquently proclaimed "the Lord is my Shepherd, I shall not want" in a mellifluous tone that delighted everyone in the hall. He finished with great aplomb and received a standing ovation with deafening applause. He then deferred to the priest and asked him to take his turn. The priest approached the microphone and in a humble and profound voice spoke the same verses "the Lord is my Shepherd, I shall not want..." The audience was spellbound. When he came to the end there was no applause, just silence, gentle

---

[7] Venerable Bruno Lanteri, *Directory of the Oblates of the Virgin Mary*, 21-22.

sobbing and reaching for handkerchiefs. The famous orator then rose and broke the silence. "My dear friends," he exclaimed, "I know the Psalm, but this priest knows the shepherd."

As priests, we especially are called to know the Shepherd. While we may cultivate oratorical skills, we are more importantly called to communicate Christ, his words, and his Spirit. Like the bride, the priest must receive the kisses of Christ's words of love, faith, and peace. Early Church Father Origen explains that "when the bride's mind is filled with divine perception and understanding ... then she may believe she has received the kisses of the Word of God Himself."[8] It is in prayer with the Word of God that we receive this divine enlightenment from the Holy Spirit. The Spirit was upon Jesus when he proclaimed the kingdom (Lk. 4:18). The Spirit is dynamic, moving us to speak with assurance about things beyond human knowledge. St. Paul and the other Apostles preached the gospel of Jesus Christ and the Christian faith, and especially the earth-shaking event of the death and resurrection of Jesus. Their message was so important that a person's response to it would determine his or her entire future. The Spirit's power in the preaching of the word of God is evident in Peter's sermon on Pentecost to his fellow Jews gathered from all the nations (See Acts 2: 14-42). When he spoke boldly and powerfully of the death and resurrection of Jesus, they were pierced in the heart by his message, asking what they should do. Peter told them to repent and be baptized in the name of Jesus Christ for the forgiveness of sins, and that they would receive the Holy Spirit. Three thousand new converts were added to the communion of the Church that day. This event in Acts shows us that the Lord's word, expressed through his preachers, is alive and powerful, and able to bring forth fruit.

---

[8] Origen, *The Song of Songs: Commentary and Homilies, Part One, the Commentary, Book One*, trans. Edmond de Pressense, manuscript date 1862, 114.

Because the character of Christ's priesthood is impressed upon the priest, God can speak through him to his people. Theologian Clement Dillenschneider asserts: "By virtue of his character, the priest participates equally in the sacerdotal power of Christ, the messenger of the Father to men. The New Testament seems to include in the priesthood the apostolic ministry of the word (Rom. 15:16)… the priest's preaching has an objective, sacred character, inalienable, a quasi-sacramental radiation."[9] When they celebrate the Holy Eucharist, priests are mediators between God and human beings. The preaching of God's Word also has a mediating function:

> The preacher represents this community by voicing its concerns, by naming its demons, and thus enabling it to gain some understanding and control of the evil which afflicts it. He represents the Lord by offering the community another word, a word of healing and pardon, of acceptance and love. … If we are able to hear a word which gives our lives another level of meaning, which interprets them in relation to God, then our response is to turn to this source of meaning in an attitude of praise and thanksgiving.[10]

Preaching has sometimes been called the "eighth sacrament" and is linked to faith in the Sacraments, especially the Holy Eucharist. To ensure the Sacraments' fruitfulness in terms of faith and living, preaching must come before, follow, and crown their dispensation. "In this celebration the proclamation of the death and resurrection of the Lord is inseparably

---

[9] Clement Dillenschneider, *Dogmatic Foundations of our Priestly Spirituality, vol. 1, Christ the Priest and We His Priests*, trans. Sr. M. Renelle, SSND (St. Louis: B. Herder Book Co., 1964), 146, 148-149.

[10] *Fulfilled in Your Hearing: The Homily in the Sunday Assembly*, the United States Conference of Catholic Bishops (Washington D.C., USCCB, 1982), 7.

joined both to the response of the people who hear, and to the very offering whereby Christ ratified the New Testament in His blood.'"[11]

The priest should speak with boldness and assurance because he has the authority and presence of Christ. The more the priest is conformed to Christ in his daily living, the more Christ will be radiated in his preaching. He becomes an instrument and co-laborer with the Lord, exercising a priestly function, which has the attribute of a liturgical offering to God. There is certainly a sacrificial element to our preaching in the time and effort expended in preparing and delivering the homily. Fr. Don Miniscalco, a Redemptorist priest who specialized in preaching missions, invited me to preach my first parish mission three years after my ordination. I wanted to just tag along and observe, but he insisted that I preach two of the evening services and two of the different morning services over the five days. I spent about a month assiduously preparing my four talks, working through several drafts, and thought I was ready. The first two nights Fr. Don was stellar, speaking with authority, boldness, and eloquence. He had a doctorate from the prestigious University of Louvain in Belgium and a wealth of life experience. There was both theological gravitas and down to earth simplicity in his message. The entire congregation of 1200 people was spellbound, and so was I. Now it was my turn. My Tuesday night topic was The Four Last Things—death, judgment, hell, and heaven, which would lead nicely into Wednesday night's repentance theme for the Sacrament of Penance. By Tuesday afternoon, I was rehearsing my talk and feeling apprehensive, convinced it didn't measure up to the standard Fr. Don had set. I decided to ask him if I could practice my talk in front of him, thinking I would gain confidence and perhaps some pointers from the master. The rehearsal was a disaster. I couldn't get through the first 2 minutes without bumbling and desperately reading from my notes. Fr.

---

[11] *Presbyterorum Ordinis*, 4.

Don seemed concerned and asked me if I wanted to go through with it—offering me an out. Not wanting to be cowardly, I said no, that I would move forward with the talk. I had a pit in my stomach and major feelings of spiritual desolation during dinner with the pastor, and we proceeded to the service. As soon as the music began and we processed down the aisle I felt all fears lifting, replaced by a confident assurance in God. As the moment arrived for me to stand and deliver, the Holy Spirit took over, anointing my words and opening the hearts of those 1200 eager people for the next forty minutes. I felt so alive and blessed by God. I knew it was his work and his words that inspired me to boldly proclaim his gospel. From that moment on I was much more profoundly convinced of the value and impact of preaching. While I realized the importance of my own preparation, I learned to become more heavily reliant on the Spirit.

There is always a tension between our own egos and humility when we preach. We are all poor in spirit when we approach the daunting task of preaching, Only God can inspire us to say anything of value and only he can open the hearts of the faithful to receive his message through the preacher. We must have true humility, which does not make us avoid the congregation's attention, but to embrace it in all our vulnerability. We must overcome any sense of our own inadequacy when we preach. God's word and the proclamation of the gospel are not just a matter of my own powers of persuasion and of my own perspiration in the pulpit. The effectiveness of preaching comes primarily from the power of the presence of God, from beyond me. The great Redemptorist preacher from Boston, Joseph Manton, wrote:

> Like all human beings I am only a sinful man, but when I stand in the pulpit, I stand and speak as an ambassador of the Almighty. I speak with courage because I am the courier of Christ, bringing not my feathery personal opinion, but His grave and majestic

message. I have just come down from the mountaintop like Moses, and I carry the law of God in my hands! I know that the pulpit is not a fence to straddle, but a tower from which to proclaim.[12]

We should avoid selling ourselves short with a sense of mediocrity and aim at excellence in preaching, cultivating a professional attitude as spiritual leaders. If we are certain that our message is valid and that it is something important for our congregation, the transmission will come across charged with enthusiasm, honesty, and significance. We preach because *we have something to say*, not because *we have to say something*. The more we are trying to live out the message we proclaim, the more convinced we will be in the value of our preaching.

How We Preach

Once we are convinced of the importance of preaching, we must be committed to preparation. I know many priests who would rather do anything *but* prepare a homily. Pope Francis insists that homily preparation is such an imperative that an extended time of research, prayer, deliberation, and pastoral creativity should be given to it. Plenty of time should be devoted to this work, even if there is less time available for other worthwhile pursuits.[13] "Trust in the Holy Spirit who is at work during the homily is not merely passive but active and creative. It demands that we offer ourselves and all our abilities as instruments (cf. Rom. 12:1) which God can

---

[12] Joseph Manton, C.S.S.R., *Ten Responsible Minutes* (Huntington, IN, Our Sunday Visitor, 1980), 46-47.

[13] Recall that the Apostles delegated the service of the poor to the deacons so that they could spend more time on prayer and the ministry of the word (cf. Acts 6:1-7).

use. A preacher who does not prepare is not 'spiritual'; he is dishonest and irresponsible with the gifts he has received."[14]

We begin by asking God what he wants us to say and what the congregation needs to hear, rather than approaching the mission with my own preconceived notions. We have faith that the Lord has a message in his inmost being that he wants to communicate to his people, and that he will reveal it to his humble servant. Then we show receptivity by opening our hearts to his word in prayer with the scriptures. We consult commentaries, notes, the Church Fathers and Mothers, spiritual masters, and literary greats, continuing to pray with the Word of God throughout the process. The person who is not in the habit of communicating with God in the intimacy of prayer is not able to effectively speak of the things of God. No matter how cultured and eloquent his words, without the inspiration of the Spirit in prayer, he will not influence or convert people. He will only be a "noisy gong or a clanging cymbal" (1 Cor. 13:1).

Just like Jesus in his parables, we need to be graphic in our proclamation. Once there was a famous rabbi who loved to illustrate a truth by means of a concrete story. One day his students asked him why he adopted this approach. He responded with the following parable. There was a time when Truth went around naked and unadorned. But the people shied away from him and gave him no welcome. So, Truth wandered through the land, rebuffed and unwanted. One day, very disconsolate, he met Story strolling along happily dressed in a multicolored robe. "Truth, why are you so sad?" Story asked.

"I am sad because I am so old and ugly that everybody avoids me," Truth replied.

"Nonsense!" laughed Story. "That is not why people avoid you. Here, borrow my robe, and see what happens."

---

[14] Pope Francis, *Evangelium Gaudium*, 145.

So Truth donned Story's multicolored robe, and lo, everywhere he went, Truth was welcomed.[15] Sometimes the naked truth can be so challenging that we are not able to take it straight. We need to decorate it. A story makes a difficult truth more palatable.

People are more moved by illustrations than anything else. Examples engage the imagination and bring real-life understanding to the ideas we convey. Relevant personal anecdotes help make the message of our preaching come alive. People can more easily recall the images that have been impressed upon their minds and sustain the message the preacher wants to convey. We should use the stories and images in our homiletics that profoundly move us. The more deeply meaningful the stories are to us, the more our heartfelt message will resonate with the audience. The great bishop and preacher St. Augustine asserts: "And in reality, we are listened to with much greater satisfaction, indeed, when we ourselves also have pleasure in the same work; for the thread of our address is affected by the very joy of which we ourselves are sensible, and it proceeds from us with greater ease and with more acceptance."[16]

Our enthusiasm for our message will be infectious and draw others to seek the Lord. The bride is not only drawn to her Lover through the kisses of his mouth and his presence, she invites others to be drawn to him (cf. Sg 1:3-4). The preaching of the ministerial priest is ordered to the service of the common priesthood of the faithful so that they too will exercise their priestly and prophetic function and preach the word in their daily life situations—at home, at work, in the marketplace—ultimately leading others to Christ. Just as for the ministerial priest this preaching will be in both

---

[15] Flor McCarthy, SDB, *New Sunday and Holy Day Liturgies*, Year A, Week 15 (Dublin, Dominican Publishers, 1998), 237.

[16] St. Augustine de *Catechizandis Rudibus, On the Catechizing of the Uninstructed*, Ch. 2 par. 4, *Church Fathers*, New Advent website, http://www.newadvent.org/fathers/1303.htm

word and deed. The lay faithful will be effective to the degree in which they are steeped in God's word. They look for opportunities to witness to Christ by their words. One day Saint Francis said to one of his young friars: "Let us go down to the village and preach to the people." So, they went. Along the way they stopped to talk to various people. They begged a crust of bread at doors of different homes. Francis stopped to play with the children and exchanged greetings with passers-by. Then Francis and the friars turned to go home. "But father," said the novice, "when do we preach?" "Preach?" repeated Francis smiling, "Every step we took, every word we spoke, every action we did, has been a sermon."[17]

The more moved the faithful are by the priest's homily, the more energized in the Spirit they will be to evangelize in the world. Cardinal O'Malley quips, "Are we preaching to the choir? Yes, but if we touch their hearts then the choir will become the messengers and inviters. ...They will become the evangelizers because we have given them the tools and the motivation."[18] The Spirit, through our preaching, makes the faithful witnesses and equips them with the gift of faith and the grace of the word. "To teach in order to lead others to faith is the task of every preacher and of each believer."[19] Others will say along with the bride, "We will exult and rejoice in you; we will extol your love more than wine" (Sg 1:4). The faithful, too, will be drawn to the Lord and desire to run in his ways (Sg 1:3).

---

[17] *Little Flowers of St. Francis*, Brother Ugolino, Christian Classics Ethereal Library, Grand Rapids, MI, https://ccel.org/ccel/ugolino/flowers/flowers

[18] Sean O'Malley, Chrism Mass Homily, *We are anointed to preach the good news to the poor*, Catholic Online, https://www.catholic.org/featured/headline.php?ID=868

[19] *ST*. III,71,4 *ad* 3.

Questions for Reflection and Discussion

1. How convinced am I of the importance of preaching in my ministry? Am I confident of the power of God's Word to change hearts?

2. Am I enthusiastic about preaching, or do I see it more as a burden? How much time and effort do I expend in preparing for preaching? What fruits do I see?

3. To what degree do I seek to be aware of and answer the deepest questions and desires of my congregation's hearts? How aware am I of addressing my own existential longings as an avenue into the hearts of others?

4. How do I make sure I am announcing God's Word and not my own, and be a more effective instrument of the Lord's?

5. How do I balance my own poverty of spirit and vulnerability in preaching with God's power to move hearts? To what degree do I seek to develop my oratorical skills to become a more effective instrument of God?

Prayer Exercises

1. Ponder the desires of peoples' hearts. Pray with Lk 4:18-22 and ask for the grace to trust in the Spirit to anoint your preaching, and to address the needs of the people.

2. Consider the survey results on the practice of the faith. Pray with Rm 10:14-17 and ask for the grace to realize the importance of the ministry of preaching.

3. Reflect on the story of the great orator and the priest reciting Ps 23. Pray with Acts 28:30-31 and ask for the grace to realize the

power of God's Spirit at work in your preaching, despite your own human weakness. Ask for the desire to speak boldly and with full assurance and without hindrance.

4. Ponder the story of the rabbi and the multicolored robe. Pray with Mt 13:10-17 and ask for the grace to preach as Jesus did.

5. Ponder the image of the herald of the king. Pray with 1 Thes 2:4-13 and ask for the grace that the gospel you preach will be received as the Word of God and not of men.

Chapter 3

Dignity Restored

I am very dark, but comely,

O daughters of Jerusalem,

like the tents of Kedar,

like the curtains of Solomon.

Do not gaze at me because I am swarthy,

because the sun has scorched me.

My mother's sons were angry with me,

they made me keeper of the vineyards;

but, my own vineyard I have not kept!

I compare you, my love,

to a mare of Pharaoh's chariots.

Your cheeks are comely with ornaments,

your neck with strings of jewels.

We will make you ornaments of gold,

studded with silver. (Sg 1:5-6, 9-11)

The Work of Mercy

Victor Hugo wrote his classic *Les Miserables* as a story of sin, mercy, and redemption set in mid-19th century France. The protagonist, Jean Valjean, is paroled after spending nineteen years on the chain gang enduring slavish manual labor—five years for stealing a loaf of bread for his sister's starving child—and fourteen more for trying to escape. He must by law display a yellow ticket which condemns him as an outcast. He goes to the rural village of Digne (to regain his "dignity"), where no one is willing to give him shelter or work because he is an ex-convict. He finally approaches the bishop's house and enters as a threatening intruder. He shouts his name and his crime in a loud harsh voice. To Valjean's surprise, the bishop welcomes him as a brother, invites him to dinner, and allows him to sleep there. Valjean wakes in the middle of the night. Anxiety about his situation and temptation overcome him. He absconds with the bishop's silverware into the foggy darkness. The police track him down, beat him, and drag him back to the bishop for justice. When Jean Valjean protests that the bishop gave him the bag of silver, the bishop concedes and further adds that he forgot to take two precious candlesticks. Valjean is overwhelmed by this act of mercy. The bishop then takes him aside, telling him, "My brother, Jean Valjean, you now belong to good rather than evil. I paid for your soul with my own. I took it out of the realm of hateful thoughts and handed it to God." In the next scene Valjean is still reeling from the bishop's lavish act of mercy. He turns to Jesus in prayer,

> Why did I let that man enter my heart and instruct me about love? He treated me equally to everyone else. He put his faith in me. He addressed me as brother. He claims my life for God above. Do such things exist? I had grown to despise the world, which had always been hostile toward me. He told me that I have a soul, how does he know? Who or what is moving my life? Could there be a different path to take?[1]

Valjean has a complete change of heart and begins to lead a life of goodness. He changes his name and becomes a factory owner who is generous to his employees. He becomes a mayor who is known for offering mercy

---

[1] See Valjean's soliloquy from the musical *Les Miserables*. A musical by Alain Boulbil and Claude-Michel Shoenberg, Lyrics by Herbert Kretzmer, based on the novel by Victor Hugo, original London production by Cameron MacIntosh and the Royal Shakespeare Company, 1985.

instead of strict justice according to the law. He cares for the prostitute Fantene's daughter Cosette. Valjean gained back his life because of the bishop's mercy and went on to make something beautiful of his life, showing mercy to others.

Most people are unaware that Hugo wrote the character of the bishop into his novel as an inspirational model of mercy for the priests of his day in France. As priests, we have all received mercy. Despite our sinful histories, despite our countless ongoing daily sins, we have still been called to share in the Lord's ministry. Like Peter, we could easily say, "Go away from me Lord, for I am a sinful man," and yet, we would hear the Lord invite us into his company and mission: "Do not be afraid; from now on you will be catching people" (Lk 5:1-10). We are especially called to show love to the world in the form of mercy. Jesus Christ is the epitome of mercy and reveals the Father as unfathomable mercy. The Incarnation is an act of mercy whereby God condescends to sinful humanity to take on our weak flesh and meet us on human terms in our misery. Jesus' ministry was one of mercy. In his proclamation of the Kingdom he speaks in terms of fulfilling Isaiah's prophecy: "The Spirit of the Lord is upon me, because he has anointed me to preach good news to the poor. He has sent me to proclaim release to the captives and recovering of sight to the blind, to set at liberty those who are oppressed, to proclaim the acceptable year of the Lord" (Luke 4:18-19). Jesus fulfilled all those promises and showed mercy to everyone he encountered. Isaiah's prophecy is especially fulfilled in the forgiveness that releases people from the prison of sin. They are restored to the spiritual vision of faith and freed from the oppression of the world, the flesh, and the devil.

Old Testament prophets spoke of sin, which is turning away, separating oneself from God in terms of adultery. God had taken his people as a bride and espoused her in faithfulness to the covenant. When Israel worshipped false gods, it was an act of infidelity that God considered adulterous. Yet God remained faithful to the covenant, continually forgiving his people, bringing them back to fidelity, and purifying them from their sins. He speaks tenderly to his bride's heart: "And I will take you for my wife forever; I will take you for my wife in righteousness and in justice, in steadfast love, and in mercy. I will take you for my wife in faithfulness; and you shall know the LORD" (Hos 2:19-20). The Song of Songs repeats this theme of God espousing his bride despite her infidelity. The bride is a figure of Israel and expresses her history of sin and its effects on her appearance. She admits that she has not kept her own vineyard. She has not avoided vice and has failed to cultivate virtue. As a result, she (Israel) has been conquered, led into exile, and subjected to hard labor. She is disfigured and burnt by the sun and yet her beauty has somehow been restored. She has been redeemed. The bride is a figure of all of us adulterous sinners who have not kept our vineyard, making a ruin of our lives. We, too, are redeemed by the mercy of God.

In the New Testament, where Jesus is the visible Face of the invisible God, we find a more graphic illustration of how God responds to infidelity. Jesus encountered a woman caught in adultery. The Scribes and Pharisees dragged her before Jesus in an act of public shaming. They insisted that the Law commanded she be stoned and demanded to know his opinion. Jesus said nothing, bent down, and traced his finger in the sand. He then stood up and responded, "Let him who is without sin among you be the first to throw a stone at her." He then bent down and wrote again in the sand. In the face of pressure from the Jewish leaders, he refuses to condemn the woman. At first, he does not even look at her to avoid shaming her. When he does look at her, his eyes of mercy meet her eyes of misery and he restores her sense of dignity. She is forgiven, and he tells her to go and sin no more.

The grand question has always been, "What did Jesus write on that day?" It matters not *what* he wrote but *that* he wrote. There is one other instance in the scriptures where God writes something twice with his finger. In Exodus 31:18, God writes the Ten Commandments on stone tablets with his finger. When Moses comes down the mountain to deliver the Law to the people, he catches them in adultery, worshipping the golden calf. He breaks the tablets, symbolizing their breaking the covenant. Moses returns to Mount Sinai to intercede on behalf of his people, and God promises to write the Commandments again on the former tablets. In between the two writings, God passes by Moses, who hides his face in the cleft of the rock. Moses witnesses the glory of God as he passes by uttering the words: "The LORD, the LORD, a God merciful and gracious, slow to anger, and abounding in steadfast love and faithfulness, keeping steadfast love for the thousandth generation, forgiving iniquity and transgression and sin..." (Ex 34:6-7). Now, Jesus also writes with the finger of God and in between writings, he shows the Lord's unfathomable mercy.

Jesus gave the Sacrament of Reconciliation to his ministers. In the upper room on Easter evening, he appeared to them through the locked doors of the upper room. Not only were they afraid of reprisals from the Jews for being followers of the Lord, but they were also afraid of reprisals from the Lord for abandoning him in his darkest hour. When Jesus appeared to them, they were not only surprised to see him, but they were also frightened. Perhaps they thought it was the ghost of Jesus to haunt them in retribution for their sin. But immediately Jesus reassured them "Peace be with you." He showed them his hands and side, the proof that it was really him, the same Jesus who had been crucified and pierced. Now, it would be by his wounds that he would heal us (cf. Isa 53:3, 1 Pet 2:23). The wounds Jesus endured on the cross for us are the signs of his undying love and the Father's mercy. John Paul II explains:

Believing in the crucified Son means "seeing the Father," (cf. Jn 14:9) means believing that love is present in the world and that this love is more powerful than any kind of evil in which individuals, humanity, or the world are involved. Believing in this love means believing in mercy. For mercy is an indispensable dimension of love; it is as it were love's second name and, at the same time, the specific manner in which love is revealed and effected vis-a-vis the reality of the evil that is in the world, affecting and besieging man, insinuating itself even into his heart and capable of causing him to "perish in Gehenna." (Mt 10:28).[2]

The cross reveals that we have marred the image of God within us. God speaks his message of mercy into the horror of sin and its disfiguring effects upon the human person. He restores us to life and dignity as sons and daughters of our heavenly Father. The image of God is restored in us through his cross and resurrection. "The Good Shepherd seeks out the lost sheep. When he finds it he places it on those same shoulders which bore the wood of the Cross, and he carries the sheep to eternal life."[3]

Jesus continues to treat sinners with mercy, especially through the ministry of priests. He breathed the Holy Spirit on the Apostles and sent them forth to absolve sins: "If you forgive the sins of any, they are forgiven; if you retain the sins of any, they are retained" (Jn 20:23). Through the Sacrament of Penance, Christ extends his forgiving words through the communication of the priest while simultaneously changing the disposition of the penitent who recognizes one's sinfulness, desiring absolution with the intent of reparation and firm purpose of amendment. In 1980, a woman named Tatiana Goricheva crossed the Russian border to freedom.

---

[2] St. John Paul II, *Dives in Misericordia*, 7. (Vatican City, Libreria Editrice Vaticana, 1980) Vatican Website, https://www.vatican.va/content/john-paul-ii/en/encyclicals/documents/hf_jp-ii_enc_30111980_dives-in-misericordia.html

[3] Gregory Nazianzus, *Orations*, 45, New Advent Website, https://www.newadvent.org/fathers/310245.htm

Once in the West, she authored a book about her change of heart while living in Russia. From her youth she was rebellious. She detested the oppression of the Russian regime, as well as people who tolerated it. She even grew resentful toward her parents for not opposing the government. Goricheva took refuge in reading books and eventually attended University. She became a star pupil and an academic. Rather than associate with her fellow intellectuals, she socialized with the down-and-out drug users and prostitutes of Russian culture. She also took an interest in Eastern mysticism and began practicing yoga.[4] One day she used the *Our Father* as a mantra, reciting the words slowly and meditatively during the stretches. Gradually the meaning of the words impacted her, and she found them to be beautiful. She now felt drawn to investigate Christianity, voraciously reading all she could on the faith. When she was baptized at age 26, though not obligated to do so, she desired to make a full confession to the priest. She describes how she told the priest about her drunkenness, her unrestrained sexual behavior, her troubled marriages, her abortions, and her inability to love anyone. When she was finished confessing, she was a changed person. She felt forgiven by Jesus and deeply healed by his loving touch. Like the adulterous woman in the gospel, she was humble and contrite, and emerged from encountering Jesus as a new creation.[5]

As priests we are privileged to dispense mercy to others. We need to receive mercy in order to give mercy, to be forgiven in order to forgive. St. Paul mentions that in the Old Testament, the high priest first offered sacrifices for his own sins, and then for the sins of the people (Heb 7:27). The faithful people could offer a goat for their sins (Lev 4:28), but the priest had to offer a bull in atonement because his sin also brought sin upon the

---

[4] I in no way recommend practicing yoga.

[5] See Mark Link, *Illustrated Sunday Homilies, Series 1, Years A,B,C,* Year C, Fifth Sunday of Lent (Allen, TX: Tabor Publishing, 1989), 27.

people (Lev 4:3). Given that the priest is representative of the people and their holiness, his sin impacts the whole people. The priest is called to a higher standard of moral life because of his dignity of sharing in the ministerial priesthood of Jesus the great high priest. The objective priestly character of being and acting *in persona Christi* demands a consistently virtuous character development and moral striving that seeks conformity with the heart of Christ. According to Jean Galot, "This means that, more so than the ordinary Christian, the priest is called to take Christ as his model in all his behavior."[6] This does not imply that a priest is better than a lay person, but because he is set apart for service as a minister and ambassador of Christ, there is a higher expectation of holiness and he is necessarily meant to be of good character.[7] The U.S. Bishops state:

> Because of the ministry entrusted to priests, which, in itself is a holy sacramental configuration to Jesus Christ, priests have a further reason to strive for holiness. This does not mean the holiness to which the priest is called is in any way subjectively greater than that to which all the faithful are called in virtue of Baptism. While holiness takes different forms, holiness is always one. The priest, however, is motivated to strive for holiness for a different reason: so as to be worthy of that new grace which has marked him so that he can represent the person of Christ, Head and Shepherd, and thereby become a living instrument in the work of salvation.[8]

---

[6] Jean Galot, *The Theology of the Priesthood* (San Francisco, Ignatius Press, 2005), 207.

[7] See David Toups, *Reclaiming our Priestly Character* (Omaha, Institute for Priestly Formation, 2008), 156.

[8] U.S. Council of Catholic Bishops, *The Basic Plan for the Ongoing Formation of Priests* (Washington D.C., USCC, 2001), 10. Cf. *Presbyterium Ordinis* 12 and *Lumen Gentium*, 41.

Manifesting Christ

While the priest's actions in conferring the sacraments remain efficacious regardless of his sinfulness, he will be a much better conductor of
God's grace if he is upright and holy. Therefore, he must frequently exam-
ine his conscience and strive for purity of heart to more fully manifest
Christ in his ministry. John Paul II presses the point:

> The priest's spiritual and pastoral life, like that of his brothers and sis-
> ters, lay and religious, depends, for its quality and fervor, on the fre-
> quent and conscientious personal practice of the sacrament of pen-
> ance. The priest's celebration of the Eucharist and administration of
> the other sacraments, his pastoral zeal, his relationship with the faith-
> ful, his communion with his brother priests, his collaboration with his
> bishop, his life of prayer—in a word, the whole of his priestly existence,
> suffers an inexorable decline if by negligence or for some other reason
> he fails to receive the sacrament of penance at regular intervals and in
> a spirit of genuine faith and devotion. If a priest were no longer to go
> to confession or properly confess his sins, his priestly being and his
> priestly action would feel its effects very soon, and this would also be
> noticed by the community of which he was the pastor.[9]

The faithful have a right to priests who are holy. That is why the clergy
sex abuse scandals are so disturbing and demoralizing to the faithful and
to us as priests. Priests are expected to be the models of virtue, and in this
case a small minority are the worst examples of depravity. *Corruptio optimi*

---

[9] John Paul II, *Reconciliatio et Penetentia*, 31 (Vatican City, Libreria Editrice
Vaticana, 1984), Vatican Website, https://www.vatican.va/content/john-paul-
ii/en/apost_exhortations/documents/hf_jp-ii_exh_02121984_reconciliatio-et-
paenitentia.html

pessima: "the best, corrupted, becomes the worst." Sadly, the sick and depraved behavior of a few has sometimes caused mistrust of the vast majority of good priests, and mistrust of bishops who oversee them. We must be careful that with the high calling to be ministers of Christ, we do not become corrupted by sin and cause scandal to God's faithful. To remain pure we need mercy more than anyone else. As priests we need to reach out to one another, especially those most in need of God's mercy, to forgive, and to spur each other on to virtue.

Back in the late 1990s a priest from New York City visited Rome to do some work for a committee in the Vatican. He happened to be walking up the steps of one of the churches not far from the Vatican and passed a man begging for money at the church entrance. He asked the man, "Do I know you?

The man replied, "I was a priest once."

Later that day, the committee was meeting in the Vatican, and had an opportunity to share with the Holy Father, John Paul II, their work. The New York priest shared with the Pope, "Holy Father, I ask your prayers for this man, a priest who has fallen on hard times and is now begging outside one of these church's in Rome, would you please pray for him."

The Pope replied, "Ask him to come to dinner, tonight."

The priest went back, found the beggar priest, relayed to him what had happened, and finally convinced him to have dinner that night with the pope. During dinner, the pope signaled for the priest from New York City to leave him in private with the beggar priest, and then asked the beggar priest to hear his confession. At first, the priest thought it was inconceivable, how could he?

"I am the Pope, I can grant you faculties."

Then the beggar priest asked the Holy Father to hear his confession. After that, the pope asked him the name of the church where he was begging outside. The Pope then assigned him as an associate pastor with a special ministry to the poor in that area. What an amazing story of redemption for that down and out priest! At the moment of his greatest shame and unworthiness, before the Holy Father himself, he is not only forgiven, but restored to his priesthood and mission. How magnanimous was Saint John Paul II in welcoming the priest to his table and taking time for him in private. How humbling of the Pope to confess his sins to this priest and remind the priest of his power to act in the person of Jesus.

When we priests experience the beauty of meeting Christ in the Sacrament of Reconciliation we are more joyfully inclined to patiently offer the same humble and demanding service to God's people. Though hearing confessions can at times be an intensive, exhausting, and monotonous toil, it remains one of my most delightful experiences to witness the conversion of hearts and to administer absolution. In our parish here in Denver, Holy Ghost, we Oblate priests offer confessions before and often during all the masses. There are long penance services at retreats and other parishes, especially during the penitential seasons. We usually spend three hours in the confessionals on Good Friday. Sometimes we drive far into the mountains on Saturday night to help with hundreds of retreat confessions, returning home at midnight and rising at dawn for Sunday masses. Whenever I tire of the confessional, I recall the heartfelt love and zeal of our founder, Venerable Bruno Lanteri, for the ministry of reconciliation. He would visit the prisons and hospitals of Turin and make himself available in churches and even at home to offer the sacrament with gentle compassion and utmost charity, especially to those in greatest need. His early Oblates would offer parish missions and spiritual exercises in the churches, hearing confessions from 4:00 AM until midnight over a two-week span. Often the number of penitents was so great that halfway through the missions they would enlist many additional confessors to help. In a time when few priests were available in the city,[10] Lanteri insisted that the Oblate community would be unceasingly ready in their churches to welcome people of all social conditions and occupations to the sacrament, especially the neediest. His exhortation was "the Oblate dies in the pulpit or the confessional."

Venerable Bruno would never consider anyone beyond the reach of God's mercy and would treat each penitent with affability and gentleness. He exhorts his Oblates regarding the manner of hearing confessions:

> They shall study in everything to imitate the divine Master in receiving, and dealing with all, especially those most in need, with the greatest gentleness and kindness....They shall never judge any, even the most hardened heart, to be invulnerable, but by continual and fervent prayer, and perseveringly applied charity, they shall do all they can to let none perish.... They shall deal with those troubled with doubts and scruples with the utmost charity and unalterable patience.[11]

We priests might be tempted to grow irritable with penitents due to what we might perceive as their weakness, lack of virtue, foolishness, or hardness of hearts. While we are called to help the penitent judge whether something confessed is a sin or not, we are never to disdainfully judge the penitent. Lanteri often felt irritability and the temptation to judge, yet his constant demeanor was one of patience and gentleness.

---

[10] Much of the Catholic Church in Europe was still tinged with the heresy of Jansenism, which held that few were worthy of the Sacraments. Priests were not readily available for the sacraments and people were not encouraged to frequent the sacraments.

[11] Ven. Bruno Lanteri, *Directory of the Oblates of the Virgin Mary*, Part II, Art. 2, ed. G.B.Isnardi (Archives of the Oblates of the Virgin Mary), 52.

Another temptation we sometimes feel as a confessor is to mechanically grind through one confession after another while not taking each penitent seriously enough. This temptation especially occurs when we have been hearing confessions for some time and the line is still long. At times, when someone seems to be explaining too much, we grow impatient and want to say, in effect, "Just the facts ma'am," which would only stifle the penitent. People sometimes need to explain themselves. One man commented on his experience of confession to a disinterested priest:

> What's really disappointing is when you've mustered up the courage to go ahead and say something and you actually want to talk about it—at least a little—and the priest just lets it hang. When it's something I was afraid of, but really wanted to talk about, I don't leave the sacrament relieved. I leave feeling I've wasted my time. Wasn't he interested—really interested—in what I was saying? Did he think I was just doing this as a matter of routine?[12]

The danger is losing our personal interest in the penitents and failing to carefully tend to their soul wounds. As priests we are called to be one with the Divine Physician and that calls for diagnosis of the illness of spirit and prescribing a cure. A doctor would want to know where the patient hurts, the symptoms of the illness, asking a question or two only to better assess the patient's condition. Certain behaviors might suggest an underlying illness. The man who is given to lustful behaviors such as viewing pornography might deep down suffer from a lack of any meaningful relationships or ability to communicate on a more profound level. A couple of questions about friendships or intimacy could help him to realize he needs

---

[12] Kurt Stasiak, O.S.B., *A Confessor's Handbook* (New York: Paulist Press, 1999), 22.

to cultivate healthy relationships, seeking to live chastity that is oriented toward love.

> In the dialogue with the penitent, the priests appreciate the personal dimension of the sacrament, which is brought to expression. It provides the opportunity to discuss with penitents the nature of sin as an offense against God and to help them to discern the causes and effects of sin in their lives. Individual confession provides a powerful sign of personal forgiveness.[13]

In the Song of Songs, the bride not only admits that she has not kept her own vineyard, but she explains the reason: Her mother and brothers were angry with her. They made her do hard labor under the sun to keep their vineyards. She can tell her story, express her own pain and explain the oppression she has felt at the hands of others. While she feels shame for her appearance, asking the Bridegroom not to look at her, she is also aware that she is dark and lovely. Sin has harmed her but has not disfigured her essential beauty. We can help our penitents to the same self-expression and self-realization.

The Sacrament of Penance is meant to be a celebration. We are supposed to rejoice with our penitents at their change of heart, their freedom from the enslavement of sin, and their restored communion with God and others. The sacrament is a spiritual rebirth, transforming the sinner into a new creation and uniting him or her in friendship for Christ. Thus, it is a well-spring of joy for those who are servants of the Good Shepherd. During Advent I like to use the example from Charles Dicken's Christmas

---

[13] United States Catholic Conference, *Reflections on the Sacrament of Penance in Catholic Life Today: a Study Document* (Washington, D.C, United States Catholic Conference, Inc, 1990), 6.

Carol of Ebenezer Scrooge's joy of repentance. Scrooge realizes what an ogre he's been and discovers generosity in his heart at Christmas. He dances, leaps, and sings for joy, sharing his delight with others. He is a new person, a new creation. So often confession is just the opposite—a grim and anxious experience. Examining our conscience seems like a chore and we approach it with dread. Facing a priest, the representative of God, with one's wretched sinfulness feels like Dorothy and her companions groveling before the terrifying Wizard.

We need to change the narrative and pastoral strategy for the Sacrament of Penance. It should be more about God's unfathomable mercy than about our sinfulness. While we should feel the weight of sin and true contrition, it should always be within the greater context of God's mercy. Sin is already selfishness. We do not want to make people more self-centered by becoming more self-absorbed and self-loathing. Liberated from sin and its effects, we become more other-centered on God and neighbor. When a person presents oneself for confession, repentance is already happening. There is already a change of heart, a turning from sin and movement toward God. We are encouraging and celebrating that movement. When Jesus spoke of repentance it was always celebratory and festive. He tells three stories in Luke 15, the parables of the lost sheep, the lost coin, and the lost son. In each case what was lost is found and there is celebration and "more joy in heaven over one sinner who repents than over ninety-nine righteous persons who need no repentance" (Lk 15:7).

Healing and Restoration Through Reconciliation

The Sacrament of Penance is not only medicinal, curing us of the disease of sin, it is also a powerful source of grace for growth in holiness. According to the Order of Penance, this is yet another cause for joy and celebration. In Christ, real friendship is a result of God's grace. Regaining harmony and fellowship with God, rejoining the Church's body, and being unified in one's own heart all happen. Even the rest of creation is at peace with us. The Christian both feels and witnesses God's forgiveness in his life. One participates in the priest's celebration of the Church's perpetually renewed liturgy." [14] The Congregation for the Clergy adds: "The Sacrament of Penance is an eloquent sign of our desire for perfection, contemplation, fraternal communion, and apostolic mission." [15]

Emilie Griffin was a Madison Avenue advertising executive when she felt attracted to the Catholic Faith. In her book *Turning*, she describes her attitude toward the sacrament of Penance:

> The notion of confessing my sins was hateful to me. It was not a question of unwillingness to confess my sins before another human being; it was in fact an unwillingness to confess my sins at all. I could not admit myself to be a sinner. Yet in some part of me I knew I was flawed...and I was profoundly ashamed. [16]

When Griffin became Catholic she was faced with confessing that she was a sinner. The moment came for her to participate in the sacrament of Penance. It was an encounter she would always remember. She wanted to leap and cry for joy over the peace and spiritual liberation that she felt in her heart. She was amazed that she found herself being forgiven not so much by the priest as by Christ himself. She reflects: "I had begun to see

---

[14] See Rituale Romanum – *Ordo Paenitentiae* (December 2, 1973), *Praenotanda* 11: edition typica (1974), 15-16.

[15] Congregation for the Clergy, *The Priest, Minister of Divine Mercy*, 10.

[16] Emilie Griffin, *Turning, Reflections on the Experience of Conversion* (Garden City, NY: Doubleday, 1980), 112.

[priests]…not as men but as Christ himself; and I remembered with what tenderness he dealt with the tax collectors and the adulteress."[17]

The bride in the Song of Songs experiences the joy of her change of heart, while acknowledging her past neglect and pain. She now has a new perspective. She recognizes her essential beauty. She is affirmed by her Bridegroom, who compares her to a mare of Pharoah's chariots. The mare was greatly valued and a good image of the speed and grace with which the bride now runs in the Lord's ways. Origen expounds on the analogy:

> Just as long ago in Egypt, Pharoah pressed forward in chariots and with horsemen in his pursuit of the people of Israel, and mine far surpassed the chariots of Pharoah and were superior thereto, for they defeated them and drowned them in the sea. Similarly, you, my neighbor and my bride, exceed all women and have come to be compared to my company of horsemen which, by comparison with Pharoah's chariots, are regarded altogether more powerful and magnificent.[18]

The image of the noble and powerful mare illustrates how conversion in the Scriptures always results in a new energy and desire to serve the Lord. The freedom from the burden of sin, the opportunity for a new beginning, the feeling of being unconditionally loved by the Lord, all fuel the heart's desire to love God and neighbor fervently.

The bridegroom also makes gold and silver jewelry for the bride, which symbolize that the shackles of her sin are now converted into ornaments of virtue, adding to her grace and beauty. Now, instead of the iron

---

[17] Ibid.

[18] Origen, *The Song of Songs, Commentary and Homilies,* Book 2, 6, trans. Edmund de Pressence, manuscript dated 1862.

rings, necklaces and armlets that once held her captive, the Bridegroom is going to place rings and necklaces on the ears and neck of his beloved, pure jewels of gold and silver. She is restored to an even greater beauty than had she never sinned. Like the redeemed woman at the feet of Jesus (cf. Lk 7:36-50), she who has been forgiven much, loves much. The bride is greatly encouraged to simply continue in the bridegroom's loving and merciful gaze.

Similarly, the priest gazes upon the penitent with compassionate love, speaking his words of mercy, extending the Lord's healing hands in blessing and encouragement. The priest is called through grace and mercy to become the beloved bride of Christ. Because of this intimate relationship with Christ, he can share in the Lord's role of Bridegroom and extend Christ's compassion and mercy to all. The French priest and poet Henri Lacordaire sums up the priest's joy of sharing the Sacrament of Penance: "To share all suffering; To penetrate all secrets; To heal all wounds; To teach and to pardon, console and bless always. My God, what a life; and it is yours, O priest of Jesus Christ."[19]

Questions for Reflection and Discussion

1. What is my own experience of having my dignity restored in the Sacrament of Penance? How do I feel revitalized to serve the Lord more fervently?

2. Am I aware of the priest's greater obligation to avoid sin and to strive for holiness due to the nature of his calling and position in the Church as a representative of Christ *in persona Christi*? Am I concerned about how profoundly my sin, as well as my holiness, impact the whole people of God?

---

[19] Henri Lacordaire, "A Priest." Roman Catholic Identity: The Art of Living. http://www.romancatholicidentity.com/2009/06/priest-by-lacordaire.html

3. What is my experience of hearing confessions? What do I enjoy and what are the challenges? What are the obstacles for me to becoming a better confessor?

4. How can I help the penitent focus more on the mercy of God than to be turned inward in shame or fear during confession? How can I help the penitent to a greater sense of rejoicing and celebration?

5. How has the Sacrament of Penance made me more fervent in service to the Lord out of gratitude for his mercy and unconditional love? Do I see this in the lives of penitents as well?

Prayer Exercises

1. Ponder the story of Jean Valjean from Les Miserables. Pray with Mk 10:46-52 and ask for the grace to know your dignity as a child of God.

2. Consider the story of Tatiana Gorisheva. Pray with Ex 34:6-7 and Sg 1:5-6, 9-11 and ask for the grace to know God's mercy.

3. Reflect on St. John Paul II's quotation about believing in mercy. Pray with Jn 20:19-29 and ask for the grace to rejoice in the gift of God's mercy in the Sacrament of Penance.

4. Ponder the quote from the U.S. Bishops about the importance of priestly holiness. Pray with 1 Pt 1:13-25 and ask for the grace to strive for holiness.

5. Consider Emilie Griffin's quotes on confession. Pray with Lk 7:36-50 and ask for the grace to love much, knowing you have been forgiven much.

Chapter 4

A Shepherd's Care

Tell me, you whom my soul loves,
where you pasture your flock,
where you make it lie down at noon;
for why should I be like one who wanders
beside the flocks of your companions?
If you do not know,
O fairest among women,
follow in the tracks of the flock,
and pasture your kids
beside the shepherds' tents. (Sg 1:7-8)

The Scottish American preacher Peter Marshall famously said that the person who doesn't stand for something will fall for anything. For people who don't believe in God or practice their faith, they will sometimes fill that void with a cause or obsession which they invest with ultimate value. It could be that a cause becomes the obsession of their lives. Even for those who believe, but are not strong in their faith, it is possible to fall for the latest philosophical trend, pop-psychology, immoral current, or New Age religion. Forty years ago, I read Christopher Lasch's groundbreaking book *The Culture of Narcissism* for a college philosophy course. Lasch cautioned that the mainstream media fosters the delusion that we are all independent individuals who determine our personal tenets and habits; that our opinions are important; and that businesses and products are created to improve our lives because we merit it. The reality is quite different. According to Lasch, contemporary culture consciously breeds dependent and frail individuals. Why? Because a feeble mind is more easily controlled by advertising and the artificial desires it arouses. The narcissist may appear to be extremely self-centered, and he is, but his selfishness is motivated by uncertainty and anxiety rather than confidence. What it means to be a Christian is the exact opposite of such conformism. Real faith demands the courage to go against the norm. The characteristics of the mature Christian are thankfulness, not avarice, faith in the Lord, not insecurity, and not phony accommodation with a heathen culture. Faith in God sets us free from our self-centered individualism. The Lord desires that we adhere to his teaching and not be swayed by passing fads. He reveals himself as a Good Shepherd who leads his people both collectively as a flock and personally as individuals. Because we are created in the image of God, God desires to establish a relationship between the human person and himself, wherein God walks with his people and cares about their well-being as a shepherd.

Sheep Must Be Shepherded

The good shepherd rises early at daybreak to lead his sheep out of the pen into fresh pastures. He stands at the gate and calls gently to his own to move outside. As each animal passes, he calls it by name, surveys it with his perceptive eye, and, if necessary, explores with discerning hands beneath its wool, to make sure everything is fine. It is a tender moment at the dawn of each new day, a period of personal and cherished connection between the shepherd and his flock. Later, in the evening, the shepherd lays his staff across the entrance to the enclosure. Each sheep passes under the rod, during which the shepherd inspects it to discern whether it has incurred any injury or illness during the day. The shepherd knows his sheep well. He can tell you the personal story of each one of the sheep, when and where it was born, the problems it has had in life, and its personal characteristics. He attends to the individual needs of each one of them. He knows which one has tender hooves, which one became ill from eating the wrong things, and which one was likely to stray from the flock. Jesus knows each one of us in an intensely personal way: "My sheep hear my voice. I know them, and they follow me" (Jn 10:27). He wants his shepherds to know and tend to their flocks with the same intimacy. He knows our life history. He knows which one of us is weak in faith, which of us is likely to become disheartened, which one of us is likely to amble away from the rest of the flock. When one of us goes astray, the shepherd will leave the other ninety-nine and go in search of us (cf. Mt 18:12).

God himself is a caring shepherd and chose shepherds to be Patriarchs. He chose shepherds to be Israel's first kings. The prophets reminded Israel that they were a flock, and that the Lord was their shepherd. The Psalms sing the joy of being the Lord's people, the flock he shepherds (cf. Ps 100:3). Even when Israel's human shepherds failed, God promised to show himself as their ultimate shepherd: "I will give you shepherds after my own heart...I will set shepherds over them who will care for them, and they shall fear no more, nor be dismayed" (Jer 3:15; 23:4).

Jesus Christ would prove to be the fulfillment of God's promise: "I am the Good Shepherd" (Jn 10:11). He is the "great shepherd of the sheep" (Heb 13:20). Jesus entrusted to the apostles and their successors the ministry of shepherding God's flock: "Tend the flock of God that is your charge, not by constraint but willingly, not for shameful gain but eagerly, not as domineering over those in your charge but being examples to the flock. And when the chief Shepherd is manifested, you will obtain the unfading crown of glory" (1 Pet 5:2-4).

The bride of the Song desires to follow in the tracks of the Shepherd of Israel (cf. Sg 1:8), who is the Lord. She represents Israel, lost in exile, seeking to return. The Lord himself promises to bring her back:

> I will rescue them from all the places to which they have been scat-
> tered on a day of clouds and thick darkness. I will bring them out
> from the peoples and gather them from the countries, and will
> bring them into their own land...I will feed them with good pas-
> ture... there they shall lie down in good grazing land...I myself
> will be the shepherd of my sheep, and I will make them lie down,
> says the Lord GOD...I will seek the lost, and I will bring back the
> strayed, and I will bind up the injured, and I will strengthen the
> weak... (Ez 34:12-16).

As shepherds seek out their flocks among scattered sheep, so the Lord will seek out his sheep. Israel the bride will be freed from her captors and will again experience the peace and joy of remaining near the Shepherd, sing-ing "The Lord is my Shepherd, I shall not want" (Ps 23:1).

The Psalmist proclaims "The Lord is *my* shepherd" (Ps 23:1) and that "we are *his people*, the sheep of his pasture" (Ps 100:3). We belong to him. Shepherd and conservationist Phillip Keller describes his venture with owning sheep. The question of paying a sum of money for his sheep was crucial and meaningful to him: "They belonged to me by virtue of the fact that I paid hard cash for them. It was money earned by the blood and sweat and tears drawn from my own body during the desperate grinding years of the depression."[1] Because of this he felt in a special way that they were truly part of him and he a part of them: "There was an intimate identity involved which, though not apparent on the surface to the casual observer, nonetheless made those thirty ewes exceedingly precious to me."[2] In a

---

[1] Phillip Keller, *A Shepherd Looks at Psalm 23* (Grand Rapids, Zondervan, 1970), 6.

[2] Ibid., 7.

present-day experience of Psalm 23, Keller discovered that sheep require perpetual attention and painstaking maintenance.

Jesus paid a great price for each of us with his body, pouring out his blood for us (cf. 1 Cor 7:23). Jesus continually extends himself for us, ever interceding on our behalf, working to provide for us, and guiding us by his Spirit. Each sheep in a flock has a distinctive and lifelong earmark cut into its ear so that it can be recognized as belonging to a particular shepherd. We, too, are marked by baptism with the Cross of Jesus and are recognizable to him as his own. Our deepest longing is to belong to someone, from the time we belong to our family, through to adulthood when we seek to attach to others. We belong first to the Lord. We are precious in his sight, even carved into the palm of his hand (cf. Isa 49:16). We belong to the Church our Mother, and our brothers and sisters within the great family of God. "Once you were not a people, now you are God's people" (1 Pet 2:10).

Threats to the Flock

As pastors, we want to show this same predilection to our flock so that they know the Lord loves them. Like the Good Shepherd we always want to be putting ourselves out for our people and assiduously caring for them. St. Patrick illustrates the pastoring charism as a missionary bishop in the 5th century A.D. to the people of Ireland. As a boy in England, St. Patrick spent six years as a shepherd. When he was sixteen, Irish pirates swept into his village, kidnapped him, and forcibly took him back to pagan Ireland where he was sold as a slave. His master ordered him to tend his sheep, which he executed faithfully. His time as a shepherd proved to be a conversion experience. He had strayed from God and returned. He had prayed infrequently, but as a shepherd learned to pray morning, noon, and night.

The teenage boy had become a holy man. He had visions. He heard the voices of the Irish people calling him back. The voices were persistent, and he eventually left his family to become ordained as a priest and a bishop with the intention of returning to Ireland and converting the Irish to Christianity. At the time, the Irish were fierce, illiterate, Iron-Age people. For over eleven hundred years, the Roman Empire had been spreading its civilizing influence from Africa to Britain, but Rome never conquered Ireland. The people of Ireland warred constantly. They made human sacrifices of prisoners of war and sacrificed newborns to the gods of the harvest. They hung the skulls of their enemies on their belts as ornaments. The slave-boy-turned-bishop decided to make these people literate and peaceful. Braving dangers and obstacles of tremendous magnitude, he finally succeeded. Of course, it was not all easy sailing. The history of St Patrick is strewn with periods of imprisonment when his teachings upset local chieftains or Celtic Druids, but he always escaped or gained freedom by presenting his captors with gifts. For twenty years, he travelled the length and breadth of the island, baptizing people and establishing monasteries, schools, and churches as he went. By the end of his life, Ireland was Christian. Slavery had ceased entirely. Wars were much less frequent, and literacy was spreading. St. Patrick was truly a shepherd who was constantly present to his sheep and willing to give his life for them.

Like St. Patrick who walked with his people, a shepherd is with his sheep 24 hours a day, 7 days a week, 365 days of the year. He is always there guiding and tending his flock, just as Jesus promised to be with us always, until the end of time. (Mt 28:20). The shepherd knows each sheep of his flock by a distinct name, usually based on some physical characteristic such as "black leg" or "floppy ears." The Lord has a particular name for each one of us. "I have called you by name, you are mine" (Isa 43:1). This is comforting in a time when society is increasingly depersonalized. People are known by their numbers: checking account and credit card numbers, social security numbers. It is consoling to be known by name. It is comforting to be seen. A shepherd has a unique way of calling his sheep and they know his voice. The sheep does not follow a stranger (cf. Jn 10:5).

A visitor to the Holy Land wanted to witness for himself if it was true that a sheep would not follow a stranger. He arranged with a willing shepherd to wear the shepherd's outer cloak and turban. Then he approached the sheep and cried out "manah," the Arabic word for "come." Not a single sheep moved. The man was fascinated and asked whether the sheep will ever respond to someone else's voice. The shepherd replied that yes, they will. Sometimes, a sheep will become so sick that it will follow anyone. When people are hurting, they will look for anything, and sometimes mistake an enemy or thief's voice for their shepherd's. Therefore, as shepherds, we must be especially on the lookout for those who are in any way wounded and hurting. This is when Jesus wants to be closest to his people and we can be his heart and hands reaching out to them.

The bride in the Song of Songs is lost and confused and wants to be shepherded. She asks where the shepherd will rest his flock at noon (Sg 1:7). According to Origen, noon is the period of repose in eternal contemplation, when God reveals to the soul all the storehouse of wisdom and knowledge. At this moment, the Sun of Justice, the enlightening Word, will be the one to draw our gaze. He imagines the bride saying:

There are other times to pasture: evening or morning or sunset. But this is the only moment that I seek, when in the fire of the day you are revealed in the fullness of light, in your dazzling majesty....Now I blush in the presence of others and veil my face because I am a very beautiful bride and I do not uncover my face for anyone but you whom I have loved for so long.[3]

---

[3] Origen, *The Song of Songs, Commentary and Homilies*, Homily 1:8.

Her contemplative repose is echoed in the Psalmists words "He makes me lie down in green pastures; he leads me beside still waters; he restores my soul" (Ps 23: 2-3).

The Reassuring Presence of the Shepherd

"He makes me lie down." (Ps 23:2) A peculiar trait of sheep is that it is very difficult to make them lie down. Because of their fearfulness they must be anxiety-free to lounge. If there is even a hint of danger from wild animals the sheep remain on alert to run away to survive. They are weak and defenseless creatures. Phillip Keller over time discovered "that nothing so quieted and reassured the sheep as to see me in the field. The presence of their master and owner and protector put them at ease as nothing else could do, and this applied day and night."[4] For us, knowing Jesus is near dispels all fear of evil and brings peace and rest to his flock. We as his shepherds are called to offer the same reassuring presence. It may be our reassuring words in pastoral counseling as someone faces a difficult trial. It might be our comforting presence and prayers in the face of loss. It could be our firm admonition and intervention amid a dangerous temptation. The faithful will know we are there to protect them.

Sheep are also kept from lying down by rivalry, tension, and competition for status and self-assertion. They must always stand up and defend their place and challenge the challenger or the intruder. An arrogant, cunning, and domineering sheep will try to bully the other sheep. The bully sheep asserts its supremacy butting and driving other sheep away from the preferred grazing or resting grounds. Keller notes, "Whenever I came into view and my presence attracted their attention, the sheep quickly

---

[4] Keller, 25.

forgot their foolish rivalries and stopped their fighting."[5] The presence of the shepherd quelled their aggressive behavior. In the Church, as in any organization, there can be rivalries and tensions over self-assertion and recognition. Jesus had to remind the Apostles, who were already vying to be greatest in the kingdom, that the greatest among them should be the humble servants of others (cf. Mat 23:11). St. Paul also dealt with prideful individuals and factions seeking power and status in the Church (cf. 1 Cor 4). He had to remind them of their humble origins and that all the members of the body should work together for the good of the whole. Our presence as shepherds helps to quell such rivalries and ambitions. We can form the faithful in humility and in surrendering control to God.

Finally, sheep will not lie down if they are hungry. "A hungry, ill-fed sheep is ever on its feet, on the move, searching for another scanty mouthful of forage to try and satisfy its gnawing hunger. Such sheep are not contented, they do not thrive, they are of no use to themselves nor to their owners. They languish and lack vigor and vitality."[6] The Lord is a shepherd who always feeds his people. The Israelites were given manna and quail in the desert. The Lord offers his very body and blood in the holy Eucharist. He promises "I am the bread of life. Whoever comes to me will never be hungry, and whoever believes in me will never be thirsty" (Jn 6:35). When we nourish our flock at the Eucharistic Table, they will be fed on God's word and body. Only then will they be contented and able to lie down in repose and experience the Lord's rest.

Recognizing the Shepherd's Voice

The time we spend every day in intimate relationship with the Lord—

---

[5] Ibid., 29.
[6] Ibid., 35.

indeed, the very gift of prayer—enables us to lie down in rest and repose. In prayer, we experience the gaze of the Lord as the Good Shepherd who always pays attention to us. The Lord is always speaking to us as a shepherd who walks ahead of his flock talking and singing so they can hear him and follow along. Yet, we must learn to discern the Lord's voice among the competing voices of the world, the flesh, and the devil. No matter how dark or stormy it gets, God makes his voice heard in our hearts. Theologian Romano Guardini questions how well we hear the Good Shepherd's voice, and how attentive we really are to it:

> Actually, I respond much more readily to the call of "others." I neither really understand Christ's summons nor follow it. Therefore, in order that I may hear, he must not only speak, but also open my ears to his voice. Part of me, the profoundest part, listens to it, but superficial, loud contradiction overpowers it. The opponents with whom God must struggle in order to win us are not primarily "the others," but ourselves; we bar his way. The wolf that puts the hireling to flight is not only outside; he is also within. We are the archenemy of our own salvation, and the Shepherd must fight first-of-all with us–for us.[7]

A profound moment of shepherding for me as a priest is offering the *Spiritual Exercises of St. Ignatius.* For the retreatant, it is a time of profound repose and listening to the voice of Christ the Good Shepherd. The journey through the Exercises creates a special bond as the director walks with his retreatant through the spiritual stages of purification, illumination, and union with God. I have offered the retreat in isolated settings over thirty-day periods, but most often offer the full retreat in daily life

---

[7] Romano Guardini, *The Lord* (Washington D.C., Regnery Publishing, 2012), 162.

over thirty weeks. I assign prayer material for each of the 240 days and meet with the retreatant for an hour each week. This becomes a very intimate hearing of the person's entire salvation history as the retreatant experiences the spiritual and psychological healing found through commending one's past to the Lord's mercy. The person is led to a close following of the Good Shepherd through contemplation of the mysteries of Jesus' incarnation, hidden life, and public ministry.

As a director, I help the retreatant listen and respond to the Shepherd's voice and to distinguish His voice from the voices of the world, the flesh, and the devil that seek to distort or drown out Jesus' call. Most retreatants experience some spiritual desolations that lead to discouragement, doubt, and distractions. These feelings and the resulting thoughts often go unnoticed by the retreatant and I play a crucial role in helping them to notice these movements, to judge them as coming from the enemy, and to reject them. It is easier for the retreatant to notice the joyful feelings and thoughts that come from spiritual consolation, which leads one closer to the Lord. Again, I play a crucial role in helping the person unpack the meaning and dwell in the divine pastureland of grace God is giving the soul. As a director I have my antenna up to be aware of any element of falsehood or deception in what the retreatant proposes at every stage of the process, teaching each of them to have discerning hearts. Discernment is a key aspect of shepherding a person through the retreat, distinguishing the shepherd's voice from the enemy, who is a thief, liar, and murderer (Jn 8:44). Finally, the enemy spirit deceives even with spiritual consolations that can lead a person off track. "Even Satan disguises himself as an angel of light" (2 Cor 11:14). Pope Francis speaks of the importance of the priest as a shepherd who helps people discern: "We need to form future priests…to this keen discernment of spirits so that they can help people in their concrete life."[8]

As priests, we must pray and discern before speaking as the Lord's representative. Jesus as Shepherd protects his sheep. He says, "Very truly, I tell you, I am the gate for the sheep" (Jn 10:9) He speaks of those who came before him as thieves and marauders who only come to kill and destroy. The Lord had long ago condemned the false shepherds of Israel for feeding themselves and not the sheep:

> You eat the fat, you clothe yourselves with the wool, you slaughter the fatlings; but you do not feed the sheep. You have not strengthened the weak, you have not healed the sick, you have not bound up the injured, you have not brought back the strayed, you have not sought the lost, but with force and harshness you have ruled them. So they were scattered, because there was no shepherd; and scattered, they became food for all the wild animals. (Ez 34:3-5)

Throughout salvation history, the people of God have confronted innumerable false prophets. By the time Jesus arrived there were many false Messiahs and insurrectionists in Palestine who promised they would restore the glory of Israel. The historian Josephus spoke of there being thousands of disturbances in Judea, tumults caused by men of war and bloody rebellions. Zealots were willing themselves to die, and they did not object to slaughtering their own loved ones for the goal of takeover.[9] Their way of war, murder, and assassination only led away from God. Jesus' way of

---

[8] Pope Francis, Interview, *The Church Must Grow in Discernment*, The Catholic New World, Sept. 4, 2016, The Chicago Catholic Website, https://www.chicagocatholic.com/international/-/article/2016/08/25/pope-francis-the-church-must-grow-in-discernment

[9] See Josephus, *Early Jewish Writings, The Wars of the Jews*, Early Jewish Writings, http://www.earlyjewishwritings.com/text/josephus/war1.html

peace, love, and life led closer to God. There are still false prophets in our own society, sometimes even in the Church, who foment violence, class warfare, hostility, anarchy, and destruction, which is never the Christian way.

Shepherding Through Self-Giving and Sacrifice

Jesus himself is the gate who protects his sheep. When the sheep were out on the hills in the warm season and did not return at night to the village pen, they were collected into sheepfolds on the hillside. The field pen consisted of a circular stone wall about 4 ft. high with a small opening for the sheep to pass through. Once they had all been herded in, instead of closing a hinged gate, the shepherd laid down across the narrow entrance acting as a barrier. No sheep could leave the pen and no thief or wild animal could get through without stepping on his body, awakening the shepherd to the danger. He was literally the gate to the sheepfold and laid himself down to protect his sheep. If necessary, the shepherd would engage in mortal combat to protect his sheep. In modern times, a young shepherd was leading his flock to pastures near Mount Tabor in Israel. Suddenly, three Bedouin bandits emerged. The shepherd, aware of the danger he faced, remained steadfast and battled to defend his flock. The struggle ended when the intruders killed the shepherd with a knife.[10] Such willingness to die to protect the flock speaks to us of Jesus' willingness to lay down his life for the sake of his sheep.

The life of the good shepherd in New Testament times was one of personal self-giving and sacrifice. His work was that of watchful care and closeness to the flock. Jesus, as the good shepherd who owns and cares for

---

[10] See Mark Link, *Vision 2000*, A Cycle (Allen, TX, Tabor Publishing, 1992), 137.

the sheep, distinguished himself from the hired hand: "The hired hand, who is not the shepherd and does not own the sheep, sees the wolf coming and leaves the sheep and runs away—and the wolf snatches them and scatters them" (Jn 10:12). For the hired hand, keeping the sheep was just the convenient and available job. He was only in it for the pay and not invested in the sheep because they were not his. He moved from flock to flock depending on the terms of service and he would not risk his life for them. Seeing wolves or thieves coming, he would run for his life and leave the flock at the mercy of the attackers. By contrast Jesus is like the shepherd-owner of the flock with whom the flock has grown up. He remains with his flock all throughout their lives. When his sheep are attacked by wolves or thieves, he risks his life and fights to defend them. He is the good shepherd who lays down his life for his sheep.

Priests are called to lay down their lives in imitation of Christ the Good Shepherd as exemplified by the life and death of Blessed Stanley Rother. In 1935, Rother was born in rural Oklahoma to a pious German farming family as the oldest of four children. He had experience with working. He fixed anything that broke on the property. He constructed things as they were required. He was a man of few words and great action. He eventually sensed and followed a call to the priesthood, and in 1963, he was ordained. He adopted a priestly maxim: "For my own sake I am a Christian; for the sake of others, I am a priest." He accepted a request to join a team of missionaries in Guatemala when he was thirty-three years old. Soon after arriving there, he was appointed parish pastor of St. James the Apostle soon after. Many days in the sweltering sun were spent by Fr. Stanley bulldozing land for a collaborative farm. With the parishioners, he planted, plowed, and harvested their crops, inspiring them to persevere in their work. In order to address their material and spiritual needs, Rother thoroughly embraced his flock as family. He helped them staff the hospital, create a radio station, and establish a cooperative of weavers. He pioneered the translation of the New Testament and developed a written form of their native Tz'utujtl language. Fr. Stanley remained close to his flock throughout. He took stock of the necessities of his congregation when he opened his rectory. He offered guidance, extracted teeth, and fostered orphans. His friendship with the indigenous people aroused the suspicion of Guatemala's oppressive regime. Catechists and priests would frequently vanish, and their corpses would never be located. If they were discovered, they had marks of torture on them.

Fr. Stanley once learned that he was number eight on the list of state enemies who would be executed. He acknowledged this in a letter, stating that the shepherd cannot flee at the first hint of peril. Fr. Stanley allowed the church to be open the evening before the feast of St. James so that six hundred men who anticipated being compelled to join the army could find refuge there. On July 28, 1981, around 1:30 a.m., Rother awakened to a knock at the door and received notification that the police were looking for him. Fr. Stanley calculated if he attempted to flee, Francisco, the young watchman, would surely be made to suffer. The Carmelite sisters on the other side of the courtyard would be in danger, too. So, he courageously went to the door and told the assailants they would have to kill him there. Gunshots erupted and Fr. Stanley was killed and left dead on the floor. When the populace learned that their priest, who spoke their language, had been murdered, thousands of locals crowded inside St. James Church. The local church was planted and grew as a result of Fr. Stanley's martyrdom. They currently have enough native priests to run the parish by themselves. St. James parish has produced nine priests who have been ordained, and seven additional men are now enrolled in the seminary. Fr. Stanley shared the life of his people and, in the words of Pope Francis, lived with the "smell of the sheep." He was a true shepherd who never abandoned his flock, even to the point of laying down his life for the sheep.

The bride who has been lost and confused is now counselled to return to her home Jerusalem. Israel the bride had been exiled and would return the same way by which she had been led out by her captors. God told Israel: "Set up road markers for yourself, make yourself signposts; consider well the highway, the road by which you went. Return, O virgin Israel, return to these your cities" (Jer 31:21). She would find her way by following the tracks of the shepherds. As with our biblical ancestors, Jesus is the Good Shepherd who leads his bride the Church, his flock, in right paths. He pastures his sheep and makes them lie down in peaceful repose, confident of his watchful eye and abiding presence, especially through his shepherds.

Questions for Reflection and Discussion

1. What do I find attractive about the image of Jesus as the Good Shepherd? Where, in my life and ministry as a priest do I most realize the qualities of the shepherd?

2. How well do I as a priest listen to the voice of the Good Shepherd? What obstacles do the world, the flesh, and the devil present to my recognizing God's voice?

3. How well do I know my flock and tend to their needs? Where is my flock most apt to go astray and how do I seek them out? How do I sacrifice myself to keep them from danger?

4. In what ways does my presence as a shepherd help the sheep to "lie down" in peaceful repose in the face of dangers, rivalries, and hunger?

5. How aware am I of the Church's teaching (especially St. Ignatius of Loyola) on discernment of spirits and discerning God's will? How might discernment help me in my own spiritual life and in ministry to God's people?

Prayer Exercises

1. Consider Christopher Lasch's critique of our conformist culture. Pray with Sg 1:7-8, and Ez 34:12-16, and ask for the grace to shepherd God's flock in the ways of Christ.

2. Reflect on Phillip Keller's paying the price for his flock. Pray with Jn 10:1-18 and ask for the grace to imitate Christ in laying down your life for his flock.

3. Ponder Pope Francis' emphasis on the importance of the priest's knowledge of discernment of spirits. Pray with Jn 10:1-10 and ask for the grace to discern the voice of Christ amidst competing voices.

4. Consider the reasons sheep find it difficult to lie down. Pray with Ps 23 and ask for the grace to be a peacemaking presence among your flock.

5. Reflect on the story of Blessed Stanley Rother. Pray with Jn 21:14-19 and ask the grace of greater love for the Lord in order to better feed his sheep.

Chapter 5

Vision of Beauty

While the king was on his couch,

my nard gave forth its fragrance.

My beloved is to me a bag of myrrh,

that lies between my breasts.

My beloved is to me a cluster of henna blossoms

in the vineyards of En-ged'i.

Behold, you are beautiful, my love;

behold, you are beautiful;

your eyes are doves.

Behold, you are beautiful, my beloved,

truly lovely.

Our couch is green;

the beams of our house are cedar,

our rafters are pine. (Sg 1:12-17)

There was once a ballerina named Donna filled with such grace and beauty that she could "blow like silk across the stage or drive like a storm through the corps de ballet." [1] However, if you questioned Donna about her own experience of dancing as a font of beauty and brilliance, she would register a void of emotion or expression. All she knew was fixation with grueling preparation to meet her perfectionist standards of performance. Her rigorism affected not just her attitude toward dancing, but the whole of her life. Donna was driven by anger over her past and especially fear.

---

[1] Martin Laird, *Into the Silent Land, The Practice of Contemplation* (New York, Oxford, 2006), 19-20.

She was afraid of negative reviews of her dancing, afraid her husband might one day walk away, afraid of her own loneliness. The tapes that played in her head were mostly from her childhood and her relationship with her mother. One day her mother had entered Donna's bedroom, found her looking at herself in the mirror and said: "I hope you don't think you're beautiful." Donna was certainly beautiful as a young girl and throughout her life. But, in her mind she could only imagine herself as ugly. She eventually won a choice scholarship to a prestigious ballet academy, which led her mother to question "How did you get that? Everybody knows you're a klutz." Despite continuously rave reviews for her dancing throughout the world, Donna still believed she had two left feet. Her mother's tape continued to loop through her head and made her life miserable. Eventually, Donna took long walks out in nature in the Yorkshire hills. The vast expansive view cleared her overwrought mind while the scent of heather soothed her tormented soul. Once, in a graced moment her anxiety was eased, and she was enfolded in God's holy presence which buoyed her spirit and the ambiance surrounding her. Donna felt reclaimed as God's beautiful and precious daughter. She became aware that her own beauty no longer hinged on her external performance but radiated from deep within.[2]

Transcendent Beauty

God seals each being He creates with its own secret mark of beauty. Love helps us to discern the beauty–and the dignity–that God has placed in each soul. In the Song of Songs, the bride becomes aware that her lover is gazing upon her and in his ecstasy cries out, "Ah, you are beautiful my love" (Sg 1:15). God looks with love on each of us as his wonderful creation

---

[2] Ibid.

and calls us beautiful. It is because he has loved us and redeemed us from the ugliness of sin that we now draw close to him, the source of all beauty. St. Augustine gushes:

> What then is this love that makes the loving soul beautiful? God, who is always beautiful, who never loses his beauty, who never changes: he loved us first, he who is always beautiful. And what were we when he loved us if not ugly and disfigured? But he did not love us to leave us to our ugliness but to change us and, disfigured as we were, to make us beautiful. How then can we become beautiful? By loving the one who is eternally beautiful. The greater the love in you, the greater your beauty.[3]

God reveals himself and draws all who contemplate his beauty to himself. The sight of beauty moves us, captivates us, ravishes our hearts. We enjoy the pleasure of beauty and are seized by it.

Through our faith, we develop a taste for true beauty. As priests, we need to cultivate and promote the truly beautiful in order to dispose people to receive the faith. There is much in our world that is opposed to the finer taste for beauty. A visitor was once being shown around an art gallery. The gallery contained some beautiful paintings, which were universally acknowledged to be masterpieces. At the end of the tour, the visitor said, "I don't think much of these old pictures." To which his guide replied, "My good man, these pictures are no longer on trial. But those who look at them are."[4] The man's reaction was not a judgment on the pictures but on his

---

[3] St. Augustine, Witnesses to Hope Website, https://witnessestohope.org/2009/09/#:~:text=dwells%20within%20us.-,St.,he%20who%20is%20always%20beautiful

[4] Flor McCarthy, *New Sunday and Holy Day Liturgies*, Year B, Fourth Sunday of Lent (Dublin, Dominican Publications, 1999), 84.

own pitiful appreciation of art. Unfortunately, much of what we consume with our senses that passes for beauty in our culture is really a more superficial glamour. It is a false artificial imitation of beauty that has no depth and does not flow out from an essential center, leading us away from wisdom. "Glamour is more glitter than light, more glitz than depth, more glisten than glory."[5] For instance, people are obsessed with Hollywood stars, their fashion and fame, which is merely glamor. Someone can put on a fancy dress and pricey jewelry and look glamorous but not necessarily beautiful. At the Easter Sunday renewal of baptismal vows, we reject the glamour of this world and embrace the true beauty of Christ.

God is the unchanging essence of beauty and the source of all created beauty. According to St. Thomas Aquinas, everything participates in the beautiful, meaning everything which exists is beautiful. To *be* is to *be beautiful.* Beauty belongs to God in a unique way beyond mere aesthetics. God is supernatural being and beautiful beyond that of our existence. His beauty is beyond our grasp, incomprehensible in its divinity, resplendent, sublime, immense, and infinite. God's beauty is the source of the beauty of all created things. All things exist and all things become because of beauty and goodness. All things look to beauty and goodness as their cause, which they possess as a rule governing their activities.[6] The closer we come to God, the more immersed in him, the more beautiful we become.

While the beauty of God in his essence cannot be seen or comprehended, he has revealed himself in his Son, Jesus Christ, who is the perfect image of the Father and the refulgence of his eternal Light (cf. Heb 1:3). God the Incomprehensible, allowed himself to be known personally. Jesus

---

[5] Donald De Marco, "Can Beauty Save the World?" *Lay Witness* (November/December, 2009): 16-17.

[6] See St. Thomas Aquinas, *An Exposition of "the Divine Names," the Book of Blessed Dionysus,* trans. Michael Augros, pars. 337-339 (Merrimack, NH: Thomas More College Press, 2021), 153, 155.

makes the beauty of God accessible. Beauty is a quality that is most fittingly attributed to God the Son. The Son is the Beauty of God; He is Beauty itself. God the Son is clearly the intelligible Word of the Father, the light and splendor of the divine mind. Jesus Christ is beautiful in his divinity and he is also beautiful in his humble human nature. St. Augustine effuses:

> Beautiful is God, the Word with God... He is beautiful in heaven, beautiful on earth; beautiful in the womb, beautiful in His parents' arms, beautiful in His miracles, beautiful in His sufferings; beautiful in inviting to life, beautiful in not worrying about death, beautiful in giving up His life and beautiful in taking it up again; He is beautiful on the Cross, beautiful in the tomb, beautiful in heaven. Listen to the song with understanding and let not the weakness of the flesh distract your eyes from the splendor of His beauty.[7]

Christ, perfect image of the Father, imparts the fullness of grace to us, making us gracious, beautiful, and lovely to God. In a stream of continuous grace, the Christian worships Christ who has restored him to life and allows himself to be transfigured by the glorious gifts he has received.

It is ironic that the beauty of Christ the suffering servant is manifest in his crucified form, seeming to lack any physical beauty (cf. Isa 53). Jesus, who was without sin, takes the ugliness of sin upon himself to elevate us to the divine beauty. "For those who wish to contemplate it, the icon of the Crucified with disfigured face contains the mysterious beauty of God. This

---

[7] St. Augustine, *Commentary on the Psalms,* 44,3 Corpus Christianorum Series Latina, 38, 496.

beauty is fulfilled in pain and sorrow, in the gift of self without personal gain. It is the beauty of love which is stronger than evil or death."[8]

The bride speaks of her beloved Bridegroom as the nard between her breasts or heart, the seat of her affections. (Sg 1:12-13) Nard must be bruised and crushed to give off its fragrance. Christ gave his bruised and broken body as a pleasing sacrificial offering to the Father. Just as precious oils were used to anoint the Body of Christ, the nard symbolizes his precious priestly death as a beautiful fragrance that continually delights the bride.

Transformative Beauty

At priestly ordination, the beauty of Christ's priestly character becomes impressed upon the soul of the sacred minister. The priest becomes an icon of Christ the Priest that is divinely written by the Holy Spirit.[9] The beauty of the priest is a share in the beauty of Christ the priest and bridegroom. We are *in persona Christi Capitis,* "in the person of Christ the Head" (of his Body, the Church). Being and acting in the person of Christ means being the face of Christ oriented toward his people. As the face of Christ, the priest must be conformed to the heart of Christ. In contemplation, we more fully enter the person of Christ and more closely identify with him. Jesus says to us: "You came to me...Therefore you became beautiful, changed as it were into my own image through some kind of

---

[8] The Pontifical Council for Culture, *Concluding Document of the Plenary Assembly, Via Pulchritudinis,* III, 3, A, Libreria Editrice Vaticana, 2006. Vatican Website, https://www.vatican.va/roman_curia/pontifical_councils/cultr/documents/rc_pc_cultr_doc_20060327_plenary-assembly_final-document_en.html

[9] See *Catechism of the Catholic Church,* 1142 (Vatican City: Libreria Editrice Vaticana, 1993), Vatican Website, https://www.vatican.va/archive/ENG0015/_INDEX.HTM

mirror…You became beautiful as soon as you approached my light, drawing to yourself, through this very approach, a share in my beauty."[10] This beauty surpasses the external; it is deeply interior. It is the loveliness of "the inner self with the lasting beauty of a gentle and quiet spirit, which is very precious in God's sight" (1 Pet 3:4). This spousal relationship with Christ leads us to embrace a life of celibacy in union with and in imitation of Christ. Celibacy is remaining unmarried to any earthly person in order to be married to God in the Holy Spirit. Marriage is the best image of the intimacy of this spousal union and speaks to the unity of our entire lives with Christ. The two become one flesh in human marriage, while the two form one spirit in Christ. "But anyone united to the Lord becomes one spirit with him." (1 Cor 6:17). The marital image also speaks of fruitfulness in generating new life, especially through the sacraments.

Jesus emphasizes that a person may remain unmarried for the sake of the Kingdom of Heaven—for a cause (see Mat 12). St. Paul highlights that marriage is renounced "for the sake of the Lord," (1 Cor 7:32-34) for a person, who embraces all persons.[11] Loving Christ who has a heart for all people opens the celibate's heart to also want to embrace all whom the Lord loves, and to be his heart for others. For those called to the ministerial priesthood, celibacy is the consequence of being seized by Christ to be one with him and share his life, vision, and mission. Celibacy is freely chosen for the purpose of serving God more completely, of giving the mind to the contemplation of divine things in the absence of family cares and with the sacrifice of family joys. Sadly, many priests accept celibacy only as a

---

[10] Gregory of Nyssa, *Homilies on the Song of Songs*, Homily 4, eds. Brian E. Daley, S.J. and John T. Fitzgerald, trans. Richard A. Norris (Atlanta, Society of Biblical Literature, 2012), 93.

[11] See Raniero Cantalamessa, *Virginity, A Positive Approach to Celibacy for the Sake of the Kingdom of Heaven*, transl. Charles Serignat (New York: Alba House, 1995), 21.

requirement of ordination without embracing its deeper meaning and power. Celibacy should be chosen as a consequence of the Father's love and as a participation in Christ's greater love for all human beings.

The great Protestant existential philosopher Søren Kierkegaard was betrothed to a beautiful young woman named Regina whom he loved deeply. Once he experienced the call to remain unmarried and devote himself to the things of the Lord in his contemplation of spiritual truths, he knew he would have to sacrifice Regina. He tried to conceal the intensity of his love for her under a veneer of flippancy and cruelty, hoping she would break the relationship, but she saw through it and would not budge. He sent her a withered rose, then returned his engagement ring. She fought against it like a tigress, but finally, with considerable anguish, he had to break it off.[12] Toward the end of his life he wrote:

> God wants celibacy, because he wants to be loved... O infinite Majesty, even if You were not love, even if You were aloof in your infinite majesty, I still could not help loving You, for I need something majestic to love. What others have complained of—namely that they did not find love in this world, and therefore felt the need to love You, since You are love (which I agree with totally)—I would like to proclaim too and apply it to the majestic. There was, and still is, in my soul a need for majesty, which I shall never grow tired or weary of adoring. In the world I found nothing of this majesty for which I yearned.[13]

---

[12] See Soren Kierkegaard, *The Journals of Kierkegaard*, Ed. Alexander Dru. Harper, Torchbooks, Tb 52 (New York: Harper & Brothers, 1959), 69-75.

[13] Soren Kierkegaard, *The Journals*, XI, A, in Cantalamessa, *Virginity*, 25.

Kierkegaard did not embrace celibacy simply for the cause of writing, but for a more intense love of Jesus Christ.

Celibacy, or virginity, is a participation in the beauty of the virginity of Christ. Virtue gives the soul spiritual beauty. Temperance is the most beautiful of virtues because it means moderation and therefore harmony and due proportion, the properties of beauty. The temperate person controls his passions which, unrestrained, make a person ugly and cruel. Self-control enables the light of reason and grace to shine through one's person.[14] Chastity is the reasoned control of the sexual passions. Virginity as a form of chastity (part of temperance) radiates an incomparable beauty. St. Ambrose says: "Who can find a greater beauty than the comeliness of the virgin, who is loved by the King, approved by the Judge, dedicated to the Lord, consecrated to God?"[15]

Christ confers the gift of celibacy on his priests so that they might belong to him alone and might choose the same love relationship with the Father and with human beings that he has chosen. Jesus remained unmarried because his relationship with the Father was most precious to him. His Father's love embraced all times and peoples and Jesus shared in that love which would not remain confined to a few. Such purity of intention is amazingly beautiful and draws us to desire to share in Christ's infinite love. A woman once confided to me that as a priest she found me very attractive. Realizing she was happily married and had no designs on me, I tried to help her grow through this infatuation. I asked her what it was about me that she found attractive? I know from my training in sexuality and celibacy that as human beings we tend to eroticize what we need, or think we lack. We often become aware that we really have in potential what we feel as deficiency and need to allow the Lord to activate it within us. She

---

[14] See *ST*, IIa-IIae, 145,4.
[15] St. Ambrose, *De virginibus* 1, 7; PL 16, 210B.

replied, "your purity." I found that interesting, especially since this woman was already living a pure and chaste life, but still needed healing from past wounds. She was eventually able to recover a sense of her own purity and dignity as a daughter of God.

What is it about purity that people find beautiful and attractive? I think it is the singular dedication to the glory of God and the nobility of his cause that is most transparent. Jesus is the beautiful King with the noble cause of Psalm 45: "You are the most handsome of men; grace is poured upon your lips; therefore, God has blessed you forever. Gird your sword on your thigh, O mighty one, in your glory and majesty. In your majesty ride on victoriously for the cause of truth and to defend the right" (Ps 45:2-4). Jesus was purely dedicated to the love of his Father and his will to save us. The priest after Jesus' own heart shares in his same purity of intention, conforming our mind and heart to the demands of God's holiness. "By purity of intention which consists in seeking the true end of man: with simplicity of vision, the baptized person seeks to find and to fulfill God's will in everything" (cf. Rom 12:2, Col 1:10).[16] Purity of heart leads to the vision of God. The pure in heart will see God face to face and be like him (cf. Mt 5:8). Even now it enables us to see according to God's vision, to accept others as God's beloved, as temples of the Holy Spirit, and manifestations of divine beauty. The priest shares in Christ the Bridegroom's response to his bride the Church, "Behold you are beautiful my love."

Celibacy is a gift to celebrate and use, but involves ongoing purification, struggle against concupiscence of the flesh and disordered desires. Only by the grace of God can we prevail.[17]

Purity involves purity of vision, both external and internal. We live purity by discipline of feeling and imagination, by refusing all complicity

---

[16] *Catechism of the Catholic Church*, 2520.
[17] See *Catechism of the Catholic Church*, 2820.

in impure thoughts that incline us to turn aside from the path of God's commandments. "Appearance arouses yearning in fools" (Ws 15:5). It takes passion to renounce disordered passion, especially when it is sexual passion.

Jesus as Chaste Spouse is the model for every priest. His virgin mother is also to be loved as the ideal woman who brings us Christ. George Maloney explains how Mary is the archetypal symbol of the feminine in all human beings:

> Mary as virgin and mother becomes the archetype of the feminine contemplative spirit that lies as the integrating, healing force between our human consciousness and our unconscious. In the symbol of Mary as virgin we see ourselves as individuals, and the Church, the community of individuals brought into unity by the Spirit of Jesus, possessing a basic potential for wholeness, a healing unto full life, a happiness that flows from the fulfillment of this potential for greater being. Virginity on this primeval level is man opening himself to God's initial love in total acceptance. It is the letting go of our lives in faith and child-like trust in God to let him have full centrality in our lives.[18]

According to Venerable Fulton Sheen, every man unconsciously loves her as the perfect woman when he loves a woman.[19]

As celibate priests, our relationship with Mary leads to fulfillment of our deepest needs for self-integration, communion with others, and bearing fruit for the Kingdom. As a human being untouched by original sin,

---

[18] George Maloney, *Mary: The Womb of God* (Denville, NJ: Dimension Books, 1976), 24.

[19] See Fulton Sheen, *The World's First Love* (San Francisco: Ignatius Press, 1996), 175-176.

Mary is totally transparent to God and perfectly manifests the feminine aspects of God. A priest can allow Mary to influence his life in a way like a husband with his wife. The priest can carry her memory in his heart wherever he goes and in whatever he does. He can commit his life to her service and strive to please her and Christ in all his actions.

While celibacy has many practical advantages, we do not embrace it for its own sake. Celibacy is oriented toward the contemplative life, pondering the beauty of God, especially in prayer. "Contemplation of divine things and assiduous union with God in prayer is to be the first and foremost duty of all religious."[20] Both religious and secular priests will be nourished and fulfilled by contemplation of divine and beautiful things. St. Thomas Aquinas explains that because every man finds delight when he has attained what he loves, it follows that the contemplative life terminates in delight, which is in the will, and this in its turn intensifies love.[21]

Contemplation of truth is the greatest of all pleasures, and every pleasure eases pain. The contemplation of truth therefore eases pain; and it does so the more perfectly one loves wisdom. This is why people find joy amid tribulation by contemplating the things of God and the happiness to come.[22] This is valuable for the priest because sacrificing the gratifications of married and family life, he still needs some enjoyments of a loftier degree to experience fulfillment in his life.[23] More importantly, contemplation stirs up that essential aspect of devotion in religion. Devotion is an act of the will by which one promptly gives oneself to the service of God.

---

[20] *Code of Canon Law* 663, Sect. 1 (Vatican City, Libreria Editrice Vaticana, 1983), Vatican Website, https://www.vatican.va/archive/cod-iuris-canonici/cic_index_en.html

[21] See *ST* II IIae, 180, 1.

[22] See *ST* I-II 38, 4.

[23] See Basil Cole, "O Priest, Who Are You?" (part I), *The Priest*, August, 1994, 10-16.

When a person contemplates God and ponders his goodness and loving kindness, he is stirred to a love of God that begets devotion and the idea of giving oneself to the service of God. The direct and principal effect of devotion is joy in God.[24]

The bride is able to gaze with adoration thanks to the bridegroom's expressive gaze of love. He first describes her as attractive before saying, "Your eyes are doves" (Sg 1:15). The bride's dove-like eyes, which are vibrant, alluring, and innocent capture the bridegroom's attention. For Israel, the dove represented love and peace. The Holy Spirit is represented by the dove in the New Testament because He came to Jesus in the form of a dove. The bridegroom suggests that the bride's eyes are similar to the Holy Spirit by likening them to doves. The bride has the ability to see spiritually now through the grace of the Holy Spirit: "The light of the countenance of Jesus illumines the eyes of our heart and teaches us to see everything in the light of his truth and his compassion for all men."[25] Origen remarks that the bride can see and comprehend spiritually with these fresh, spiritual eyes. She can see the beauty of God's Word when she looks more intently into her Spouse's beauty with her dove-like eyes. Only those with a truly spiritual understanding—that is, those with dove's eyes—can truly comprehend the marvelous majesty of the Word.[26] The supernatural powers of faith, hope, and love are given to the bride, and as a result, her eyesight is significantly enhanced, and her eyes are drawn farther above the natural horizon. In the person of the Holy Spirit, the Lord's benevolent gaze endows her eyes with the splendor of spiritual vision. We also require the gift of the Holy Spirit, who opens our supernatural vision to divine reality, in order to ponder Christ and genuinely see his inner

---

[24] See *ST* II-II 82, 1-4.

[25] *Catechism of the Catholic Church*, 2715.

[26] See Origen, *Commentary on the Song of Songs*, Part One, Book Three, 171-173.

beauty.

Contemplation of beauty leads to greater love of the Lord and greater holiness, which in turn becomes attractive to others to follow Jesus. Jesus teaches that he is "the way, the truth, and the life" (Jn 14:6). The inner experience of holiness and virtue is (1) glorious freedom, (2) luminous insight, and (3) abundance of life. *(1) Freedom:* St. Augustine said, "Love and do what you will." As long as we are profoundly loving God, obedience and faithfulness, right thinking and action will follow, and we will experience the freedom and grace to love others. Jesus tells us that the truth will set us free (Jn 8:31-36). When we live by the Spirit, we are no longer subject to the stifling restrictions of the Law. The fruits of the Spirit are" love, joy, peace, patience, kindness, generosity, faithfulness, gentleness, and self-control" (Gal 5:22-23). *(2) Insight:* Jesus is the light of the world. When we follow his way, we become children of the light and understand the things of God. The Lord becomes a light to our path in the way of goodness and eternal life. *(3) Life:* Holiness and virtue also lead to greater abundance of life. The glory of God is a human being fully alive with God's grace who, burning with love, is more deeply humble, generous, strong, and gentle. "Beauty sparks an animation of spirit. A deeply rooted enthusiasm, a vibrant response to reality, is born of a capacity to appreciate the beautiful and to respond with love."[27] Beauty lies far beyond external appearance and is often perceived in a person's life energy that radiates from within.

Pavel Florensky, a Russian singer and martyr of the 20th century, comments on Jesus' exhortation to let your good works radiate before others (cf. Mt 5:16): "Your 'good deeds' does [sic] not really mean 'good acts' in the philanthropic and moral sense: *tà kalà érga* means 'beautiful acts,' luminous and harmonious revelations of spiritual personality—above all a

---

[27] Thomas Dubay, *The Evidential Power of Beauty* (San Francisco, Ignatius Press, 1999), 339.

luminous face, beautiful of a beauty that lets the interior light of men shine forth to the outside. That is when, beaten by this irresistible light, men give glory to the celestial Father and His image shines over all the earth."[28] By grace, the Christian's life is to become an occasion of conspicuous beauty to awaken wonder and reflection and provoke transformation. Beauty is the brilliance of truth and the blossoming of love.[29]

Salvific Beauty

In the liturgy of the Church, we encounter Christ and the beauty of his love. The reality of Jesus' life, death, and resurrection is manifest to us and illuminates our lives with meaning and beauty. We become more fully alive members of his Body and participate in his beauty. There is an old story about the roots of the Christian faith in Russia. Prince Vladimir I of Kiev was searching for a national religion. He sent ambassadors to neighboring countries to seek out the respective virtues of Judaism, Christianity, and Islam. During their fact-finding Journey, the prince's men had occasion to attend a Eucharistic celebration in the great Church of Hagia Sophia in Constantinople. They were overcome with awe. They went back home and filed this report: "We came to the Greeks, and we were taken to the place where they worship their God. ...We do not know whether we have been in heaven or on earth. ...We know only that God dwells there among men."[30] Not long after that, Vladimir was baptized and exhorted all his countrymen to be baptized, too. Joseph Ratzinger asserts,

---

[28] Pavel Florensky, *Les portes royales. Essai sur l'icône*, Milan 1999, 50, in *Via Pulchritudinis*, III, 3, A.

[29] See *Via Pulchritudinous*, III,3, B.

[30] See The Rus Primary Chronicle (Cambridge: Mediaeval Academy, 1953), in Ratzinger, *Pilgrim Fellowship of Faith* (San Francisco: Ignatius Press, 2005), 90–91.

It is in effect certain that the internal force of the liturgy played an essential role in the diffusion of Christianity...That which convinced...was true, was not a missionary style argument whose elements appeared more convincing to those disposed to listen than those of any other religion. No, that which struck home was the mystery in itself, a mystery that, precisely because it is found beyond all discussion, imposes on reason the force of truth.[31]

Everything related to the Eucharist should be marked by beauty. Special respect and care must also be given to the vestments, the furnishings, and the sacred vessels, so that by their harmonious and orderly arrangement they will foster awe for the mystery of God. They will manifest the unity of faith and strengthen devotion.

For those of faith, beauty surpasses the merely aesthetic, for

[i]t permits the passage from 'for self' to 'more than self.' The liturgy which...does not seek to celebrate God for Him, through Him and in Him, is not beautiful, and therefore not true. It should be 'disinterested' in putting oneself before God and placing one's eyes on Him who shines with the divine light on the things that pass. It is in this austere simplicity that it becomes missionary, that is, capable of witnessing to observers who let themselves be taken over by the invisible reality that it offers.[32]

---

[31] Joseph Ratzinger, *Eucharistia come genesi della missione*. Conference at the XXIII Eucharistic Congress of Bologna, 20-28 September 1997 in "Il Regno" 1 Nov 1997, no. 19, p. 588-589.

[32] *Via Pulchritudinous*, III, 3, C

The French writer Paul Claudel was drawn to the internal power of the liturgy in testifying to his conversion during the singing of the Magnificat at Vespers on Christmas Eve at Notre-Dame de Paris:

> It was then that the event happened that has dominated all my life. In an instant, my heart was touched, and I believed. I believed with such force, with such relief of all my being, a conviction so powerful, so certain and without any room for doubt, that ever since, all the books, all the arguments, all the hazards of my agitated life have never shaken my faith, nor to tell the truth have they even touched it.[33]

The beauty of the liturgy cannot be reduced to mere ceremonial beauty.

> It is first of all the deep beauty of the meeting with the mystery of God, present among men through the intermediary work of the Son, 'the fairest of the children of men' (Ps 45:2) who renews without end His sacrifice of love for us. It expresses the beauty of the communion with Him and with our brothers, the beauty of a harmony which translates into gestures, symbols, words, images and melodies that touch the heart and the spirit and raise marvel and the desire to meet the resurrected Lord, He who is the *Door of Beauty*.[34]

In putting on Christ, we learn to see with his eyes, the eyes of the Spirit, to see the true beauty and dignity of each individual. The movie *Mask* is

---

[33] Paul Claudel, *Ma conversion* in *Contacts et circonstances*, Gallimard, 1940, p. 11ss; cf. also in *Ecclesia, Lectures chrétiennes*, Paris, No 1, Avril 1949, p. 53-58P, in *Via Pulchritudinis*, III, 3 C.

[34] *Via Pulchritudinis*, III, 3, C.

based on the true story of a teenage boy named Rocky Dennis. Rocky was born with a rare disease that caused his skull and facial bones to grow abnormally large and disfigured. As a result, people tended to shy away from Rocky and were embarrassed to look at him. Some cruel and insensitive people even made fun of him. In the face of such avoidance and ridicule, Rocky never grows bitter or offended. Though he feels bad about his appearance, he never pities himself; rather, he accepts his condition as his lot in life. One day, Rocky and his friends visit an amusement park and enter a hall of mirrors attraction. His friends laugh at the way the mirrors distort their face and bodies. Then something startling happens. As Rocky looks at himself in the mirror, it so distorts his face that it looks normal. Rocky even looks strikingly handsome. His friends see his reflection and are amazed. Now they see Rocky in a whole new light. They see him on the exterior as he is interiorly, a beautiful young man.[35] When we look upon others with the eyes of Christ and his gaze of love, we see them as children of God with infinite dignity.

Divine Beauty

The keener the love the deeper the appreciation of the beauty of each person. One sees with the truth and compassion of the eyes of Christ. Thomas Howard wrote of the British novelist Charles Williams' perspicacity:

> The eye with which he looked at ordinary things was like the eye of a lover looking at his lady. The lover sees this plain woman crowned with the light of heaven. She walks in beauty. Her eyes

---

[35] See Mark Link, *Illustrated Sunday Homilies, Years A,B,C, Series I,* Second Sunday of Lent, Year C, 21.

are windows of Paradise to him. Her body, every inch of it, is an incarnation and epiphany of celestial grace. In her he finds the ecstatic vision that his heart has sought. All this passionate intensity, Williams would argue, is not illusion. The ecstatic vision of beauty thus vouchsafed to that love is true, not false. The lady is glorious as he sees her to be. It has been given to him who loves her, to see the truth about her. The rest of us bystanders, mercifully, have not had our eyes thus opened, else we would all go mad. It would be an intolerable burden of glory if we all saw unveiled, the splendor of other creatures, all the time...We cannot bear very much reality, said Eliot [William's friend].[36]

Christ the Bridegroom fixes his gaze upon his bride with the same fervor of love and deep appreciation of her interior beauty. As priests who identify with Christ and who ask him to be our vision, we see with his spiritual eyes and ponder deeply the dignity and splendor of each person. As contemplatives of divine beauty, we become "permeable to and receptive of the deep meanings of things."[37] Loving genuinely, priests are able

to see their beloved [faithful] in a wholly different way from others because the beloved's profound interior self is manifested to them in all its utterances and appears as that which is really precious and worthy of love. Every gift, every word speaks of this, and every reply they give contains their whole self. Exterior exchanges are only bridges by which the souls pass over into one another.[38]

---

[36] Thomas Howard, "Discovering Charles Williams ... and the Nuptial Dance, *New Oxford Review*, April 1981, p. 11.

[37] Hans Urs Von Balthasar, *The Glory of the Lord*, Vol. 1 (San Francisco: Ignatius Press, 1982), 445.

[38] Ibid.

We demonstrate Christ's spousal love by loving people with pure and magnanimous hearts, with genuine self-detachment, with complete and steadfast commitment to their well-being.

Priests in the person of Christ the Bridegroom are called to love the bride of Christ, the Church. Christ gave himself for her to purify her and present the Church to himself in splendor (Eph 5:25-27). What is Christ's also belongs to the priest. He must lay down his life for the Church and understand that he has entered a permanent relationship, analogous to marriage, for his whole life. "The Church as Spouse of Jesus Christ, wishes to be loved by the priest in the total and exclusive manner in which Jesus Christ her Head and Spouse loves her. Priestly celibacy, then, is the gift of self in and with Christ to his Church and expresses the priest's service to the Church and in the world."[39] In the wedding feast of the Lamb (Rv 19:7-8), the holy Eucharist, the consummation of this union already takes place as Christ is made one flesh with his body, the Church, through the mediation of the priest.

Seeing Christ's beauty and the beauty of his spouse, the Church, we begin to see the beauty of Christ in all things. The poet Joseph Plunket wonderfully expresses our spiritual perspective:

> I see His Blood upon the rose,
> And in the stars the glory of His eyes;
> His Body gleams amid eternal snows,
> His tears fall from the skies.
> I see His Face in every flower.
> The thunder and the singing of the birds
> Are but His voice and, carven by His power,
> Rocks are His written words.

---

[39] St. John Paul II, *Pastores Dabo Vobis*, 29.

All pathways by His feet are worn,

His strong Heart stirs the ever beating sea,

His crown of thorns is twined with every thorn,

His Cross is every tree.[40]

As an invitation to see, the experience of beauty is apostolic. All the faithful are called to bear witness to the world of the beauty of Christ at the heart of all creation. Through our baptismal consecration we are called to ponder the things of God and to thereby manifest their beauty in our lives.

Contemplated with a pure soul, beauty speaks directly to the heart, turning astonishment to marvel, admiration to gratitude, happiness to contemplation. Thereby it creates a fertile terrain to listen and dialogue with men, engaging the whole man—spirit and heart, intelligence and reason, creative capacity, and imagination. It is unlikely to result in indifference; it provokes emotions, it puts in movement a dynamism of deep interior transformation that engenders joy, feelings of fullness, desire to participate freely in this same beauty, making it one's own in interiorizing it and integrating it into one's own concrete existence.[41]

As we taste divine beauty our hearts are filled to overflowing and we speak to others out of the abundance of our hearts. As priests, "there is nothing more beautiful than to know Him and to speak to others of our friendship with Him. The task of the shepherd, the task of the fisher of men, can often

---

[40] Joseph Plunkett, *I See His Blood upon a Rose.*
[41] *Via Pulchritudinis*, II, 3.

seem wearisome. But it is beautiful and wonderful, because it is truly a service to joy, to God's joy, which longs to break into the world."[42]

Questions for Reflection and Discussion

1. To what degree do I cultivate a taste for beauty in my life? What things do I find beautiful? What things do I find to be shallow beauty or mere glamour that I can let go? What do I find beautiful about God and the things of God? How do I experience the beauty of Jesus Christ? In what ways do I find my life growing in beauty by drawing closer to the Lord?

2. Have I tended to embrace celibacy for the sake of a cause – for the Kingdom of God, or more for the sake of a person–Jesus Christ? Have I been seized by Christ to be one with him and share his life, vision and mission? Have I approached celibacy as more of a requirement for ordination or a consequence of the Father's love and a participation in Christ's greater love for all human beings?

3. How have I experienced the struggle for purity of intention, of chastity, and of doctrine? How has passion for the Lord helped me to renounce disordered passions? How has my relationship with Mary helped me to greater purity? How has contemplation of divine things brought me delight and intensified my love for God?

4. What care do I take to make the liturgy as beautiful as possible, with vestments, furnishings, music, and vessels? Do I see the liturgy as a missionary activity to take people into the beauty of the mystery of God?

---

[42] Benedict XVI, *Homily at the Mass for the Inauguration of his Pontificate*, April 24, 2005 (Vatican City, Libreria Editrice Vaticana, 2005), Vatican Website, https://www.vatican.va/content/benedict-xvi/en/homilies/2005/documents/hf_ben-xvi_hom_20050424_inizio-pontificato.html.

5. How do I demonstrate Christ's spousal love by loving people with a pure and magnanimous heart, with genuine self-detachment, with complete and steadfast commitment to their well-being? Do I love genuinely and regard every gift, every word, and every reply I offer as a gift of self?

Prayer Exercises

1. Ponder the Augustine quote about the soul's beauty. Pray with 1 Pet 3:4 or Sg 1:12-17 and ask for the grace of awareness of your own beauty when you come into union with God.
2. Reflect on the Augustine quote about God's beauty. Pray with Sg 1:12-17 or Ps 45 and ask for the grace of experiencing the beauty of Jesus Christ.
3. Consider the Kierkegaard quote about celibacy. Pray with 1 Cor 7:25-35 and ask for the grace to be seized by Christ in your life of celibacy to be one with him in life, vision, and mission.
4. Ponder the Maloney quote on Mary. Pray with Mt 5:8 and ask for the grace of purity of heart in imitation of Jesus and Mary.
5. Reflect on Psalm 45:1-9 considering its fulfillment in Jesus Christ. Pray with Col 3:1-17 and ask for the grace to delight in the contemplation of divine truth and beauty.

Chapter 6

Consuming Love

As an apple tree among the trees of the wood,
so is my beloved among young men.
With great delight I sat in his shadow,
and his fruit was sweet to my taste,
He brought me to the banqueting house,
and his banner over me was love.
Sustain me with raisins,
refresh me with apples;
for I am sick with love.
O that his left hand were under my head,
and that his right hand embraced me!
I adjure you, O daughters of Jerusalem,
by the gazelles or the hinds of the field,
that you stir not up nor awaken love
until it please. (Sg 2:3-7)

I once heard a story about a man whose brother decided to join the seminary. The brother's reason was that God had been so good to his family that he felt obliged to give back to God as a priest. As noble as that sounds, it would not be likely to sustain a man in the priestly vocation. In fact, the man left the seminary a couple years later. The only solid basis for priesthood is the experience of God's love. My own call to the priesthood came on Divine Mercy Sunday 1987, the Marian Year. I had been praying the Divine Mercy Novena for nine days. I made what I thought was a good confession to a priest that morning and then attended the Holy Mass with my friends. After receiving Holy Communion, I knelt to pray and felt over-come with God's love for me. I looked up and saw the priest purifying the vessels and for the first time ever, the thought of the priesthood came into my mind. I had always admired the priests and the priesthood as a noble calling, but never felt drawn to it in the least. I had always prayed about getting married and assumed that it would be my vocation in life to be a husband and a father. Christ's love for me completely changed that, and I did a 180-degree turn. While celibacy had always been a non-starter, it now seemed attractive because it was about love. The Lord's love is most strongly manifest in the Holy Eucharist.

Love's Banquet

The Holy Eucharist as the Sacrament of God's love has its roots in He-brew tradition. In Jesus' day, it was traditional for Jewish men to travel to Jerusalem three times a year to celebrate the major feasts of Passover, Pen-tecost, and Tabernacles (cf. Ex 23:17; 34:23). Scripture scholar Brant Pitre notes how the priests in the Jerusalem Temple would remove the Golden Table and the Bread of the Presence from inside the Holy Place in order for the Jewish pilgrims to witness it.[1] When they took out the holy bread, the priests would lift it up and exclaim "Behold, God's love for you." This practice, even though a seeming breach of Temple etiquette, is well docu-mented.[2] The reason why the Bread of the Presence is so bound to the love of God is because it is a sign of the covenant of God with his people. The Bread was not only the most holy sacrifice of the Sabbath, but also the vis-ible symbol of God's perpetual covenant with Israel (cf. Lv 24:5-9). "As the

---

[1] Brant Pitre, *Jesus and the Jewish Roots of the Eucharist* (New York, Double-day, 2011), 130-134.

[2] See Ibid., 130 -133.

visible sign of this everlasting covenant, the Bread of the Presence was also the visible sign of the divine Bridegroom's love for his Bride. Perhaps that is why the priest could say to the people when they held up the bread, 'Behold, God's love for you!'"[3]

While most of the English translations of the bible say that the men going to the Temple should "appear before God," the literal Hebrew is translated "see the face of the Lord." The Hebrew word for the "face" of God is *panim*, the same word used for the "Bread of the Presence" or "Bread of the Face" (Ex 25:30). God's presence and his face were revealed in a kind of public theophany as the holy Bread. "This holy Bread was the primordial sacrifice of Melchizedek, the miraculous food of the Holy Place, The Bread of the Face of Almighty God. Last, but not least, this holy bread was a living, visible sign of love for his people."[4]

In the Song of Songs, the bride is brought into the banqueting hall where the Bridegroom's intention toward her is love. She is swooning with love and needs to be refreshed with fruit. She is intoxicated by the wine that symbolizes the blood of the Covenant, made new with Christ's blood, the pledge of his undying love. Just as the priests had raised the Bread of the Presence and proclaimed God's love for Israel, so now at the Eucharistic banquet, Jesus' love is manifest. This love is overwhelming. A more literal translation of "his intention toward me was love" (Sg 2:4) would be "his army against me is love." Blaise Arminjon insists: "The God of the armies has, in the last analysis, only one weapon. It is neither thunder, not the sword of justice, to which too many preachers had recourse. It is love. God does not conquer our hearts except through the excess of love."[5]

---

[3] Ibid., 131.
[4] Ibid., 133.
[5] Arminjon, 153.

Jesus' Last Supper is the new bread and wine of God's presence which forges the New Covenant in his blood. It is offered by Jesus, the High Priest and eaten by the disciples, who are also priests. It is eaten not at the Golden Table in the Jerusalem Temple, but at Jesus' Table in the Kingdom of the Father (cf. Lk 22:19-20).

Jesus, in his Last Supper discourse, told his disciples, his first priests, of his love for them: "As the Father has loved me, so I have loved you; abide in my love" (Jn 15:9). He told them to live in him as he lives in them. (cf. Jn 15:4). According to St. Francis de Sales, "in no other action can the Savior be considered more tender or more loving than in this one, where he annihilates himself, so to speak, and reduces himself to food, in order to penetrate our souls and to unite himself to the hearts of his faithful."[6] Jesus promised his disciples he would remain with them always, even until the end of time (cf. Mt 28: 20). The Eucharist, the Body and Blood of Jesus poured out for us, would be the new mode of Christ's presence to us. "Like the priests in the Temple before him, by means of the Last Supper, Jesus was saying to the disciples: 'Behold, God's love for you.'"[7]

In the Eucharist, we encounter the God of unconditional love and truly experience love. No wonder the Eucharist is called the sacrament of charity. St. John Paul II reminds us: "Man cannot live without love. He remains a being that is incomprehensible for himself, his life is senseless, if love is not revealed to him, if he does not encounter love, if he does not experience it and make it his own, if he does not participate intimately in

---

[6] St. Francis de Sales, *Introduction to the Devout Life, Part 2, Ch.1, Christian Classics Ethereal Library, https://ccel.org/ccel/desales/devout_life/devout_life. i.html*

[7] Pitre, 144.

it."[8] There is no greater love than to lay down one's life for one's friends (cf. Jn 15:13). Jesus showed his love to the end in willingly giving his life for us. The Eucharist is not only thanksgiving and communion, but also sacrifice. The Last Supper was not complete until Jesus died on the Cross. After drinking the third cup of the Passover meal, Jesus went out to his Agony and Passion. It was only when he drank from the wine on the hyssop at his death on the Cross that Jesus pronounced "It is finished" (Jn 19:30). His offering of his body and blood at the Last Supper was fully accomplished in his dying for us. This is the moment of consummation of the union with his bride the Church. Jesus' marriage bed is the Cross. The Church as bride emerges from Jesus' pierced side in the sleep of death, just as Eve was formed from Adam's side as he slept. We become one with Jesus in this mystery, bone of his bone, flesh of his flesh (cf. Gn 2:23) as members of his body and his bride, the Church. It is the consummation of his nuptial union with us.

Our response to the Lord's advance of love to us should be like the bride in her total intoxication, wonderment, and surrender to so great a love. St. Francis de Sales exclaims:

> Knowing that Jesus Christ, true God, has loved us so that he suffered death, and death on a cross, for us, doesn't that put our hearts in a vise, and make them feel its force, and squeeze love from them, but with a power that, the stronger it is, the more delightful it is…Why then, don't we cast ourselves on Jesus crucified, to die on the cross with him, who has chosen to die for love of us? I will hold him (we should say), and I will never let him go; I will

---

[8] St. John Paul II, *Redemptor Hominis*, 10 (Vatican City: Libreria Editrice Vaticana, 1979), Vatican Website, https://www.vatican.va/content/john-paul-ii/en/encyclicals/documents/hf_jp-ii_enc_04031979_redemptor-hominis.html

die with him and will be consumed in the flames of his love. One flame will consume this divine Creator and his wretched creature. Jesus gives himself unreservedly to me, and I give myself unreservedly to him. I will live and die in his loving arms; neither life nor death shall ever separate me from him. O eternal love, my soul longs after you, and chooses you forever. Come O Holy Spirit and inflame our hearts with love. O to love! O to die! To die to all other loves, and to live only for the love of Jesus Christ! O Redeemer of our souls, grant that we may eternally sing, long live Jesus, whom I love. I love Jesus, who lives for ever and ever.[9]

Like St. Francis desires to give himself in complete sacrifice, even to the point of dying, to the Lord who has sacrificed himself in dying for us, we desire to offer ourselves wholeheartedly to the Lord.

The Eucharist's Inherent Mutuality

The Holy Eucharist is both a *sacrament* and a *sacrifice*. Whoever offers a sacrifice must share in it. Hence, the priest who offers the Eucharistic Sacrifice (that is, the Mass), must receive the Eucharist as sacrament. Otherwise, the sacrifice would not be complete.[10] Venerable Cardinal Francis Xavier Van Thuan was a Catholic priest from Vietnam. He became a bishop in 1975, and shortly thereafter, the North Vietnamese invaded Saigon and took Van Thuan prisoner. He was imprisoned for thirteen years, nine of which involved solitary confinement under the most trying conditions. He had to flee with empty hands when he was first detained. He was

---

[9] St. Francis de Sales, *Treatise On the Love of God*, Bk 7, Ch. 8, trans. Henry David Mackey, O.C.D. (New York, Benzinger Brothers, 1884), Christian Classics Ethereal Library, https://ccel.org/ccel/desales/love/love

[10] See *ST*, III, 82, 4.

allowed to write to his flock the following day to request the most basic items, such as clothing and toothbrush. He requested some wine from his fellow believers in a letter to treat his "stomachache." The faithful knew immediately. For Mass, they sent him a tiny bottle of wine with the note, "Medicine for Stomach Pain." Additionally, they sent several hosts, which they concealed in a flashlight to keep out the dampness. He was questioned by the police about his stomach pain, and they gave him the medication. He was ecstatic. He would conduct Mass each day while holding three drops of wine and one drop of water in the palm of his hand. His cathedral and altar were here. It was a genuine cure offering both soul and body immortality, a means of overcoming death and ensuring eternal life in Jesus. In his book *Testimony of Hope*, he writes of his experience: "Each time I celebrated the Mass, I had the opportunity to extend my hands and nail myself to the cross with Jesus, to drink with him the bitter chalice. Each day in reciting the words of consecration, I confirmed with all my heart and soul a new pact, an eternal pact between Jesus and me through his blood mixed with mine. Those were the most beautiful Masses of my life!"[11] Von Thuan offered his own sacrifice as he celebrated and received the sacrament. He gave his blood together with Jesus' at the consecration and gave his life for Christ during his miserable prison existence.

The priest, acting in persona Christi, offers himself together with Jesus to the Father and to his people as chaste Bridegroom. The more he celebrates the holy Eucharist with love, gratitude, and reverence, the clearer and more profound it will be to the faithful. He will manifest the memorial, sacrifice, and presence of Jesus to the congregation. The more the priest reflects on the words he is saying and makes them his own, the more he will offer himself in union with Jesus. The Venerable Bruno Lanteri, as a

---

[11] Francis Xavier Van Thuan, *Testimony of Hope*, Spiritual Exercises Given to Pope John Paul II (Boston, Pauline Books and Media, 2000), 131.

newly ordained priest, resolved to recollect himself during the Holy Eucharist by keeping in mind certain Scriptural personages and images:

> In going to the altar, I will imagine seeing Simeon who went in the Spirit to the temple for the presentation and circumcision of Jesus, or I will imagine seeing some other fervent saint. In the mass, at the *Introit* I will have the sentiments and the heart of the publican, at the *Gloria* that of the Angels, at the *Oremus* that of an ambassador for the Church, at the *Epistle* and the *Gospel* that of a disciple, at the *Creed* that of the Martyrs, at the *Offertory* that of Melchizedek, at the *Preface* that of the Heavenly Court, at the *Consecration* that of Christ, at the *Pater Noster* that of a beggar, at the *Agnus Dei* that of a guilty man, at *Communion* that of one in love, at the *Ite* that of an apostle. All of this with lively faith, hope, charity, with pauses, emphasis, affection. I will go forth from the altar as if breathing fire.[12]

Lanteri takes on the sentiments of each of the biblical characters as a means of entering more fully the mystery of the Holy Eucharist. In so doing, Lanteri disposes himself to the Holy Spirit's action of bringing about greater identification with Jesus in celebrating the Eucharist.

Jesus promised to remain with us always in the Holy Eucharist. He promised to send the Holy Spirit to abide with us as well. The priest is one with the Holy Spirit, who brings about the marvelous change of the elements of the bread and wine into the Body and Blood of Christ. According to St. Cyril of Jerusalem,

---

[12] Ven. Bruno Lanteri, *The Spiritual Writings of Venerable Pio Bruno Lanteri, a Selection*, ed. David N. Beauregard, OMV (Boston: Oblates of the Virgin Mary, 2001), 43-44. For an exposition of this passage, see Timothy Gallagher, *A Biblical Way of Praying the Mass* (Irondale, AL, EWTN Publishing, 2021).

We call upon God in his mercy to send his Holy Spirit upon the offerings before us, to transform the bread into the body of Christ and the wine into the blood of Christ. Whatever the Holy Spirit touches is sanctified and completely transformed.[13]

Saint John Chrysostom, too, notes that the priest invokes the Holy Spirit when he offers the sacrifice: like Elijah, the minister calls down the Holy Spirit so that "as grace comes down upon the victim, the souls of all are thereby inflamed."[14]

At the *Epiclesis,* the priest implores the Father to send his Spirit upon the offerings to make them holy that they may become the Body and Blood of Our Lord Jesus Christ. As a result, the community as one will become ever more the body of Christ. This is the phenomenon I have noticed most as a priest. As I celebrate the holy Eucharist, there is an increasing feeling of unity among all of us as the body of Christ. This unity is not something we can produce on our own; it can only come from the Holy Spirit. As the celebrant calls down the Spirit upon the gifts of bread and wine placed on the altar, the faithful are gathered by the Spirit into one body and made a spiritual offering pleasing to the Father.[15] At Holy Communion, Saint Augustine exhorts the faithful to say *Amen* not only to the truth that the consecrated host is the Body of Christ, but also to the truth that they, too, as individuals and as a collective, are the Body of Christ: "If you, therefore, are Christ's body and members, it is your own mystery that is placed on the Lord's table! It is your own mystery that you are receiving! You are saying 'Amen' to what you are: your response is a personal signature, affirming your faith. When you hear 'The body of Christ', you reply 'Amen.'

---

[13] St. Cyril of Jerusalem, *Catechesis* XXIII, 7: PG 33, 1114ff.

[14] See John Chrysostom, *On the Priesthood,* VI, 4: PG 48, 681; III, 4: PG 48, 642.

[15] See Benedict XVI, *Sacramentum Caritatis,* 13.

Be a member of Christ's body, then, so that your "Amen" may ring true… Be what you see; receive what you are."[16]

How We Experience the Eucharist

Sadly, many Catholics do not believe in or understand the real presence of Jesus in the Blessed Sacrament.[17] Psychologists speak of a phenomenon called habituation which might partially explain the lack of faith. If our minds were attentive to all the information coming in through our senses—the sounds, colors, smells, skin sensations, etc.—we would lose our sanity. The mind, to protect itself, becomes accustomed to these regularities and obstructs them from our consciousness. We can then better focus on immediate concerns. But there is a pitfall to habituation. We tend to become dull to all the amazing realities that we encounter daily: the beauty and intricacies of nature and even the wonder of our beloved family and friends.[18] We can become dull to spiritual realities, including the sacraments, and the miracle of the Body and Blood of Christ offered for us and to us. Priests even fall into a routine of saying the Mass, losing a sense of celebration, wonder, and awe. That is why, when we pray, it is so important to remain perceptive and responsive to the reality of God in our midst.

The Mass itself is obviously a prayer, but it is good to reflect often on the mysteries we celebrate. The Last Supper discourse is Jesus' final message of love that conveys to us all that he desires to share with us in the

---

[16] St. Augustine, *Sermon 272, On the Feast of Pentecost*, PL, 38, 1247.

[17] Pew Research Poll, *Just one-third of U.S. Catholics agree with their church that Eucharist is body, blood of Christ*, Gregory A. Smith, Aug. 5, 2019, Pew Research Center Website, https://www.pewresearch.org/fact-tank/2019/08/05/transubstantiation-eucharist-u-s-catholics/

[18] See Mark Link, *Illustrated Sunday Homilies, Year A,B,C, Series II*, 67-68.

Holy Eucharist. By focusing on this message, we burn into our minds the person we love and always remember him or her. We want to burn into our minds the last image of Jesus seen on earth—his loving his disciples to the end at the Last Supper and in his passion, death, and resurrection. Just as we remember our final, most profound moments with loved ones, we want to remember Jesus' last days on earth with us and how much love he showed us. He commands us to "do this in remembrance of me" (Lk 22:19).

Not only the celebrant but all the Christian faithful are invited to a deeper appreciation of what they celebrate and receive, becoming more prayerful during the Holy Eucharist. Receiving Holy Communion is a wonderful moment. It becomes even more precious when we set it in the middle of a prayer experience, like an exquisite diamond set on a gold band. For some, Communion has become dissociated from prayer. To remedy this, we can make acts of devotion before receiving Holy Communion and prayers of thanksgiving afterward. At the moment of communion, St. Teresa of Avila advises: "When you have received Holy Communion, close your bodily eyes so that you may open the eyes of your soul. Then look upon Jesus in the center of your heart."[19] We can speak to Jesus in this intimate moment as a close companion who forgives us and loves us deeply. We can express our needs, problems, and deepest desires, knowing that he understands and is willing to help us. Thus, we will avoid growing dull and habituated to Jesus and his sacrifice for us.

When I lived on the East Coast, I made some retreats at Wernersville, PA, and would often visit and pray at the tomb of the Jesuit priest Walter Ciszek, who spent 23 years in Russian prison camps. The Stalinist regime forbade any expression of faith, so Ciszek had to say Mass secretively. He

---

[19] St. Theresa of Avila, *Beauty of Carmel* Website, https://www.beautyofcarmel.com/eucharistic-life-of-carmelite-saints

relates: "We said Mass in drafty storage shacks or huddled in mud or slush in the corner of a building site foundation....Yet in these primitive conditions, the Mass brought us closer to God than anyone might conceivably imagine."[20] Jesus was present even in those miserable conditions through the change of those elements of bread and wine into his Body and Blood. Mass was in some ways more profound and beautiful than if it had been celebrated in a magnificent cathedral. The prison inmates so desperately wanted communion that they made heroic sacrifices. In those times, Catholics abstained from food and drink from midnight until receiving Communion the following day. Fr. Ciszek relates: "Sometimes that meant we would only see them when we returned to the barracks at night before dinner. Yet these men would actually fast all day long and do exhausting physical labor without a bite to eat since dinner the evening before, just to receive the Holy Eucharist—that was how much the sacrament meant to them."[21] For those men, supernatural food was more important and sustaining than natural food. How much we need to recover such a great appreciation for the Holy Eucharist.

To better appreciate the Holy Eucharist, we can consider Jesus' role as a servant. Jesus washed the feet of his disciples at the Last Supper as he instituted the priesthood. In so doing, he hearkened back to the ritual of washing the feet of Aaron and his sons before being anointed priests of the Old Covenant (cf. Ex 29:4, 30:17-21, 40:30-32). In an act of utter humility, Jesus lays aside his garment, just as he lays aside his divine dignity to assume our humanity, to become a servant to us, and to die for us. In Jesus' day, only slaves performed foot washing as an act of hospitality. It was nasty and self-abasing work. In the ancient world, feet were dirty objects.

---

[20] Walter Ciszek, S.J., *He Leadeth Me* (San Francisco: Ignatius Press, 1995), 126-127.

[21] Ibid., 130.

Sandals were commonly worn, and they often tramped over dirt roads that sometimes served a dual purpose as sewers and channels of refuse. Often the roads were shared by herdsmen moving their livestock to market and traders transferring goods using oxen and camels. The dirt was often mixed with dung. Any measure of walking could cover one's feet with a dirty, stinking combination. Thus, having clean feet, especially upon entering a home, was significant.[22] Jesus shows humble love and service by lowering himself to do such a task. He teaches us that in serving others we must do things that we might think are beneath us. Jesus teaches us the ultimate lesson by dying for us on the Cross, washing us clean of sin. Priests, acting in the person of Christ, and as leaders of the faithful, bring the saving effects of Jesus' redemption to the faithful. We should adopt Jesus' self-emptying attitude and be prime examples of his service.

As leaders of men, priests tend to their needs in service that knows no bounds, teaching others to do the same in imitation of Jesus. There is a beautiful passage in *The Beloved Captain* by Donald Hankey, which describes how the revered captain cared for his men after long marches. He describes the captain as "a superior man of finer fiber" than the army. That was how he could be so humble without losing his dignity. No trouble of the men was too small for him to take care of as though it was his own. After long marches, he went into the barracks to routinely inspect the feet of his soldiers. But for him it was no routine. He would kneel to take a good look at the worst cases, as though he were a doctor. Then he would himself administer the remedy. If a blister needed lancing, he would usually lance it himself. He knew the men's feet were important and that they could be careless. The men saw something quite sacred in his care for their feet.

---

[22] See Epriest, *Homily Packs, Holy Thursday,* Epriest Website, https://epriest.com/homily_packs

There was no pretense about it. It spoke of the character of Christ, and the men loved and admired him for it.[23]

The power to serve and to love one another as Jesus loves us does not come from ourselves, but from the Lord himself. Jesus says to live in him as he lives in us, and that without him we can do nothing (Jn 15:5). Through the holy Eucharist, we receive the strength to love like Jesus. As we receive Jesus in holy Communion, he is not so much digested and transformed into us, but we into him. We share more and more in the nature of God himself. Think of the chain of life and food. Chemicals are absorbed from the ground and changed into plant cells, becoming an integral part of a plant by absorption through the root system of the plant and the photosynthesis of its leaves. Plants are eaten by animals and are transformed into the cell life of the animals through digestion and assimilation from the intestinal system into the animal's bloodstream and are then distributed to different parts of its body. Animals are eaten by humans and, in a similar manner, their meat is digested and absorbed from our intestines by our blood to become an integral part of our bodies. By contrast, the Body of Christ is eaten by us, and a reverse transformation occurs. Instead of our assimilating Christ's Body into our bodies, as we normally do with the food we eat and digest, the Eucharist transforms and "deifies" us by assimilating us into the very nature and life of God himself. Medieval mystic John Ruysbroeck asserts: "He enters the very marrow of our bones.... He consumes us without ever satisfying this illimitable hunger and immeasurable thirst.... He swoops upon us like a bird of prey to consume our whole life, that he may change it into His."[24]

---

[23] See Donald Hankey, *The Beloved Captain* (London: Forgotten Books, 2015), 15.

[24] John Ruysbroeck, *Flowers of a Mystic Garden* (London: Watkins, 1912; reprinted Llanerch Publishers, 1994), 69-70.

We transform ordinary food into our own bodies, but the food of the Eucharist transforms us into the body of Christ. St. Augustine heard the Lord saying to him in prayer: "I am the food of grown men; grow and you shall feed upon me; nor shall you change me, like the food of your flesh, into yourself, but you shall be changed into me."[25] When we consume the Body and Blood of Christ, we truly become what we eat. St. Thomas Aquinas explains that material food first changes into the one who eats it, and then, as a consequence, restores to him lost strength and increases his vitality. Spiritual food, on the other hand, changes the person who eats it into itself. Thus, the effect proper to this Sacrament is the conversion of a man into Christ, so that he may no longer live, but Christ lives in him; consequently, it has the double effect of restoring the spiritual strength he had lost by his sins and defects, and of increasing the strength of his virtues.[26] The Lord Jesus speaks of the gift of his life and assures us that "if any one eats of this bread, he will live forever" (Jn 6:51). This "eternal life" begins in us even now, thanks to the transformation effected in us by the gift of the Eucharist.

We must consciously and intentionally open ourselves to be interiorly transformed. It does not happen automatically. We pray in the Eucharistic Prayer that through our partaking of the Paschal Mystery, the almighty Father will give us life through his Spirit and *conform us to the image of his Son*. Fr. Theodore Dobson shows us an example of this conversion from his own life as a priest. He had a difficult relationship with an elderly colleague; they were always on opposite sides of any issue. They had a particularly angry discussion just before Dobson went off to a conference. Then, soon after he returned, he was at Mass when the other priest was presiding.

---

[25] St. Augustine, *Confessions*, Book VII, 10, 16: PL 32, 742.

[26] See St. Thomas Aquinas, *Commentary on Book IV of the Sentences*, d.12, q.2, a.11.

During the celebration, he felt all his negative feelings about this priest rising within him. At the presentation of gifts, he kneaded into the bread the angry words he had used towards this man. He poured into the chalice his negative feelings of hurt and anger, and he asked forgiveness. At the time of communion, he asked the Lord to let him know how he could find a way to be reconciled with his colleague. Sometime later, he noticed this priest was having difficulty climbing some stairs because of his weak heart. Dobson asked if he could help, and the other man allowed Dobson to assist him. This was the beginning of a happier relationship.

Dobson makes the very bold statement that transformation is the heart of the Eucharistic mystery, that the heart of the mystery of the Eucharist is this: "As the bread and wine are transformed and made sacred, so are we transformed and made sacred, if we unite ourselves consciously and prayerfully with these symbols of the sacrifice."[27]

Newly transformed, we go forth from the Eucharist as Christ's witnesses. There was once a teacher who asked her fifth-grade religion class which part of the mass was the most important. Immediately, hands were raised with likely answers: the consecration, when the priest says the words "this is my body…;" the Great Amen, when the priest offers the sacrifice of Jesus to the Father; Holy Communion, when we receive Jesus into our hearts. The teacher confirmed all these answers. Eventually, one of the students named Billy said: "When the mass is over and the priest says, 'Go forth.'" The teacher was surprised at this answer and suspected he was being snarky. She asked Billy why he chose that moment, to which he replied: "Because we go forth to bring Jesus to the world."[28] Billy was right in one

---

[27] Theodore Dobson, *Say But the Word: How the Lord's Supper Can Transform Your Life* (Ramsey, NJ, Paulist Press, 1984), 31.

[28] Mark Link, *Illustrated Sunday Homilies, Year A,B,C, Series II*, Easter, 3A, 36.

sense. While the Mass orients us to love God, when it is ended it orients us toward others, to love and serve God in human beings.

What the Eucharist Demands of Us

The English word "Mass" comes from the Latin word *missa*, which means to be "sent." The word has been used since the sixth century during the conclusion of the celebration when the priest or deacon says in Latin, *Ite, missa est.* The literal translation of that phrase is, "Go, it has been sent." Saint Thomas Aquinas writes: "And from this the Mass derives its name…the deacon on festival days 'dismisses' the people at the end of the Mass, by saying: 'Ite, missa est,' that is, the victim [Jesus] has been sent to God through the angel, so that it may be accepted by God."[29]

Pope Benedict XVI expands on the spiritual meaning of the phrase: "In antiquity, *missa* simply meant 'dismissal.' However, in Christian usage it gradually took on a deeper meaning. The word 'dismissal' has come to imply a 'mission.' These few words succinctly express the missionary nature of the Church. The People of God might be helped to understand more clearly this essential dimension of the Church's life, taking the dismissal as a starting point."[30] Instead of seeing the words of the priest or deacon as a conclusion to the celebration, Pope Benedict saw them as a beginning. He made that abundantly clear when he developed new words for the dismissal at Mass. Pope Benedict approved the phrases, *"Go and announce the Gospel of the Lord"* and *"Go in peace, glorifying the Lord by your life."* Both dismissals focus on the missionary character of the Mass

---

[29] *ST*, IIIa q 83, a 4, ad 9.

[30] Benedict XVI. *Sacramentum Caritatis*, 51 (Vatican City, Libreria Editrice Vaticana, 2007), Vatican Website, https://www.vatican.va/content/benedict-xvi/en/apost_exhortations/documents/hf_ben-xvi_exh_20070222_sacramentum-caritatis.html

and how those in the pew are meant to go out in the world, sustained by the Eucharist they just received. Viewed in this framework, the Mass is not just a single celebration on a Sunday or weekday or feast day, but a starting point for a lifelong journey of Christian witness. The priest, in the place of Christ, sends forth his parishioners into the world so that they may be beacons of light, set on a hill for all to see. The Holy Spirit transforms and sanctifies us. He re-awakens in the disciple the strong desire to proclaim boldly to others all that he has heard and experienced, to bring them to the same encounter with Christ. Thus, the disciple, sent forth by the Church, becomes open to a boundless mission.

The spirituality of the Eucharist demands that we do something practical for other people. The Mass pours into us an abundance of spiritual energy which is given to carry the good news to others, especially the most neglected in our communities. Pedro Arrupe, the former leader of the Jesuits, believed:

> If there is hunger anywhere in the world, then our celebration of the Eucharist is somehow incomplete everywhere in the world.... In the Eucharist we receive Christ hungering in the world. He comes to us, not alone, but with the poor, the oppressed, the starving of the earth. Through him they are looking to us for help, for justice, for love expressed in action. Therefore, we cannot properly receive the Bread of life unless at the same time we give the bread of life to those in need wherever and whoever they may be.[31]

The liturgy encourages all to apostolic works, that they may permeate the world with the spirit of Christ and be the leaven of its sanctification.

---

[31] Pedro Arrupe, S.J., *Address at Eucharistic Congress*, Philadelphia, August 2, 1976.

St. Thomas More, English Statesman and Lord Chancellor in 1529, rose early in the morning and attended mass every day, receiving Holy Communion. He said: "The first hour of the day belongs to my heavenly king, the other hours will be for my earthly king." He was scrutinized by a government official for using up time by attending daily mass. More replied,

> Your reasons for wanting me to stop this practice are the very reasons why I receive Holy Communion. Many times during the day I am tempted to sin, and it is due to the reception of the Eucharist that I do not. I have many difficult tasks and decisions to make together with duties to fulfill; I need the strength and the light to deal with them. In Holy Communion, I receive that light and strength.[32]

The new worship of the Christian comprises and transforms every feature of life: "whether you eat or drink, or whatever you do, do everything for the glory of God." (1 Cor 10:31). Christians, not just in prayer, but in all their deeds, are called to render fitting worship to God. Benedict XVI explains:

> Here the intrinsically eucharistic nature of Christian life begins to take shape. The Eucharist, since it embraces the concrete, everyday existence of the believer, makes possible, day-by-day, the progressive transfiguration of all those called by grace to reflect the image of the Son of God (cf. Rom 8:29ff.). Here we can see the effect of the radical renewal brought by Christ in the Eucharist: the worship of God in our lives cannot be relegated to something

---

[32] St. Thomas More, in Rev. John A. Crowley, *A Day with then Lord, vol. 2, Lent and Eastertide* (Huntington, IN: Our Sunday Visitor, 1991, 135.

private and individual, but by its nature it permeates every dimension of our lives.[33]

The Lord renews us at his table with the bread of life, strengthening us in love and service to others. The poet says you can talk Eucharist, you can philosophize about it, you can teach about it, but most importantly, you can pray it and do it. Sometimes, you laugh it, sometimes you cry it, often you sing it. Sometimes, it's wild peace, then crying hurt, often humiliating, never deserved. You see Eucharist in another's eyes, give it in another's hand to hold tight, squeeze it with an embrace. You pause Eucharist in the middle of a busy day. You listen Eucharist when you have a million things to do, and a person wants to talk. You are saying, "I give you my supper, I give you my sustenance. I give you my life, I give you me, I give you Eucharist."[34] As priests, we are privileged to confect the holy Eucharist and give it to others in the Sacrament and in our every action. The bride, prefiguring the Church, has been wounded by the army of the Lord's love at his banquet table. She surrenders herself completely to him and is ready to bear fruit in serving him in all her deeds.

Questions for Reflection and Discussion

1. How do I see the Eucharist as Christ's love for me? How do I seek his presence or "face" in the Eucharist? How have I been conquered by his love?
2. Do I perceive Christ's sacrifice in the Eucharist? In what way do I participate in that sacrifice as a victim? How do I understand

---

[33] Benedict XVI, *Sacramentum Caritatis*, 71.

[34] Arthur LeClair, CPPS, *Wonder in the Wild, A Collection of Pertinent Essays for Christian Living* (Cincinnati: St. Anthony Messenger Press, 1969).

Christ's sacrifice in the Eucharist as a consummation of marital union, and myself as united with Christ and his people?

3. In what sense do I assent to the fact that I am the body of Christ and what does it mean to me? How do I experience being transformed into him in the Eucharist?

4. Have I ever become "habituated" to the holy Mass, taking it for granted? How can I be more reflective and appreciative, especially at the moments of Consecration and Holy Communion?

5. How can I grow into the Lord's service that knows no bounds to others? How do I live the Eucharist throughout my day?

Prayer Exercises

1. Ponder the Levitical priests holding up the Bread of the Presence as God's love for his people. Pray with Jn 15:9-17 and ask for the grace to know the Lord's love for you in the Eucharist.

2. Reflect on the bride's words translated as "His army against me is love." Pray with Sg 2:3-7 and ask for the grace to be conquered by the Lord's love.

3. Consider Archbishop Van Thuan's experience of saying Mass in prison. Pray with Lk 22:14-23 and ask for the grace to share in Christ's sacrifice.

4. Ponder the phenomenon of "habituation" and Bruno Lanteri's contemplation of each part of the Mass. Pray with Jn 17:6-26 and ask for the grace of a greater appreciation of the mysteries of the Eucharist and Priesthood.

5. Reflect on the Eucharist as mission and Le Claire's poem about living the Eucharist. Pray with Jn 13:1-20 and ask for the grace to live a eucharistic spirituality in daily life.

Chapter 7

My Portion and My Cup

The voice of my beloved!
Behold, he comes,
leaping upon the mountains,
bounding over the hills.
My beloved is like a gazelle or a young stag.
Behold, there he stands
behind our wall,
gazing in at the windows,
looking through the lattice. (Sg 2:8-9)

In the years before Vatican Council II, a seminarian would be welcomed into the clerical state in a tonsure ceremony. The bishop would speak the words of Psalm 16 and the candidate would repeat them: "The LORD is my chosen portion and my cup; you hold my lot. The boundary lines have fallen for me in pleasant places; I have a goodly heritage" (Ps 16:5-6). In the Old Testament, men were also ordained to the priesthood using this psalm. A portion of the Promised Land as was required to support each family from each of Jacob's tribes would be given to them. The lone exception was the priestly Levites, who were not given any land as a legacy. The main purpose of the Levite's life was to serve God, hence he had to subsist only on the sacrifices that the other tribes saved for God. Priests still serve God today and live for him, living from the offerings of the people and sharing with them the Bread of Life and the Word of God. A priest gives up living for himself and accepts God as his only source of support and security. God is the priest's foundation for life and the "land" of his existence.

A Priest's Dwelling Place

The priest forsakes his own land, home, and family in order to follow Jesus. "The Son of Man has nowhere to lay his head" (Mt 8:20). Benedict XVI reflects on how the word of God must become the priest's own so that he becomes at home with it, and it can become his home. The Lord is his portion and cup (cf. Ps 16:5). The cup recalls the celebratory cup that was passed around at the sacrificial meal. For us priests now, the Lord shares his life with us in the Eucharistic Chalice of his blood. The Eucharist is the land which has become the priest's lot and of which he can say, "The boundary lines have fallen for me in pleasant places; I have a goodly heritage" (Ps 16:6). Pope Benedict recalls his own moment of tonsure:[1] "I suddenly understood what the Lord expected of me at that moment: he wanted to have my life completely at his disposal, and at the same time, he entrusted himself entirely to me."[2]

The New Covenant priest does not possess any land or house. Wherever he is sent, he must find his home in God. His realm is God and the divine things, and he encompasses humanity in it. As a result, the priest's mission is to extend the reign of Christ as the Lord's special presence to his people everywhere he goes. The Bridegroom in the Song of Songs is present to his bride, bounding over the hills to come to her. His speed, alacrity, and traversed distance speaks to us of God's coming to us an infinite distance from heaven to earth. The Bridegroom comes from the higher level

---

[1] Before Vatican Council II, *Tonsure* was a Roman Catholic rite of admission to the clerical state by the clipping or shaving of a portion of hair on the head.

[2] Pope Benedict XVI and Cardinal Robert Sarah, *From the Depths of Our Hearts*, trans. Michael Miller (San Francisco: Ignatius Press, 2020), 48.

of the mountain of the temple of the Lord, which is established as the highest mountain, raised above the hills (cf. Is 2:2). Departing from his eternal dwelling, he traverses the entire course of the sky: "In the heavens he has set a tent for the sun, which comes out like a bridegroom from his wedding canopy, and like a strong man runs its course with joy" (Ps 4-5). God who is transcendent reveals himself to be immanent: "You were more inward to me than my most inward part and higher than my highest"[3] The priest, in the person of Jesus, participates by grace in God's transcendent nature and power, while also drawing near in immanence to God's people: "How beautiful upon the mountains are the feet of the messenger who announces peace, who brings good news, who announces salvation, who says to Zion, 'Your God reigns.'" (Is 52:7). The priest inhabits both the divine and human worlds, extending the divine into the human.

Human beings, in the image of God, have a transcendent and immanent nature. According to the renowned psychologist Adrian Van Kaam, we are *transcendent* in going beyond or above the range of normal or merely physical human experience, surpassing the ordinary into the exceptional. We are also *immanent*, existing or operating within, sometimes retiring within, our own selves. Human beings have the immanent capacity to close themselves within a safe and constant degree of their self-development, while also having the transcendent disposition to become more truly themselves, disposed to the potential of their ongoing transformation.[4] There is a tension between who we are and who we are becoming as we are transformed, especially by the grace of the Holy Spirit. "All of us...are being transformed into the same image from one degree of glory to another; for this comes from the Lord, the Spirit" (2 Cor 3:18).

---

[3] St. Augustine, *Confessions* 3.6.11, New Advent Website, https://www.newadvent.org/fathers/1101.htm

[4] See Adrian Van Kaam, *In Search of Spiritual Identity* (Denville, NJ, Dimension Books, 1975), 172-176.

We always have the tendency to shut off the transformation of our emerging selves by remaining too static in immanence. One could fixate where one is, relax in one's immanent nature, and stop growing, stop transcending.[5] My immanent self enjoys being secure and safe, like remaining in my mother's womb. It enjoys being at rest. The danger is that this dimension could rule my life. When I am spiritually alive, I am always transcending or going beyond my present appearance, like a child being born to a new level of existence. In transcending, I am opening all the time to new projects of life, new insights, experiences, and growth. The priest must maintain a healthy balance of transcendence and immanence. The priest can easily fall into complacency in his human, intellectual, pastoral, and spiritual growth. He could easily settle for the status quo and remain a functional administrator. Often, attachment to our work, while it seems active, is a form of lethargy which can be stifling to personal growth and transcendence. We like to keep control and manage a safe environment. A priest once said he made a deal with God soon after his ordination, "If you don't bother me, Lord, I won't bother you." Fortunately, he added, "God didn't keep his end of the bargain and directly intervened in my life. Boy, am I glad he did!"[6] We are made for much more than bureaucracy and a merely functional care of souls. We need to go out to where the people are, to spend time with them and really get to know them. As priests, we enter the transcendence of God to reveal his immanence to people, mirroring the incarnational principle. As we relate to people and serve them, we are affirmed in who we are, while being challenged to grow. Because Jesus has drawn close to us in the Incarnation, he extends his presence to us through

---

[5] Ibid.

[6] Stephen Rosetti, *The Joy of Priesthood* (Notre Dame, IN, Ave Maria, 2005), 39.

his local priests, who become part of people's everyday lives. In the Eucharist, the Lord enters the very fiber of our being and dwells within us.

We can find greater meaning in our apostolic work by looking at some of the terms that define the scope of our ministry. The parish priest is the expansion of the bishop or *Ordinary* of the diocese. *Ordinary* is derived from "order" or the administrator who has direct authority. Ordinary also refers to dealing with people in a conventional manner. The priest has direct spiritual authority to provide for those who live in his parish, notwithstanding the fact that the bishop is primarily the presence of Christ. *Diocese* derives from a Greek word that implies administration of a residence or housekeeping. As an apostle and priest, St. Paul provides guidance on how to conduct oneself in the household of God (cf. 1 Tim. 3:15). The priest performs the same duties in the local parish of God. *Parish*, a word derived from the Greek, which means "close alongside" or "someone living near to others as a transient dweller." Until we all enter our everlasting home, the priest continues to live temporarily among his flock. The priest is like Jesus who, as the Word made flesh, "tabernacled" among us (cf. Jn 1:14). Jesus "pitched his tent" in our midst as one of us. Retreat Master Paul Keyes declares: "The radical presence or witness of the parish priest is to be the fundamental or original presence of God's care, God's dwelling beside or near the ordinary and common household of his people…. To be an ordinary priest carries the great dignity and responsibility of being called by Christ to live or dwell near ordinary people in their common, everyday spiritual and temporal needs."[7]

In my first assignment as an associate pastor at St. Andrew's in Avenel, NJ, I had the privilege of working alongside Fr. Dave, our pastor. Fr. Dave was around all the time, available to his people. The rectory was a large,

---

[7] Paul Keyes, *Personal Presence and the Diocesan Priest* (Whitinsville, MA: Affirmation Books, 1978), 18.

old convent and we had the parish offices on the main floor in the front. Fr. Dave would open the first floor of the rectory to the people as a kind of parish home. When you arrived at the offices, chances were you might see Fr. Dave gardening in the front and strike up a conversation. He would open the rectory chapel for the earlier of the two daily masses. He opened the dining room for the bereavement group in the evening and allowed use of the large conference table in one of the priest's offices for RCIA. He would always try to be present and familiar with the participants. He had a knack for involving people who were unchurched, and to eventually welcome them into the fold. His sense of humor was infectious, and he brought cheer to those around him. He would also have us go out to meet people where they were most in need. He and I were diligent in visiting the hospitals on a weekly basis and looking not only for our own parishioners, but anyone who might be Catholic and in need of a communion call. We went out to the prisons, the developmental center for the handicapped, and the poor in surrounding areas. I learned from him to be engaged with people, to be interested in their lives and families, to collaborate with them in ministry. I learned to go out to the margins, as Pope Francis often exhorts, where people are living far from God, to bring them near. To be a priest is to draw close to people, to be their companions on the journey of faith.

Occasionally we encounter, by contrast, the phenomenon of the "fatherless parish." Here the pastor is cold and distant. The people can never find the pastor whose office is hidden away in the back of the rectory and who is only available during office hours, and by appointment only. Even when he is physically there, he is emotionally or spiritually isolated, and his ministry is paralyzed. Nothing could be further from the spirit of the priesthood. Author Stephen Rosetti defines the essence of the charism of the parish priest as being a compassionate presence to his people:

The diocesan priest is someone who lives with the people, and each becomes a part of the other's life. ... We priests do not have a calling apart from the People of God whom we serve. We live among them and, as the years pass, our lives, and the lives of the people whom we serve, become inextricably intertwined. The radical witness of the secular parish priest rests in Christ's call to root his priestly presence in the rhythm of commonplace, everyday life.[8]

St. John Vianney exemplifies the priest who is close and available to his people. He arrived in the small rural village of Ars in 1818 for his first assignment. His bishop told him that there was almost no religious fervour and little love in the town parish, and that John would be the one to put it there. Realizing that he would have to be the presence of Jesus and his saving mercy, Fr. Vianney asked the Lord to convert his parish at the price of his own lifelong suffering. He decided to physically live in his parish church. He entered the church before dawn and remained until after the evening *Angelus,* except when out serving the needs of his people. He could usually be found there whenever he was needed. Vianney also knew how to animate the entire area of his parish. He consistently called upon the sick and families, arranged popular missions and patronal feasts, gathered and distributed funds for his charitable and missionary endeavours, adorned and equipped his parish church, tended to the orphans and teachers of the "Providence" (an institute he founded). He endowed children's education; founded societies of apostolic life, and enlisted lay co-operators. He invited people to encounter the real presence of Jesus in the Eucharist: "We know that Jesus is there in the tabernacle: let us open our hearts to Him, let us rejoice in His sacred presence. That is the best prayer."

---

[8] Rosetti, 135-136.

And he would urge them: "Come to communion, my brothers and sisters, come to Jesus. Come to live from Him in order to live with Him."[9]

John Vianney became the real presence of Jesus to his people. He made sure he was with them, meeting them in their own circumstances. According to author Fr. John Cihak, Vianney quickly started circulating himself in the community whenever and wherever he knew most people would be available. Even though they often resisted him, the community perceived their new pastor to be considerate, jovial, and friendly. Vianney was available and approachable. People always knew they could find him at the church, and if not there, out praying his divine office or the rosary.[10]

As much as Vianney loved his quiet solitude, he never minded being interrupted or engaging with people. He went out looking for his people and blended in with them. He was always fervent and joyful in his mission, in his element as a priest. Vianney would visit his flock in their own territory and land on topics that were interesting to them as farmers and laborers, such as livestock, plantings, and work projects. He would always seek to know about peoples' families and children, and their relationship to other families. Entering in by their door in conversation, he would lead them to exit through his door toward the things of God. He ended his visits with some faith questions to assess their level of catechesis and probe the fundamental spiritual issues. Sadly, the people were poorly catechized and disinterested in their faith, especially those born around the French

---

[9] Benedict XVI, *Letter Proclaiming a Year for Priests on the 150th Anniversary of the "Dies Natalis" of the Cure of Ars,* June 16, 2009, Vatican Website, http://www.vatican.va/content/benedict-xvi/en/letters/2009/documents/hf_ben-xvi_let_20090616_anno-sacerdotale.html#_ftn14

[10] Fr. John Cihak, S.T.D., "St. John Vianney's Pastoral Plan," Ignatius Insight Website, http://www.ignatiusinsight.com/features2009/print2009/jcihak_stvianneyhpr_june09.html

Revolution.[11] He loved people in their concrete circumstances and led them to Christ through a ministry of presence. In this way, he resembled Jesus who met people where they were and led them to ways beyond. Jesus could speak with the common person about farming, fishing, shepherding, eating and drinking, the weather, and family life. He attended weddings, festivals, dinners, and public gatherings. He drew from ordinary life, persons, and events to teach life lessons. He did not speak about abstract concepts in an esoteric way, from a safe distance, but entered into daily life and realities.

A Ministry of Presence Manifest's God's Gaze

As priests we are called to imitate Jesus in being close to our people. We share in their joys and sufferings; we learn from them, and we teach them. It all begins with a compassionate presence, animated by a close relationship with Christ. In the potency of this relationship, the priest is positioned to be a faith presence for others. This involves being with others in a way that is open and inviting, accepting and respectful, sharing and learning. The priest's presence, availability and visibility are symbols of God's invisible presence and availability. We help people discover God's sacred presence revealed in human relationships, reflecting on God within the ordinary events of life. Henri Nouwen spoke of the privilege of being available to practice a simple ministry of presence:

> More and more, the desire grows in me simply to walk around, greet people, enter their homes, sit on their doorsteps, play ball and be known as someone who wants to live with them. ... Still it is not as simple as it seems. My own desire to be useful, to do

---

[11] Ibid.

something significant, or to be part of some impressive project is so strong that soon my time is taken up by meetings, conferences, study groups and workshops that prevent me from walking the streets. It is difficult not to have plans, not to organize people around an urgent cause, and not to feel that you are working directly for social progress. But I wonder more and more if the first things shouldn't be to know people by name, to eat and drink with them, to listen to their stories and tell your own, and to let them know with words, handshakes, and hugs that you do not simply like them, but you truly love them.[12]

Our culture of virtual relating militates against Nouwen's aspirations. In today's culture, we have lost the sense of true communion with one another because we are so attached to our phones and screens. It is challenging for us to disengage from social media platforms and truly be present to one another because they keep us so preoccupied. We are restless, driven individuals who cannot sit alone and are used to monitoring our phones every five minutes. These secular trends take our attention away from the truth's source, the living God. They assail our capacity to engage in dialogue with the Lord who is the only one with the authority to shield us from spiritual deceptions, fraudulent signs, and misleading lights which threaten. We wonder about the effect of all this screen time on our brains and on our souls as human beings. It is certainly affecting the quality of our relationships and connection to society as a whole.

The other side of the coin of addiction to social media and screen time is the debasing addiction of workaholism and functionalism. Instead of masters of our work and schedules, we are slaves to them. Although social

---

[12] Henri Nouwen, *Gracias, A Latin American Journal* (Maryknoll, NY: Orbis Books, 1993).

media is a product of the 21st century, functionalism is not. In the gospel, Jesus reminds us that we are human beings, not "human doings." Jesus told Martha, who was obsessed with her work, that Mary had chosen the "better part" of leisure (cf. Lk 10:38-42). Mary at the feet of Jesus, conversing with him, represents true leisure that contemplates God and is willing to spend time with people. Work and leisure are two important aspects of life that need to be balanced. In our American culture, work ethic and utilitarian values dominate. "Accomplish something or die" was the attitude of utilitarian philosopher John Stuart Mill. We need to instead cultivate an authentic attitude of leisure, which is not a slothful idleness, but a contemplative stance toward reality. Work is active, always concerned with producing something, justified by its results. Leisure is more receptive to reality, not concerned with producing, not needing any justification. Leisure drinks in reality with a sense of wonder and leads us to the depths of our being.

As a priest, I recognize how subtle these influences are. In my daily Examen prayer, I must continually consider how dominant these attitudes and habits are shaping my own daily routines and interaction. As a priest, I can take the time for people and value their inner selves when I am more at ease and accessible to them. They are no longer regarded as instruments for completing my projects or as disruptions with issues that need to be resolved. They are magnificent works of art, full of promise, boundless dignity, and rich in character. They will feel at ease around me, drop their guard, become more vulnerable, and express themselves as a result. My respect for them as God's children encourages them to accept themselves as the special sons and daughters of God that they are, rather than the individuals I might wish them to be. Paul Keyes explains "In the presence of the other, when I am truly there with him or her in a deep sense of personal care, I am there as one who is learning to wait upon his guest. The other is not my property or possession in any way. I cannot manage or control him or her, for he or she is God's secret. He or she is the *shekinah* or the tenting place of God's mysterious dwelling in my day-to-day world."[13] As a priest, I need to let go of the impulse to constantly instruct or argue my point of view if I want to listen to our people better. Then I am free to embrace them in the wonder of who they are. They feel accepted and more conscious of who they truly are because I give them my whole attention and do it with welcome in my heart. I am invited to remain vigilant in order to shepherd the basic intrinsic worth of the person with humble receptivity to his or her current life.

It is interesting that in the Song of Songs, the bride experiences her Bridegroom "gazing in at the windows, looking through the lattice" (Sg 2:9). She perceives that he can see her interiorly, in the profundities of her heart. She is open to his penetrating, loving gaze. This gaze affirms her in her identity and uniqueness, and she is free to become the person she is. The priest is meant to mirror this gaze of God, looking into the window of the soul. I am so blessed to be part of a community, the Oblates of the Virgin Mary, whom people perceive as approachable and affirming. I was very gratified to hear a woman describe her experience with one of our priests: "A spiritual father helps me 'become me' in the Lord. My own father wasn't supporting me. There was a place in myself that needed a spiritual father at the time to affirm me." She continued to reflect: "They have such a reverence, gentleness, tenderness of a spiritual father. „, You're allowing them to hold your soul in a way that no one else can. They know their sacred and holy responsibility. They hold your soul so reverently."[14] A man said of the Oblate priests, "I want to tell you, as the one really, truly most important thing, these are the kindest, gentlest, most patient, most

---

[13] See Keyes, 71.

[14] Cabrini Pak, Ph.D., *Sons of Mary, Men of Mercy, The Lanterian Way* (Cabrini Pak, 2019), 37.

respectful people I have ever met in my life. I see how that fits into their idea of everyday spirituality and wanting to make the world a more spiritual place one day at a time. They do that by just being who they are and carrying that love and honor of God and Christ in them like a little flame, every day, everywhere they go."[15] Finally, another person mentioned about the Oblates: "Their presence is very particular; they meet you in your life, where you are; they see Christ in each other; they are with each other at table; totally available; affectionate with all reverence and respect."[16]

Often, we priests are unaware of how people perceive us, and what an amazing difference we can make in their lives by simply listening to them reverently and affirming their goodness. When someone realizes that God loves them as they are and wants to meet them where they are—with no preconditions – it makes an impression and breeds a familiarity. The people of God will then express a confidence and sincerity with their priests and approach God just as they are. The Oscar winning British actor Sir Alec Guinness had an eye-opening experience while filming *The Detective* in a rural village in France. Despite not being Catholic, Guinness was cast as a priest. After an extensive time of filming, he was still sporting his priest's cassock as he made his way back to his hotel through the village streets. A young girl, on her way home, a young girl who was running errands on the same street went up to his side right away. She sprang straight alongside him, held him by the hand, and walked with him because she thought he was a priest. She prattled endlessly about various topics as though he were a close friend. Even though Guinness couldn't speak French and couldn't respond, it didn't matter. She chatted on for a few blocks before veering off in a new direction. She released his hand, waved him off, and ambled home. Guinness remained enthralled on that street

---

[15] Ibid, 34.
[16] Ibid. 35.

corner for quite some time, enchanted by the Catholic religion and the priesthood that had the power to evoke such trust and gladness.[17] He brought his newfound appreciation into his movie role, and it became the first step that brought him into the Catholic Church.

While cultivating relationships with people, we should always maintain appropriate boundaries. When those limitations are present, they foster the ability to love in the appropriate way.

Unique Challenges of the Priestly Vocation

Stephen Rosetti notes that priests have special vulnerabilities. They sometimes meet with people in the context of privacy. They get involved in intimate areas of peoples' personal lives. Meetings can sometimes be emotionally charged, as people express deep feelings. People have many needs. The priest might also have needs that can muddle an already intense situation. For instance, a priest at mid-life might have recently lost parents and feel more vulnerable to unsuitable relationships, seeking comfort in ill-chosen situations.[18] A good rule to follow is to ask yourself "would I feel comfortable maintaining this relationship out in the open, especially in the view of my confreres?" Clergy must take responsibility for their own spiritual, physical, mental, and emotional well-being. They are also responsible for maintaining professional competence and for meeting the commonly recognized professional standards of their particular roles. Psychological boundaries are necessary as well. There is the reality of transference, or the projection of unconscious feelings and material between the priest and the person being helped. Priests must try to be aware of their own

---

[17] See Epriest, *A British Actor Converts*, Homily Pack Illustration, Good Friday, Years A, B, C, Epriest Website, https://www.epriest.com/homily_packs/illustrations/view/96

[18] See Rosetti, 97.

issues and needs and keep them separate, dealing with them professionally in another setting. They should seek the necessary help when either personal or professional areas of their life need attention. When we are tending to our own needs in a healthy way there will be no obstacles to shepherding people tenderly.

The Lord sought to be close to people and he sought to form the heart of his pastors to also be close to the people whom they serve. Unlike the secular profession, such as doctors or lawyers, the diocesan priest finds his calling in living among the people, which sometimes challenges his pastoral boundaries. Rosetti notes:

> The separation between what is personal and what is professional is blurred by the nature of this life. We are companions to the people. We socialize with them. We attend their parties and family functions. We meet them in the rectory as well as in their homes. We see them on the ball fields and in the schools. Our vocation calls us to be present to the people in the daily fabric of their lives. It is impossible to set up a clear boundary between our personal lives and our public ministry. Setting typical professional boundaries is not only impossible, but it would be contrary to our charism.[19]

Herein lies the challenge—the built-in tension: the parish priest lives among his people, therefore responsible boundaries must be maintained. Relationships are at the foundation of ministry and are central to Catholic

---

[19] Ibid., 139.

life. Healthy and safe relationships are founded upon and demonstrate sincere love, respect, and compassion for all of those who are served.[20]

It is a great privilege to have deep encounters with others, and these moments are profoundly gratifying. Like the Bridegroom gazing at the bride through the window, the priest has the privilege of gazing into the window of a person's soul. These can be moments of beautiful and chaste intimacy with others, and we as priests are grateful to God for them. However, priests must be careful not to seek to have their needs for intimacy met by the people they serve. Psychologists distinguish between the love of friendship and functional love. In the love of a personal friendship, the celibate priest welcomes on an equal level his friend's love and affection. By contrast, functional love is expressed toward many individuals with feelings of tenderness, kindness, and compassion. Our apostolic duties are the source of functional love. Although we could experience affection in functional love, its foundation is appreciation for advantages gained, such as the experience of intimacy with others or people expressing gratitude. If the priest tries to sustain either an excessive number of merely functional relationships or an excessive concentration of them at one time, he faces the danger of becoming emotionally spent. Therefore, a vital motive for the priest maintaining strong interpersonal friendships is the necessity to recharge his emotional reserves.

---

[20] Some general rules: While offering pastoral counseling to one or more people with whom one has a relationship, the priest should make clear the nature of the relationship, recognize any possible difficulties, and consider how to resolve them. Sessions for pastoral counseling should take place in suitable areas and at appropriate times. Sessions should not take place in settings or at times that could leave the client unclear about the nature of the connection they are in with the priest. Physical contact is usually discouraged during pastoral counseling or spiritual direction since it could be misunderstood. Each physical interaction should be appropriate in both its character and length.

Friendships and Closeness with the People of God

The Lord Jesus invites us into his personal friendship and deep intimacy. There is nothing we cannot share with Jesus, knowing that he hears and understands us. In his real humanity, he also wants us to hear and understand him. He thirsts for our friendship. We also need to cultivate friendships with our fellow priests. It is not good for man to be alone (cf. Gn 2:18). By sharing with friends, we learn to multiply our joys and divide our sorrows. Celibate chastity is ordered toward friendship as a flowing of affective maturation. Friends share not only on the more superficial level of circumstances, but also at the deeper level of desires, hopes, and dreams for one's life. Friends are vulnerable to sharing deeper feelings, even the more negative fear, anger, and sadness. A friend will encourage you while providing a sympathetic, understanding ear. Friendship will sometimes be tested with differences of opinion, or when we hurt each other and seek and offer forgiveness.[21] The greater the degree of sharing such matters of the heart, the greater the experience of intimacy.

Priests should cultivate friendship with the very priests in their midst, not just talking about common ministry, but about each other's lives. Paul Keyes explicates:

It means sharing what is really going on in one's ordinary confusion and anxiety. It means finding the time to be with one's common weaknesses in another's presence and letting the other offer a friendly healing. It does not mean that one becomes an open book that lets all his hang-ups stand out in naked openness. ... Friends have to preserve their separate selves as well as be

---

[21] See Matthew Kelly, *The Seven Levels of Intimacy* (New York: Beacon Publishing, 2005), 173-202.

together. True encounter calls for being with others while at the
same time preserving one's separateness.[22]

Certainly, dining and praying together can foster this bond of friendship. It is also good to have a common rectory space where we can gather
occasionally, and even invite mutual friends. Sharing our common mission in a parish or another apostolic setting can deepen our companionship.

The Lord sent his disciples together on mission so that they could love
one another as companions even as they loved the people they served.
Saints Basil the Great and Gregory of Nazianzen began their model friendship while at school in Athens and later became bishops. When Basil first
arrived as a freshman, Gregory shielded him from the usual subjection and
ridicule of new students. This was the kindling spark of their friendship,
and they felt affection for one another. Realizing they shared the same
goals of philosophy and pursuit of eternal life, Basil and Gregory became
all in all to one another, housemates, table companions, and close friends.
They were driven by equal hopes in the pursuit of letters, which Gregory
considered a field easily prone to envy. Instead, they strove to emulate one
another in virtue, struggling not to gain first place, but to yield it to the
other, more concerned about the other's reputation. Their friendship was
an experience of having one soul inhabiting two bodies, seeming to live in
and with each other. The sole interest of each was virtue, living for the life
to come, having no desire for the things of this world. Basil and Gregory
sharpened their weapons of virtue (cf. Prov. 27:17) with each other, becoming a rule and a standard of right and wrong to each other.[23] Their

---

[22] Keyes, 72-73.

[23] See Saint Gregory Nazianzus, *Sermon* (Oratio 43, in *Laudem Basilii Magni*,
15. 16-17, 19-21; PG 36, 514-423, in *Liturgy of the Hours*, Office of Readings, Jan
2.

friendship was a close sharing of life, pursuits, and love. They spurred each other on to virtue and helped one another remain true to the Lord's calling. Basil and Gregory show us the potential for friendship in Christ that is considerably enriching to us as priests.

Friendship's creative, ennobling effect results from making ourselves more available to the other, and so becoming more our real friendship, we discover, and we reveal who we are and even more, who we are capable of becoming. The mutually enriching opportunity of entering the mind of another also enables each friend to extend love more easily to the whole of humanity. Its imperfections and limitations notwithstanding, friendship represents one of the most precious values of human life. It is worth the effort to commit ourselves courageously to the experience of friendship. We need to experience the joy of intimacy described in Sg 2:8-9. We priests need to refresh ourselves with friendships, especially when we feel exhausted from our labors.

Jesus forms in his priests a pastoral attitude of closeness to the People of God. The priest's presence carries the image of Christ in the lives of his people. Through the priest's presence, the Church as bride perceives Christ as her beloved bounding over the hills to be with her. Her Beloved now comes to her leaping over all heights and even to the valleys of her own inner misery to bring his healing love. Jesus in his resurrection brings her a transcendence with an unlimited horizon. Christ elevates his bride, shares with her his ability to transcend all limitations and enables her to begin to experience eternal life.

Questions for Reflection and Discussion

1. To what degree is the Lord "my portion and my cup," especially in the Holy Eucharist? How have I learned to find my home in

Him? What is my experience as a priest of inhabiting both the divine and human worlds, extending the divine into the human?

2.   How do I experience the tension between who I am and who I am called to be? How do I tend toward a secure and safe status quo in my self-development, and how am I tran-scendently disposed to the potential of my ongoing transformation? What is my healthy balance in this regard?

3.   In what way as a priest do I live the fundamental presence of God's care by dwelling near ordinary people in their common, everyday spiritual and temporal needs? How well do I circulate in the community and know my flock? How available am I at the church or offices?

4.   How much am I affected by social media and other distractions that keep me from deeper encounters with others? What is the quality of my relationship with others? How do workaholism and functionalism adversely affect me? How can I take time for meaningful leisure and relationships?

5.   How appropriate are my boundaries, both physically and psychologically, with parishioners and others? What are the challenges and tensions I face? How are my pastoral relationships enriching and demonstrating sincere love, respect, and compassion for all of those who are served?

6.   How are my friendships with other priests and lay people? Am I able to share what is really going on in my joyful moments and in my difficulties? Am I able to find the time to be vulnerable with my weaknesses in another's presence and let the other offer friendly healing? How do my friendships inspire me to virtue?

Prayer Exercises

1. Reflect on the old tonsure ceremony and Benedict XVI's words. Pray with Ps 16:5-6 and ask for the grace to experience the Lord in the Eucharist as your portion and your cup.

2. Consider Fr. Rosetti's description of the essence of the life of the parish priest. Pray with Jn 1:1-18 and ask for the grace to be a close presence to your people.

3. Ponder Henri Nouwen's words on the ministry of presence. Pray with Jn 1:35-51 and ask for the grace to be a part of the lives of Christ's people.

4. Reflect on Fr. Rosetti's quote about the difficulties for priests in setting boundaries. Pray with Jn 21:11-18 and ask for the grace to maintain healthy boundaries as a means of respectfully loving people.

5. Consider Basil and Gregory's friendship. Pray with Jn 15:12-17 or Sir 6:5-17 and ask for the grace of true friendship with the Lord and others.

Chapter 8

Hidden Sojourn

My beloved speaks and says to me:
"Arise, my love, my fair one,
and come away;
for lo, the winter is past,
the rain is over and gone.
The flowers appear on the earth,
the time of singing has come,
and the voice of the turtledove
is heard in our land.
The fig tree puts forth its figs,
and the vines are in blossom;
they give forth fragrance.
Arise, my love, my fair one,
and come away. O my dove, in the clefts of the rock,
in the covert of the cliff,
let me see your face,
let me hear your voice,
for your voice is sweet,
and your face is comely. (Sg 2:10-14)

Years ago, an unknown author circulated a tongue-in-cheek memorandum addressed to Jesus, son of Joseph, Woodcrafters Shop, Nazareth, from the Jordan Management Consultants, Jerusalem regarding a staff aptitude evaluation:

Thank you for submitting the resumes of the twelve men you have picked for management positions in your new organization. All of them have now taken our battery of tests, and we have not only run the results through the computer, but also have arranged personal interviews for each of them with our psychologist and vocational aptitude consultant. It is the staff opinion that most of your nominees are lacking in background, education, and vocational aptitude for the type of enterprise you are undertaking. They do not have the team concept. We would recommend that you continue your search for people of experience in the managerial ability and proven capability. Simon Peter is emotionally unstable and given to fits of anger. Andrew has absolutely no qualities of leadership. The two brothers, James and John, the sons of Zebedee, place personal interest above company loyalty. Thomas demonstrates a questioning attitude that would tend to undermine morale. Matthew (we feel that it is our duty to tell you) has been blacklisted by the Greater Jerusalem Better Business Bureau. James, the son of Alphaeus, and Thaddeus definitely have radical leanings, and they both registered a high score on the manic-depressive scale. Special note: One of the candidates shows great potential. He is a man of ability and resourcefulness, meets people well, has a keen business mind and has contact in high places. He is highly motivated, ambitious, and innovative. We recommend Judas Iscariot as your controller and right-hand man. All the other profiles are self-explanatory. We wish you every success in your new venture. Sincerely, Jordan Management Consultants.

The disciples were hacks, failures by worldly standards. Only Judas would have made the cut in terms of professional ability! The first disciples of Jesus were initially far from perfect. They needed a lot of formation.

They were keenly aware of their unworthiness for so noble a calling and their inadequacy to perform the task. At first, they might have been over-confident, but through their failures over many years they learned to rely on God's wisdom and strength.

I, too, was overconfident in my own abilities and of my progress as a disciple when I joined the seminary. I felt I had achieved a lot in my marketing career, making a substantial income. I was now thrown in with other young men from all over the country, some older, some younger, some with no college and little work experience, some with very advanced degrees and having held elite positions. It was easy to compare myself with others and think that I was better or worse than them. I could, I thought, always fall back on what I had accomplished in my career. Little did I realize that scarcely mattered. God wasn't calling me so much for my strengths, but because I was weak. St. Paul reminds the leaders of the fledgling Corinthian Church:

> Consider your own call, brothers: not many of you were wise by human standards, not many were powerful, not many were of noble birth. But God chose what is foolish in the world to shame the wise; God chose what is weak in the world to shame the strong; God chose what is low and despised in the world, things that are not, to reduce to nothing things that are, so that no one might boast in the presence of God. He is the source of your life in Christ Jesus, who became for us wisdom from God, and righteousness and sanctification and redemption, in order that, as it is written, 'Let the one who boasts boast in the Lord'. (1 Cor 1:26-31)

Far from making us proud, our calling should humble us before God and others.

Emerging from the Winter of Sin

In the Old Testament, the bride in the Song hears the call from her arriving Bridegroom as he bids her to come forth: "Arise my love, my fair one, and come away" (Sg 2:10). He calls her to experience the springtime of love that is the exodus from Egypt, the entrance into the promised land, the time of Passover. It is also a time of renewal and conversion. The long winter was a time of exile and trial for Israel.

> Winter is a symbol of many trials of coldness, darkness, and sense of being close to death. There have been the spiritual rains, cold and snow abounding in the bride's experiences of her beloved. There has been the lifelessness of winter sins that have gripped her and throttled to death that loving presence of Christ in her.[1]

Winter is the time of sleeping and torpor of soul. The bride is still wounded by her suffering and perhaps slow to respond. The Lord now calls her to let go of all her negative experiences that have happened to her. It is a call to come out of herself. He calls her to come forward to labor more diligently to bring forth the fruit of new life.

In the Gospel, Jesus issued the same summons to his disciples to come away and bear fruit. He invited Andrew and John to "come and see" where he stayed. When Jesus called Peter with the miraculous catch of fish, Peter was humbled and ashamed to face Jesus. He fell to his knees, saying "Go away from me Lord, for I am a sinful man" (Lk 5:8). My experience of this gospel passage was during my first seminary retreat, when I felt consolation at Peter's words. In my own acknowledgement of myself as a sinner,

---

[1] George Maloney, *Singers of the New Song, A Mystical Interpretation of the Song of Songs* (Notre Dame, IN: Ave Maria Press, 1985), 52.

I felt hope in God's grace and call. All of us as priests have known that feeling of awe and unworthiness at the Lord's presence and call. Like Peter, we fall to our knees and are tempted to say, "depart from me Lord." We are like Isaiah in the Old Testament who, when he was called to be a prophet, said: "Woe is me! I am lost, for I am a man of unclean lips, and I live among a people of unclean lips; yet my eyes have seen the King, the LORD of hosts!" (Isa. 6:5). God touched a burning coal to Isaiah's tongue to purify him by grace. Our call to follow the Lord always involves personal conversion, awakening and responding to the Lord. In our most honest and vulnerable moments, we discover the persistent love of God. Like St. Augustine, we can exclaim:

> O God, the strength of my salvation! I go astray and you call to me over and over again; I resist You and You invite me; I am idle and You rouse me; I am converted and You embrace me; I am ignorant and you instruct me; I am sad and You cheer me; I fall and You lift me up; You restore me after the fall; You give me all I ask You for; You let me find You when I look for You and You open the door when I call. So that, Lord of my life, I do not know what excuse I could have. Now, Father of mercies and God of all consolation…grant me the joy of Your countenance that by loving You I might receive all that You promise me … inspire me as to what I must think of You, teach me what words I must use to invoke You and give me works with which to please You.[2]

Augustine shows us that this ongoing call of the Lord is a continuing process of conversion that wakes us from our complacency. It is a call from

---

[2] St. Augustine, *Meditations*, in Arintero, 295.

the winter of our sins and trials to be with him in the springtime of his life and love.

Fraternity and Apostolic Action

Jesus calls us first to companionship with himself, and later to mission. He is not so much interested in what we can do for him, but in our receiving his heart. Jesus was with the Apostles all the time, establishing a deep bond of friendship. Though Jesus was divine and knew what was in the hearts of men (cf. Jn 2:25), he came to know them in a thoroughly human way. He joyfully affirmed them in their positive qualities and virtues and patiently tolerated their weaknesses and defects. His love was unconditional, and they felt they could be themselves, blurting out whatever was in their hearts: "Lord, show us where you are going, we do not know the way," (Jn 14:5) or "God forbid Lord that you should have to suffer" (Mt 16:22). I, too, began to learn to be vulnerable in expressing my true feelings and thoughts in conversation with the Lord.

My own experience of being called to come away with Jesus was delightful, but arduous. Being in the seminary felt as it must have been for the disciples gathered to learn from the Master. Jesus was our Master, and he had some great assistance from our formation staff and teachers. On the human level, we were all thrown together in community life like gemstones thrown into a rock polisher. Each of us had our rough edges that needed to be smoothed, improving one another. We learned to love one another as the Lord strengthened within us the virtues of patience, forgiveness, kindness, and consideration. It is difficult and sometimes painful to confront ourselves with self-knowledge, as if noticing in the mirror all our defects. We recognized our failures, the areas in which we needed to grow, and how difficult it was to change. We grew in dependence on God and his grace just to have this self-knowledge at all. Self-knowledge is meant to lead to self-acceptance, which leads to self-gift. Living in community we learned to cultivate an atmosphere of trust and sincerity, to be willing to help one another, and to not be judgmental.

Meals in common were special moments of fraternity and love in joy and simplicity of spirit. The time for sports and recreation also built community and helped us relax with one another. Manual labor, house cleaning, and maintenance kept us grounded in the redemptive law of work. We remained abreast of the culture: the arts, sciences, and politics. Singing together in a choir symbolized unity, harmony, and diversity of gifts. Companionship led to friendships. Overall, we grew in the capacity to relate to one another, developing the human and affective maturity fundamental for a person of communion. We were formed to develop balanced personalities and self-control. We learned openness and vulnerability with a capacity to dialogue, which made us "bridges"[3] for communicating Jesus Christ to the people of our world.

St. Irenaeus, an early Church Father, once wrote that "the glory of God is a man fully alive." Our spiritual formation engaged the whole person, animated by the Spirit, in union with God. The *Spiritual Exercises of St. Ignatius* were our formative instrument. It is the retreat experience par excellence, endorsed by every recent pope throughout the 20th and 21st centuries. Ven. Bruno Lanteri founded our congregation to give the Spiritual Exercises, writing: "In short, the Exercises of St. Ignatius are in general a most powerful instrument of Divine Grace for the universal reform of the world, and in particular a sure method by which everyone can become a saint, a great saint, and quickly."[4] The Exercises are not only a retreat experience, they initiate a person into a complete spirituality following the traditional stages of growth in the spiritual life. In the purgative way, we

---

[3] See St. John Paul II, *Pastores Dabo Vobis*, 43.

[4] Ven. Bruno Lanteri, *The Spiritual Writings of Ven. Bruno Lanteri*, 19.

are confronted with our own sinfulness, and by grace uproot our vices, experiencing so much of God's mercy. In the illuminative way, using the gift of imaginative prayer, we gain a more intimate knowledge of Jesus, to love him more and follow him more closely. Especially for seminarians, one of the greatest gifts of the Spiritual Exercises is greater clarity about our calling and how to live it. In the unitive way, we are conformed to Christ in his suffering, death, and resurrection, as we participate in these realities through contemplation and daily living.

One of the greatest outcomes of Ignatian spirituality and the Spiritual Exercises is discovering God present in all things, not only in our essential prayer time, but in all the events of our daily lives. Ignatius even wrote to the rector of the seminary in Coimbra, Portugal, to keep the overzealous students to their regular regimen of prayer, but that also:

> they can exercise themselves in seeking the presence of our Lord in all things—for example, in conversing with someone, in walking, looking, tasting, hearing, thinking, and in everything that they do, since it is true that his Divine Majesty is in all things by his presence, power and essence.... This splendid exercise will dispose us for great visitations from the Lord, even during a short prayer.[5]

Ignatian spirituality continues to teach us to be contemplatives in action, realizing that God is seeking to communicate himself to us through all the circumstances, events, and persons in our lives.

The Spiritual Exercises also instructed us in Ignatius' teaching on discernment of spirits. We learned how to recognize and reject the action of

---

[5] St. Ignatius of Loyola, *Letter to Father Anthony Brandeo*, June 1, 1551, in *Letters of St. Ignatius of Loyola*, trans. William J. Young (Chicago: Loyola University Press, 1959), 240-241.

the evil spirit, first, insofar as he causes spiritual desolation and discouragement, and then in deceiving with spiritual consolations to lead one astray under the appearance of good. We also learned the characteristics of the good spirit of God and his holy angels in granting consolations to draw one closer to God in encouragement, and to remain in the Lord's grace and service. It was also important for us not to become one-dimensional in our spirituality. Our formators introduced us to the great spiritual traditions of other saints and movements within the Church. We especially imbibed the teaching of the Carmelite doctors such as St. Theresa of Avila, St. John of the Cross, and St. Therese of Lisieux, which intertwined so well with St. Ignatius.

We constantly nourished ourselves with the reading of Sacred Scripture and with daily practice of mental prayer, the true "school of the union of the soul with God,"[6] which became our foremost delight. By reading and meditating on the scriptures, we learned "the surpassing value of knowing Christ Jesus," (Phil 3:8) and penetrated more deeply the mystery of salvation for which we were to be both messengers and witnesses. The zenith of our day was always the celebration of the Eucharist Mystery which would become the heart of our priesthood. The Eucharist was the sun of our day in offering perfect adoration to God. It was also the wellspring of our zeal to build up the Church and make it grow. Adoration of the Lord in the blessed Sacrament kept us in the Lord's loving embrace and in his merciful gaze. We celebrated in common the Liturgy of the Hours, in which the Church renders the Lord incessant praise and intercedes for the salvation of the entire world in song and prayer.

The seminary was very much a participation in the hidden life of Jesus. Jesus spent 30 years in anonymity, obedient to his parents, growing in wisdom and grace before God and men, as he prepared for his public mission.

---

[6] Ven. Bruno Lanteri, *Directory of the Oblates of the Virgin Mary*, 16.

He was in silence and prayer, engaged in manual labor and study. Jesus came to know the great rabbis of Israel and their sayings. While at once fully human and divine, he developed his divine relationship with his heavenly Father. The seminary was similarly a time of deepening in prayer, scripture, and theology to prepare us as future priests for public ministry. The long period of preparation certainly tested our patience, but, like Jesus, we had to be fully prepared and had to wait until the time was right. We had to be fully conformed to Jesus, and by our ordinary daily actions we entered fellowship with him.

Just as the seminary is a participation in the hidden life of Jesus, the bride is hidden in the clefts of the rock. The Bridegroom calls to her, desiring that she let him see her lovely face and let him hear her sweet voice (cf. Sg 2:14). She bravely decides to return to her Bridegroom, not averting her face but turning it toward him, not silent, but responding to his call. The bride dwells in the clefts of the rock, which symbolizes Christ (cf. 1 Cor 10:3-4). Saint Francis de Sales comments:

> Let us go, arise, says the bridegroom, get out of yourself, fly toward me my dove, my very beautiful love ... Come my dearly beloved, and to see me more clearly, come to the window through which I am looking for you; come to contemplate in my heart the gap cut in my side when my body, like a demolished house, was so sadly destroyed on the tree of the Cross. Come and show me your face.[7]

George Maloney elucidates that "mystics throughout all of Christianity are led to come out of themselves and enter into the pierced heart of Christ and there to have the exchange of 'hearts,' where two consciousnesses are

---

[7] St. Francis de Sales, *Treatise on the Love of God*, Book V, Ch. VII, 215.

made one."[8] Jesus' side was pierced by a soldier's spear and from his heart flowed blood and water (cf. Jn 19:34). Jesus had invited all to come to him to drink from his heart fountains of living water (cf. Jn 4:14), which symbolizes the Holy Spirit, the gift of the Father and the Son to us.

The bride must pass from her poor refuge of self into this deep cave in the body of Christ, her true "rock" which is the wound in his heart. Saint Bernard says: "How can one not see through these openings, the secret of his Heart that is bared in the wounds of his body."[9] Saint John of the Cross exhorts us to remain in these openings:

> We will go up to the high caves of rock that are deeply hidden. In these caves the soul wants to go deeper and deeper, to be absorbed, to get intoxicated, to be deeply transformed in the love that the knowledge of the mystery will give to it and to hide in the bosom of her beloved. The latter, indeed, invites her in the Song of Songs to enter into the gaps of the stone, into the caves of the wall.[10]

Spiritual formation for me was coming to Christ, to enter his Sacred Heart, to dwell there and receive the total outpouring of his love and the infinite abyss of his mercy. At the same time, the Lord was calling to me to reveal myself to him, desiring to see my face and hear my voice. He deeply desired my friendship and wanted me to love him not only in my goodness, but

---

[8] Maloney, *Singers of the New Song,* 54.

[9] St. Bernard, *Sermons on the Song of Songs,* Sermon 61, in *Life and works of Saint Bernard, Abbot of Clairvaux: Volume 4: Cantica Canticorum Eighty-Six Sermons On The Song Of Solomon,* ed. Jean Mabillon, trans. Samuel J. Eales, editor Eales, Samuel J. (Samuel John) (London, J. Hodges, 1889), Internet Archive Website, https://archive.org/details/LifeAndWorksOfSaintBernardV4

[10] Saint John of the Cross, *Spiritual Canticle,* Stanza 36, *The Collected Works of John of the Cross,* trans Kieran Kavanaugh, O.C.D. and Otilio Rodriguez, O.C.D. (Washington, D.C.: ICS Publications, 1991), 611--612.

also from the depths of my misery. He was offering his heart to me and desired that I share mine with his, no matter what was in it. My tendency was to hide myself and my deepest feelings. I was afraid certain desires might sound ridiculous and go unfulfilled. I was ashamed of negative emotions and thoughts. The Lord invited me to pour out my heart to him, to cast all my cares on him, knowing he cares for me. (cf. 1 Pet. 5:7). In the heart of Christ, I could discover and be my authentic self. I continue today to pour out my heart to the Lord who desires to see my face and hear my true voice.

As religious, we discovered the power of the evangelical counsels of poverty, chastity, and obedience, counsels which every priest is encouraged to live in some fashion.[11] In poverty, we learned dependence on God and the congregation for all we need. Beyond the material aspect, poverty taught us that we are nothing without God and to treasure that emptiness that could only be fulfilled in Christ. Poverty led us to share not only material goods, but also our natural talents and spiritual charisms, sharing in the richness of life in Christ. Through chastity, we devoted ourselves to God alone with an undivided heart in virginity or celibacy, for love of the kingdom of heaven and as a source of spiritual fertility. Chastity enlarged our hearts to love all our brothers and sisters with the same love of Christ. In obedience, we surrendered our autonomy to better imitate Jesus, who became obedient unto death, and to cooperate with him in his work of redemption. Obedience sealed the union among us as brothers, in seeking and fulfilling the will of God, assuring the unity of apostolic action. Our holy mother Mary was, and continues to be, our model and help in all aspects of religious life. She is a model of poverty, chastity, and obedience

---

[11] See Code of Canon Law, 207, Sect. 2; CCC 1973-74, 2103. Some would suggest that diocesan priests need these counsels even more than religious priests. Jesus' rudimentary exhortation to these counsels is found in Matthew 19.

and an inspirational help to living these counsels. Mary's maternal presence invited us to draw closer to her Son and to each other in community.

Knowledge, Understanding, and Cooperation in Pastoral Work

Human intelligence "participates in the light of God's mind" and "seeks to acquire a wisdom which in turn opens to and is directed toward knowing and adhering to God."[12] The theologian is a believer who asks himself questions about his own faith with the aim of reaching a deeper understanding of the faith itself.[13] Intellectual formation, the study of sacred scripture and theology, was mentally exhilarating. God's Word came alive in amazing ways, making me fall in love with scripture. All our theology was rooted in the scriptures and I feasted on every subject from the Church Fathers to all the fields of theology: The Holy Trinity, Christology, Ecclesiology, Morality, the Sacraments, etc. Christ's pure light expanded my mind beyond the concrete things I was learning to the expanse of the infinite. Theologian William Dych comments on the subjective transcendence of the human person who is open to God: "This transcendence brings us not to a content of knowledge which we grasp, but to an absolute question. This experience of the unattainable and the incomprehensible we call the experience of mystery."[14] The little portion of infinite truth that I was able to grasp was deeply satisfying, while simultaneously engendering a

---

[12] Vatican Council II, *Gaudium et Spes,* 15 (Vatican City, Libreria Editrice Vaticana, 1965), Vatican Website, https://www.vatican.va/archive/hist_councils/ii_vatican_council/documents/vat-ii_const_19651207_gaudium-et-spes_en.html.

[13] See St. John Paul II, *Pastores Dabo Vobis,* 53.

[14] William Dych, "Theology in a New Key," in *A World of Grace,* ed. Leo O'Donovan (New York, Crossroad, 1991), 7.

desire to know more. The more understanding I gained, the more it elevated me to ever-greater heights of the infinite mystery of God.

Most importantly, I would pray about these divine mysteries to better understand them, to relish their beauty, and to come to greater conviction about them in my heart. I would often take my meditation time in the chapel before the celebration of Mass, savoring some of the key teachings I had absorbed during the morning classes. I truly feel that to know God is to love him; that to love him is to want to know him better. St. Bonaventure exhorts: "Let no one think that it is enough for him to read if he lacks devotion, or to engage in speculation without spiritual joy, or to be active if he has no piety, or to have knowledge without charity, or intelligence without humility, or study without God's grace, or to expect to know himself if he is lacking the infused wisdom of God."[15] Our theological studies were not detached speculations that were bound to the classroom; they had a definite pastoral orientation. Our instructors sought to connect theoretical knowledge with a practical wisdom, so that we could serve the people of God more effectively. It was faith seeking understanding, propelled by love for the people. Finally, through my theological studies I was able to cultivate what St. Ignatius of Loyola calls the *sentido verdadero* or "genuine attitude" in the Church.[16] This habitual attitude of mind means fundamentally an intellectual loyalty, but also includes an interiorized sensing or feeling about the Church as a whole, its officials, and doctrinal teachings.

All our intellectual training had a pastoral thrust, always oriented toward the mission of serving the people of God. From the moment we

---

[15] St. Bonaventure, *The Mind's Road to God*, Prologue, 4, Trans. George Boas, Christian Classics Ethereal Library Website, https://www.ccel.org/ccel/b/bonaventure/mindsroad/cache/mindsroad.pdf

[16] Saint Ignatius of Loyola, *The Spiritual Exercises of St. Ignatius of Loyola, A Translation and Commentary*, George Ganss, S.J. (St. Louis, Institute for Jesuit Sources, 1992), par. 352.

arrived at the seminary we were given apostolic opportunities. We began a kind of street evangelization, setting up racks of pamphlets and tracts on the Christian faith, and striking up conversations with people passing by. I greatly valued the presence of my fellow seminarians in that endeavor, sharing the mission, depending on one another for support. I also learned the value of spiritual dialogue and learned to listen to people more deeply to address their needs. We spent time building friendships with the handicapped, visiting the elderly in nursing homes, ministering to the sick in hospitals, and serving food to the poor. I spent one summer in Clinical Pastoral Education at a local hospital, where I learned not only how to minister more effectively, but also how to reflect deeply on the experience to grow personally.

We spent the other summers in parishes staffed by Oblates of the Virgin Mary, receiving a taste of our future life in an apostolic community. At the end of the first summer assignment, I made my annual Ignatian eight-day retreat. Our director encouraged us to pray through the gospels and see the parallels between our ministry and that of Jesus'. I was amazed and humbled as I became aware that I was living his mysteries—or rather, that he was living his mysteries in and through me. By third theology, I was helping in the Family Life Office of the Archdiocese of Boston, learning marriage preparation, divorced and separated ministry, and bereavement ministry. My eyes and my heart were being opened to a greater horizon of human need for Christ's love and healing. There, my female mentors taught me how to address people's hardships and to become a more compassionate, caring presence. Like the bride who is called out of her comfort zone in the hidden clefts of the rock, the Lord was leading me into challenging new experiences to become his face and voice to the world. By my fourth year of theology, I helped to offer parish missions, an important part of our Oblate apostolate, with one of our experienced priests. I was learning how to be a spiritual director in a year-long course. I undertook two courses on giving the Spiritual Exercises and began offering spiritual direction and directing weekend Ignatian retreats. Specializing in our specific Oblate charism was enlivening. I felt amazed and privileged to witness people's most intimate relationship with God. Most importantly, I was learning to be a co-laborer with Christ, who invited me to share in his mission. I experienced the joy of proclaiming his Kingdom and his building his people into a holy temple (cf. Eph 2:21).

Our Ignatian charism and spirituality is especially geared to apostolic life. The Spiritual Exercises are associated with an active Christian life and enable us to respond wholeheartedly to the call of Jesus Christ to "be with him" in active mission. The climax of the Exercises, the "Contemplation to Attain Divine Love," transforms our whole conception of reality. Just as the bride finds her Lover present in every aspect of her life, we learn to find God in all things, in all persons, circumstances, and events. We see all spiritual gifts as descending from God above.[17] Ignatian spirituality is a mysticism of service, geared toward action, mission, and everyday practice. We are to be people for others. We are meant to maintain a reflective attitude toward our work, to become "contemplatives in action." The Exercises became for me a framework within which to present the faith, to usher people into the experience of God. In all our apostolic ministry, we Oblates use the Exercises as a valuable means of pastorally assisting people according to their needs. We encourage the faithful to make the Exercises and teach Ignatian prayer and discernment both during and outside the retreat.

My summer retreat before fourth theology was geared toward discerning final vows and diaconate. Mary sang her Magnificat in my heart and her words, "my soul proclaims" (Lk 1:46) took on a deep significance. Her song summed up for me all the blessings of my creation, redemption, and

---

[17] See St. Ignatius of Loyola, *Spiritual Exercises*, 237.

call to mission, especially as an Oblate of the Virgin Mary. In gratitude, captivated by divine grace, I could more easily say:

> I see the beauty of your grace, I contemplate its radiance, I reflect its light; I am caught up in its ineffable splendor; I am taken outside myself as I think of myself; I see how I was and what I have become. O wonder! I am vigilant, I am full of respect for myself, of reverence and of fear, as I would be were I before you; I do not know what to do, I am seized by fear, I do not know where to sit, where to go, where to put these members which are yours; in what deeds, in what works shall I use them, these amazing divine marvels![18]

I took final vows and was ordained a deacon that Autumn. I was primed to be ordained a priest in my final summer. Toward the end of my final spring semester, I received the news that the formation team wanted me to do a pastoral year before ordination. It was not about any deficiencies of mine, they explained, but they were finding that our newly ordained priests weren't well enough prepared for ministry. I was deflated but accepted it, feeling it to be a real participation in the Lord's cross, which strengthened me. The situation afforded me the opportunity to spend the summer working on a master's thesis that captured my experience of seminary formation and at the same time shaped my more specialized apostolic focus for the coming years. It was titled *The Experience of Wholeness and Integration in the Spiritual Exercises of St. Ignatius*. I was grateful to have the opportunity to complete it.

In September 1994, I arrived with great anticipation at Our Oblate community in Avenel, New Jersey, where we staffed a parish and a nearby

[18] St. John Paul II, *Vita Consecrata*, 20.

retreat house. We had a gifted community of five priests and deacons all in their thirties. They were zealous for the Lord and really put themselves out there for the people. Their zeal was contagious, and I desired to always be poised to serve generously. Our ministries were many and varied. I became involved in youth group, religious education of youth and adults, RCIA, teaching Bible Study, ministry to the handicapped, service to the poor, and prison ministry. I also began officiating weddings, baptisms, and funeral services. I was amazed at how well prepared I was for all these apostolic works and felt that seminary formation had been immensely valuable. I greatly enjoyed the people and especially those lay people with whom I collaborated. In many cases, they were leaders of particular ministries and I would assist them. Saint John Paul II emphasizes:

> Awareness of the Church as 'communion' will prepare the candidate for the priesthood to carry out his pastoral work with a community spirit, in heartfelt cooperation with the different members of the Church. Such a cooperation presupposes a knowledge and appreciation of the different gifts and charisms, of the diverse vocations and responsibilities which the Spirit offers and entrusts to the members of Christ's body. It demands a living and precise consciousness of one's own identity in the Church and of the identity of others. It demands mutual trust, patience, gentleness, and the capacity for understanding and expectation. It finds its roots above all in a love for the Church that is deeper than love for self and the group or groups one may belong to.[19]

---

[19] St John Paul II, *Pastores Dabo Vobis*, 59.

Cooperation with the laity was important and enriching to me. I learned to listen to lay people, to consider their wishes, and to recognize their expertise in different fields of human activity.

Sanctified by the Hands of the Lord

By June 10 of 1995, the Solemnity of the Most Holy Trinity, I was finally ready for ordination. What better feast day could there be for an ordination, in communion with the three persons of the Holy Trinity?[20] As I lay face down on the floor before the sanctuary, I pondered my own nothingness, my unworthiness before the all-holy Trinity. I desired to die to my old self, to live for God in a new and profound way as his minister. I had recognized my own inadequacy for the task and learned to rely on God's wisdom and strength. I pondered St. Irenaeus' image of the Son and the Spirit being the two hands of the Father that extend his love and mercy to us. As the bishop laid hands on me, I was in the space of the Father's love. His Holy Spirit came upon me and made me one with Jesus Christ in his ministerial priesthood. Pope Benedict affirms:

> At the center [of priestly ordination] is the very ancient gesture of the imposition of hands, with which [Christ] took possession of me saying: 'You belong to me.' But along with this, he also said: 'You are under the protection of my hands. You are under the protection of my heart. You are kept in the palm of my hand and

---

[20] "The priest, by virtue of the consecration which he receives in the sacrament of orders, is sent forth by the *Father* through the mediatorship of *Jesus Christ*, to whom he is configured in a special way as head and shepherd of his people, in order to live and work by the power of the *Holy Spirit* in served of the Church and for the salvation of the world." St. John Paul II, *Pastores Dabo Vobis*, 12

because of this, you find yourself in the vastness of my love. Remain in the space of my hands and give me yours.'[21]

The gesture of laying on of hands was as simple as it was profound. At Holy Communion, the choir sang a haunting rendition of "The Lord is my Shepherd" by John Rutter. I rejoiced and gave thanks for the Lord's shepherding me throughout my formation in preparation for this moment. I knew he would walk beside me always throughout my priestly ministry. I felt hope and confidence that I would dwell in the house of the Lord all the days of my life (cf. Ps 23:6). The Lord had desired to see my face and hear my voice in the clefts of his heart. Now I would be his face, voice, and heart to his people.

Questions for Reflection and Discussion

1. What was my experience of entering seminary? How was I prepared or unprepared for the experience of formation? What were the biggest changes and challenges I faced?

2. How was seminary formation a participation in the hidden life of Jesus of Nazareth? How was the experience an entry into the heart of Jesus to become one in mind and heart with him?

3. In what ways has poverty or simplicity of life led you to greater dependence on the Father? How has celibacy given you an undivided heart and greater adherence to Christ? How has obedience kept you in the ways of the Spirit in doing God's will, and led to greater fruitfulness in my ministry?

---

[21] Benedict XVI, *Homily at the Chrism Mass* - April 13, 2006, Libreria Editrice Vaticana, Vatican Website, https://www.vatican.va/content/benedict-xvi/en/homilies/2006/documents/hf_ben-xvi_hom_20060413_messa-crismale.html.

4. Did you experience intellectual formation as a participation in the light of God's mind? How did learning about God increase your love for him and your desire to know him better? To what degree did your intellectual formation have a pastoral bent and how well did it translate into ministry?

5. Recall your experience of priestly ordination. What touched you about the ceremony and gestures? How have you experienced belonging to Christ and being led by him in your priestly life?

Prayer Exercises

1. Ponder the Jordan Management Memo. Pray with 1 Cor 1:26-31 and ask for the grace of humility and wonder that God has chosen you for priesthood and mission.

2. Reflect on the quotes from St. Francis de Sales and George Maloney on entering the heart of Jesus. Pray with Sg 2:10-14 and ask for the grace to exchange hearts with Jesus in his hidden life and become one in consciousness with him.

3. Consider Jesus' exhortation to the evangelical counsels and the Catechism of the Catholic Church paragraphs 1973-74, 2103. Pray with Mt 19 and ask for the grace to adhere more closely to Jesus and his way of life.

4. Ponder St. Bonaventure's quote about learning the things of God. Pray with Rom 11:33-36 and Eph 3:14-21 and ask for the grace of wonder at the enlightenment and love from God.

5. Reflect on Pope Benedict's words about the gesture of laying on of hands at ordination. Pray with Sg 2:10-14 or Ps 23 and ask for the grace of greater belonging to Christ as a priest.

Chapter 9

Listening to Life

Catch us the foxes,
the little foxes,
that spoil the vineyards,
for our vineyards are in blossom."
My beloved is mine and I am his,
he pastures his flock among the lilies.
Until the day breathes
and the shadows flee,
turn, my beloved, be like a gazelle,
or a young stag upon rugged mountains. (Sg 2:15-17)

A farmer who had reluctantly agreed to attend a workshop on Christian faith was asked if there had ever been a particular time in his life when he felt overcome by a sense that something greater than himself was at play, something he couldn't explain, a time when something seemed like a gift given from beyond himself. The farmer's expression for the first time during the lengthy session indicated curiosity, and after some time he offered a recollection: "Sometimes in the early mornings when I am out in the center of a wheat crop and I am holding a grain of young wheat in my hand, I get that same feeling." He continued by saying that even though the incident had occurred many times, he had never previously spoken to anyone about it. He was convinced that others would not comprehend what he was talking about because the experience had been so intense as to be practically indescribable. The farmer attended church frequently and occasionally prayed, but it became evident as the conversation went on that, up until this point, he had never directly linked his experience with his wheat crop to anything related to his Christian faith.[1] The farmer's experience speaks to us of the gap that is sometimes found between faith and life. Christians can attend mass on Sunday and remain oblivious to God's presence for the rest of the week. There is in our society an artificial division between the secular and the sacred. Even though we priests deal regularly with the things of God, we can sometimes lose our sense of the sacred in all that we do.

Greater Awareness Through Introspective Reflection

We are always in God's presence, but we often lack awareness. The experience of God is real and often unconscious. When we have a conscious religious experience, it affects our whole person, mind, imagination, will, emotions, and bodies. Yet, like the farmer, we can remain oblivious to this. We can reflect on our experience to understand the meaning and discern the direction it is taking us. Otherwise, we admit, with T.S. Eliot, "We had the experience, but we missed the meaning."[2] Eliot understands the human tendency to ignorance, illusion, and negligence of essential things. He continues: "And approach to the meaning restores the experience in a different form." When we understand our experience in light of God's grace and revelation, it transforms us. According to Denis Edwards, "the concept of experience as an encounter which yet needs interpretation allows that the original encounter has to receive concrete life in a person

---

[1] See Dennis Edwards, *Human Experience of God* (Ramsey, NJ, Paulist Press, 1983), 27.

[2] T.S. Eliot, "Dry Salvages," II, *The Four Quartets*, David Gorman Four Quartets Website, http://www.davidgorman.com/4quartets/3-salvages.htm.

through the mediation of the person's reflective consciousness."[3] When we reflect on the meaning of an experience, it can have its vital influence upon us.

The Examination of Conscience prayer of St. Ignatius of Loyola (often referred to as *The Examen*) is a moment for quiet, introspective prayer each day when we can discover the spiritual value in our circumstances. In all the persons, places, and events of our day, we find the hand of God at work. Ignatius had the wisdom and awareness to recognize that everything contains traces of God, the source of all reality. He understood that because we are highly preoccupied as humans, we can miss the presence of God in our day-to-day activities. When we forget about God, we can get into trouble. The Bridegroom in the Song engages the bride to "Catch us the foxes, the little foxes, that ruin the vineyards" (Sg 2:15). Throughout literature, including the Bible, foxes are cunning, deceitful creatures that cause havoc. Jesus called the evil Herod, "that fox." (Lk 13:32). Just as the foxes trample the plants and eat the grapes of the vineyard, so, too, in the spiritual life, within and without, our spiritual enemies of the world, the flesh, and the devil seek to undermine and destroy our relationship with God. This can happen especially at the early stages of spiritual growth when a person is naïve and poorly guarded. The fully-grown foxes eat the fully grown fruit, while the little foxes nibble at the flowers and the beginning of the fruit on the vine. St. John of the Cross elucidates:

> The devil, who in his great malice is envious of all the good he sees in the soul, knowing of her prosperity, now employs all his ability and engages all his crafts to disturb this good, even if only a slight part of it. ... He is sometimes the cause of many movements of the

---

[3] Denis Edwards, *Human Experience of God* (Ramsey, NJ, Paulist Press, 1983), 9.

sensory part of the soul and of many other disturbances, spiritual as well as sensory.[4]

The bride must defend against any movement of heart that would allow any detrimental power to damage their bond of love. Jesus warned against evil thoughts and deeds which come from within the heart of a person (cf. Mt 7:21-23). We can remain vigilant in the spiritual life and not lose our recollection in the Lord. By reflection on the presence of God and our interior state, The Examen enables us to be recollected in the Lord. It keeps us from straying too far from his presence and grace. Whereas contemplative prayer with scripture ponders God's word and applies it to our lives, the Examen prayer is listening to what God is saying in our relationships and in the events of life itself. Aristotle once said that only the reflective life is worth living. The Examen prayer is just that, reflecting on our lives in the light of God's grace.

We could begin by reflecting upon ordinary experiences of encountering the divine. When we walk, we are changing, searching, moving toward a goal yet to arrive. "In him we live and move and have our being" (Acts 17:28). In sitting down, we rest, often from exhausting activities. We long for eternal rest in our eternal homeland, where we belong. We sit to be quiet and read or to contemplate as a higher form of activity. Eating is transforming something dead into something alive—ourselves. It can bring communion with others and even God. Jesus compared eternal life to a banquet (cf. Mt 22:1-14). Sleeping takes up one third of our lives. It is inner relaxation where a person is open to God speaking through dreams. It is an act of trust in God and his goodness to let go of our conscious life and activity. It is also a rehearsal for death and resurrection. Laughter is

---

[4] St. John of the Cross, *Spiritual Canticle*, Stanza 16, par. 6, in *The Collected Works of St. John of the Cross*, 540.

freeing and springs from a childlike and joyous heart. It involves taking oneself lightly. It is said that angels fly because they do not take themselves too seriously. Work is being a co-creator with God. It involves both joy in creativity and suffering in toil and expenditure of energy. Work often ends in the satisfaction of achieving a good and a better world.

In Thornton Wilder's *Our Town*, Emily, who dies giving birth to her child, is allowed to go back to one special day in her life and relive it. Emily laments that amid all that is happening, her mother doesn't even look at her in a way that she really sees her daughter. As she witnesses the basic activities of daily life—the freshly-ironed clothes, clocks ticking, food and coffee, and hot baths, she realizes how much she and her family take it all for granted. She exclaims: "Oh, earth you're too wonderful for anyone to realize you! Do any human beings ever realize life while they live it—every, every minute?"

"No," replies the stage manager. Then he pauses and adds, "The saints and poets, maybe—they do some." [5]

The Examen helps us to fathom the meaning of life as we live it and to really grasp God's love and providential care for us. We are open to God's revelation in the ordinary and appreciate the beauty of our life in God. We experience God's grace especially in significant moments of self-transcendence when we experience the fullness and richness of God beyond ourselves—moments such as love, creativity, mercy, and appreciation of the beauty of nature.

The Carmelite Brother Lawrence of the Resurrection was known for his ability to discover God's presence in the ordinary moments of life. He was granted an exceptional grace which took place while he was still in the world at eighteen years of age. One day while looking at a tree stripped of

---

[5] Thornton Wilder, *Our Town, A Play in Three Acts* (New York, Harper & Row, 1957), 100.

its leaves, he considered that before long its leaves would grow back again, and then its flowers and fruits would bloom. With that realization he received an insight into the providence and power of God which never left his soul. The experience gave him a tremendous love for God that remained throughout his religious life.[6] Lawrence experienced grace in the simple act of looking at a bare tree and perceived its positive potential. We can easily lapse into a focus on the negative, what is missing from the tree that is our life. St. Paul counters that attitude by encouraging us to focus on the goodness of being as a threshold to God: "Finally, brethren, whatever is true, whatever is honorable, whatever is just, whatever is pure, whatever is lovely, whatever is gracious, if there is any excellence, if there is anything worthy of praise, think about these things" (Phil 4:8). We can choose to focus on the goodness and virtue in other people. Even in others' weaknesses we can see Christ in need and be compassionate.

It is not only in the joyful experiences of life that we discover God's grace. God is to be found in situations that are limiting and seemingly negative, such as moments of vulnerability, death, failure, alienation, and loneliness.[7] Cardinal Von Thuan recounts further details of his long years of imprisonment and reveals the secrets that allowed him to hope amid despair. During those nine years of solitary confinement, he was in a windowless cell. His torturers left the lights on for days at a time, and then left him for days in complete darkness. At times he feared he would suffocate from the heat and humidity which nearly drove him insane. As a young bishop for eight years, he was sleepless at the thought of being separated from his flock, that his many pastoral works were being neglected and lost.

---

[6] See Brother Lawrence of the Resurrection, *The Practice of the Presence of God, The Best Rule of a Holy Life*, First Conversation (New York, Fleming H. Revell Company, 1895), 7.

[7] See Edwards, 33-38.

His entire being rebelled against it. One night he heard a voice in the depths of his heart:

> Why do you torment yourself like this? You must distinguish between God and the works of God. Everything you have done and desire to continue doing—pastoral visits, formation of seminarians, of men and women religious, of the laity, of the youth, construction of schools, foyers for students, missions for the evangelization of non-Christians—all these are excellent works. These are God's works, but they are not God! If God wants you to leave all of these works, do it right away and have faith in him! God can do things infinitely better than you can. He will entrust his works to others who are much more capable. You have chosen God alone, not his works![8]

Von Thuan was filled with peace and enlightened with a new way of thinking that enabled him to surmount tremendous obstacles. A new strength filled his heart that remained throughout those thirteen years. Keenly aware of his own human weakness, the Cardinal renewed his commitment to the Lord in the face of grim circumstances, always remaining at peace. Von Thuan came to know his own poverty of spirit and powerlessness as preparation to receive the Lord's strength and love.

The Experience of Participating by Remembering

Prayer is about remembering who God is, who we are, and the relationship we have with Him at every moment. Because it is practically our nature as human beings to forget the Lord who is the source of our being

---

[8] Francis Xavier Van Thuan, *Testimony of Hope,* 42.

and all our gifts, we must discipline ourselves to remember his presence. "We must *remember* God more often than we draw breath."[9] Jesus taught us "the need to pray always and not to lose heart" (Lk 18:1). In his poverty of spirit, Ven. Von Thuan remembered God's presence and power and gained strength of heart. The people of Israel felt it to be a religious imperative to remember God's mighty deeds. "However, take care and be earnestly on your guard not to forget the things which your own eyes have seen, nor let them slip from your memory as long as you live" (Deut. 4:7-9). Israel remembered the Exodus as the central event of their history that constituted their identity as a people. They interpreted their ongoing story in its light. Their return from Exile was considered a new Exodus. When they celebrated Passover, they re-enacted and relived the Exodus event, and its power was again made present. Jesus celebrates a new Passover, the Holy Eucharist, wherein he is the Lamb of sacrifice, and he saves us by his blood. Jesus tells us to "Do this in remembrance of me" (Lk 22:19). Whenever we do this, we participate in his sacrifice, and we relive it. In the Mass, we practice the *Anamnesis*, the "holy remembering" wherein Christ makes himself and his sacrifice present to us.

> In the Liturgy of the Word the Holy Spirit 'recalls' to the assembly all that Christ has done for us. In keeping with the nature of liturgical actions and the ritual traditions of the churches, the celebration *'makes a remembrance'* of the marvelous works of God in an *anamnesis*. ... The Holy Spirit who thus awakens the memory of the Church then inspires thanksgiving and praise.[10]

---

[9] St. Gregory of Nazianzus, in *Catechism of the Catholic Church*, 2697.
[10]*Catechism of the Catholic Church*, 1103.

Sometimes it seems that memory is where we keep things out of sight and out of mind. Often, we tend to forget the things we do not like or do not want to remember. On the other hand, our love for others is kept alive by remembering moments of love. Do we remember the moments when we have been touched by God's action? To remember Jesus is to call upon his Spirit without whom we can neither love nor serve him. In prayer, we use our memory to pray over our experiences and to bring the light of the gospel to bear upon them. Mary is the first New Testament figure to do this. Luke mentions two instances in the infancy narratives where Mary ponders the events that have just taken place and their meaning. First, at the Nativity she ponders the visit of the shepherds and the words the angels told them (cf. Lk 2:19). And when Mary returns with Jesus to Nazareth, and she treasures the events of the Presentation and Finding in the Temple. By "pondering" Mary meditated on their meaning, penetrated their inner reality, and saw their unity. She came to greater acceptance and understanding of these events in wonder. Sometimes the meaning of experiences is ambiguous and not immediately evident. For instance, Jesus' remaining behind without telling his parents was painful, but ultimately for the purpose of obedience to his heavenly Father. Mary did not understand Jesus' actions or words to her and had to continue to ponder them (cf. Lk 2:51). We ought not to seek quick answers or solutions to our problems and unresolved situations. Sometimes it is more important to live the question being proposed in our lives and remain open to whatever God will reveal.

When we pray over our life experiences, it is not so much the pious sentiments that matter, but our need to be open to God's truth revealed in the event. According to Christian Brother Joseph Schmidt:

To pray our experiences is not to pray to win or succeed, or to obtain the things we think we need in order to be content and happy. It is not to pray for what is external to our deepest concerns. It is rather to pray for enlightenment and courage and acceptance and gratitude. Praying our experiences is praying to know ourselves as God knows us in a particular experience of our life, to accept ourselves as God accepts us, to love ourselves and others as God loves us, and to act in a Christlike way in response to what we come to know to be God's call in that particular experience. This form of prayer is not worrying or planning or aimlessly daydreaming. It is not devising a strategy or rationalizing about a memory. It is coming to know that we are held in God's infinite love and mercy as that all-encompassing truth is focused and revealed in particular experience. Our God is always with us. We come to know God in and through our daily life experiences because God is the source of our existence and God's mercy is the very heart of our life.[11]

The bride in the Song of Songs is most aware that she and her Beloved belong to each other. As the day breathes and the shadows flee, she desires his presence, that he turn like a stag on the mountains and come to her (cf. Sg 2:16-17). His presence is all that she needs to be known, accepted, and loved by him. The most important thing we need to be aware of is God's presence and compassion. Once we have that, all else will fall into place.

The Examen Prayer Step One: Gratitude

The first step of The Examen prayer is to focus on gratitude for God's presence and blessings, something we often neglect. Two old friends

---

[11] Joseph Schmidt, *Praying our Experiences* (Winona, MN, St. Mary's Press, 2000), 11.

bumped into one another on the street one day. One of them looked for-
lorn, almost on the verge of tears. His friend asked, "What has the world
done to you, my old friend?"

The sad fellow said, "Let me tell you. Three weeks ago, an uncle died
and left me forty thousand dollars."

"That's a lot of money."

"But you see, two weeks ago, a cousin I never even knew died, and left
me eighty-five thousand free and clear."

"Sounds like you've been blessed."

"You don't understand!" he interrupted. "Last week my great-aunt
passed away. I inherited almost a quarter of a million."

Now he was really confused. "Then, why do you look so glum?"

"This week, nothing!"

Like this character, we blithely take God's gifts for granted and fail to
count them. Often, we only notice them if they are momentarily withheld.
Sometimes, we are so filled up with so many things and distractions that
we fail to recognize our own poverty and dependence upon God. We lose
sensitivity to his continuous gifts and blessings.

It is easy to get so caught up in our own exertion of effort and calcula-
tion in our endeavors that we fail to notice God's presence and action. This
can easily lead to prideful thinking, as though our accomplishments were
entirely our own. In the movie *Shenandoah*, Charlie Anderson is the pa-
triarch farmer who leads grace before the family meal. With his children
gathered around the supper table—and one conspicuously empty place set
for his dead wife, Charlie begins a litany they obviously have heard before:
"Lord, we cleared this land. We plowed it, sowed it, and harvested. We
cooked the harvest. It wouldn't be here, we wouldn't be eatin' it, if we had-
n't done it all ourselves. We worked dog-bone hard for every crumb and
morsel. But we thank you just the same anyway, Lord, for this food we're
about to eat. Amen." Charlie fails to recognize that God is giving him the

very life and ability to labor, the land to work, and the growth of his crops. God is just an afterthought to his own arrogance and conceit.

Gratitude is a humble perspective toward life, a pervasive spirit that saturates our thinking and compels our doing. It is a way of life that flows naturally from the awareness that all of life is a gift, that all we have and are is due to divine grace. Gratitude is linked etymologically with *grace* (Greek *charis*), which means that which affords joy, delight, and loveliness. Gratitude shows reverence to God's grace with thanks. One must notice the gift, come to greater admiration, leading to thankfulness toward the giver. Thankfulness is not only with words, but with deeds. God is generously pouring out his gifts in abundance. The more we recognize it and take time to deepen our appreciation, the more grateful we will be. Gratitude leads to emotions of love, peace, and happiness. It is a great motivator to do good in return for all one has received. Gratitude also opens our heart to receive more of God's gifts. When we receive a gift of grace from God, and express gratitude to him, he reciprocates our thanks by bestowing more blessings.

Thank means "thought" in Old English. We ought to make a deliberate effort to have thankful thoughts in our mind, to look for opportunities to give thanks throughout our day. The Peruvian Jesuit Padre Martinez was so enthusiastic about gratitude as a response due to God's largesse that he disciplined himself to say thank you to God four hundred times each day, urging others to do likewise.[12] As Catholics, we celebrate the holy *Eucharist*, a Greek word which means "thanksgiving." We thank Jesus for the supreme sacrifice he made for us, dying to save us from our sins, rising to lead us to everlasting life. Jesus offers the perfect sacrifice of thanksgiving to the Father by

---

[12] Raoul Plus, S.J., *Some Rare Virtues*, trans. Sr. Mary Meyer, O.S.F. (Westminster, MN: Newman Press, 1950), 11.

offering his very life, paying our debt of gratitude. Therefore, gratitude should characterize the whole of our lives.

We should also cultivate gratitude for seemingly negative things. St. Paul exhorts us to give thanks in all circumstances (1 Thes 5:17), good and bad. We know that God uses all things for good for those who love him (cf. Rom 8:28). Usually, we have difficulty seeing and trusting in the hidden good that God is working in our lives through our trials, sufferings, and weaknesses. Through our trials we come to greater trust and dependence on God. St. James reminds us,

> Count it all joy, my brethren, when you meet various trials, for you know that the testing of your faith produces steadfastness. And let steadfastness have its full effect, that you may be perfect and complete, lacking in nothing. Blessed is the man who endures trial, for when he has stood the test, he will receive the crown of life which God has promised to those who love him. (Jas 1:2-3, 12)

God is making us stronger in virtue through our trials. That is why we can train ourselves to thank God for the challenges in our lives.

By contrast, ingratitude is one of the worst vices and ill-disposes us to receive God's grace and gifts. St. Bernard called ingratitude "a searing wind which dries up the springs of pity, the dew of mercy, the streams of grace."[13] God might even withhold his gifts from us if he perceives we have no appreciation for them. "How sharper than a serpent's tooth it is," wrote William Shakespeare, "to have a thankless child."[14] *When We Dead*

---

[13] St. Bernard of Clairvaux, in *Gratitude*, Donald de Marco, Catholic Education Resource Center Website, https://www.catholiceducation.org/en/culture/catholic-contributions/gratitude.html#:~:text=St.%20Bernard%20has%20said%3A%20%22,is%20most%20pleasing%20to%20God.

[14] William Shakespeare, King Lear, I, 4.

Awaken by Henrik Ibsen follows the existential musings of professor and renowned sculptor Arnold Rubek as he meets up with Irene, his former mistress. Both characters lack a strong sense of the importance of their own lives. Rubek is oblivious to his surroundings because he is so focused on producing his brilliant masterpieces. Irene, his loyal mistress, feels devalued by him because she does not fit his ideal of a woman, and he does not appreciate her. Towards the end, Irene begins to speak to Rubek but abruptly changes the subject: "We only recognize the things we've lost, when," Rubek looks at her with intrigue and asks her to finish her statement, "when we dead awaken." He nods sadly, then asks: "And, then— what do we see?" "We see," Irene continues, "that we have never lived."[15] Rubek and Irene lack gratitude for their lives and their potential for love in the real circumstances of their lives. Instead, they seek unattainable ideals they will never possess. We beg God that we cultivate better appreciation of our lives to truly live them. The poet George Herbert writes: "Thou hast given so much to me. Give me one more thing—a grateful heart."[16]

The Examen Prayer Step Two: Prayer for Enlightenment

The next stage of The Examen is to ask for light from God to be aware of the movements of spirit in our day. Where have I felt consolation leading me closer to God, and where have I experienced desolation leading me away from God? Are there any faults of mine that may have contributed to the spiritual desolation? We need God's enlightenment because we are often blind to our own sins and failings. Only in the light of Christ can we

---

[15] Henrik Ibsen, *When We Dead Awaken*, in *The Wild Duck and other Plays*, trans. Le Galliene (New York: Modern Library, 1961), 489.

[16] George Herbert, "Gratefulness," in *A Priest to the Temple*, 1633, Christian Classics Ethereal Library Website, https://www.ccel.org/h/herbert/temple/TempleFrames.html

know our faults, that we need to rely on God's grace at this stage. Our tendency is to be oblivious to God's promptings, or to hide from him in our sins and woundedness. The coming of light ought to be welcome in our lives, but we often prefer to avoid it. The Simon Community operates shelters for the homeless in London. Each night volunteers bring soup and sandwiches to those who prefer not to come to the shelters. They search for them in rundown buildings and under bridges. They bring a torch, because often there is no light where the homeless live. Most of the homeless greet the volunteers as friends, while some refuse to interact with them. The volunteers can immediately gauge which type of person they are by their reaction to the light—some welcome it, others fear it. In one sense, the light judges them, revealing the darkness of their lives—the darkness of alcoholism, misery, despair, and crime. In truth, however, it does not judge them. The light is friendly and illumines their lives with comfort.[17] The coming of the light is the coming of friends. Likewise, Jesus offers friendly enlightenment and nourishment, not judgment or condemnation. Jesus will highlight the goodness in our lives and being. He will also gently show us our darkness or weakness of character, which we often prefer not to acknowledge. We can overcome our tendency to maintain our respectability at all costs, by welcoming the light of Christ and not hiding from it.

The Examen Prayer Step Three: Review the Day

The next step of The Examen is to review our day, paying attention to the moments when we felt movements of feeling in our hearts. My own Examen from my parish days would often look something like the following: I would begin with thanksgiving for moments of blessing. I felt

---

[17] See Flor McCarthy, *Litrugies for Sundays and Holy Days*, Fourth Sunday of Lent, 86-87.

gratitude for some amazing insights I'd had while preparing for a bible study, which had set my heart on fire with love for the Lord. I followed up on those insights in prayer and would tell the Lord I could hardly wait to present them in our class. I might be grateful for the opportunity to sit with a needy person who came to our door looking for some conversation and some help. Often, I would give out food vouchers to the poor for which they were grateful. Their day was brightened and so was mine. I would often thank God for showing me his presence in these poor folks.

Next, I would ask the Lord for enlightenment for anything in my heart that was hurtful, either to me or because of me, anything which might be an obstacle to his love. I recall one afternoon meeting of our St. Vincent de Paul Society when one of the older members who was treasurer at the time, and a bit of a curmudgeon, was giving me resistance about how much money I was giving out. He seemed to be happier when fewer people came and was skeptical of their real neediness. I remember feeling some anger and impatience well up within me, and I was tempted to judge him as insensitive to the poor. I also felt hurt that he seemed to question my judgment and leadership of the society. Instead, I took solace in the fact that I enjoyed the support of most of the members. I was able to process the experience with the Lord and concluded that I had no basis or right to judge this man. I was able to turn the task over to the Lord to soften the treasurer's heart. I asked the Lord's forgiveness and felt he understood me and was merciful. I looked to the future with hope and a feeling of peace.

The Examen Prayer Step Four: Forgiveness

The fourth step is to ask forgiveness for faults, and for healing in the places one feels hurt by others. As we review our day, it is not necessary to make a catalogue of sins. We can, however, pay attention to the few that stand out, perhaps small neglects or failures, or sins of omission where we could have performed a charitable act, but did not. These are the "little foxes" that could destroy the vineyard (cf. Sg 2:15). It is through the struggle to overcome ourselves in little things that we become faithful in greater things and keep from backsliding into greater faults. This is often the moment of The Examen where we feel most bonded with the Lord. The compassionate Lord who shows mercy in our weakness reveals himself as unconditional love. We experience the Lord present where we need him most as a friend who never abandons us. Instead, he draws us closer to his heart in friendship. Venerable Bruno Lanteri speaks of the Lord's endless mercy:

> Let us not measure God by our own limitations, imagining him to be what in reality he is not, since in such fashion we do him a great wrong, and injury, but at our own expense, reducing the bounds of his mercy as though he were a wretched man like me, and therefore not daring to go and seek his forgiveness when we fail in our good proposals and return to our former sins, having such concept of his Divine Majesty as if he were of our condition and would grow weary of so much instability, weakness, and forgetfulness, and therefore would revenge himself upon our sins by taking away his helps, and allowing us to fall into even greater ruin, and believing that we, by our sins, hinder him from granting us graces, and other such similar foolish things, worthy of our ignorance. Our God is not so; let us attribute to him that which truly befits him, that is, that he is good, merciful, compassionate, a loving father who bears with us, and forgives us; with this understanding of God, as is properly his due, he allows himself to be obliged to be merciful in dealing with us.[18]

---

[18] Ven. Bruno Lanteri, *The Spiritual Writings of Venerable Pio Bruno Lanteri,* 46.

God loves to offer his forgiveness and is always waiting for us to return to him with confidence in his mercy. We can be more generous and freer in loving others, knowing the Lord will always forgive us when we fail. Knowing that we are forgiven, we can more easily extend God's mercy to others who have hurt us.

The Examen Step 5: Renewal and Hope

Knowing God's mercy and unconditional love renews us with energy to serve him and leads to the final step of The Examen, looking ahead to the future with hope. Throughout the New Testament, those who experience God's mercy are moved to respond in gratitude. Jesus affirms that the repentant woman who weeps at the feet of Jesus loves much because she has been forgiven much (cf. Lk 7:47). As we look forward to our next day, next event, or next encounter with someone we have struggled to love, we ask God's help in whatever way we need it. Let us return to the example of my parish Examen. Looking ahead to my next St. Vincent de Paul Society meeting with that difficult person, I could ask God's help to see him in a different light. I could focus on his diligent and dedicated service over the years. He had done this work for a long time and perhaps had been deceived by enough charlatans that he was justifiably jaded. I could consider my own naivete and need for input from experienced veterans. I could also begin to let go of my fear of criticism and need for approval. Finally, I would be able to look forward with hope for improvement in our relationship and trust in the Lord for a good outcome that would enable us to serve the poor more effectively.

Most important is the regained sense that God accompanies me in all my activities and wants me to depend on him. The bride expresses this sense of belonging to her Beloved and being shepherded in her daily life: "My beloved is mine and I am his; he pastures his flock among the lilies"

(Sg 2:16). Amidst her day, she can turn to the Lord and know his presence. When she calls upon him, he will quickly be present and answer her: "Until the day breathes and the shadows flee, turn, my beloved, be like a gazelle or a young stag on the cleft mountains" (Sg 2:17).

The Examen prayer empowers us as priests to surrender in trust to the Lord's plan. As Pope John XXIII said before retiring each night, having done his best to serve: "Lord, it's your Church, I'm going to bed." Ultimately our ministry is the Lord's work, and we are merely cooperative instruments. The Examen prayer sustains us moving forward with trust. During the bombing raids of World War II, thousands of children were orphaned and left to starve. The fortunate ones were rescued and placed in refugee camps where they received food and good care. But many of these children having lost so much could not sleep at night. They feared waking up to find themselves once again homeless and without food. Nothing seemed to reassure them. Finally, someone hit upon the idea of giving each child a piece of bread to hold at bedtime. Holding their bread, these children could finally sleep in peace. All through the night the bread reminded them, "Today I ate, and I will eat again tomorrow."[19] That is what the Examen does for us.

Summary of Steps of The Examen:

1. Gratitude for Blessings Received
2. Prayer for Enlightenment
3. Review of Day: Noticing God Present, Sins, and Faults
4. Seek Forgiveness and Healing
5. Asking Help for the Future: Renewal and Hope

---

[19] See Dennis Linn, Sheila Fabricant Linn, Matthew Linn, *Sleeping with Bread, Holding What Gives You Life* (Mahwah, NJ, Paulist Press, 1995), 1.

Questions for Reflection and Discussion

1. Do I ever experience a split between faith and life? Though as a priest I deal with the things of God regularly, do I often forget God in my daily life? How could practicing The Examen prayer unite faith and life for me?

2. To what degree do I find God present in seemingly negative experiences of life such as trials and sufferings?

3. To what extent does gratitude characterize my attitude toward life? How do I tend to forget God's blessings, or attribute my success to my own abilities? Do I ever experience ingratitude? How does gratitude make me a humbler, happier person and more receptive to God's gifts?

4. How open am I to the light of Christ revealing areas of sinfulness in my life? How do I experience that light? Where do I sense resistance on my part?

5. How often do I seek God's mercy? When I sin, how am I tempted to give up and even turn away from God? How can I be more confident in his mercy and receive new energy to serve him?

6. How do I look to the future, especially in The Examen prayer? What do I ask for? Do I experience hope in God? How does God's mercy for my past fill me with hope for the future?

Prayer Exercises

1. Reflect on the farmer's experience holding grain in the field. Pray with Phil 4:8 and ask for the grace to know God's presence in your ordinary life.

2. Ponder Archbishop Van Thuan's experience in solitary confinement. Pray with 2 Cor 4:7-16 or Jas 1:1-8 and ask for the grace to find God in seemingly negative experiences.

3. Consider Joseph Schmidt's quote on praying our experiences. Pray with Lk 2:19, 51 and ask for the grace to ponder in your heart all the events of your life in light of God's revelation.

4. Reflect on gratitude and greater receptivity to God's gifts. Pray with Col 1:3-8 and ask the Lord to give you a grateful heart.

5. Ponder the story of the Simon community bringing light to the homeless. Pray with Mt 4:12-17 and ask for the grace to welcome the light of Christ in examining your conscience.

6. Consider Ven. Bruno Lanteri's quote on the mercy of God. Pray with Lk 18:9-14. Ask for the grace of a repentant heart and to experience God's mercy daily.

7. Reflect on the story of the orphans sleeping with bread. Pray with Heb 6:13-20 and ask for the grace of an increase of hope moving forward using The Examen prayer.

Chapter 10

The Sacrificial Impulse

Upon my bed by night
I sought him whom my soul loves;
I sought him, but found him not;
I called him, but he gave no answer.
"I will rise now and go about the city,
in the streets and in the squares;
I will seek him whom my soul loves."
I sought him, but found him not.
The watchmen found me,
as they went about in the city.
"Have you seen him whom my soul loves?"
Scarcely had I passed them,
when I found him whom my soul loves.
I held him, and would not let him go
until I had brought him into my mother's house,
and into the chamber of her that conceived me.
I adjure you, O daughters of Jerusalem,
by the gazelles or the hinds of the field,
that you stir not up nor awaken love
until it please. (Sg 3:1-5)

A man once had a dream that time was coming to an end. On a vast plain in front of God's throne, untold billions of humanity were awaiting judgment. Some were afraid, while others were enraged. "How can God judge us?" a woman questioned, "How is He mindful of suffering? We suffered horror, assaults, torture, and death." She then raised her sleeve to reveal a tattooed Nazi concentration camp number on her arm. Then a black man exposed an unsightly rope scar on his neck by lowering his shirt. "What do you think of this?" he questioned. Lynched for no other reason than being black. We have suffocated in slave ships, been torn from loved ones, labored until liberated by death. A girl who had the term "illegitimate" tattooed across her forehead declared, "To bear my disgrace was beyond shame," before others picked up where she left off. Everyone was angry with God for allowing them to endure wickedness and pain throughout their existence on earth. How fortunate God was to be in heaven where everything was joy and peace, where there was no crying, terror, starvation, or hostility. What was God's comprehension of human travail?

They came to the conclusion that God should be sentenced to live as a man. But because he was God, they imposed restrictions to ensure that he could not use his omnipotence for personal gain. Let him be a Jew at birth and let the legitimacy of his birth be called into question. Give him a project so challenging that even his relatives will think he is crazy if he attempts it. Let the residents of his town repudiate him. Make it so his closest companions desert and betray him. Let him be falsely charged, tried by a biased jury, and found guilty by a spineless judge. Finally, make him experience what it's like to be utterly forsaken by all other living things. Let him be beaten and insulted. Then force him to experience an agonizing and degrading death. Make him perish so that there will be no room for uncertainty. Let there be many witnesses to attest to it and make certain he is dead and buried. Loud shouts of approbation rose from the large crowd of humanity as their judge proclaimed each part of the punishment God should serve.[1]

---

[1] See Flor McCarthy, *New Sunday and Holy Day Liturgies, Year A*, Passion (Palm) Sunday, 97.

The Nature of Our Suffering

Ever since Adam committed sin when he ate the fruit of the tree of knowledge of good and evil, the entire human race has been plagued by sin. In justice, an infinite price to an infinitely good God must be rendered to redeem us. Therefore, only God had the ability to pay the price. God made atonement for our transgressions in Jesus Christ, who bore the punishment for our sins and became the innocent victim in our place.[2]

Jesus took on the weakness of our human flesh and transformed it into our redemption and his glory. He swallowed up sin in love and turned it into victory. In contrast to Christ's beauty, the ugliness of human sin is most exposed by his passion. At the last supper he suffers a most painful betrayal by Judas, his dear chosen apostle. "Even my bosom friend in whom I trusted, who ate of my bread, has lifted the heel against me" (Ps 41:9). Jesus does not prevent him, but encourages him to do what he must do, quickly (cf. Jn 13:27). Peter is rash and cowardly. He protests that he will never deny Jesus, then proceeds to do so three times. Three of the apostles, Peter, James, and John, display an egregious sloth. They fall asleep during Jesus' agony, his hour of greatest need, when his soul was overwhelmed with sorrow, even unto death (cf. Mt 26:38). He had only asked that they stay and watch with him. Jesus' enemies then come out for him with clubs and swords, as though he is a thief or outlaw. He had spoken openly in the streets but they would not arrest him there. Jesus then suffers the most brutal form of violence in crucifixion, at the hands of wicked men. He endures hatred from his enemies and his own people, in the form of insults and false accusations. Yet he remains silent instead of fighting

---

[2] In Luke's gospel, Jesus is proclaimed to be innocent on four separate occasions: first before the Sanhedrin, then by Pilate, then by Herod, and finally by the people. It is the supreme irony that they release Barrabas, a murderer and an insurrectionist, who is in sharp contrast to Jesus' innocence and peace.

back (cf. Mt 26:63, Is 53:7).

Jesus shows sin for what it is as its full force is unleashed upon him. Jesus as the prince of peace, suffers hostility to reconcile us with God, to bring about peace in the kingdom. But he changes viciousness into love by his willingness to suffer innocently. Hans Urs von Balthasar declares:

> This is a war for God's beloved creation. Sin has so corrupted the interior of the world that it is trapped in an abyss of self-consumed lust. Its only hope is to be redeemed from the inside out: God will enter into the heart of His creation, exposing His love-filled heart to all the powers of evil, for only love can overcome this damnation.[3]

Jesus, in his suffering and death, fulfills the figure of the Bridegroom of the Song of Songs. The bride is on her bed, awaiting the Bridegroom's coming to consummate their marriage. Ordinarily the Bridegroom would disappear from the crowd at a wedding to go to the bridal chamber. In this case, instead of going into the chamber, he disappears into the night. The bride goes out to seek him. This corresponds to Jesus' words to his disciples about his impending passion and death. He tells them "The days will come when the bridegroom will be taken away from them" (Lk 5:35). Jesus disappears in his passion and death. Ironically, this becomes the moment of consummation of his marriage with his bride, the Church. The Church is born from the blood and water which flowed from pierced side of Christ as he dies. The water and blood symbolize the sacraments of Baptism and Eucharist, which make the Church and nourish her. As Eve was formed from Adam's side as he slept, so the bride, the Church, was formed from

---

[3] Hans Urs von Balthasar, *Heart of the World*, trans. Erasmo S. Leiva (San Francisco, Ignatius Press, 1979), 48.

Christ's side in the sleep of death on the Cross. Jesus' marriage bed was one of pain, not pleasure. St. Augustine wrote, "Like a bridegroom Christ went forth from his chamber. … He came to the marriage bed of the cross, and there in mounting it, he consummated his marriage. And when he perceived the sighs of the creature, he lovingly gave himself up to the torment in place of his bride, and joined himself to her forever."[4] The medieval German mystic St. Mechtilde of Magdaberg affirms this notion in stating that Christ's "noble nuptial bed was the very hard wood of the Cross on which he leaped with more joy and ardor then a delighted bridegroom"[5]

Redemptive Suffering

In the Old Testament, Isaiah foretold the saving effects of the Lord's passion: "He was wounded for our transgressions, he was bruised for our iniquities; upon him was the chastisement that made us whole, and with his stripes we are healed" (Is 53:5). Jesus took on our sins and the punishment that was due to us and gave us love in return. The cross is foolishness to the those who are perishing, but the power of God to those being saved (cf. 1 Cor 18). In contemporary Russia, the *yurodivy*—a holy idiot who purposefully behaves foolishly in front of men—exemplifies this gracious folly. The phrase suggests actions that are not careless or dimwitted, but rather intentional, annoying, and sometimes provocative. When Russia was communist, there were some Christians who called themselves "yurodivys" and were frequently detained as political prisoners. A yurodivy

---

[4] St. Augustine, *Sermon on the Lord's Nativity*, numbered 120, 8 in the appendix, PL vol. 39, 1987.

[5] Mechtilde of Magdaberg, *Resounding the Faith Website*, https://resoundingthefaith.com/2019/10/greek-%CE%BD%CF%85%CE%BC%CF%86%CE%AF%CE%BF%CF%82-nymphios-latin-sponsus-latin-vir/

would desire to receive the stripes of the whip when another prisoner was about to receive punishment from a jail guard. He believed that the guilty would hate back, thus raising the level of hatred in the world. But the content of the world's love would increase when one absolved and swallowed hatred. It can be said that Christ was the first "holy fool," bearing our sins and turning suffering and hatred into love.

When we accept suffering in imitation of Jesus, and continue to love, we, like the yurodivys, absorb hate and mitigate pain—whether it be spiritual, psychological, or physical. Chiara Lubich, founder of the Focolare movement, proclaimed:

> When our pure love comes in contact with suffering, it transforms it into love. In a certain sense, it divinizes the suffering. We could almost say that the divinization of suffering, that Jesus brought about, continues in us. And after each encounter in which we have loved Jesus forsaken, we find God in a new way, more face to face, with greater openness and fuller unity. Light and joy return; and with the joy, that peace which is the fruit of the Spirit.[6]

Lubich's point is evident in the life of the priest. The priest, in persona Christi, takes the sin, guilt and pain of the world upon himself and changes it into mercy and love. He enters every situation of human suffering as the presence of Jesus. He endures those difficult situations and brings healing, comfort, peace, and an increase of faith in God. While there is a certain heaviness in these experiences that can feel burdensome, there is also the joy of bringing God into peoples' lives.

---

[6] Chiara Lubich, "Nailed to the Cross, We Become Mothers and Fathers of Souls," Rome, March 18, 2008, Zenit Website, https://zenit.org/articles/chiara-lubich-s-heroic-lesson-of-love/

While living in Boston, I would occasionally monitor a beeper for hospital calls for five local hospitals on the weekend. On one of the first Saturday nights that I was on duty, I was beeped at 2:00 a.m. while in the middle of a deep sleep. A man was dying and needed the Sacrament of Anointing of the Sick. I replied that I would be right over. I grudgingly dressed in a half-daze. I got into a cold car on a winter night, grumbling to God, wondering why they couldn't have called me earlier when they might have known he was going to die and I was still awake. I moaned to myself that I would have to rise again in a few hours to go for Sunday Masses across town. I arrived at the hospital and the family was very pleased to see me. Their loved one perhaps only had a slight awareness of what was happening, but I felt strongly that the Sacrament would bring him peace of heart at this moment of death. It certainly brought more peace to his family, and they thanked me profusely. As I drove home, I was filled with joy and felt privileged to bring God's presence at such a critical moment. I also felt ashamed of my initial whining and reluctance. The words of the Psalm came to mind, "Those who sow in tears reap with shouts of joy" (Ps 126). A small sacrifice on my part bore great fruit by God's grace. I resolved not to complain so much in the future. The Lord forgave me and gave me encouragement and hope that I would be more disposed to sacrifice for him and others in times ahead.

Moments like that hospital experience helped me realize that sacrifice of self for God and others leads to fulfillment. The priest manifests the fact that as human beings we are made for sacrifice. The philosopher Max Scheler wrote about the "sacrificial impulse" as an original constituent of life which precedes any specific aspirations we might later impose on it: "We have the urge to sacrifice before we ever know why, for what, and for whom? Jesus' view of nature and life, which sometimes shines through his speeches and parables in fragments and hidden allusions, shows quite clearly that he understood this fact."[7] Jesus, by his actions more than by his teachings, shows us the meaning of sacrifice. Our lives are now drawn into Christ's sacrifice, which saves us and preserves us. The sacrifice of others has brought us into being and nurtured us, and we need to accept that sacrifice in gratitude and poverty of spirit. We cannot earn the immense love of Christ, but we can only accept it as a complete gift.[8] Only then can we participate in his sacrifice and share it with others.

Sacrificial Suffering

People often view the priest's life as one of sacrifice, and it is. But it is not so much what we don't have as what we do have that becomes an oblation. The emptiness we make in our lives by the evangelical counsels of poverty, celibacy and obedience becomes filled up with gratitude and praise to God for all that he does for us and through us. In my own priesthood, I experience the wound of Christ's sacrificial love. I have given up material possessions and received the riches of God and friends. The sacrifice of married life gave me Christ as an unfailing spouse and the Church as a beautiful bride. To renounce personal autonomy over my life in my vow of obedience was most excruciating but has been abundantly fruitful in adhering to God's will. Going forth to minister is a sacrifice, especially when we enter other people's pain. But that sacrifice is ultimately joyful and brings solace to those most in need. I have felt the peaceful wounding of Christ's love in compassionately sitting with the poor. When I help a married couple work through a painful relationship and re-commit their lives to God and one another, I feel privileged to be the presence of Christ

---

[7] Max Scheler, *Ressentiment*, ed. Lewis A. Coser, trans. William W. Holdheim (New York: Free Press of Glenco, 1961), 89.

[8] See Joseph Ratzinger, *Introduction to Christianity* (San Francisco, Ignatius Press, 2004), 267.

to them. What an honor it is to anoint dying persons and forgive their sins to prepare them to meet the Lord in peace. I relish helping a spiritual directee to persevere in prayer through darkness and trials and thus to discover God more profoundly. Entering prison to console the incarcerated feels so freeing. Feeding the spiritually hungry and preaching God's word to the faithful is a Sunday sacrifice that overflows my chalice with gratitude. All these precious experiences of priesthood are enough to make my heart burst with joy—that is the "torment" of the priest.

Jesus *willingly* embraced the suffering of the Cross, and so must we. "I lay down my life in order to take it up again. No one takes it from me, but I lay it down of my own accord" (Jn 10:17-18). We can merely tolerate difficulties or decide to wholeheartedly embrace them. St. Thérèse of Lisieux did not like having her projects interrupted. Sometimes, she was asked to do jobs requiring quite a lot of focus such as drawing a picture or writing a theatrical play on her community's behalf. The program of daily activities of the Carmelite community was so packed that she had little time available. When she was able to find a chunk of time to dedicate to the project, she adopted an accommodating attitude, saying, "I accept this interference." If one of her sisters visited her asking for help, rather than saying "I'm too busy right now," Therese decided to welcome the intrusion with patience and attentive caring for her sisters. If she was able to work without disruption, she welcomed it with gratitude as a delightful gift from God. No matter what transpired she remained at peace and unperturbed by external circumstances. Her will was always to accept what God desired and manifested to her in her concrete situation and she thus passed the days peacefully and was never upset.[9] In everything she felt free to accept God's will, and it brought her the Lord's consolation.

---

[9] See Jacques Phillipe, *Interior Freedom*, tr. Helena Scott (New York, Scepter, 2007), 56.

St. Francis de Sales rejoiced in his own suffering as a participation in Jesus' sufferings:

> And I, exposed to the sorrow that I received through the compassion from the unique travails of my divine Savior, am all covered with distress and pierced with pain. However, since the pains of the one I love come from this love, they make me suffer in compassion and delight me out of kindness in the same measure. For how could a faithful, loving soul not be extremely happy when knowing that she is so loved by her heavenly Bridegroom? For this reason, therefore, the beauty of love resides in the ugliness of pain.[10]

Similarly, the bride, realizing her beloved has gone forth to suffer, runs out into the city streets in search of him. She desires to accompany him and to share his suffering. When she finds him, she will not let go of him. We are reminded of the Blessed Virgin Mary, St. Mary Magdalene, and the Beloved Disciple, who go out in search of Jesus during his Passion, accompanying him on the Way of the Cross and standing faithfully at the foot of the Cross (cf. Jn 19:25-26). They only desire to suffer along with him.

Comfort Through Suffering

When we suffer with Jesus, we will experience Jesus' comfort in our sufferings, as did St. Paul. He experienced many problems, disappointments, and sufferings in his ministry. He was stoned by his fellow Jews and persecuted by Gentiles in the face of spreading the gospel. Paul had difficulty understanding why a majority of his fellow Jews would not accept the gospel, and it caused him great anguish, even to the point of wishing

---

[10] St. Francis de Sales, *Treatise on the Love of God,* Book V, Ch. V.

that he could be separated from Christ so that the Jews might benefit (Rom 9:3). He also felt anxiety for the Churches as he longed for their unity and harmony, that they might be of one heart and mind in Christ Jesus. In many cases they were divided due to rivalries and jealousies about who had the most prestige and should therefore lead the church. In some cases, Paul was rejected as a leader and his credentials were called into question. Some broke into factions, saying they belonged either to Paul, Apollos, Peter, or Christ (cf. 1 Cor 1:12). Paul, as a ministerial priest, must have struggled with frustration, fatigue, anger, and disappointment. Amid his sufferings, he experienced the comfort of the Lord: "who consoles us in all our afflic-tion, so that we may be able to console those who are in any affliction with the consolation with which we ourselves are consoled by God" (2 Cor 1:4). According to Cardinal Carlo Martini:

> These are no longer Paul's sufferings, but Christ's, and we under-stand that the Apostle instinctively experiences his sufferings not as a solitary personal fate, but as Christ's sufferings in him, be-cause they occur within the ministry that the Lord has entrusted to him. In this way his life is united to Christ's. He calls them Christ's sufferings in himself, because their cause is his entering the ministry for love of the Lord. [11]

We too embrace sufferings on behalf of the Lord's ministry and experience Christ's suffering in and through us.

Martini makes a connection between suffering and the comfort we re-ceive when facing challenges in ministry. In the course of our pastoral work, we encounter a wide range of different experiences and reactions,

---

[11] Carlo Martini, *In the Thick of His Ministry*, trans. Dinah Livingstone (Col-legeville, MN: Liturgical Press, 1990), 17.

from tiredness to irritability, to aversion and resistance of people and situations. We can experience these feelings and responses without numbing ourselves or suppressing them. We can drink the cup of bitterness and sorrow to the very last drop. Jesus asked James and John, "Are you able to drink the cup?" (Mt 20:22). We have to ingest our experiences and enable the Lord to change them into his comfort rather than simply tasting and spitting them out.[12] Only if we remain in the heart of Jesus will that be possible. These encounters are not incidental; they are frequently woven into the fabric of our service. According to the apostle Paul, "you became imitators of us and of the Lord, for in spite of persecution you received the word with joy inspired by the Holy Spirit" (1 Thes 1:6).

His Holiness Pope John Paul II died in April of 2005 after having led the Church for about twenty-seven years. He came close to dying when he was shot in an attempted assassination in 1981. He developed colon cancer in 1992. Also in 1992, he hurt his shoulder, and in 1993 damaged his hip. His appendix was removed in 1996. In 2001, he developed Parkinson's disease. He experienced trembling in his hands, arms, legs, jaw, and face. His arms, legs and trunk stiffened, and his movement slowed. He suffered from poor balance and coordination, as well as speech difficulty. As he approached death, he was clearly in pain. He united his sufferings with those of Christ and carried his burden with amazing composure. Once, in the middle of a press conference, a reporter challenged him: "Holy Father, kindly excuse me for being bold. You are aged, your hands are shaking due to Parkinson's disease, your voice is feeble and inaudible, and you find it difficult to walk. You are suffering a lot and you are incapacitated in your work. Why don't you resign and take rest, and make way for the others to take over?"

---

[12] See Martini, Ibid., 18.

The saintly pope replied, "If Jesus had come down from the cross, I, too, would have resigned. Since, He remained on the cross and suffered, I too, am holding on to my responsibility, and am suffering."[13]

St. John Paul II accepted his cross and persevered in his ministry, and so should we. Our greatest cross is the cross we reject. The more we resist and fight it, the more anguished we become. We prefer our comforts and routine. We look for admiration and things, but avoid God, lacking trust that he knows what is best for us. St. John Vianney exhorts us:

On the Way of the Cross, you see, my children, only the first step is painful. Our greatest cross is the fear of crosses . . . We have not the courage to carry our cross, and we are very much mistaken; for, whatever we do, the cross holds us tight—we cannot escape from it. What, then, have we to lose? Why not love our crosses, and make use of them to take us to heaven?[14]

We cannot expect to be spared our share of the hardship of the gospel, but we must bear it willingly with the strength provided by God. Complaining often only makes things worse and is often unrealistic. We should be hopeful with St. Paul who wrote: "I consider that the sufferings of this present time are not worth comparing with the glory about to be revealed to us" (2 Cor 4:17). Etty Hillesum, a Dutch Jew, sent to Auschwicz spoke of embracing sufferings:

I now realize, God, how much You have given me. So much that was beautiful and so much that was hard to bear. Yet whenever I

---

[13] Epriest, Homily Pack, *Divine Mercy Sunday*, Epriest Website, https://epriest.com/homily_packs

[14] St. John Vianney, *Little Catechism of the Cure' de Ars*, Part 1, 11. (Charlotte, NC: Tan Books, 2011).

showed myself ready to bear it, the hard was directly transformed into the beautiful. And the beautiful was sometimes much harder to bear, so overpowering did it seem. To think that one small human heart can experience so much, oh God, so much suffering and so much love, I am so grateful to You, God, for having chosen my heart, in these times, to experience all the things it has experienced.[15]

Hillesum shows us that it is not by avoiding suffering that we are transformed. Only when we accept it in union with Christ, who loves us in suffering can we find value in it and mature as Christians. Saint James encourages us to rejoice in facing suffering and trials because when we are tested in our faith it leads to perseverance. Perseverance leads to our perfection, maturity, and growth in virtue. We grow in humility, courage, and hope, as well as empathy toward our neighbors. When we recoil from suffering, we become stuck in our selfish attitudes and fail to achieve our human potential. Paul speaks of making up what is lacking in the sufferings of Christ. The only thing that could be lacking is that I, myself experience suffering in union with Christ and, in love, share in his redemptive action.

Jesus underwent hardship to become "perfect" (cf. Heb 2:10), and so must we. Jesus was conceived sinless and led a life free from sin. Yet, he experienced the effects of entering a sinful world and was afflicted in every way we are. Even as an innocent man he experienced suffering and death. Moral righteousness is a certain kind of perfection. A different form of perfection or wholeness, however, can only be attained by experience. Jesus fully experienced the afflictions of this world and overcame them. The

---

[15] Etty Hillesum, *An Interrupted Life and Letters from Westerbork,* trans. Arnold Pomeran (New York: Henry Holt and Company, 1996), 197-198.

atrocities he endured completed the experience of his life spent on earth. He was made human in every way to become a merciful and faithful high priest in service to God and to make atonement for our sins (cf. Heb 2:17).

Strength in Suffering

Suffering keeps us humble. It makes us realize that God's ways are not our ways. We are not masters of our own destiny. I learned this lesson in 1994, when I was a deacon, expecting to be ordained a priest soon, at the end of our fourth year of theological studies. At the same time, as I mentioned in chapter eight, I was told by the formation staff that my ordination would be postponed, and that they wanted me to do a pastoral year in one of our parishes. Apparently, some of the newly ordained were having difficulty transitioning into parish work. I felt like that was their problem being projected onto me, and that I was ready. I had already spent nearly seven years in formation. My family and friends were expecting my imminent ordination and would be wondering what the problem was, which would cause me embarrassment. I felt anger that this was being imposed on me against my will. With all this in my mind and heart, I went to our upstairs chapel. As I poured out my heart to the Lord, the image of St. Francis receiving the stigmata on Mt. Alverna came to me. Like Francis, I felt a union with Jesus in his sufferings and the ability to let go of my will and accept this cross. I was energized and strengthened to move forward in peace. Many good things happened as a result. I was able to finish my master's thesis that summer, which shaped my future ministry. I then spent nine months as a deacon in my first parish and emerged better prepared for priesthood.

St. Paul believed that if we die with Christ, we shall also live with him (cf. Rom 6:8). He firmly believed that nothing—not adversity, not persecution, not even death itself—could stand in the way of his friendship with

Jesus (cf. Rom 8:38). He was free from anxiety about the present and the future as a result. He seemed to operate under the guiding principle that "what doesn't kill me makes me stronger." He also understood that his sufferings were for the benefit of others in unison with Jesus' sacrifice (see Rom 6:7-9). When he was distraught, he knew it was for the solace and salvation of his church; when he was comforted, he knew it was for their comfort, enabling them to peacefully undergo the same pains he suffered. The cross has the ability to impart life to others. Paul saw the release of a force and dynamism of love on behalf of his cherished church whenever someone made a sacrifice.[16] Others received new life as a result, as stated in 2 Corinthians 4:11: "For we who live are continually being given up to death for the sake of Jesus, so that the life of Jesus may be manifested in our mortal flesh." God's might was so clearly visible through the gloom of the cross that he was certain the gospel was wholly sufficient. Paul refused to impose any further biblical law or observance on Gentile converts despite intense pressure. Others might take pride in rituals like circumcision and other religious rites, but he refused to take pride in anything other than the cross of Christ. Paul would glory only in the wounds and scars in his body that he could show as the results of whippings, floggings, chains, and torture that he endured in view of the gospel. "But may I never boast except in the cross of our Lord Jesus Christ, through which the world has been crucified to me, and I to the world. ... From now on, let no one make troubles for me; for I bear the marks of Jesus on my body. (Gal 6:14, 17)

Paul experienced every possible obstacle to the preaching of the gospel from within and without:

---

[16] See Joseph Grassi, *The Secret of Paul the Apostle* (Maryknoll, NY: Orbis, 1978), 102-103.

Are they ministers of Christ? I am talking like a madman—I am a better one: with far greater labors, far more imprisonments, with countless floggings, and often near death. Five times I have received from the Jews the forty lashes minus one. Three times I was beaten with rods. Once I received a stoning. Three times I was shipwrecked; for a night and a day I was adrift at sea; on frequent journeys, in danger from rivers, danger from bandits, danger from my own people, danger from Gentiles, danger in the city, danger in the wilderness, danger at sea, danger from false brothers and sisters, in toil and hardship, through many a sleepless night, hungry and thirsty, often without food, cold and naked. And, besides other things, I am under daily pressure because of my anxiety for all the churches. (2 Cor 11:23-28)

The paradox of the cross was that all the obstacles, events, and people that seemed to upset all his plans and stand in the way instructed Paul. He learned that with the failure of human schemes the divine plan unexpectedly emerges.[17] Therefore, he could confidently exhort his flock to rejoice in the face of trials and anxiety. They could then become one with Christ crucified and experience being transfigured from glory to glory in him. Through all these obstacles and trials, Paul keenly felt his own weakness and was able to experience the power of God and surrender to it. "Therefore, I am content with weaknesses, insults, hardships, persecutions, and calamities for the sake of Christ; for whenever I am weak, then I am strong" (2 Cor 12:10). Christ conquered through weakness on the cross and would continue his triumph in the same way. Han urs Von Baltahasar elucidates:

---

[17] Ibid., 104-105.

For his weakness would already be the victory of his love for the Father, and as a deed of his supreme strength, this weakness would far surpass and sustain in itself the world's pitiful feebleness. He alone would henceforth be the measure and thus also the meaning of all impotence. He wanted to sink so low that in the future all falling would be a falling into him, and every streamlet of bitterness and despair would henceforth run down into his lowermost abyss.[18]

The Triumph of the Cross

The irony of the cross is that this utter defeat and miserable tragedy is turned into a triumph beyond our wildest imagining. Jesus rises from the dead, his same body that was brutally destroyed is now raised up. In Southern Scotland, near the town of Dumfries, there is preserved an old stone cross, the famous, Ruthwell Cross. It was carved sometime around 700 AD, some 1300 years ago. And on that cross are some lines from an old Anglo-Saxon poem, called the "Dream of the Rood," that is, the Dream of the Cross. In the course of that poem, the tree is cut down so that it can be used as the cross on which Christ is crucified. It participates in the crucifixion of Christ, undergoing all that Christ undergoes. It is raised up, it is pierced with nails, it is covered with blood, it is even buried. But then finally, with Christ, it is transformed from an ordinary tree into a tree sparkling with jewels and gold. So, the cross is called "the triumph tree, the tree of glory." We are like that cross, crucified with Christ. The more we identify with Christ crucified, uniting our suffering and pain to his, the more we will be glorified with him, raised up in triumph. We all have our sufferings, our crosses to bear. We must love our cross, it is our means of sharing

---

[18] Von Balthasar, *Heart of the World*, 48.

with Christ, being close to God, experiencing his life. "How splendid the cross of Christ! It brings life, not death; light, not darkness; paradise, not its loss. It is the wood on which the Lord, like a great warrior, was wounded in hands and feet and side, but healed thereby our wounds. A tree has destroyed us, a tree now brought us life."[19]

Whenever we experience the Cross, we can be sure God is at work and triumphing. Edith Stein was a convert from Judaism and became a Carmelite nun, taking the religious name Sister Theresa Benedicta of the Cross. In 1942, immediately after the Dutch bishops wrote a pastoral letter condemning the Nazi treatment of the Jews, the Nazis made a reprisal and arrested 1200 Catholic Jews, among them was Edith Stein. She was gassed at Auschwitz six days later. In her book *Science of the Cross*, she explains how important the cross of Jesus Christ is in our daily lives for our own sanctification and for the salvation of souls. Edith Stein's final words were smuggled out of Auschwitz on a note which stated, "One can only learn the science of the cross if one feels the cross in one's own person. I was convinced of this from the very first and have said it with all my heart: 'Hail to the cross, our only hope.'"[20] Even as her life was threatened, she was able to trust in God's designs:

> Whatever did not fit in with my plan did lie within the plan of
> God. I have an ever deeper and firmer belief that nothing is merely
> an accident when seen in the light of God, that my whole life down
> to the smallest details has been marked out for me in the plan of
> Divine Providence and has a completely coherent meaning in

---

[19] St. Theodore of Studious, *The Liturgy of the Hours*, Office of Readings, Easter week 2. The Liturgy Archive Website, https://www.liturgies.net/Liturgies/Catholic/loh/easter/week2fridayor.htm

[20] See Edith Stein, *Self-Portrait in Letters 1916-1942*, trans Josephine Koeppel (Washington, D.C.: ICS Publications, 1993), 341.

God's all-seeing eyes. And so I am beginning to rejoice in the light
of glory wherein this meaning will be unveiled to me.[21]

Edith Stein is like the bride who goes out to meet her Bridegroom in the
night of his suffering and death. She finds him and will not let him go (Sg
3:4), taking his hand in trust of his Providence that he will lead her through
the valley of the shadow of death to dwell in the house of the Lord for all
eternity.

Questions for Reflection and Discussion

1. What is my response to Jesus' willingness to suffer the penalty due
    to me for my sin? As I ponder the response of the various charac-
    ters to Jesus' passion and death, what is my response to all that he
    suffers?

2. How have I felt more united with Christ in my sufferings? How
    does the Lord reveal himself to me amid trials? As a priest, how do
    I feel more united with my parish congregation by sharing in their
    sufferings?

3. In what way do I experience the "sacrificial impulse" in my life as
    a priest? In what ways and in what particular instances are my sac-
    rifices joyful and fulfilling? How does love transform suffering for
    me?

4. Have I ever sensed that Christ is suffering in and through me as I
    perform my ministry on his behalf? To what degree do I accept
    suffering as part of my life and ministry? Do I tend to avoid suf-
    fering or embrace it? How do I experience God's consolation in

---

[21] Ibid.

my suffering? Where is the power of God in the weakness of my suffering?

5. How have what I have perceived as obstacles to God's will and plan ultimately instructed me in God's ways? How has the Cross brought the triumph of God's will in my life?

Prayer Exercises

1. Ponder Jesus' serving the sentence that we deserved, the innocent for the guilty. Pray with Lk 23:1-25 and ask for the grace of gratitude to Jesus for redeeming you.

2. Reflect on the quotes by St. Mechtilde and St. Augustine about Jesus' consummation of his marriage to his Church on the Cross. Pray with Sg 3:1-5 and ask for the grace to remain united to God's people through your trials and sufferings.

3. Consider the sacrificial impulse and the sacrifices involved in being a priest. Pray with Heb 5:1-10 and ask for the grace to sacrifice yourself willingly in union with Christ.

4. Ponder the Martini quote about embracing suffering. Pray with Col 1:24-29 and ask for the grace to embrace suffering.

5. Reflect on the Edith Stein quote about the science of the Cross. Pray with 2 Cor 11:23-28 and ask to know the wisdom and power of God in the Cross.

Chapter 11

Love Rules

What is that coming up from the wilderness,
like a column of smoke,
perfumed with myrrh and frankincense,
with all the fragrant powders of the merchant?
Behold, it is the litter of Solomon!
About it are sixty mighty men
of the mighty men of Israel,
all girt with swords
and expert in war,
each with his sword at his thigh,
against alarms by night.
King Solomon made himself a palanquin
from the wood of Lebanon.
He made its posts of silver,
its back of gold, its seat of purple;
it was lovingly wrought within
by the daughters of Jerusalem.
Go forth, O daughters of Zion,
and behold King Solomon,
with the crown with which his mother crowned him
on the day of his wedding,
on the day of the gladness of his heart. (Sg 3:6-11)

The fantasy classic *The Lord of the Rings* by J.R.R. Tolkien explores the
authority to rule over others. One of the heroes of the story is Aragorn, a

descendent of the King of Gondor, a nation of men. Aragorn is the heir to the throne of the kingdom of Gondor, but at the beginning of the trilogy, he hides this identity and lives in the wild as a ranger named Strider. Tolkien's epic chronicles Aragorn's transformation from ranger to king. All his life he has quietly been preparing for the time to publicly reveal his identity and ancestry. As the story progresses, Aragorn gains more responsibility as others look to him for support and direction. As he gains more responsibility, he grows in confidence and self-awareness. Openly claiming his kingship and revealing his reforged sword, he encourages and aids the people of Rohan to defeat their adversaries so that all can come to the aid of Gondor which will soon be overrun by the Dark Lord Sauron's vast armies. Aragorn cements himself to the role of king and gains his first followers. At the massive battle in Gondor's capital city, Aragorn makes the last stunning entrance with his newfound reinforcements. As he unexpectedly emerges onto the battlefield from the enemy ships he captured, Aragorn is truly the conquering king returned. But he also proves the healing king after the battle, when he heals the sick and wounded of the city simply by touch and breath. It is at this point that all the citizens of Gondor recognize him for who he is. When Aragorn is finally officially crowned, the ceremony is only symbolic—Aragorn has already proven himself to be the true and rightful king.

Jesus, in his Resurrection is revealed to us not only as the true king of Israel, but also as the king of the Universe. Like Aragorn during his years of obscurity and preparation, Jesus' identity as king was hidden during his earthly life. Jesus was born in a humble cave and lived his "hidden life" for thirty years. Even as he worked miracles and forgave sins in his public life, he maintained the "messianic secret," not allowing people to tell others of his miracles and divinity. He did not want people to seek him for sensationalist motives, but instead to take up their crosses to follow him. His divine authority was called into question. Some asked, "who can forgive sins but God alone?" (Lk 5:22). Jesus then showed his power to forgive by healing the paralytic. When Jesus cast out demons, he did not recite elaborate incantations against the evil spirits, but simply and authoritatively spoke: "Be quiet and come out of the man!" (Lk 4:35), and the spirits obeyed. Jesus taught with authority, not like the Scribes and Pharisees. Other teachers were required to back their opinions by referencing the thinking of two or more expert rabbis. Jesus only referred to his Father as his witness, along with the deeds he performed, as evidence of his authority (cf. Jn 5:36-37). During his passion, Jesus' authority and kingship was especially hidden because his kingdom was not of this world (cf. Jn 18:36). When he rose from the dead, his glory and power were manifest. Before he ascends into heaven, he tells the Apostles "all authority in heaven and on earth has been given to me" (Mt 28:18).

In the Song of Songs, the Bridegroom, with his retinue, emerges as the King on his throne of power (3:9). The bride watches with admiration and awe as he approaches with a column of smoke and incense, symbolizing the Lord's holiness and divinity throughout the Old Testament (cf. Ex 19:18, Is 6:1-6, Ps 45). The angel told Mary that she would bear a son who would assume a throne: "The Lord God will give to him the throne of his ancestor David. He will reign over the house of Jacob forever, and of his kingdom there will be no end" (Lk 1:32-33). Jesus would manifest the Lord's kingship in his incarnation, death, and resurrection. Jesus is the king of the universe, and he occupies the throne of authority. The throne is made of elements which symbolize divinity: the wood of Lebanon cedar signifies incorruptibility, the gold implies divinity, the purple suggests royalty. Jesus said that he would be seated at his throne at the right hand of the power of God (Lk 22:69). The Song of Songs emphasizes that the King has made the throne himself. No one gave it to him; it is his own handiwork, showing that Jesus has always had divine authority. Only at his resurrection was it fully recognized.

The Warrior King and His Infantry

Jesus, like Aragorn, is a warrior King. The King and his throne are surrounded by sixty warriors (Sg 3:7), double the number that circled King Solomon's throne. They are the King's imposing sentinel. These sixty champions demonstrate the gallantry of their commander. In Solomon's time, these warriors were experienced over a long period of service. Similarly, in the Song they have become skilled and educated veterans, wise and discriminating. They are experts in war, equipped with swords against the terrors of night, especially the dark enemies who threaten with surprise attacks. They represent the valiant battle of the Lord against the forces of darkness. Jesus did battle with Satan and triumphed over sin and death:

> Since, therefore, the children share flesh and blood, he himself likewise shared the same things, so that through death he might destroy the one who has the power of death, that is, the devil, and free those who all their lives were held in slavery by the fear of death. (Heb 2:14-15)

As we sing in the Easter hymn *Victimae Paschali Laudes*, "Death and life have contended in a wondrous duel: the leader of life, though dead reigns alive." Jesus, in his passion, destroyed death and the kingdom of Satan. Biblical scholar Scott Hahn notes that the original Hebrew meaning of *redeemer* is "the man sent by a clan or tribe to rescue a family member who had been captured or imprisoned by an enemy."[1] The *Messiah* "referred to the promised deliverer, whom many people believed would be a

---

[1] Scott Hahn, *Many Are Called, Rediscovering the Glory of the Priesthood* (New York, Doubleday Religion, 2010), 90.

priest and many others believed would be a warrior-king."[2] Jesus fulfills both of those roles. In his resurrection, he is vindicated from his enemies and now reigns in glory. Just as Aragorn was a humble ranger who proved himself a great warrior in the battle against the evil Sauron, assuming his rightful throne as King, so, too, Jesus humbled himself to become a man and defeated Satan and his kingdom, assuming his place as King at the right hand of God.

As priests, we are called to do battle with the powers of darkness:

> For our struggle is not against enemies of blood and flesh, but against the rulers, against the authorities, against the cosmic powers of this present darkness, against the spiritual forces of evil in the heavenly places. Therefore, take up the whole armor of God, so that you may be able to withstand on that evil day, and having done everything, to stand firm. (Eph 6:12-14)

We triumph by the name of Jesus and his power. Like the skilled warriors around the king, we should be wise in the ways of discernment of spirits. We ought to know the deceptions of the devil and help people to resist and overthrow the devil. By the power of Christ, we must do battle against the fleshly desires which can disrupt our relationship with God. "For what the flesh desires is opposed to the Spirit, and what the Spirit desires is opposed to the flesh; for these are opposed to each other, to prevent you from doing what you want" (Gal 5:17). The flesh is more than our body; it is also our weak human nature, body *and* soul, insofar as it rebels against God. We also do battle with the world, which, though created good, opposes God due to the sins of humanity. The world is defined in this negative sense as

---

[2] Ibid.

the many ways human society organizes itself against God, in terms of hedonism, materialism, relativism, and other false systems of thought.

The military feature of the priesthood was present throughout the history of Israel. Adam was called to be the first warrior-priest in his family. Yet, he failed to protect the garden dwelling from Satan's contamination, allowing Eve to be tempted and paradise to be ruined. The Old Testament patriarchs who served as priests also protected their families and even fought wars against enemy tribes (cf. Gn 14:14-16). Eventually, when Israel worshipped the golden calf near Mt. Sinai, the Levites were the only ones to emerge and punish the sin of idolatry (cf. Ex 32:28-29). Therefore, God appointed the Levites to the role of priesthood for all of Israel.

Hahn explains that under the Law of Moses, God instructed his people in how to conduct battles. The priests had the most important role of carrying the Ark of the Covenant into battle, sounding the Lord's presence with shouting, and blaring of trumpets. At the Ark's departure for battle, Moses would say, "Arise, O LORD, let your enemies be scattered, and your foes flee before you." (Nm 10:35). Priestly combat reached its pinnacle in the seize of Jericho as Joshua led his people to conquer the promised land. The Israelites were greatly outnumbered by fearsome enemies with superior weapons. The city's inhabitants taunted the Israelites as they attempted to invade their well-fortified city. The Lord instructed Joshua:

> You shall march around the city, all the warriors circling the city once. Thus, you shall do for six days, with seven priests bearing seven trumpets of rams' horns before the ark. On the seventh day you shall march around the city seven times, the priests blowing the trumpets. When they make a long blast with the ram's horn, as soon as you hear the sound of the trumpet, then all the people shall shout with a great shout; and the wall of the city will fall down flat, and all the people shall charge straight ahead. (Josh 6:3-5)

The plan succeeded and the walls came tumbling down. The priests played the decisive role.[3]

In our contemporary culture, priests are on the front lines in the battle against evil, waging spiritual, not physical warfare. We do battle against evil in so many ways, such as freeing people from the bondage of sin in the Sacrament of Penance or confronting falsehood in the world and the Church. In the Forty Days for Life campaign, priests lead their parishioners in marching around Planned Parenthood, the nation's biggest abortion provider, while praying the rosary. Often, we priests will even say Mass across from the abortion mill. Because of this prayerful march, which in some ways resembles the siege of Jericho, many women have turned away from choosing abortion. Many of the medical and administrative staff have renounced practicing abortion, and clinics have been closed. In my own experience of praying the rosary at the clinics, in the face of counter demonstrations, the opposition grows silent when I, as a priest, lead the prayer. Our own prayer warriors and sidewalk counselors are inspired by our witness. God exercises his divine authority in confronting evil, especially through the ministry of his priests.

Justified by His Resurrection

Through the hands and feet and voices of his Mystical Body, the Beloved Son of the Father, the Incarnated and Risen Christ, continues to exercise his authority as ruler over the entire universe:

He is the image of the invisible God, the firstborn of all creation; for in him all things in heaven and on earth were created, things visible and invisible, whether thrones or dominions or

---

[3] See Ibid., 88-89.

rulers or powers—all things have been created through him and
for him. He himself is before all things, and in him all things hold
together. He is the head of the body, the church; he is the beginning, the firstborn from the dead, so that he might come to have
first place in everything. For in him all the fullness of God was
pleased to dwell. (Col. 1:15-19)

The incarnated Son of God—within his earthly ministry—gained the loyalty of his Apostles and continues to call his disciples throughout the centuries until now. Jesus Christ also delegates his authority to his Apostles
and disciples, who rule in his stead: "when the Son of Man is seated on the
throne of his glory, you who have followed me will also sit on twelve
thrones, judging the twelve tribes of Israel" (Mt 19:28). In his Resurrection
appearances, Jesus instructed the Apostles on how to govern the Church.
As the office of Apostle was passed on to bishops and, in the extension of
the bishop's authority, priests. Jesus identifies himself with those whom he
sends: "Whoever listens to you listens to me. Whoever rejects you rejects
me. And whoever rejects me rejects the one who sent me" (Lk 10:16). The
people are bound to obey their religious leaders in matters of faith and
morals, so long as it does not violate their properly formed consciences:
"Obey your leaders and submit to them, for they keep watch over you as
men who must render an account" (Heb 13:17). Jesus is present to the
leaders in a special way, aiding them in their exercise of his authority. He
sends his Holy Spirit to abide with them: "I will ask the Father, and he will
give you another Advocate to be with you always, the Spirit of truth" (Jn
14:16).

   Jesus justifies us by his resurrection, wherein his authority is clearly
manifest:

All authority in heaven and on earth has been given to me. Go therefore and make disciples of all nations, baptizing them in the name of the Father and of the Son and of the Holy Spirit, and teaching them to obey everything that I have commanded you. And remember, I am with you always, to the end of the age. (Mt 28:18-20)

Jesus' authority brings about newness of life and spiritual growth. St. Augustine notes that by Jesus' death we are seeded; by his resurrection, we bud forth in justice to walk in the newness of life.[4] The Lord's resurrection becomes a source of overflowing spiritual life for us as he communicates the Holy Spirit to us. As priests, we share in the authority of Christ. The word authority comes from the Latin *augeo*, which means to grow, to increase, and to enrich. An *auctor* is a causal influence, a sponsor, or promoter of this increase of life. An author possesses a fullness whereby he aids his fellow men and women in achieving fulfillment in their lives. He shows particular concern for the well-being and growth of every member of the kingdom. He embodies God's providence, looking ahead, looking out for members, alert and vigilant to notice needs, helping whoever is not growing. His authority must give the impression that spiritual growth is expected of people.

God authors the spiritual growth of his Church by raising up great saints. St. Ignatius of Loyola exercised his authority to foster extraordinary growth in holiness when he founded the Jesuits in 1540. The Jesuits hugely impacted the renewal of the Catholic faith throughout Europe, as well as the revival of the Church's missionary activity. Historian Outram Evenett asserts:

---

[4] See St. Augustine, *Sermon 236*, PL 38, col. 1120.

Of this active, virile, exacting religious outlook of counter-reformation Catholicism, with all its strengths as well as with what it had of weakness and insufficiency, the Jesuits were the outstanding representatives. It was because they were so fully representative of all its main characteristics, so fully aware of all the supreme urgent necessities of the new epoch and its new climate—so far as the preservation and expansion of Catholicism were concerned—that they became the outstanding force in the whole counter-reformation movement; that they became its modernizers.[5]

The growth of the Jesuits was amazing. Their initial band numbered seven. Sixteen years later, at the time of Ignatius' death, the membership had grown to a thousand. In the year 1580, there were five thousand members in twenty-one provinces. By 1615, they had grown to thirteen thousand.

Leadership Through Service

As a servant-leader, St. Ignatius oversaw the growth of his new Society of Jesus for fifteen years as superior general in Rome. This was, according to historian Jerome Williams, a time of veritable martyrdom for him. He had longed to preach the gospel in foreign lands and was now compelled to live in the Eternal City, a slave to his desk. He painstakingly composed the Jesuit Constitutions, praying and laboring over each sentence to ensure the direction of the fledgling society. He wrote an endless series of letters to guide the plethora of activities of the Jesuits emerging throughout the world.[6] According to his contemporary, Pedro de Ribadeneyra, Ignatius

---

[5] H. Outram Evenett *Spirit of the Counter-Reformation* (Notre Dame, IN, Notre Dame Press, 1991), 72.

[6] See Jerome K. Williams, *True Reformers, Saints of the Catholic Reformation* (Greenwood Village, CO: Augustine Institute, 2017), 79.

showed his love for his subjects "by looking into and trying to understand their good inclinations, in order to govern them according to these inclinations and so lead them more smoothly to total perfection."[7] For Ignatius, a key principle of government appeared to be listening to the heart of its subjects. Knowing their desires, spiritual gifts, talents and limitations, Ignatius could better deploy his priests and brothers to advance Christ's Kingdom.

As a warrior for Christ, Ignatius requested that the Holy Father not restrict the Jesuits with certain responsibilities:

> The other religious orders of the Church's army are like frontline troops drawn up in massive battalions. We are like light armed soldiers ready for sudden battles, going from one side to the other, now here, now there. And for this we must be unencumbered and free from all responsibility of this type.[8]

In a time known for its ignorance and worldliness of priests, highly trained and devout Jesuit priests were to be found everywhere:

> [P]reaching and giving retreats, building churches, founding colleges and training young men, establishing missions around the world, providing theological expertise at the Council of Trent, engaging in polemics with Protestants, serving as directors of souls, shedding their blood for the Faith; all in the service of Christ, the Church, and the Holy See. They were the most talented, disciplined and impressively

---

[7] Pedro Ribadeneyra, *Life of B. Father Ignatius of Loyola, 1616*, trans. Michael Walpole, S.J. (Illkey, England: Scolar Press, 1976), 57.

[8] Paul Doncouer, S.J., *The Heart of Ignatius* (Baltimore: Helicon Press, 1959), 66.

prepared group of men ever assembled for a single cause in the history of the world.[9]

Their training was long and thorough, and it laid the groundwork for their tremendous growth and impact, thanks to the visionary authority of St. Ignatius. Our times are no less challenging and demand everything we as priests have to offer the Lord, each according to our own gifts.

The hallmark of St. Ignatius and his early Jesuits' spirituality was service to God and neighbor, following Christ's example. At the Last Supper, Jesus said "I am among you as one who serves" (Lk 22:27). The priest's pastoral authority has its basis in this self-emptying in service for the faithful. After his resurrection, Jesus told Peter that Peter would stretch out his hands and be led where he would rather not go in self-sacrifice (cf. Jn 21:18). Priests desire to serve the faithful, lay down their lives as the Good Shepherd, every day, if necessary, rather than lose one or diminish God's life in them. In gratitude for all Christ in his mercy has done for me, and desiring others to share in his life, I am more disposed to lay down my life in service to others. In the words of the pioneer of the servant leadership movement, Robert Greenleaf:

> The first and most important choice a leader makes is to serve, without which one's capacity to lead is severely limited. ... The servant-leader is servant first. ... It begins with the natural feeling that one wants to serve, to serve first. Then conscious choice brings one to aspire to lead. ... The best test [of a servant-leader], and difficult to administer, is this: Do those served grow as persons? Do they, while being served, become healthier, wiser, freer, more autonomous, and more likely themselves to become ser-

---

[9] Jerome K. Williams, *True Reformers*, 77.

vants? And what is the effect on the least privileged in society? Will they benefit, or at least not be further harmed?[10]

We must be more concerned with the enrichment of persons than with performance and results.

According to leadership professionals Sipe and Frick, there are seven major qualities of the servant-leader, which we can all aspire to. While no one possesses all these qualities of servant-leadership to a high degree, an adequate measure of them will enrich the servant-leader and those he serves. The first is that he is a person of character who makes insightful, ethical, and principle-centered decisions. He maintains integrity, demonstrates humility, and serves a higher purpose. Second, he puts people first and helps others to meet their highest priority development needs. In so doing, he displays a servant's heart, is mentor-minded, and shows care and concern. Third, he is a skilled communicator who listens earnestly and speaks effectively. He demonstrates empathy, invites feedback, and communicates persuasively. Fourth, he is a compassionate collaborator who strengthens relationships, supports diversity, and creates a sense of belonging. He expresses appreciation, builds teams and communities, and negotiates conflicts. Fifth, he has foresight, imagining possibilities, anticipating the future, proceeding with clarity of purpose. He is a visionary who displays creativity and takes courageous and decisive action. Sixth, he is a systems thinker, who thinks and acts strategically, leads change effectively, and balances the whole with the sum of its parts. He is comfortable with complexity, demonstrates adaptability, and considers the greater good. Seventh and finally, he leads with moral authority as one worthy of respect who inspires trust and confidence and establishes quality standards for

---

[10] Robert Greenleaf, *The Servant as Leader* (Indianapolis: The Robert Greenleaf Center for Servant Leadership, 1970), 7.

performance. He accepts and delegates responsibility, shares power and control, and creates a culture of responsibility.[11]

Back in my first parish assignment as a priest, I learned how to exercise servant leadership with the St. Vincent de Paul Society. When I took charge, our parish Society was on life support, with just a few aging members who had served faithfully over the years, but who had little energy left to help anymore. I was the only one working with needy clients at the rectory door, mostly counseling them and giving out food vouchers. We had a large transient population in the cheap motels along Route 1 in our New Jersey township of Woodbridge. We also had many poor people in our neighborhood and trailer parks. Many needed help, both materially and spiritually. I decided to recruit some new blood, eager younger men and women, which delighted the older members. The new volunteers had good organizational skills and wanted to run with new programs. I listened to their ideas and proposed some of my own, which we began to implement. We began to look for opportunities to serve in our own parish and in the poorer neighboring towns like Perth Amboy, where there was a parish that needed help staffing their food pantry. We also helped to organize clothing drives for the poor. The diocesan branch of the Society helped us obtain furniture for families in need, and my pastor and I would sometimes carry heavy pieces up staircases to destitute families. We involved the youth group in serving hot meals to hungry street people. The diocesan coordinator helped us obtain matching funds to help more people pay their bills in our own parish. We began a "friendly visitor" program to relieve full-time caregivers of the homebound ill. In all these new endeavors, I was delighted to engage directly with those in need, leading our parishioners to do the same. I included a spiritual formation component at each month-

---

[11] See James Sipe and Robert Frick, *The Seven Pillars of Servant Leadership*, New York/Mahwah, NJ: Paulist Press, 2009), Kindle Version, 7%.

ly meeting to help our volunteers grow spiritually and develop a compassionate perspective toward the poor. Our number of regular volunteers grew from 6 to about 50 people, and we soon developed close bonds of friendship through the ministry. The bishop, observing the wave of charitable works, asked our chapter to address the diocesan body at their annual gathering. The Lord gave us a vision based on our hands-on work as servant-leaders among the needy and the volunteers. The Holy Spirit raised up willing and gifted helpers to multiply his work.

Leadership is influencing people by our example so that they will willingly and enthusiastically reach their goals. Leadership is part of management, but distinct. We need a healthy balance of both. Management is a discipline of systematically organizing and coordinating matters in an efficient way. The manager is usually concerned more with accomplishing things: finishing tasks, organizing, administrating, and executing plans. One is an executive, a planner, and a decision maker. There is something laudable about a pastor who administrates well, and priests are often evaluated based on how well they get things done. Leadership, a vital component of management, has its basis in trust, with an accent on the power to inspire people. Leadership attracts followers, and wins support for a cause, vision, idea, or proposal. It can be based on natural endowment or charismatic gifts. Leaders stand out because they seem to incarnate in their persons the common vision and aspirations of the group. Proposals, discussions, pro and con arguments, and charismatic insights should come from the whole community, according to their information, experience, and insight. But input is not yet a decision or course of action. A leader must be decisive, or people will not bother to initiate anything. Leadership is usually oriented toward encouraging change in a proactive way. The leader considers the broader perspective, ensuring the clarity of the values and focus of the group, as well as its high morale. A leader is concerned about peoples' feelings, encouraging the weary and distressed, allowing for feedback, and making peace where there is conflict. Good leaders will accomplish many things, too, mainly through motivating people interiorly and ensuring their happiness.

A pastor needs to maintain a healthy balance and harmony between leadership and management. It takes more than efficient administration and smart delegation to move peoples' hearts. He needs to inspire and reassure, love and care for people to help the Holy Spirit to transform souls. I have been privileged to assist pastors in spiritual leadership by offering retreats and seminars to parish staff and volunteers and leaders of ministry. Nothing helps servant leaders more than the opportunity to reflect together on their relationship with God, their gifts, and their mission in the Church. I can see the pastor's delight when we offer his servants something more than a task to efficiently accomplish, but the fire of the Holy Spirit to fulfill their calling. Our Oblate parishes have become known for this spirit of expressive leadership that creates a culture of compassionate understanding and care. One woman described the congregation's reaction:

> When they come here, and when they see the priests, they can see something special. They're always around, and they're visible. They feel that there's something here; the welcome depends on the needs of the people: prayers, a friendly ear, or something else. The Holy Spirit works with us. They feel something they can't describe.[12]

People are drawn in by the spirituality and leadership of the priest.

We opt to approach people with an attitude of friendliness and persuasion as good servant-leaders. To ensure the peace and security of the flock, we must also be prepared to employ the shepherd's rod of strength

---

[12] Cabrini Pak, *Men of Mercy, Sons of Mary*, 36.

when required (cf. 1 Cor 4:21). We can use that authority in a calm manner while being conscious of our own shortcomings. The self-aware individual recognizes and accepts his flaws. A capable servant-leader is aware of his vulnerability. When he is humble, he can admit that he does not know all the answers or that he needs to be right in order to seem good. Even when acting in an official capacity, he exhibits strength in tenderness and gentleness in strength. The priest doesn't feel too pressured to uphold high standards of perfection. St. Francis de Sales, the bishop whose trademarks were patience, humility, and gentleness, counsels us to both self-acceptance and self-improvement: "Have patience with all things, but chiefly have patience with yourself. Do not lose courage in considering your own imperfections, but instantly set about remedying them—every day begin the task anew."[13] Never should we equate our humanity with our shortcomings. Simply by virtue of our existence, we are absolutely valuable, inventive, and worthwhile individuals. No number of successes or setbacks can ever change that. A priest who is kind is a lovely companion to his flock. Instead of feeling threatened by his presence, they warmly accept it. They can feel at ease with the Lord, who is present in both one's strengths and weaknesses, if they feel at home with the priest. St. Francis de Sales concludes:

> Keep this ever before you and remember constantly that God's loving eyes are upon you amid all these little worries and vexations, watching whether you take them as He would desire. Offer up all such occasions to Him, and if sometimes you are put out,

---

[13] St. Francis de Sales, *Maxims and Counsels for Every Day in the Year,* trans. Ella McMahon (Dublin: Gill and Co., 1884), Digitized by Google, Internet Archive Website, https://archive.org/stream/MaximsAndCounselsOfStFrancisDeSales/MaximsAndCounselsOfStFrancisDeSales_djvu.txt

and give way to impatience, do not be discouraged, but make haste
to regain your lost composure.[14]

Jesus exercised his authority as a gentle servant, not wrangling or crying out loud, not breaking a bruised reed or quenching a smoldering wick,
while bringing justice to victory (cf. Mt 12:19-20). Jesus is strong and
mighty to save. He can fight the strongest of our enemies and always be
certain to triumph. The spiritual forces that align against us have no
chance of enduring. Yet, Jesus is amazingly gentle and considerate with us.
He is compassionate toward our injuries and weaknesses, treating us with
the greatest sensitivity and affection. Even with his enormous strength, he
is someone we can trust with our most tender bruises and fragility.

His Heart's Joy

The Bridegroom has thus been revealed as the king who prefigures Christ
the King. The Risen Lord took his seat upon his throne as the warrior king
who sacrificed his life to conquer evil and death on behalf of his bride the
Church.

> Christ loved the church and gave himself up for her, in order to
> make her holy by cleansing her with the washing of water by the
> word, so as to present the church to himself in splendor, without
> a spot or wrinkle or anything of the kind—yes, so that she may be
> holy and without blemish. (Eph 5:26-27)

As the king in the Song of Songs approaches his bride in glory, she is
awestruck and prepared to submit to his authority and his every desire. He

---

[14] Ibid.

abandons himself to her as his heart's joy, acknowledged as king and beloved Bridegroom. He utters a love declaration, a song of passionate admiration for his dearly beloved bride who is always present to his heart. His governance is an act of love toward his bride and his people. As priests, we govern in the Lord's name according to his law of love. As warrior-priests, we battle alongside Christ for the purity of his bride, the Church. We share in his kingship in the spirit of his humble servant leadership. By passionately loving the bride, the Church, we inspire her to love Jesus in return and submit to his transcendent authority.

Questions for Reflection and Discussion

1. How do I perceive Jesus as a warrior who defeats the forces of evil and death itself? How do I see myself as a priest involved in a spiritual battle to protect my flock? How can I become a more skilled warrior?

2. In what way do I understand the authority of Christ as ruler of the universe and author of growth in the Church? How do I understand my priesthood as a share in Christ's authority?

3. In what ways do I consider myself a servant-leader? Am I ever tempted to lord my authority over others? How do I notice my choice to serve others helping them become healthier, wiser, freer, more autonomous, and more likely themselves to become servants?

4. How well do I maintain a healthy balance and harmony between leadership and management? Beyond efficient administration and smart delegation do I seek to move hearts? How much do I seek to inspire and reassure, love and care for people, and to help the Holy Spirit to transform souls?

5. How patient and gentle am I with myself and with others? Can I acknowledge that I do not have all the answers, or must be correct, or to have to appear good? Do I tend to lose courage when considering my imperfections rather than remedying them? Can I consider that I am a perfectly valuable, creative, and worthwhile person simply because I exist?

Prayer Exercises

1. Ponder Aragorn as the warrior king and Christ as warrior against evil and death. Pray with Sg 3:6-11 and ask for the grace to be a skilled warrior in service to Christ the warrior king.
2. Reflect on the meaning of authority as ruling and causing growth in one's subjects. Pray with 1 Col:15-19 and Mt 28:1-4 and ask for the grace to share more effectively in Christ's authority.
3. Ponder the qualities of servant leaders. Pray with Lk 22:24-30 and ask for the grace to greater develop these qualities.
4. Reflect on the comments about the Oblate priests by their parishioners. Pray with Jn 21:15-19 and ask for the grace to serve the Lord's flock out of love.
5. Consider the St. Francis de Sales quotes on patience with self and others. Pray with Mt 12:15-21 and ask for the grace to learn from Jesus to be gentle of heart.

Chapter 12

Foundational Character

Behold, you are beautiful, my love,
behold, you are beautiful!
Your eyes are doves
behind your veil.
Your hair is like a flock of goats,
moving down the slopes of Gilead.
Your teeth are like a flock of shorn ewes
that have come up from the washing,
all of which bear twins,
and not one among them is bereaved.
Your lips are like a scarlet thread,
and your mouth is lovely.
Your cheeks are like halves of a pomegranate
behind your veil.
Your neck is like the tower of David,
built for an arsenal,
whereon hang a thousand bucklers,
all of them shields of warriors.
Your two breasts are like two fawns,
twins of a gazelle,
that feed among the lilies.
Until the day breathes
and the shadows flee,
I will hasten me to the mountain of myrrh
and the hill of frankincense.

You are all fair, my love;
there is no flaw in you.
Come with me from Lebanon, my bride;
come with me from Lebanon.
Depart from the peak of Ama'na,
from the peak of Senir and Hermon,
from the dens of lions,
from the mountains of leopards. (Sg 4:1-8)

Back in high school, I read the book *Kon Tike*, about the Norwegian sea adventurer Thor Heyerdahl. In 1947, Heyerdahl sailed 5,000 miles across the Pacific Ocean from South America to the Tuamotu Islands in a hand-built raft. The expedition was designed to demonstrate that ancient people could have made long sea voyages, creating contacts between societies. What people did not know was that Thor, as a young man, had a ghastly fear of water. He was cured of his terror during World War II when he was training with his Norwegian regimen in Canada. One day, Thor was paddling his canoe down a precarious river that ended with a waterfall. The canoe unexpectedly capsized, and Thor plummeted into the violent river. As he fell, Thor immediately thought that he would quickly find out which of his parents was correct in their view of eternal life. His father was a believer, and his mother was not. Something else came over Thor as he was being carried along by the swift current—the words of the *Our Father* went through his mind. He began to pray the words sincerely and desperately. Suddenly, his body surged with energy. He started to fight against the current. An inexplicable power came to his aid, and before long he swam to the shore. Thor emerged a believer in God. It was as though he had been baptized by falling into those raging waters of the river. He had previously had questions about God and eternal life, but now he did not. He began to believe and sought actual baptism as a Christian. And he was no longer afraid of the waters of death again, as proven by his sea adventures.

The New Life of Baptism

Thor's experience is a good image of what happens to us in the sacrament of Christian Baptism. In baptism, we are plunged into the waters, symbolizing death, which is a consequence of sin inherited from our first parents. We rise again from the waters, symbolizing new life in Christ. We die with Christ to live with him. Baptism is an immersion into the paschal mystery, the death and resurrection of Jesus. Like the Israelites who passed through the Red Sea, we are liberated from the slavery of our former way of life and journey toward the promised land of eternal life in God. St. Paul tells us:

> God, who is rich in mercy, out of the great love with which he loved us even when we were dead through our trespasses, made us alive together with Christ—by grace you have been saved—and raised us up with him and seated us with him in the heavenly places in Christ Jesus. (Eph 2:4-6)

Like Thor, we no longer need fear death; we are energized by the Spirit for bold undertakings.

The new life of baptism is reflected in the vibrance of the bride in the Song of Songs. Her vivacious eyes are doves, a symbol of the Holy Spirit, who is the Lord and giver of life. By the power of the Spirit, she now has the mind of Christ and discerns the things of God.

> Now we have received not the spirit of the world, but the Spirit that is from God, so that we may understand the gifts bestowed on

us by God. And we speak of these things in words not taught by human wisdom but taught by the Spirit, interpreting spiritual things to those who are spiritual. (1 Cor 2:12-13)

The bride's hair, often considered the glory of a woman, is alive like goats frisking down the slopes of Gilead.

> The bride's long, freely flowing hair symbolizes her freed spirit under the love of her groom in obedience and submission to him. This is her glory now, to obey her beloved in every detail of her life, in her thoughts, imaginations, words and deeds.[1]

Her teeth, which chew the food that will sustain her life, are like a flock of ewes that have come up from the washing. Shepherds would wade sheep through the water to wash the wool before the sheep were shorn. The bride is cleansed of her sins through the baptismal bath, washed in the blood of the Lamb. Though her sins were red as crimson, they have become white as wool (cf. Is 1:18). Each of the ewes is bearing twins, a further suggestion of the fullness of life that has come to the bride. The bride is wholly beautiful and without blemish. Baptism cleanses the bride of sin to make her spotless. By grace we are cleansed of sin and called to live without sin in righteousness. At baptism, we are called to bring our garment of salvation unstained into eternal life.

Baptism is also a sacrament of enlightenment: "Having received in Baptism the Word, 'the true light that enlightens every man,' the person baptized has been 'enlightened,' he becomes a 'son of light,' indeed, he becomes 'light' himself" (cf. Jn 1:9; 1 Thes 5:5).[2] The baptized person

---

[1] Maloney, 71.

[2] St. Justin, *Apology*, in *Catechism of the Catholic Church*, 1216.

becomes a partaker of the divine nature (cf. 2 Pt 1:4), infused with the virtues of faith, hope, and love. While we are enlightened, there is something unknown that happens to us, a subtle transformation. St. Augustine, in his *Confessions*, described a very close and dear friendship he had as a young man. They had played together as children, went to school, and enjoyed a bond that was sweeter than life. The brilliant Augustine led the friend into errors, and together they mocked the Christian faith—which Augustine's mother bewailed. At one point, his dear friend became very sick, with a high fever, long unconscious in a deathly sweat. His loved ones despaired of his life, and he was baptized. Augustine mused that "naturally he knew nothing of it, and I paid little heed, since I took for granted that his mind would retain all that he learned from me and not what was done upon his body while he was unconscious."[3] However, it turned out differently. His friend's fever left him, and he recovered. As soon as they could speak, Augustine began to mock, assuming his friend would join in mocking, supposing the baptism was received without sense or feeling. The friend instead looked at Augustine as if he was his deadly enemy. In a burst of independence, he warned Augustine that if he wished to continue as his friend, he must cease that kind of talk. Augustine was stupefied and deeply perturbed but postponed telling him until his friend's full recovery. Within a few days, his friend relapsed into his fever and died. Augustine was not there. His heart was black with grief, and he wept bitterly. Eventually, the episode helped to lead him to conversion.

It is interesting that Augustine's friend had no awareness of baptism, and yet it changed him. It made his faith solid and unwavering and gave him courage to resist Augustine's mockery. Because most of us were bap-

---

[3] See St. Augustine, *Confessions*, Book 4. Ch. 4, trans. Edward B. Pusey, D.D., Christian Classics Ethereal Library, https://ccel.org/ ccel/augustine/confess/confess.v.iv.html

tized as infants, we were unaware of what was happening. Yet, God still made his mark on us, claiming us as his own beloved sons and daughters. Our faith was given to us and changed us into believers. Baptism opened a whole new spiritual realm of existence to us, which we gradually appropriated through catechesis. We became a new creation in Christ and members of his Body, the Church.

John's prologue has been described as an overture to a marvelous symphony, a statement of the main theme of the Gospel. The prologue converges on the key phrase about Jesus, "But to all who received him, who believed in his name, *he gave power to become children of God*, who were born, not of blood or of the will of the flesh or of the will of man, but of God" (Jn 1:12-13, emphasis added). The central message is that those who are born again as Christians by baptism become, by grace, children of God. "From his fullness we have all received, grace upon grace" (Jn 1:16). Grace means divine favor, goodness bestowed, the life of God himself dwelling within us. We are imbued with a new divine quality of life, making it possible to believe and to hope in Jesus, and to love as he loves us. We are no less than God's children, because we now share in his very nature. If we are now children of God, we must grow and learn to act like God.

By baptism we are adopted to become children of God, members of Christ's body and co-heirs of his eternal life. The basis of our vocations as ministerial priests is to be beloved sons of our heavenly father. Jesus, after he was baptized, came up from the water, and as the heavens were opened, he saw the Spirit of God descending like a dove upon him. And a voice came from the heavens, saying, "This is my beloved Son, with whom I am well pleased" (Mt 4:17). At the beginning of Jesus' ministry, we learn the most foundational thing about who he *is* (not just what he *does*) as the Son of his Father. His love relationship with his Father characterized his identity and his actions—doing the will of his Father. His Father was at the origin of his existence, caring and providing for him. Jesus continues to refer to himself as "the Son" who knows the Father, "All handed over to me by my Father. No one knows the Son except the Father" (Mt 11:27). The Jews understood God as Father: "You, O LORD, are our father; our Redeemer from of old is your name" (Isa. 63:16). However, Jesus referred to his Father as *Abba*, which in Aramaic means "daddy." One can still hear children call their fathers Abba in the Holy Land today. The use of such a familiar term to address God was unprecedented and excluded among the Jews as a reference to God. According to biblical scholar Joachim Jeremias, "Abba, as a way of addressing God, is *ipsissima vox*, an authentic original utterance of Jesus. We are confronted with something new and astounding. Herein lies the great novelty of the gospel."[4] Jesus intends to include us in relationship so we can say Abba too, and experience great familiarity with our Father.

> For all who are led by the Spirit of God are children of God. For you did not receive a spirit of slavery to fall back into fear, but you have received a spirit of adoption. When we cry, "Abba! Father!" it is that very Spirit bearing witness with our spirit that we are children of God, and if children, then heirs, heirs of God and joint heirs with Christ—if, in fact, we suffer with him so that we may also be glorified with him. (Rom 8:14-17)

St. Paul, who knew the meaning of Roman legal adoption, understood what a privilege and what a huge transformation it was for the adopted party. Its consequences were momentous. The adopted person's rights in his old family were cancelled, and he gained all the rights as a rightful son in his new family. He received a new father in the most requisite manner.

---

[4] Joachim Jeremias, *The Parables of Jesus* (New York, Charles Scribner, 1970), 128.

The adopted person became the beneficiary of his father's wealth and property. Even if new sons were later born, he remained undeniably a co-heir. Legally, the old life of the adopted person was completely cancelled. His debts were rescinded, and his slate wiped clean. His past no longer determined his identity; he began a new life as a new person. Legally, he was categorically the son of his new father. Finally, the adoption ceremony was performed in the presence of seven witnesses. If the adopting father died and there was an argument about inheritance rights, one of the witnesses could testify to the reality.

The Holy Spirit himself is witness to our adoption. The Spirit witnesses with our spirit that we really are his children (cf. Rom 8:16). The lesson of the Roman adoption law applies to us. We have been delivered from our old life of sin into the new life of an adopted son or daughter. We now belong to God the Father as his complete and special possession. Our past is cancelled, and its debts are wiped out. We now have a new life with Christ and inherit the wealth of heavenly riches. We also share the life that Jesus Christ lived, inheriting his suffering, but also his new life of glory. God the Father has adopted each of us poor, lost, helpless and debt-laden sinners. He has cancelled our debts and granted us his inheritance. "But you are a chosen race, a royal priesthood, a holy nation, God's own people. Once you were not a people, but now you are God's people; once you had not received mercy, but now you have received mercy." (1 Pt 1:9a-10).

As adopted children, we share in the same relationship with the Father that Jesus shares with the Father by his divine nature and filiation, as the following example illustrates. There was once a 12-year-old son of a wealthy man. The boy had everything he ever wanted, except for what he longed for the most, a brother—someone with whom he could spend time, play, speak, and share his father's gifts. The boy's father listened compassionately but made no guarantees that it would ever happen. One day, the father surprised his son by going to an agency to adopt a poor, 11-year-old boy. Right away the two boys got along famously, as if they were brothers by birth. They were both thrilled beyond belief. The blood son now had a brother to call his own, and the adopted son now had a family with which to belong. One day, the two boys were outside playing catch with a football. At one point, the adopted son said to his new brother "Gee, I wish my old friend Kenny had a football like this. He really likes football, but his father can't afford to get him one." Then, he told his new brother about what a great guy his friend Kenny was. His brother responded,

> Don't forget! My dad is now your dad, too! He gives me whatever I need. He wants me to communicate with him and to let him know how I feel and what I think I need. If he thinks that some-thing isn't good for me, he tells me. And sometimes he gives me even more than I ask for. Dad wants you to do the same thing. He wants you to communicate with him. You're his son now, just as I am. He wants you to let him know how you feel and what you think you need.[5]

That day the adopted son learned what it meant to have a loving father.

The Experience of Sonship

As priests, before we are fathers, we are first beloved sons of our heav-enly father. In my second year as assistant director of the Lanteri Center, our director took a three-month sabbatical one autumn, leaving me in charge. By the middle of November, I had been on a nearly constant tread-mill of teaching and giving retreats, while administrating the center. I went

---

[5] See Monsignor Arthur Tonne, in Mark Link, *Illustrated Sunday Homilies, Year A,B,C, Series II*, Year C, Seventeenth Sunday in Ordinary Time, 92.

into the chapel the Sunday before Thanksgiving and poured out my soul to the Lord, telling him I needed a break. I knew there was a Friday and Saturday after Thanksgiving that was free, but that I'd probably fill those days up with things to get done. I told the Lord I needed a place to go and something to do and some friends with whom to do it. Hours later, a couple approached me after mass and told me they wanted to offer me their time-share condominium in the mountains for half of the upcoming week—exactly the days I had free. I smiled and told them, "Sometimes, when you tell the Lord what you desire, he answers your prayer right away. This is exactly what I need right now!" I went on to have a very relaxing weekend and felt rejuvenated when I returned, ready for Advent season to begin. Our Father so generously provides for us.

As children, we are called to have a close relationship with our Father and not take his gifts for granted. Some children take advantage of their fathers for the sake of having a residence. They assume their father's patronage without giving anything back. The father has sacrificed and worked hard to give his child opportunities that the child takes for granted. When he leaves home, the child does nothing to remain in contact. If he does return home, it is only to spend time with old friends while barely acknowledging his parents. The home and parents have served their purpose. There is no closeness of love relationship with the father. On the other hand, there is a child who appreciates everything the father has done. The child responds with gratitude by being the kind of son that makes his father proud. Over the years, the two grow closer in a bond of intimacy and a sharing of lives. When the son leaves home, he is aware that he is forever indebted to his father for all he has received from him. We as priests need to understand what it is to be a good son before we can be good fathers. We realize how much love we have received from our extravagant Father, and, in gratitude, desire to lavish his love on others.

Our own image of God as Father is conditioned, for better or worse, by our experience of our own fathers. If a father was an alcoholic, and a child never knew whether he would be home, or if bills would be paid, or if his father often exhibited rage, then basic trust and security are harmed, making it difficult for the child to trust God. When we pray to God and consider his providence, we discover that God really is a Father who cares. We then feel confidence and security, felt deep down, resulting in a true image of self as a treasured child surrounded with concern.

There is a problem today with absent fathers and a lack of recognition that the first role of the father is to be there for his children. Back in the 2000s, a study was done to determine the amount of interaction between fathers and their small children. First, the fathers were asked to estimate the amount of time they spent each day with the child. The average answer was about fifteen to twenty minutes. Next, microphones were attached to the father so that each interaction could be recorded. The results of this study were shocking: The average amount of time spent by these middle-class fathers with their small children was thirty-seven seconds per day. Their direct interaction was limited to 2.7 encounters daily, lasting ten to fifteen seconds each! Such lack of interaction can easily lead to false images of God as a cold, aloof Father, who is uninterested and uncaring. Such an image may result in distrust and weak hope, even despair.

Our own false image of self may be that we are neglected children, unwanted or uncared for. My own father loved me and provided for our family, and I deeply respected him. Yet, I was the youngest of eleven children, so it was easy to get lost in the crowd, so to speak. For all my father's many virtues, he was still not the type to develop a close personal relationship, or to say "I love you." Love needs to be expressed verbally with words of affirmation. When we say "Our Father," we are entering into that intimacy of Jesus and his Father. We each need to hear the Father calling us his precious son. A Detroit priest named Edward Farrell took his annual vacation in Ireland to be present for his uncle's eightieth birthday. On the actual day, the two of them rose before dawn and dressed quietly. As they walked the shores of Lake Killarney, they paused to watch the sunrise. They gazed at the rising sun in silence, shoulder to shoulder. His uncle then wheeled about and hopped along the road, grinning and glowing. His nephew asked him why he was so happy? The uncle replied, "You see, me Abba is very fond of me."[6] The uncle was aware that God took great delight in his life and personality. He felt deeply affirmed in who he was. That is what the Father's love does for us.

Ironically, it's often at a place of greatest weakness, where we are most helpless, most in need of mercy, that we discover God as Father most profoundly. God certainly loves us for our gifts, but most importantly, he loves us for our weaknesses. The Barcelona Olympics of 1992 provided one of track and field's most incredible moments. Britain's Derek Redmond had dreamed all his life of winning a gold medal in the 400-meter race. Derek's father Jim came along with him to the Olympics, as he did for all his big races. They were tight, even inseparable as father and son, so much so that Derek felt like his father ran alongside him. Derek was close to achieving his dream as the gun sounded and the race began. He was running a tremendous race and could see the finish line as he rounded the turn into the final curve. Suddenly, he felt a searing pain along the back of his leg. He collapsed onto the track with a torn right hamstring. As the medical attendants were approaching, Redmond fought to his feet and started hobbling down the track. The other runners had finished the race, with Steve Lewis of the U.S. winning the contest.

---

[6] Brennan Manning, *Abba's Child, the Cry of the Heart for Intimate Belonging* (Colorado Springs, CO: NavPress, 2015), 64.

Everyone was shocked to discover that Redmond was continuing the race despite hobbling off to the side of the track. No, he persisted in advancing to the finish line on one leg, all by himself. The crowd slowly stood up and started yelling in complete shock. The roar increased in volume. Redmond walked along, one agonizing step at a time, each one a bit slower and more terrible than the one before, his face contorted with pain and tears, while the crowd, many of whom were in tears, encouraged him. When Redmond arrived at the stretch, a big man wearing a T-shirt emerged from the crowd, shoved aside a security guard, and raced up to embrace Redmond. It was Redmond's father, Jim, who cradled his son while softly saying, "I'm here, son, we'll finish together." Derek wept as he wrapped his arms around his father's shoulders. Father and son crossed the finish line arm in arm as 65,000 spectators applauded and wept. Jim let go of his son Derek just before the finish line, amid the insane cheering of the crowd, allowing him to finish on his own. He embraced Derek once more as they both wept, joining the crowd and television viewers.[7] Derek did not leave with a medal, but he exited with an amazing memory of a father who, when he saw his son in pain, drew close in compassion, solidarity, and help. Our Father does that for us.

When we are experiencing pain and seeming failure as priests, when we are struggling to finish the race, we can be confident that we have a loving Father who won't leave us alone. Jesus knew his Father's loving presence during his crucifixion. His cry "My God, why have you abandoned me" should be taken as an expression of trust. These are the first words of Psalm 22, which is a hymn of trust in God's presence and care. The Hebrews implied the entire psalm when they quoted the

---

[7] See Wayne Rice, "Finish the Race," *Hot Illustrations for Youth* (El Cajon, CA: Youth Specialties, Inc., 1994), 93-94.

first line. Jesus also implies the second half of the psalm, which includes the gratitude and praise of God who is close and delivers him: "you have rescued me. I will tell of your name ... in the midst of the congregation I will praise you. You who fear the LORD, praise him! All you offspring of Jacob, glorify him; he did not hide his face from me, but heard when I cried to him" (Ps 22:22-24). Jesus took upon himself our own alienation from God so that he might reunite us with our Father.

The Seal of Confirmation

Our priestly vocation is also built upon and rooted in the Sacrament of Confirmation. Before we receive the strengthening grace of the priesthood, Confirmation strengthens us in union with Jesus and in his service. "By the sacrament of Confirmation, [the baptized] are more perfectly bound to the Church and are enriched with a special strength of the Holy Spirit. Hence, they are, as true witnesses of Christ, more strictly obliged to spread and defend the faith by word and deed."[8] As a prelude to Holy orders, Confirmation also involves the ritual of laying on of hands, imparting the gift of the Holy Spirit that completes the grace of Baptism. Confirmation in a certain way perpetuates the grace of Pentecost in the Church.[9] Confirmation and Baptism both involve anointing with oil, which is a sign of plenitude and joy. Priests, prophets, and kings were all anointed with oil as a sign of the spirit of God rushing upon them. Oil makes the skin glow and radiate beauty, health, and strength. Oil was used to help athletes and wrestlers remain flexible. Warriors smeared themselves with oil for

---

[8] *Lumen Gentium,* 11.

[9] See Paul VI, *Divinae consortium naturae,* 659; (Libreria Editrice Vaticana, 1971), Vatican Website, https://www.vatican.va/content/paul-vi/la/apost_constitutions/documents/hf_p-vi_apc_19710815_divina-consortium.html, cf. *Acts* 8:15-17; 19:5-6; *Heb* 6:2.

protection so that arrows would more easily glance off their bodies, and enemies could not easily grasp them. Oil also helps to heal bruises and wounds. By this anointing, the confirmand receives the "mark," the *seal* of the Holy Spirit: "A seal is a symbol of a person, a sign of personal authority, or ownership of an object. Hence soldiers were marked with their leader's seal and slaves with their master's. A seal authenticates a juridical act or document."[10] Christ proclaimed that the Father had set his seal upon him (cf. Jn 6:27). The Lord has also set his seal upon us as Christians: "But it is God who establishes us with you in Christ and has anointed us, by putting his seal on us and giving us his Spirit in our hearts as a first installment" (2 Cor 1:21-22). The Holy Spirit's mark seals our complete belonging to Christ, our eternal enlistment in his service, and the promise of divine protection in the final test of our faith (cf. Rv 7:2-3; 9:4; Ez 9:4-6).[11]

I personally felt the presence and effects of the Holy Spirit during my own confirmation. My family had moved back to Chicago from Florida after nine years. It was difficult to lose all my friends from six years of grade school and move to a new neighborhood and school. I experienced a difficult two years trying to fit in at a new school during junior high. I was a sensitive boy and the kids in my new school were often cruel and unaccepting of me. Our family was experiencing some crisis and division, which affected me deeply. By the end of eighth grade, I was weary of the trials, still trying to adapt to so many changing circumstances and relationships. The one thing that gave me consolation and a feeling of being bonded to my classmates was our religion class as we prepared for Confirmation. There was even a small group of us who would gather with the seminarian teacher after lunch and ponder the deeper questions of life. During these times I felt greater intimacy with the boys and girls who were

---

[10] *Catechism of the Catholic Church*, 1295.
[11] See Ibid., 1296.

becoming my friends. When the evening of Confirmation came, my brother William, who was my sponsor, accompanied me to the front of the sanctuary and put his hand on my shoulder. The bishop imposed his hands on my head and anointed my forehead with oil. The presence of the holy Spirit was palpable, and I felt a powerful experience of love. My burdens were lifted. I felt united with my classmates and family and healed of the pain that had gone before. I was empowered to begin Catholic high school and strive toward adulthood with an increase of faith, hope, and love.

Confirmation gives us a special strength of the Holy Spirit to spread and defend the faith by word and action as true witnesses of Christ. We are empowered to confess the name of Christ boldly, and never to be ashamed of the Cross.[12] According to St. Thomas Aquinas, Confirmation produces a special perfection in coming to full strength and maturity in the spiritual life. As baptism permanently equips one to live by grace, confirmation equips one for successful combat against the enemies of his soul and of the faith. As Christians we do battle with the evil forces of the world, the flesh, and the devil. Confirmation gives a person the power of the soldier of Christ, impressing this power upon one as an indelible character. The person confirmed is anointed with chrism on the forehead, so that one may show to all that he is a Christian, fearless of all the enemies of Christ.[13] When I reached young adulthood and began to take my faith more seriously, I felt the grace of the Holy Spirit help me fearlessly witness to my Lord Jesus Christ. There were many fallen away Christians who were indifferent to the faith, and even people hostile to Christianity in my new workplace and social circle. I felt the grace of the Holy Spirit to stand up for my faith and to explain it to others, sometimes in the face of antagonism. The zeal I felt for Christ enabled me to befriend others and help lead

---

[12] See *Lumen Gentium*, 11.
[13] See *ST* IIIa, 72, 3, 5, 9.

them to Jesus. The grace of Confirmation had been available to me all along, and I was now experiencing it in action.

In the Song of Songs, the Bridegroom describes the bride's neck as strong and powerful as a fortress, like the prominent watchtower of David, which overlooked Jerusalem (Sg 4:4). The Psalmist encourages: "Walk about Zion, go all around it, count its towers, consider well its ramparts; go through its citadels, that you may tell the next generation that this is God, our God forever and ever. He will be our guide forever" (Ps.48:12-14). The bride's neck is ringed with two thousand bucklers, each a shield of a hero. The medals invoke the shields of the valiant warriors of Israel, which are displayed around the walls of the city and inspire respect when viewed both from within and from afar. The bride is involved in spiritual battle. Christ makes her into a fortress of strength, like the invincible bastion of King David. The shields hung on her tower remind us of St. Paul's advice: "take the shield of faith, with which you will be able to quench all the flaming arrows of the evil one. Take the helmet of salvation, and the sword of the Spirit, which is the word of God." (Eph 6:16-17). In her faith she is surrounded by a "cloud of witnesses" (Heb. 12:12) to the faith, thousands of warriors who have helped strengthen her by their heroic achievements in abandoning themselves completely to Christ. St. Paul enumerates numerous Old Testament heroes, "who through faith conquered kingdoms, administered justice, obtained promises, shut the mouths of lions, quenched raging fire, escaped the edge of the sword, won strength out of weakness, became mighty in war, put foreign armies to flight" (Heb 11:33-34). The bride has also bravely warded off with her shield the enemies from within, the false self, rooted in the flesh that wars against the spirit.[14] She is able to achieve peace through strength. St. Francis de Sales notes that this militaristic language is in the service of a fundamental

---

[14] See Maloney, 73.

peace: "Though she is belligerent and warring, she is altogether so peaceful that, among the armies and the battles, she goes on singing songs of unsurpassed melody."[15]

St. Maximilian Kolbe maintained remarkable peace in the face of adversity. He was a brilliant student who earned his first doctorate at age 21. He took an interest in science while he was in seminary and even designed spacecraft prior to World War II. After ordination, he created a sizable media apostolate to spread the gospel and combat erroneous communist beliefs. Early in the war, when the Nazis invaded Poland, Kolbe loudly denounced their ruthless tyranny, along with its lies and misdeeds, in his magazines and on the radio. He was eventually detained, warned, and released. After continuing his tirade of criticism, he was once more imprisoned and this time sent to Auschwitz for hard labor. To help his fellow captives, he made it known throughout the prison camp that he was a Catholic priest. Because of this, the staff at the camp attacked him. He was made to endure humiliations such as beatings, dog attacks, heavy and filthy work, carrying corpses, and other degradations. He persisted in assuring his fellow prisoners during these trials, saying: "No, they will not kill our souls … They will not be able to deprive us of the dignity of being a Catholic. We will not give up. And when we die, then we die pure and peaceful, resigned to God in our hearts."[16]

Finally, the commander announced that he would be selecting ten individuals to be starved to death. Among the group that was chosen was a man by the name of Francis Gajowniczek. When he was chosen, he began sobbing with despair and cried out that he had a wife and children. Without hesitation, Kolbe took a few steps forward and informed the prison

---

[15] St. Francis de Sales, *Treatise on the Love of God*, VIII: 12.

[16] See Epriest, *Homily Pack, Thirty-second Sunday in Ordinary Time, Year C,* Epriest Website, https://epriest.com/homily_packs/archive

official that he would like to offer himself in place of Gajowniczek. The German official asked him his profession, and Kolbe responded that he was a priest. The German official approved, and Gajowniczek was told to return to his place in line with the others who had been spared. And with that, Kolbe and the other unfortunate prisoners were taken to a bunker in a barracks to be starved. The bunker was a desolate and cold place, and the prisoners were ordered to strip naked. Over the following days, the prisoners' bodies slowly deteriorated as dehydration and starvation set in. Within days, most of the group had perished, and the ones left were experiencing hallucinations and constant, severe anguish. However, those who passed by the bunker later claimed that Kolbe seemed to be exempt from these ailments. Indeed, he was reported to be in a constant state of meditation and prayer. When a fellow prisoner died, he would pray over them. Maximilian helped prepare the souls of the condemned men and encouraged them by constant reminders that they would soon be in heaven. After two weeks of starvation and dehydration, the guards were ordered to clear the prison cell. Kolbe was the only one left alive, and on August 14 the guards gave him a lethal injection of carbolic acid. It is said that Kolbe extended his arm and willingly accepted his fate. [17]

Kolbe was strengthened by the Holy Spirit through Confirmation and Holy Orders to remain at peace and sacrifice his life for his neighbor in Auschwitz. He showed himself a true warrior, a soldier of Christ and a beloved son of his heavenly Father. Like the champions of faith whose shields decorated the tower of David, and the neck of the bride, his heroic love inspires us all. The Sacraments of Baptism and Confirmation are foundational to the priest who is called to filial relationship with the Father before he becomes an icon of God's fatherly love to others.

---

[17] See Andre Frossard, *Forget Not Love* (San Francisco: Ignatius Press, 1991), 185-187, 193-197.

Questions for Reflection and Discussion

1. How have I been enlightened by Christ through Baptism? How have I been enlivened and emboldened to share the gospel?

2. As a priest, how do I experience sharing Jesus' sonship before the Father? In what way is it important to me to be a son before I can be a father to others? What kind of son am I?

3. In my life and ministry, how do I experience the Father's love and providential care for me as a son?

4. How has my own experience of being a biological son of my earthly father impacted by my relationship with my heavenly Father?

5. In what way has Confirmation matured me in the Spirit and prepared me for spiritual battle?

Prayer Exercises

1. Reflect on Thor Heyerdahl's experience of coming to faith. Pray with Eph 2:4-6 and ask for the grace of gratitude for the gift of faith and salvation.

2. Consider St. Augustine's story of his friend's baptism. Pray with Sg 4:1-3 and ask for the grace of increased life and light in Christ.

3. Ponder the legal ramifications of Roman adoption and the story of the adopted boy and his brother. Pray with Mt 3:13-17 or Rom 8:14-17 and ask for the grace to know yourself as loved by God, as a spiritual son of God your Father.

4. Reflect on Derek Redmund's Olympic race. Pray with Ps 22 and ask to know the Father's presence and help amid trials.

5. Consider St. Maximilian Kolbe's sufferings and martyrdom. Pray with Sg 4:5-8 and ask for the grace to be a Christian warrior in the battle against evil.

Chapter 13

Priestly Pray-orities

You have ravished my heart, my sister, my bride,
you have ravished my heart with a glance of your eyes,
with one jewel of your necklace.
How sweet is your love, my sister, my bride!
how much better is your love than wine,
and the fragrance of your oils than any spice!
Your lips distil nectar, my bride;
honey and milk are under your tongue;
the scent of your garments is like the scent of Lebanon.
A garden locked is my sister, my bride,
a garden locked, a fountain sealed.
Your shoots are an orchard of pomegranates
with all choicest fruits,
henna with nard,
nard and saffron, calamus and cinnamon,
with all trees of frankincense,
myrrh and aloes,
with all chief spices—
a garden fountain, a well of living water,
and flowing streams from Lebanon. (Sg 4:9-15)

Catherine Maurice wrote a book in 1993 about her daughter's improvement from autism and her own struggle as a mother treating her child. She titled the book *Let Me Hear Your Voice*, a quotation from the Song of Songs (2:14), God's love song to his people. It was a groundbreaking book that dealt with the causes of autism, its symptoms, diagnosis, and treatment, at a time when little was known about the disease. Catherine employed behavioral therapy that improved her daughter Anne Marie in about a year. Catherine described her daughter's condition as a metaphor for fallen humanity. Her daughter had no interest in her mother. She did not trail her mother or emulate her in any way. She never appealed to her mother or called for her. She constantly looked away from her mother, or looked at her with a blank stare, preferring to be alone. Encroachment on her personal space was met with strong reaction. The daughter was unable to see the whole of things and fixated on parts. Her motor skills were uneven, and she engaged in self-stimulating behaviors, such as head banging, head shaking, hand flapping, and crying fits. At one point, when her daughter refused to acknowledge her, Catherine went into crisis, despairing over Anne Marie's condition.[1]

Catherine emerged from her grief even more resolved to storm her daughter's situation with dogged resolve, until her daughter was restored to an animated, attentive, communicative, and loving existence. Catherine learned that the most necessary condition for her daughter's recovery was eye contact. Only the continuous, caring human presence with its tender look, voice, and touch could achieve restoration. It was Anne Marie's gaze that returned first. The doctor confirmed her recovery:

'Congratulations,' he said softly. He knew. Even before we'd said anything, or gone through the videotaping, the parent interview, the Vineland test ... There is a quality to the gaze of a normal child... a connection, a recognition of the other as a person, an

---

[1] See Catherine Maurice, *Let Me Hear Your Voice, A Family's Triumph over Autism* (New York: Random House, 1993), 1-93.

interest, that flashes out in the very first moments of a meeting. ...
Dr. Cohen was seeing the absence of autism.[2]

Catherine only desired her child's loving gaze, to be recognized as her
mother. Then her daughter would be able to receive her love and they
could live together in a relationship.

The Lord's Loving Gaze

Prayer begins with an awareness that the Lord is gazing upon us in
love. Too often we have been like the autistic child, who prefers to be alone,
to control one's own life, to engage in mindless, repetitive activities that
momentarily satisfy our passions and neuroses. We avert our eyes from
God and become self-absorbed, reactive if God should intrude into our
routine machinations. We fixate on the parts of our lives and fail to see the
whole. Meanwhile, God is passionately pursuing us, fixing his gaze upon
us, speaking his words, if only we have eyes to see and ears to hear. Pope
Francis invites us to consider: "How does Jesus gaze at me today? How
does Jesus look at me? With a call? With forgiveness? With a mission?" We
are certain that "on the path that He made, we all are under Jesus' gaze: He
always looks at us with love, asks us for something, forgives us for something and gives us a mission."[3] Our gaze at the Lord in return ravishes his
heart, our love for him casts a spell upon him. He is effusively overflowing
in his love for us, becoming one with us through his Incarnation. God is

---

[2] Ibid., 107.

[3] Pope Francis, *Three manners of gaze*, Morning Meditation in the Chapel of
the Domus Sanctae Marthae, Friday, 22 May 2015 (*L'Osservatore Romano*,
Weekly ed. in English, n. 22, 29 May 2015), Vatican Website, https://www.vati-
can.va/content/francesco/en/cotidie/2015/documents/papa-francesco-co-
tidie_20150522_three-manners-of-gaze.html

approaching us passionately. He is dizzy and intoxicated with love for us, to the point of losing his reason. "Our beloved was mad,"[4] writes Therese of Lisieux. Jacques Maritain speaks of "mad" or radical love wherein one transcends self by freely giving all that one is, not merely all one has or does, to the other. Jesus loves us madly be giving himself completely for us in dying on the cross. Whenever we pray, a simple glance toward the Lord evokes his outpouring of love upon us.

In the Song of Songs, the bride has become aware of her Bridegroom's loving gaze upon her. All that he desires is her gaze in return: "You have ravished my heart with a glance of your eyes" (Sg 4:9). The Bridegroom is totally focused on the bride's eyes, her voice, her fragrance, and her words and finds her utterly delightful, more so than the finest wine or scent. His intense focus on his bride has led to her response of total attentiveness to his presence, awareness of her own beauty, and wholehearted surrender to his love.

We might be apprehensive about how God looks at us. Encountering the living God can be a fearsome experience, so we might keep God at a distance. One of Aesop's fables is entitled *The Hunter and the Woodman*. A hunter was searching for the tracks of a Lion. He asked a man felling oaks in the forest if he had seen any marks of the lion's footsteps or knew where the lair was. "Oh yes," said the Woodman, "I will take you to the Lion himself." The hunter turned pale from fear and stuttered, "No, thanks. I did not ask that; it is only his track that I am looking for, not the Lion himself." In our relationship with God we are often like this hunter. We are searching for God, but perhaps reluctant to pursue a full encounter. The good news is that God is already hunting for us and pursuing our

---

[4] St Therese of Lisieux, *Letter of St. Therese of Lisieux*, Letter 169 (Washington, D.C.: ICS Publications, 1988), 882.

meeting. Indeed, God is already at work preparing our hearts to receive him in prayer.

We don't even arrive at prayer unless the Lord is already drawing us to His Sacred Heart. Jesus says, "No one comes to me, unless the Father beckons" (Mt 11:28). Stephen Rosetti tells the story of a religious priest who overcame many addictive behaviors through a powerful experience of God in prayer. After many years of religious life, he had not yet had any direct encounter with God. One afternoon, he entered his cell of his monastery and was overcome with an awareness of God's presence. In fear he retreated from his room, but, thinking better of it, came back. God had not left and graced him with healing. Though he was fearful, he ended up transformed by the experience.[5]

Like that religious priest, we might avoid prayer because we are afraid of what will surface. We all have wounds and past sins that we may have stuffed into the basement of our souls. Resentments fester from continually repressing certain emotions and affect that are normal parts of human nature. A priest is often expected to control his negative emotions such as anger, revenge, and hatred, at least exteriorly. He is expected to represent the image and principle of peacefulness and sanctity. He suffers in silence rather than confronting difficult people and situations. These expectations contribute to resentment. Also, in prayer we face those current pains and addictions we would rather not admit to the Lord. He gently enlightens us and will not show us more than we can handle, always desiring our healing. We must be honest with ourselves and God, stripping away our masks or personas. Self-knowledge and healing will lead to self-acceptance as God accepts us the way we are. Father Hugh Kennedy was putting his life back together again when he noticed:

---

[5] Rosetti, 38.

Often, driving back to the Cenacle at night, I found that I could think about things I hadn't really thought about for years ... passing through the strange quiet and clear shining darkness of the desert night, I would suddenly become aware of a stillness which was something quite apart from the stillness of the night. It was an interior stillness, a stillness inside me, a stillness in which there was the absence of all distractions and unrest, a stillness in which, quietly and without effort, I seemed to come together, to be focused and attentive, to be really present, so to speak, a stillness from which it seemed natural, even inevitable, to reach out, to pray, to adore ... at last I came to terms with myself and God.[6]

Through our many activities and trials, we can become fragmented persons, split off from ourselves. In prayer, God reconstitutes us; he puts us back together to make us whole and holy human beings.

Our Image of God

False images of God often emerge in prayer. Frequently, these false images are associated with negative feelings within. Often, we are not even conscious of these false images; they have an unconscious effect upon us. We may profess a certain image of God, while we might operate out of a very different image of God in our psyche. I might profess that God is a loving creator who chooses to make me unique and unrepeatable, but deep down I might feel worthless, loathing myself as a deeply flawed being. I might profess that God loves me unconditionally as I am but live my life trying to earn God's approval and convince myself and others that I only

---

[6] Edwin O'Connor, *The Edge of Sadness* (Boston: Little, Brown and Co., 1961), 155-156.

have worth based on what I do. In prayer, some of these false images might arise with their concurrent negative feelings. They can tell us a lot about how we really perceive God, as illustrated by the following example.

Fred was viewed as a role model for Christians. He was a young, married man who, in addition to his professional career, was a member of several volunteer organizations and had a keen interest in religion. Fred lived a spartan existence, rarely going out to eat or to the movies or the theater. He and his wife spent most of their vacation time attending conferences. He arrived to make a personally directed retreat during one of his holidays. He was guided to pray by picturing events from the Gospel in his mind's eye and engaging the scene as though it were currently taking place and he himself was a participant. He would describe what he had encountered in those contemplations at the conclusion of each day. During one prayer period he was ruminating about the wedding feast in Cana. He had a creative mind and had seen food-filled tables spread out under a clear sky. There was a lot of dancing going on and everyone was having a fantastic time. Fred's spiritual director asked him if he saw Jesus in the scene? "Yes," he replied, "Christ was looking disapproving as he sat upright on a straight-backed chair, wearing a white robe, holding a staff, and bearing a crown of thorns on his head."

Praying with the imagination revealed a lot to Fred about how he really saw God. If you asked Fred beforehand who God was, he probably would have replied that Jesus is his personal savior who is merciful and desires to forgive him. He would perhaps see himself as Jesus' disciple who is chosen and called to follow in Jesus' footsteps. Subconsciously, his operative image of God was as the judgmental one, who disapproved of celebration and extravagance. Deep down, Fred could not let himself enjoy his life or ministry. All his good works were like a clanging gong meant to justify himself before God and others. His feelings of guilt, defensiveness and resentment were the result of trying to appease a strict and angry god, not the truly merciful and compassionate Lord. This agonizing image finally showed Fred that he needed to renounce his oppressive, authoritarian image of God and embrace the truth of Jesus Christ in the scriptures. Once we recognize false images, their hold over us is weakened. Then we need to replace the false images of God with true and beautiful images based on revelation. We then find our image of self is much improved in relation to the truth about God. In the Song of Songs, the bride becomes aware that she is beautiful in the affirming gaze of her Beloved. He says her love is better than wine and her scent more enticing than any perfume. She can accept his affirming words as the truth about herself.

Prayer is a the most important thing we can do to foster our relationship with God. Nobody was more active and effective in ministry than Jesus of Nazareth, proclaiming the kingdom, healing the sick, casting out demons, feeding the hungry crowds. And yet for Jesus, prayer was the most important part of his life. He rose early in the morning, even before dawn and went to a quiet, secluded place to offer the first fruits of his day in communion with his Father. If Jesus required that time for prayer, how much more do we as poor sinners need time for prayer? It is especially necessary to pray when we are full of activity. St. Francis de Sales once commented that an ordinary Christian needs a half-hour of prayer every day, except when one is busy. When one is busy, one needs an hour of prayer! Busyness is no excuse not to pray, but a stronger reason to pray. St. Frances Cabrini used to ask, "Who is doing this, God or us?" In our digital age, we are overwhelmed with the stress of busyness and multitasking, which has become the norm. Overstimulation leads to overwhelming fatigue, fear, depression, and occasional anxiety attacks. We suffer from hurry sickness and try to do a million things at once. We are overly plugged in to our devices and take our work with us everywhere. As a result, we might develop perpetual fatigue, feeling exhausted, irritable, and depressed. A continual restlessness comes over us and threatens to disrupt our tranquility. Prayer is more important than ever to detach from the world and its restlessness and to rest in the Lord. We need to hear the Lord say: "be still and know that I am God" (Ps 46:10). Ironically, the more we step back and put things in God's hands, the more ordered our day becomes and the more productive we are. "Unless the LORD builds the house, those who build it labor in vain. It is in vain that you rise up early and go late to rest, eating the bread of anxious toil; for he gives sleep to his beloved" (Ps 127:1a-2).

The most notable characteristic in the farmer St. Isidore's life was trust in prayer. He would typically get up before sunrise and spend the morning visiting churches throughout Madrid. According to the narrative, St. Isidore's employer, Master de Vargas, grew bothered about the time the monk was taking apart from his work and decided to verify whether or not the rumors he had heard were accurate. He crept into the field early one morning where the saint was supposed to be working. St. Isidore's work was unfinished while the other laborers had done their tasks and left the area. Despite feeling inclined to correct the saint, Master de Vargas decided to wait and see what would transpire. The saint got to work and appeared to be moving along quite productively. The employer observed and realized why: Two angels were working beside the saint, each driving a plow and competing in a holy contest to see who could do the most. Thereafter, whenever there were any inquiries concerning St. Isidore's productivity, Master de Vargas would reply simply, "He is assisted by angels." When we take time for prayer as most important, God accomplishes more than we could ask or imagine (cf. Eph 3:20).

The Need for Solitude

One of the conditions for prayer is solitude. Priests are men of communion. They are also men of profound solitude. That solitude can easily become loneliness if we are not given to prayer. It is in prayer that we encounter the Lord as we truly are, not according to some ideal. We have been formed as men who strive for perfection, and that is laudable. The sad truth is that we fall far short of what we are called to be. It is painful to realize that we do not live up to our high ideals. But it is liberating when we discover that the Lord loves us as we are and always forgives us. In our extreme poverty of spirit, we come to realize all we have done is *his* work. If a priest cannot face this truth about himself, he will find it hard to face his loneliness. Father Paul Keyes admits:

> Therefore, a great deal of my life as a priest can be an unconscious and even a conscious running away from the experience of loneliness in which I must face my real self. I rescue others from loneliness because I cannot face loneliness and what it may tell me about my own life. I find it difficult to stand by lonely persons and give them a personal presence that enables them to let their loneliness be in order to commune with the insights that lie hidden in its depths. As a parish priest, it becomes more and more difficult to spend an evening alone in my rectory room, for such an experience means facing the possibility of meeting loneliness face to face. If I have time off, then I must be with priest friends or parishioners who will see to it that I am not alone. In a pathetic way, the free time of my celibate state may become filled with various ways to overcome ever experiencing myself as alone. Celibacy, which should give me time to be with myself and time to be with God in prayerful intimacy becomes a burden that I carry, a burden that haunts my very existence with the terror of being the lonely one.[7]

---

[7] Keyes, 50.

Loneliness is a gift because it forces us to confront ourselves and God. Rather than run away from loneliness, or try to fill it up with distractions, we need to sit with our loneliness. This can be painful, but fruitful. When we are with God in our loneliness, we eventually discover solitude, a state of being alone, but with an intuition that we are with God. Prayer dissolves loneliness. I discover I am friends with God and with my own self. I sense God delights in me and loves me as I am.

A retreat is a profound moment of entering into solitude with God. Once, when I was rector of out Oblate seminary in Boston, I made my yearly retreat in Mystic Seaport, Connecticut, under the direction of a wise nun. I was trying to grow comfortable in my new role as religious superior for twenty-five men, both priests and seminarians in formation. I was considering who I was as a leader and how they perceived me. During my first meeting with my director, I expressed these thoughts and feelings, and she advised me to let go of such concerns and simply to be myself and relate to the Lord. Soon I was out for a morning walk in the neighborhood. A landscaper had opened the back doors to his van and music was blaring out. I heard the song, "Just the Way You Are," but tried to ignore it, because I was keeping silence during the retreat. I had always loved that song going back to my teenage years, and the lyrics came into my head. Pretty soon I was struck to the heart by the meaning of the words. Jesus was telling me he loved me just the way I was. I didn't have to perform or try to be someone I was not for these men who looked up to me. For the rest of the retreat, I soaked in that message and surrendered to the Lord. It was liberating to know how much the Lord loved me for who I was and not who I was supposed to be in my own mind, or in the eyes of others. The bride discovers how much she is loved in just the glance of her eye toward the Bridegroom. His heart is ravished by her presence and the slightest amount of attention she shows. The Lord similarly delights in us whenever we look his way.

Why and How We Pray

In prayer we become aware of who we really are in God's loving gaze, just as the bride becomes aware of her beauty and goodness in the gaze of the Bridegroom. His gaze makes her aware that she is his unique possession: "But now thus says the LORD, he who created you, O Jacob, he who formed you, O Israel: Do not fear, for I have redeemed you; I have called you by name, you are mine" (Is 43:1). The Lord personally calls each of us by name. Each of us is a unique, unrepeatable person with both our endearing qualities and our limiting characteristics. The Lord loves us even more in our weakness than in our strengths, showing us his mercy. He continues to create us in his image and fashion us into his likeness until we reach full maturity in Christ. As we pray over time, the Lord reveals the features of his unique relationship with each of us as his beloved priests. He dealt with Peter in a way that was quite different than with John. He has a way of calling each of us in a peculiar way that we call the personal vocation.

All of us have our common vocations as priests, but a singular personal calling. The Lord speaks to each of our hearts with tender affection, in a particular way known only to us. Father Herbert Alphonso, head of the Ignatian Center in Rome, explains an encounter he had with one of his fellow Jesuits. The priest came to Father Alphonso in a sad condition regarding his prayer life. The priest felt as though, when he prayed, that he was only present bodily and "checked out" mentally. Father Alphonso asked the priest if he had ever had any significant intuitions about God in the past. "Oh yes," the priest volunteered, "whenever I think about the goodness of God I feel consoled."

Fr. Alphonso then asked him, "My friend, have you ever spent time praying on the goodness of God?"

"Why no," replied the priest, "besides, how long do you think I could pray on such a simple theme without getting bored?"

Alphonso reminded the priest, "Well you've just told me how significant the goodness of God has been for you, why not give it a try?"

The priest reluctantly agreed and departed. A week later he burst into Fr. Alphonso's office and exclaimed, "Herbie, I can pray on the goodness of God. It has revived my life of prayer!" Alphonso commended him and together they unpacked the experience. Six months later, the priest walked gingerly into Fr. Alphonso's office and whispered, "Herbie, I can always pray on the goodness of God." The theme had become sacred and deeply meaningful to him and he could always savor it. Father Alphonso was impressed and congratulated the priest, intimating that he had found his personal vocation.[8]

The more we pray, the more we become aware of God's personal message to each of us. We discover our deepest identity in Christ. In fact, we reflect something about Jesus Christ in our own unique way. As members of Christ's body, we put on Christ and identify with his mind and heart, we then radiate some aspect of who Jesus is. We are to let the same mind be in us that was in Christ Jesus (Phil 2:5), to become one with him and radiate his presence and glory. This way of being with Christ and reflecting Christ then characterizes all our ministry. For instance, St. Francis de Sales knew Jesus as the one who was eternally patient, gentle, and kind toward him. In turn, de Sales himself became known for his patience, gentleness, and kindness toward others by his presence and in all that he did.

Jesus tells us to persevere in prayer lest we lose heart (cf. Lk 18:1). Theresa of Avila was not always given to prayer. In her early years of religious life her convent was very worldly, with many visitors and distractions that made recollection and prayer difficult. She experienced dryness in prayer

---

[8] See Herbert Alphonso, *The Personal Vocation* (Mahwah, NJ, Paulist Press, 2001), 11-14.

for about 20 years. Sometimes, she had to drag herself to prayer in the face of great interior resistance. She would have preferred the most difficult penances to her scheduled prayer. Nevertheless, she persevered in prayer. It was while praying with the mystery of the Lord's agony in the garden that she had a breakthrough moment. Eventually, the Lord led her to the heights of mystical prayer and to the reform of the Carmelite order. Had she given up on prayer, she would have been lost.

Venerable Bruno Lanteri exhorts us to be resolved to pray—no matter what:

> We do not ask with enough perseverance; we become immediately wearied, if the taste for prayer is lost, and the long tests to which we have put the practice of God are counted as nothing and we cannot sustain the merciful postponement. ... Prayer is the weapon for salvation of salvation "the arrow of deliverance, take up the arrows, strike with the javelin" (cf. 2 Kgs 13:17-18). Let us not cease from the battle. If you had struck five times, or six, or seven times, you might have struck until you were victorious.[9]

Lanteri's determination reminds me of a story from the California gold rush. Two brothers sold all they owned and went gold digging. They located a vein of brilliant ore, staked a claim, and started working on extracting the precious gold from the mine. At first, everything went smoothly, but then something peculiar occurred. The seam of gold ore vanished! They had reached the rainbow's end and there was no gold treasure. The brothers kept picking away unsuccessfully. They eventually gave up in despair. For a few hundred dollars, they surrendered their

---

[9] Ven. Bruno Lanteri, *The Spiritual Writings of Venerable Pio Bruno Lanteri*, 130.

property rights and equipment, then boarded a train to return home. Now the owner of the claim engaged an engineer to look at the mine's geological layers. The engineer instructed him to keep on digging where the previous owners had stopped. Soon, the new owner reached gold three feet deeper. Had they persevered, the two brothers themselves would have struck the mother lode. Could the same be true for us when we pray? When we're tempted to give up, we could be close to a big discovery. Or perhaps when we take a little more time than our minimum amount of meditation—maybe we are on the verge of a breakthrough? There's "gold" in each of us waiting to be discovered in prayer. The bride discovers herself to have a heart of gold in her lover's eyes. He extols her as an enclosed garden, a sealed fountain, and an orchard of fruit and spice trees. (cf. Sg 4:15).

Prayer is meant to be the motive force behind all our life and activity. Paul exhorts us to "rejoice always, pray without ceasing, give thanks in all circumstances; for this is the will of God in Christ Jesus for you." (1 Thes 5:16-18). There are ways to keep God in mind and implore his help throughout the day. We pray always by continually looking for opportunities to thank God and to rejoice in his presence and gifts. Joy and thanksgiving become ways of abiding in God's presence. We can also pray as we engage in activities. St. John Chrysostom explains that "it is possible to offer fervent prayer while walking in public or strolling alone, or seated in your shop, . . . while buying or selling, . . . or even while cooking."[10] He who unites prayer to works and good works to prayer realizes the principle of praying without ceasing.[11] It is good to pray before beginning an activity, asking the Lord's strength and guidance. During an activity, we can occasionally shoot a glance of love or plea for assistance. At the end of an activity, we can express gratitude to God for its accomplishment and ask

---

[10] St. John Chrysostom, *Ecloga de oratione* 2: PG 63.
[11] See Origen, *De oration*, 12: PG 11.

his mercy for any defects.

It will be impossible to constantly keep our minds fixed on God during activities, unless God should grant us some extraordinary grace. According to the Dominican friar Matthew Leonard, when Paul exhorts us to pray constantly, he is referring to a permanent disposition that is rooted in trustful surrender, joining our wills to God's. An attitude of inner peace accepts whatever happens as God's good will for our life. We attain this peaceful, permanent attitude of constant prayer mainly through regular moments of prayer. Leonard explains:

> Constant prayer is fed by *acts* of finite prayer which operate on the "surface" of the soul. Think of constant prayer as glowing embers down in your soul. They're always hot, but not inflamed, so to speak. Finite prayers are like little gusts of wind that come down, blowing across these embers, igniting a fire of love in our hearts that bursts into flame. Finite prayers feed the flame so that we develop a life of *constant* prayer. Of course, the reverse is also true. Constant prayer feeds and fuels our acts of finite prayer so they become more focused and fruitful. And when we can establish a state of constant prayer, submitting ourselves gladly to God's will, everything we do becomes an act of prayer.[12]

For priests, the fundamental act of finite prayer is the Divine Office or Liturgy of the Hours. By praying the Divine Office, the Church, especially its ministers, offers the Lord unceasing prayer and intercession for the entire world in prayer and song. Praying the Divine Office at regular intervals

---

[12] Matthew Leonard, *How to Achieve Constant Prayer*, SpiritualDirection.com Website, January 8, 2019, https://spiritualdirection.com/2019/01/08/how-to-achieve-constant-prayer

throughout the day, we sanctify time and open our lives to the reality of God's presence through his word at every moment. Time, which is something concrete, living, and personal, is transformed into a sacred reality. We acknowledge the absolute dominion of our Creator by giving him what is most personal and precious to us. Sometimes it may feel like we are too busy, or like it will be a waste of our time. Then it will be a greater sacrifice. "Through him, then, let us continually offer a sacrifice of praise to God, that is, the fruit of lips that confess his name" (Heb 13:15). The regular recitation of the Liturgy of the Hours is that continuous sacrifice of praise to the Lord. There is an essential harmony between the Liturgy of the Hours and the holy sacrifice of the Mass. The Liturgy of the Hours prepares us for the Mass and continues it, applying its fruits to rest of the day. Mass should inspire in us devotion for the Liturgy of the Hours. We can better achieve this by taking steps to improve our understanding of the liturgy and of the scriptures, especially the Psalms. According to St. Ambrose:

> In the book of Psalms there is profit for all, with healing power for our salvation. There is instruction from history, teaching from the law, prediction from prophecy, chastisement from denunciation, persuasion from moral preaching. All who read it may find the cure for their own individual failings. All with eyes to see can discover in it a complete gymnasium for the soul, a stadium for the virtues, equipped for every kind of exercise; it is for each to choose the kind he judges best to help him gain the prize."[13]

The Bridegroom extols his bride for the fragrance of her perfumes and scent of her garments, symbolizing the temple worship of pleasing sacrifice

---

[13] Saint Ambrose, *Explanations of the Psalms* Ps 1, 9-12: CSEL, 64, 7, 9-10.

with incense of prayer rising. The ongoing sacrifice of praise in the psalms of the Liturgy of the Hours is our prayer that is pleasing to the Lord. The Bridegroom mentions the honey under the bride's tongue (Sg 4:11). Ezekiel found that same taste of honey when consuming the Scriptures. The Lord said to him: "Mortal, eat this scroll that I give you and fill your stomach with it. Then I ate it; and in my mouth it was as sweet as honey" (Ez 3:3). Therefore, the Word of God must have become the bride's own word, and she must have assimilated it perfectly for the Bridegroom to find in it the same taste of honey that Ezekiel found. "Above all the joy, all the sweetness and intoxication that she brings to him at any moment, the Bridegroom puts this rare privilege: she whom he loves is exclusively his, she is all his, only his; she is exclusively vowed, dedicated, consecrated to him."[14] She is "a garden locked, a fountain sealed, a well of living water, and flowing streams from Lebanon" (Sg 4:12, 15). When we come to Jesus in prayer we will experience, like the bride, rivers of living water flowing from within us." (cf. Jn 7:38). "The water that I will give will become in them a spring of water gushing up to eternal life" (Jn 4:14).

> The sealed fountain becomes the spring of gardens, not anymore the sole interior garden of the bride, but all the gardens of the world; becoming 'a well of living water' and 'streams flowing from Lebanon,' with all the depth of a well and the free outpouring of running waters.[15]

Through prayer, like the bride, we will have all the depth of a well and the perpetual mobility of the river.

---

[14] Arminjon, 223.
[15] Ibid., 226.

Questions for Reflection and Discussion

1. Ponder Catherine Maurice's struggles to care for her autistic daughter. Pray with Lk 18:18-26 and ask for the grace to be aware of the Lord's loving gaze upon you.

2. Consider the prayer experience of Fr. Hugh Kennedy. Pray with Sg 4:9-15 and ask for the grace to experience inner peace with God and self.

3. Reflect on the story of Herbie Alphonso's priest friend. Pray with Mt 16:13-20 and ask for the grace to know how God calls you by name.

4. Ponder the story of the gold prospectors. Pray with Lk 11:5-13 and ask for the grace to persevere in prayer.

5. Ponder the quote on unceasing prayer by Matthew Leonard. Pray with 1 Thes 5:16-18 and Lk 18:1 and ask for the grace to pray always throughout the day.

Prayer Exercises

1. How aware am I of the Lord's loving gaze upon me? What difference does it make in my life? What are the obstacles to opening myself more to awareness of his gaze? How am I distracted or too much in control of my own life? Am I in any way fearful of encountering the Lord and of what he might ask of me?

2. What false images of God do I contend with? What false image of self do I struggle with as a result? Have I ever professed a true image of God while operating out of a false image of God? How has prayer healed me with true images of God and self?

3. Do I value prayer as the most important thing I do each day? What priority do I assign to my prayer? Do I fall into the trap of working too much and lose my balance and perspective on life and God's place in it? If so, how can I regain the balance?

4. To what degree do I enjoy and cultivate solitude? Do I run from loneliness? How does celibacy afford me the opportunity to pray and help me to appreciate solitude?

5. How do regular prayer times throughout the day keep me rooted in God and his will? Could I say that my life is a prayer? Do I enjoy praying the Divine Office? How are the Psalms a "gymnasium" for my soul?

Chapter 14

A New Pentecost

Awake, O north wind,
and come, O south wind!
Blow upon my garden,
let its fragrance be wafted abroad.
Let my beloved come to his garden,
and eat its choicest fruits.
I come to my garden, my sister, my bride,
I gather my myrrh with my spice,
I eat my honeycomb with my honey,
I drink my wine with my milk.
Eat, O friends, and drink:
drink deeply, O lovers! (Sg 4:16–5:1)

Back in 1994, my congregation, the Oblates of the Virgin Mary, held a seminar on how to give the *Spiritual Exercises of St. Ignatius* featuring Fr. Herbert Alphonso, S.J. Fr. Alphonso was head of the *Center for Ignatian Spirituality* in Rome and a leading expert on the Spiritual Exercises. His enthusiasm for the Exercises was infectious and his presentations inspiring. He penetrated the core meaning of each of the weeks or themes of St. Ignatius' retreat, teaching us how to guide people and to process their spiritual movements. Our entire American Province participated, both experts and beginners in giving the retreat. We shared our collective wisdom and enthusiasm for this endeavor. The Holy Spirit fell upon us mightily and we were on fire with love for God and zeal for his kingdom.

The Spiritual Exercises of St. Ignatius

The Spiritual Exercises are at the heart of our charism as Oblates of the Virgin Mary. We undertake the complete thirty-day Spiritual Exercises during novitiate. The Exercises form us in prayer, discernment, and the ability to discover God in all things. Our mission is to promote the Spiritual Exercises and Ignatian spirituality. Sadly, our congregation, like many, fell away from its founding charism for many years. It is only since Vatican Council II that we, like many congregations, returned to our founding charism and began to practice it faithfully and vibrantly. Personally, I had been preparing to offer the Spiritual Exercises throughout my formation and Father Alphonso's seminar further enkindled the flame of my desire.

As I have lived my priesthood, I have discovered that the more I plunge my roots into the charism of our congregation to promote the mercy of God through the Spiritual Exercises, the more efficacious is my ministry. The Holy Spirit has imbued us with this charism in order that we might faithfully live it. Our charism also fits well with the gift and purpose of priesthood, which is directed toward the unfolding of the baptismal grace—a life of faith, hope, and charity, a life according to the Spirit—of all Christians.[1] Christ uses the ministerial priesthood as the means to continuously build up and lead his Church.

The Spiritual Exercises unleash the power of the Spirit upon those who make them. The Exercises help the retreatant recognize and develop one's gifts, while growing in faith, hope, and love. Saint Pius XII related: "The tiny but immense book of the Exercises of St. Ignatius will always be one of the most efficacious means to achieve the spiritual regeneration of the

---

[1] See *Catechism of the Catholic Church*, 1547.

world and its return to right order."[2] Saint John Paul II presented a copy of the Spiritual Exercises to the then Jesuit General Peter Kolvenbach, emphasizing that the Exercises reformed the Church once, and they can do it again. He went on to call them the "lungs" or "oxygen" of the spiritual life for souls and for Christian communities:

> The Exercises are, in fact, a set of meditations and prayers in an atmosphere of contemplation and silence, and above all a special interior impulse—deriving from the Holy Spirit—to open ample spaces of the soul to the action of grace. In the strong dynamic movement of the exercises, the Christian is helped to enter within the ambit of the thoughts of God and his plans, in order to entrust himself to him, Truth and Love, so as to take binding decisions in the following of Christ, clearly measuring his gifts and his own responsibilities.[3]

St. Ignatius himself strongly urged people to make his Exercises: "For I know that the Spiritual Exercises are the best means I can think of in this life both to help a man benefit himself, and to bring assistance, profit, and advantage to many others … You will see how they help you to serve others beyond anything you ever dreamed of."[4] All the Jesuit saints, by their writings and lives, testify to this forceful influence of the Exercises.

---

[2] St. Pius XII, in Herve Coathalem, *Ignatian Insights, A Guide to the Complete Spiritual Exercises* (Taiwan, Kuangchi Press, 1971), 21.

[3] St. John Paul II, Address. in *What Do the Popes Say about the Spiritual Exercises?*, Servants of the Lord and the Virgin or Matara Website, https://www.ssvmne.org/en/spiritual-exercises/what-do-the-popes-say-about-them/

[4] St. Ignatius of Loyola, *Letters,* To former confessor at Alcala' and Paris, Dr. Miona, 27.

The Exercises have always been a most powerful means of reform and sanctification of the clergy as well. St. Francis de Sales prepared for consecration as bishop with the Exercises and drew up a plan of life which he adhered to with great fidelity. Early in his priesthood he remarked that the book of St. Ignatius had contributed to more numerous conversions than it contained letters in its text. St. Vincent de Paul knew de Sales and gave the Exercises personally to more than 20,000 people in the form of retreats and popular missions. St. Philip Neri was good friends with the first Jesuits in Rome. During the cold winters he would help the poor along with St. Francis Xavier. Ignatius introduced him to the interior life through the Exercises, during which Phillip remembered Ignatius' glow. For St. Charles Borromeo, the Exercises were the decisive turning point in his vocation that moved him toward perfection. As Cardinal, he became a zealous promoter of the Exercises among clergy and laity. He made the Exercises the spearhead of the Catholic Counter-reformation. St. Alphonsus Liguori was greatly affected by the Exercises and his Redemptorists offered the retreat to the multitudes in the form of popular missions. Liguori called them a treasure which God has set open for his Church in these last ages, for which we should show abundant gratitude. Our founder, Ven. Bruno Lanteri, together with St. Joseph Cafasso administered the Exercises to train priests at the Convitto Ecclesiatico in Torino, Italy, forming holy priests of heroic virtue such as St. John Bosco.

The Exercises unleash the power of the Holy Spirit by conforming one's heart to the Heart of Jesus. The dynamic presence of the Holy Spirit is revealed in the personal salvation history of the one seeking God. Giles Cusson, a master retreat director and author, explains how the Exercises are an experience of Pentecost for the retreatant as "a progressive insertion into the movement of the Spirit acting in our time."[5] The retreatant is immersed into the life of the Spirit in prayer and daily life, coming to greater awareness of His presence, understanding better the movements of the Spirit as he seeks to advance the Kingdom of God. Everything Jesus did in his earthly life, his Incarnation, hidden life, public ministry, passion, death, and resurrection, led to the culmination of the Pentecost event, to the outpouring of his Spirit within us. Christ's Spirit was one with Jesus and the Father throughout Jesus' entire life, death, and resurrection, and was then given to his Apostles and disciples to make them other Christs, to imbue them with Christ's own mind and heart, and to extend his Kingdom on earth as it is in heaven. It is interesting that the Spiritual Exercises take the retreatant through Jesus' entire earthly and risen life up until the point of his Ascension to his Father's right hand, the moment when the Holy Spirit descended.

The Divine Character

Just as the Spirit was upon Jesus, so he reproduces Jesus in each one of us as we live Jesus' mysteries. We are called only to become one with Jesus, for he enables us as the members of his Body to share in what he lived for us in his flesh as our model. According to St. John Eudes,

> We must continue to accomplish in ourselves the stages of Jesus' life and his mysteries and often to beg him to perfect and realize them in us and in his whole Church. ... For it is the plan of the Son of God to make us and the whole Church partake in his

---

[5] Giles Gusson, S.J., *The Spiritual Exercises Made in Everyday Life* (St. Louis, Institute for Jesuit Sources, 1989), 125.

mysteries and to extend them to and continue them in us and in his whole Church. This is his plan for fulfilling his mysteries in us.[6]

Christ lives his mysteries for us and continues to live them in us as members of his body. This is especially true for us as priests, who act in the person of Christ the Head. It is this same priest, Christ Jesus, whose sacred person his ministerial priest truly represents. Now the minister, by reason of the sacerdotal consecration which he has received, is truly made like Christ, the high priest, and possesses the authority to act in the power and place of the person of Christ himself.[7] The Holy Spirit impresses this divine character on the soul of the priest, empowering him to identify with Christ the high priest and act with his power and authority.

In the Song of Songs, the bride now calls upon the Spirit as wind: "Awake, O north wind, and come, O south wind! Blow upon my garden that its fragrance may be wafted abroad. Let my beloved come to his garden and eat its choicest fruits" (Sg 4:16). According to St. John of the Cross:

> The soul means by this wind the Holy Spirit and says that it awakens love because when the divine wind breathes over it, it sets it afire, recreates it and animates it. ... Breathing with its Divine Spirit over her flowery garden, it thus opens all the buds of virtue, discovers the perfumes of the gifts, the perfections and riches of

---

[6] St. John Eudes, *On the Kingdom of Jesus*, in *The Liturgy of the Hours, Office of Readings*, vol. IV, Second Reading, Week 33, The Internet Archive Website, https://www.liturgies.net/Liturgies/Catholic/loh/ week33fridayor.htm.

[7] See *Catechism of the Catholic Church*, 1548.

the soul; and opening this treasure and this inner domain, it un-veils all its beauty.[8]

The bride calls her garden his garden, one and the same. All that is hers belongs to him and the more she belongs to him the more she is self-pos-sessed. Her only desire is to surrender more completely to his loving pres-ence. Elizabeth of the Trinity expresses well the identification of the soul with Christ:

> I realize my weakness and beseech thee to clothe me with thyself, to identify my soul with all the movements of thine own. Immerse me in thyself, possess me wholly; substitute thyself for me, that my life may be but a radiance of thine own. Enter my soul as Adorer, as Restorer, as Savior! O Eternal Word, Utterance of my God! I long to pass my life in listening to thee, to become docile that I may learn all from thee.[9]

This ongoing incarnation, as it were, is accomplished by the Holy Spirit. Elizabeth continues:

> O consuming fire! Spirit of love! Descend within me and repro-duce in me, as it were, an incarnation of the Word; that I may be to him another humanity wherein he renews his mystery. And thou, O Father, bend down toward thy poor little creature and overshadow her, beholding in her none other than thy beloved Son in whom thou hast set all thy pleasure.[10]

---

[8] St. John of the Cross, *Spiritual Canticle*, Stanza 27, par. 6, in *The Collected Works of Saint John of the Cross* (Washington D.C.: ICS Publications, 1991).

[9] Elizabeth of the Trinity, in M. M. Philipon, O.P., *The Spiritual Doctrine of Sister Elizabeth of the Trinity* (Westminster, MD: Newman, 1947), 54.

[10] Ibid.

Christ is reproduced in her by the Holy Spirit's power. She becomes *alter Christus*, "another Christ." She offers herself as the first fruits of the Pentecost or ingathering of the harvest.

The Bridegroom comes to his garden to taste his fruits. The bride becomes the one to prepare the banquet for her beloved. She becomes a beautiful and delightful fruit, offered to the gardener for his joy. The Holy Spirit reveals his presence in the soul of the bride. She is the garden of the Spirit in which the living water of the Spirit flows, in which the mighty and sweet wind of the Spirit blows, in which the fragrance of the Spirit's manifold gifts float. St. Cyril of Jerusalem teaches us the many and varied effects of the Spirit upon us:

> Water comes down from heaven as rain, and although it is always the same in itself, it produces many different effects, one in the palm tree, another in the vine, and so on throughout the whole of creation. In the same way the Holy Spirit, whose nature is always the same, simple and indivisible, apportions grace to each person as he wills. The Spirit makes one person a teacher of divine truth, inspires another to prophesy, gives another the power of casting out devils, enables another to interpret holy Scripture. The Spirit strengthens one person's self-control, shows another how to help the poor, teaches another to fast and lead a life of asceticism, makes another oblivious to the needs of the body, trains another for martyrdom.[11]

---

[11] St. Cyril of Jerusalem, *Catechetical Oration in Cat. 16 De Spiritu Sancto 1, 11-12, 16: PG 33, 931-935, 939-942), vol. 2, Office of Readings, Seventh Week of Easter, Monday,* Divine Office Website, https://divineoffice.org/easter-w07-mon-or/.

Cyril shows that the Spirit's action is different in different people, but the Spirit himself is always the same in each person. The Spirit makes his presence known in a particular manner for the benefit of everybody. The Spirit comes with the kindness of a real friend and guardian to save, heal, teach, counsel, strengthen, and comfort. The purpose of the Spirit's visit is to first illuminate the recipient's mind before passing through him to enlighten the minds of others. The bride only desires that the Spirit blow upon her garden to produce its fruit and stir up a pleasing fragrance for her Bridegroom.

For us priests, the sacred mark of ordination is always present in the depths of our beings, as a constant invocation of the Holy Spirit. According to Benedictine Abbot Dom Marmion:

> Every morning, strong in your faith, *fortes in fide*, raising your thanks towards heaven, you can exhibit to the Lord your soul marked with the seal of Christ. The priesthood of Christ, His blood and His death are engraved on your souls. When you present your soul before God with this mark upon it, you invoke the Holy Spirit and ask him to revive in you the grace received at your ordination.[12] (cf. 2 Tim. 1:6)

Throughout our priestly lives, in every action of our sacred ministry, we can call upon the sanctifying influence of the Holy Spirit. We may be more or less aware of the effects of the Spirit in our own lives and in the lives of our faithful people. There are times when we wish to offer the Lord a banquet of a fruitful harvest, yet we come before him empty handed. Often the Spirit brings us to an awareness of our poverty of spirit to know that we

---

[12] Blessed Columba Marmion, O.S.B., *Christ, The Ideal of the Priest* (San Francisco, Ignatius Press, 2005), 304.

can produce nothing on our own, that it must be his work. The disciples were convinced of their own powerlessness after Jesus' Resurrection and Ascension. They realized they could only wait on the Lord in prayer—not thinking, saying, or doing a great deal.

Renewed by the Spirit

There are times when we feel powerless to achieve anything in the Lord's service, times when we can only wait in prayer and trust in his workings. When we are physically and mentally exhausted from our labors, the Spirit can revive us. Elijah won a great victory over the priests of Baal on Mt. Carmel when his sacrifice to Baal was consumed by fire from heaven even though it had been drenched with water. Then, as a consequence of Elijah's prayers, the terrible drought the Lord had sent came to an end. But this victory was followed by a defeat so total that it sent Elijah retreating into the wilderness disheartened and bewildered. Queen Jezebel, enraged at Elijah's destruction of her priests, hounded him mercilessly, renewed her persecution of Yahweh, and drove Elijah out of the land of Israel, an isolated and homeless refugee. Wandering by himself in the desert Elijah fell into such a state of despair that he prayed for death. "Enough, Lord, take away my life, for I am no better than my ancestors" (1 Kgs 19:4). Elijah was exhausted. He had exerted his best efforts, but, in spite of the immense energy he expended, all had apparently been lost. Then, totally drained, he only wanted death, convinced that he was a failure and no better at doing the Lord's work than the unsuccessful people who had preceded him. However, the Lord was unimpressed with Elijah's sense of failure because he does not see the situation as man sees it; He sees it from His divine perspective. So, he sent his angel to rouse Elijah, feed him, and set him on his way on a long journey to Mt. Sinai. Elijah traveled many days and finally ascended the flank of the sacred mountains to a cave. Here he entered and huddled in a dark corner. He then waited for a manifestation of the divine will.

Then there ensued a dialogue between God and Elijah. God asked the prophet, "what are you doing here, Elijah?" And the discouraged prophet told him his story, how the sons of Israel had forsaken the Lord's covenant, how his work had failed, and then, he said, "I alone am left, and they are seeking my life, to take it away" (1 Kgs 19:10). God then told Elijah that he should return to the land of Israel, and that he was to anoint new people to be royalty and leaders in place of Ahab and Jezebel. Most important, he informed Elijah that not everyone had lost faith in Him, for there were seven thousand people who had not bowed to Baal nor kissed Baal's idols. Elijah, his heart renewed, his sense of failure overcome, returned to Israel and completed his work. This story shows how a sense of failure can consume our energy and leave us depleted. It shows that our feeling that we have failed may be a mistake. God did not think that Elijah had failed; He was impressed that there were seven thousand who were faithful to Him and reckoned this more than enough to continue the work. And Elijah did continue the work, but only because he had been able to talk with God. His vital energies were replenished.

As priests we need proper nourishment of our souls if we are to help people in need. The Holy Spirit is refreshment. In hard labor, the Spirit is rest, and in the heat, he is the cool breeze that best refreshes us. He gives us solace in our woe.[13] Even Jesus who had been healing people needed refreshment in his own humanity. He rose early before dawn and communed with his Father in prayer. He realized he had to leave that area where he was healing and bring the good news to others. As important as that healing was, it was not the only thing that mattered.

---

[13] See *Pentecost Sunday Sequence*, Roman Missal.

The Spirit produces a rich harvest in our lives. In the Song of Songs, the Bridegroom now enters the bride's garden, which is his garden, as she has become his possession. This is fulfilled in Christ coming to claim his bride in marital union, partaking of all that is of the bride, all that she has brought forth in the garden of her interior life, and claiming it as his own. He gathers his myrrh and his spice. He eats his honeycomb with his honey. He drinks his wine with his milk. He gathers his fruits and consumes them. This is the great harvest of Pentecost, the ingathering and enjoyment of the fruits which the Holy Spirit has brought forth from his faithful people. The Bridegroom now invites his friends who are invited to the wedding banquet to eat and drink deeply, even to become drunk with love. The wedding banquet implies the banquet of the Lord's body and blood in the Holy Eucharist. The first Pentecost happened in the Upper Room, the place where Jesus had eaten the Last Supper with his Apostles. This was the place where they had felt closest to Jesus, in the total outpouring of his love to them. He had spoken intimately of his love for them. He told them to remain in him as he remained in them. Jesus would not leave them orphans. He promised to send the advocate and consoler, the Holy Spirit, while celebrating the Eucharist with them (cf. Jn 14:26). It seemed fitting for the Apostles to return to the place where they had received the greatest grace to remain in his love and receive an even greater outpouring of grace. Now the Holy Spirit would invade their very hearts and reproduce Christ in each of them.

The Holy Spirit is most active during the most sublime moment of the priest's day, the celebration of the Holy Eucharist. St. Paul highlights how Christ's sacrifice at Calvary was accomplished under the influence of the Holy Spirit: "Christ, who through the eternal Spirit offered himself without blemish to God" (Heb. 9:14). We as Christ's ministers are under the same influence of the Spirit to offer Christ's sacrifice. Abbot Marmion instructs us in the ways that the gifts of the Holy Spirit are poured out upon us and operative in the Holy Eucharist. The priest cultivates the attitude of a holy fear of the Lord as he approaches the holy mystery of the Holy Eucharist. Out of filial love and a desire to see God's name glorified, we pray that we refrain from offering anything that is evil or offensive to God. We seek to be innocent and holy in his sight just as we offer the spotless, innocent victim, Christ. As words and images vanish and we stand silently before the Lord who is near, our holy fear grows until it evolves into a pure, childlike adoration of our loving Father. A deeper understanding of God's love for us results in a perspective of wonder and awe that extends to all people. St. Theresa of Calcutta once pointed out to her sisters that they should care for the poor with the same reverence and care with which the priest handled the Holy Eucharist during Mass. One of the nuns came back at the end of the day rejoicing that she had handled Christ's body in caring for the poor with reverence that day.

The Gifts of the Holy Spirit

The Spirit's gift of Piety empowers us as faithful, loving sons to offer worship to God as our completely perfect and all-loving Father. As adopted sons in Jesus Christ we enter with confidence into his eternal Sonship and perfect worship of the Father. We experience the loving delight that the Father expresses toward Jesus: "This is my Son, the beloved, with whom I am well pleased" (Mt 3:17). Piety also offers honor and reverence toward parents, family and loved ones, as well as toward ecclesial and civic leaders and one's country. During the Mass we show them the greatest charity of the heart of Jesus by interceding for them and all their needs. We remain attuned to the great suffering of so many in our communities and in the world, especially in the prayers of the faithful. We intercede for the sick and sorrowful, the infirmed and dying, the immigrant and refugee, those who are persecuted and those who lack faith. The high point and culmination of the Liturgy of the Word is the Prayers of the Faithful in which we beg divine mercy for those who are in most need. During the Eucharistic Prayer we implore the Father to rain down Christ's grace and peace for the Church and the entire world.

The Spirit's gift of Fortitude moves us to steadfastness in danger in pursuing the good and enduring evil. It also gives us confident hope of eternal life in the end. Fortitude moves us to virtuous living, which is difficult, and gives us the spiritual desire for the works of justice. "It is this same gift which gives us the courage to offer ourselves each day to God as victims dedicated to all the desires of His will, even the most crucifying."[14] We call upon the Spirit's gift of Fortitude especially when our cross seems too heavy to bear, asking for the spiritual fortitude which permeated Jesus at his sacrifice on the cross. St. Theresa of Avila, after receiving Holy Communion, heard the Lord asking her what she had to fear, considering that he would be with her through her difficult task of beginning two new foundations according to the reformed Carmelite rule. The priest is also subject to the danger of temptations against the faith as he confects the most holy Eucharist. He is in the most immediate contact with the Body and Blood of Christ, hidden under the appearances of bread and wine. The devil can tempt against the faith of the priest, who will "need the gift of Fortitude to maintain his faith at the level of the act which he is accomplishing, to triumph over all temptation, and to convince himself that in all truth he is in the presence of his Savior, as though he saw Him with his own eyes."[15]

The Spirit's gifts of Understanding and Knowledge are closely allied and are operative in the celebration of the holy Eucharist. The Spirit enables us to penetrate all things, even the deep things of God, in the depths of our souls. By the gift of supernatural understanding one knows the mys-

---

[14] Marmion, 308.
[15] Ibid.

teries of the faith surely, but imperfectly, and one assents with conviction to their truth on God's word. When others walked away, Peter believed Jesus' word on the holy Eucharist, saying, "Lord, to whom can we go? You have the words of eternal life." (Jn 6:68). We may know all the theology of transubstantiation, but to penetrate its meaning, we need the gifts of Understanding and Knowledge. The gift of Knowledge is concerned with human and created things to the extent these pertain to the faith in any way. Through knowledge we become convinced of the surpassing value of Christ in the Holy Eucharist as the pearl of great price, selling all to possess that treasure. We say with St. Paul: "I regard everything as loss because of the surpassing value of knowing Christ Jesus my Lord. For his sake I have suffered the loss of all things, and I regard them as rubbish, in order that I may gain Christ" (Phil 3:8).

The gift of Counsel is, in a particular manner, a help to the supernatural virtue of prudence to practice our faith in such a way as to reach heaven. As *natural counsel* is the research of reason which precedes the decision of the will, and is therefore a kind of self-advice, so *supernatural counsel* is the divine advice and guidance imparted by the Holy Spirit. The priest has many decisions of great significance to make in his pastoral ministry that impact the welfare of individual souls, and his whole flock. He will need to implore the Holy Spirit for guidance in those decisions. St. Ignatius made his discernment of many weighty matters regarding his Society by bringing them to the altar at Mass to receive divine light. St. Thomas More, as lay chancellor for the king, testified that he received the light and strength in Holy Communion to make difficult decisions throughout his day. As a spiritual director and pastoral counselor, I rely on the gift of supernatural counsel to guide souls in the ways of the Lord. During the Holy Eucharist, I ask God's grace to bring the Spirit's counsel to those I will meet throughout the day. I am later amazed and humbled at the way the Lord offers counsel either directly to people or through me as their spiritual guide.

The Spirit's gift of Wisdom enables a person to judge divine things rightly, and to judge other things according to the divine law of charity which is in him. When we celebrate the Holy Eucharist, the wisdom of the Holy Spirit focuses our attention completely on the Lord. The inspiration of wisdom is the Holy Spirit's communication of the heavenly vision at the heart level. We see God himself, not with our physical sight or even our intellects. The Spirit' enlightens our hearts to enjoy a foretaste of what we will one day experience in heaven. Even a small glimpse of heaven at the heart level makes us soar beyond what we can know or feel about God while in this world. Savoring God's presence, the human heart prefers the beatitude of union with God to all the joys of this earthly life. By the gift of Wisdom, we can say: "How lovely is your dwelling place, O Lord of hosts! My soul longs, indeed it faints for the courts of the Lord; my heart and my flesh sing for joy to the living God. ... For a day in your courts is better than a thousand elsewhere" (Ps. 84: 1-2, 10a). The gift of wisdom also produces an inner peace in the heart which supports the priest during life's trials and sorrows.

The Holy Spirit's gifts are given to us to empower us to fulfill all righteousness in charity and to pursue Christ as our goal now and for all eternity.

> The liturgy likes to see in the Holy Spirit the supreme consoler; frequently it makes us ask that we may at all times enjoy His consolations. How desirable for the priest is this peace coming from God! Thanks to it, during the sacred sacrifice, he will feel in the depths of his heart the effects of the eternal goodness.[16]

---

[16] Ibid., 312.

We should remain at peace in all circumstances through our worship of God in the Holy Eucharist. The story is told of one of Napoleon's generals, Massena, who with his army of 18,000 soldiers besieged an Austrian town that had no defenses whatsoever. The town council met to discuss how to surrender. Just then the priest and pastor of the town church reminded the council that it was Easter and suggested that they hold the usual Easter Mass and put the problem in God's hands. The council took his advice, went to the church, and rang the church bells to assemble the townsfolk for worship. During the celebration of Mass, the priest and congregation experienced great peace, without any fear of capture or death. They surrendered their destiny to the Lord's will and worshipped him in Spirit and in truth. Napoleon's approaching forces heard the joyful ringing of the bells and concluded that the Austrian forces had arrived to rescue the town. Immediately, they broke camp and beat a retreat, and the town was saved. They were faithful in surrendering themselves completely to God by worshiping him in righteousness.

The bride offers the gift of herself and all she has brought forth from her garden in her interior life and virtues to be offered to her Beloved. As fulfilled in Christ, the repast she offers him is now transubstantiated into the meal he offers for the many. In the offertory of the Mass, the faithful bring forth the fruits of their lives, their prayers, works, joys and sufferings to be offered in union with the bread and wine of the Lord's sacrifice. The priest then invokes the Holy Spirit over the bread and wine, asking him to make holy these gifts that we bring for consecration, that they may become the Body and Blood of the Lord. His sacrifice, offered once and for all on the cross, is made sacramentally present to us. According to the theologian Jean Corbon:

At this point the Father's compassion embraces the sufferings of men and causes his Spirit to flow forth from the side of his beloved

Son. It is this gift that comes to us in the epiclesis: the Spirit of Jesus permeates the death of men in order to give them his life. He pours himself out upon all flesh that offers itself to him, and his transforming energy gives the flesh a share in the Resurrection of Jesus; the wounded members are united to the incorruptible body and draw life from it. By the power of the Holy Spirit, those who partake in the body and blood of Christ become one body and one spirit in Christ.[17]

This epiclesis "brings the power of this eucharistic Pentecost to everything we offer to the Father. ... In its epiclesis, the Church gives her most free and most detached consent to the life-giving Spirit."[18] The bride has called upon the Holy Spirit to blow upon her garden, to awaken her devotion and self-offering. Now, the Bridegroom enters the garden of her soul and consumes her fruit. He takes her gift of self and unites it with his in a perfect sacrifice.

Questions for Reflection and Discussion

1. Have I ever made the Spiritual Exercises of St. Ignatius in some form? How did they impact me? What is the importance of an annual retreat for me?

2. How do I sense the Holy Spirit making me into another Christ as the Lord lives his mysteries in me as a member of his body? How do I especially feel conformed to the priesthood of Jesus Christ?

---

[17] Jean Corbon, *The Wellspring of Worship* (San Francisco, Ignatius Press, 2005), 152.

[18] Ibid., 153-154.

3. How have I felt the Spirit's comfort and encouragement in my own poverty of spirit and weakness as a priest? How have I also experienced a rich harvest in my ministry by the power of the Holy Spirit?

4. Which of the gifts of the Holy Spirit am I aware of being operative in my life? Which of the gifts of the Spirit do I need to receive in greater abundance? Have I ever implored the gifts of the Spirit during Mass?

5. In what way do I experience the peace and compassion of the Risen Lord in the Holy Eucharist? How does the Spirit permeate all that I am and do as a self-offering? To what degree do I freely and fully offer myself to God in the Holy Spirit?

Prayer Exercises

1. Ponder the St. John Eudes quote. Pray with Gal 2:20 or Jn 15:4-9 and ask for the grace to experience Christ living his mysteries in and through you.

2. Reflect on te statements of St. Elizabeth of the Trinity about Christ incarnating himself in her to make her *alter Christus*. Pray with Rom 8:28-30 or Sg 4:16—5:1 and ask for the grace to be conformed more into the likeness of Jesus.

3. Consider the restoration of Elijah. Pray with 1 Kgs 19:1-18 and ask for the grace to know the Lord's refreshment amid your weakness and exhaustion.

4. Ponder any of the gifts of the Holy Spirit. Pray with Is 11:1-16 and ask for whichever gift you need in greater abundance.

5. Reflect on the Corbon quotes. Pray with Acts 2:1-13 and ask for the grace that the Spirit make a more free and complete offering of all that you are and do.

Chapter 15

Soul Doctor

I slept, but my heart was awake.
Hark! my beloved is knocking.
"Open to me, my sister, my love,
my dove, my perfect one;
for my head is wet with dew,
my locks with the drops of the night."
I had put off my garment,
how could I put it on?
I had bathed my feet,
how could I soil them?
My beloved put his hand to the latch,
and my heart was thrilled within me.
I arose to open to my beloved,
and my hands dripped with myrrh,
my fingers with liquid myrrh,
upon the handles of the bolt.
I opened to my beloved,
but my beloved had turned and gone.
My soul failed me when he spoke.
I sought him, but found him not;
I called him, but he gave no answer.
The watchmen found me,
as they went about in the city;
they beat me, they wounded me,
they took away my mantle,

those watchmen of the walls.
I adjure you, O daughters of Jerusalem,
if you find my beloved,
that you tell him
I am sick with love. (Sg 5:2-8)

The ideal pastor preaches exactly 10 minutes long and hits all the major themes. He harshly slams sin, but never offends anyone. He is the janitor for the church and works from 8 a.m. to midnight. The ideal pastor earns $700 per week, looks good, drives a nice car, purchases nice books, and gives $300 per week to the church. He has forty years of experience and is twenty-nine years old. Moreover, he is handsome. The ideal pastor spends much of his time with the elderly despite having a strong desire to work with youth. He always maintains a serious expression while grinning, thanks to his sense of humor, which keeps him seriously committed to his faith. He goes to fifteen homes each day, and he's always available in his office. The ideal pastor is available to serve on the church council and all its committees. He never passes up a church organization meeting and is constantly engaged in evangelizing the lapsed Christians. The next church over always has the ideal pastor![1]

This little vignette illustrates that perhaps in no other profession, does a man face so many expectations from so many people than priesthood. To complicate things, those expectations vary widely. Some expect their priest to be a great teacher. Others want him foremost to be a faithful pastor. Others hand him the task of being a financial wizard. Some want him to maintain the old traditions. Just as many want him to be pleasingly forward-thinking. Some expect him to devote himself to calling on the sick, or making house calls, or attending community social functions, or being

---

[1] See *The Rochester Journal*, "The Perfect Pastor," September 1981.

concerned with the poor or civil rights. Others want him for a personal counselor or want him to be a distinguished preacher. The list continues. Clearly no one man can be so gifted, energetic, and varied in his interests that he can hope to fulfill all these expectations. As much as we try to be all things to all people (cf. 1 Cor 9:22), we inevitably fall short and wish we could be more for everyone.

The priest has an enormous and challenging job that is at once invigorating and exhausting. At my first parish assignment, I usually performed one mass daily and two masses on Sunday which involved a few hours of homily preparation. I offered confessions Saturday mornings and afternoons, and before one of the Sunday masses, while also being available to help with confessions at other parishes. I performed baptisms on Sunday afternoons and did Saturday baptism preparation classes. There were regular funerals, which could take up most of my day with the burial and reception, and the evening before with the wake and funeral preparations. I also hosted a bereavement group for grieving families. Weddings were frequent. I remember celebrating twelve weddings in my first three months of priesthood, each of which involved four sessions of marriage preparation with the priest. I was also chaplain and presenter at Pre-Cana and Engaged encounter marriage preparation weekends, usually four per year. There was a morning of hospital calls once a week. There were regular Communion calls to the homebound and nursing homes. I prepared and led a bible study every other week. Every week I taught RCIA (now OCIA) to adults and Confirmation class to eighth graders. I ministered to the handicapped every Saturday morning at the developmental center. I engaged in prison ministry at two nearby prisons, making multiple visits each week for masses, counseling, and catechism class. As leader and point man for the St. Vincent de Paul society, I was daily helping poor people at our door and in our outreach. I was chaplain to four hundred men in the Knights of Columbus. I helped with youth group activities. People came to me regularly for pastoral counseling and spiritual direction. I offered the Ignatian retreat in daily life at the parish and occasionally helped conduct weekend retreats. There were parish events, pro-life and other social justice activities to plan and attend. People would invite me to attend their family activities and celebrations, or to come and do house blessings. Each family had its own story, and its own set of needs. Then there were out-of-the-blue calls to anoint the sick and the dying, sometimes in the middle of the night. For the most part, all these activities were invigorating, but occasionally burdensome.

Parish life was a rollercoaster of activities and sometimes of feelings. I might perform a funeral in the morning and weep with those who weep, and then perform a wedding in the afternoon and rejoice with those rejoicing (cf. Rom 12:15). Through it all, prayer was my inspiration and stabilizing force. God was my rock who grounded me in love. Only he could order my life and keep me well disposed to meet the demands of his people. The Lord was in need as the one who was about to receive; and he was in abundance as the one who was going to fulfill.[2]

The Wounds of Love

The Lord presents himself as the one in need to the bride in the Song. He knocks at her door and begs her to open to him. According to Blaise Arminjon:

> He is miserable love, waiting in the cold night on her doorstep. He
> does not come in an imposing manner, but he implores; he is not

---

[2] See St. Augustine, *Commentary on the Gospel of John*, XV:12, Ed. Phillip Schaff, Nicene and Post Nicene Fathers, Series 1, Vol. 7, p. 590, Christian Classics Ethereal Library Website, https://www.ccel.org/ccel/s/schaff/npnf107/cache/npnf107.pdf

a lord and master; he does not rush in with strength and splendor—and she would only be able to kneel lovingly before him. But this time he comes in dressed as the poorest and most pitiful of all. With this face of a humiliated servant, which should also be hers! And he is begging, he is asking for compassion even though he is the richest and happiest of all.[3]

The Bridegroom calls to his bride with the tenderest of names: "my sister, my love, my dove, my lovely one." (Sg 5:2). Yet she seems unmoved and prefers her own comfort. She replies rather indifferently that she has taken off her tunic and would rather not put it on again. She has already bathed her feet and does not want to dirty them. She prefers not to be inconvenienced. After all she has received from his bounty of love, she proves herself hesitant and unfaithful in love. The Bridegroom thrusts his hand through the opening in the door, and she finally rises to open to him. Her hands are now dripping with myrrh, the symbol of his presence and especially his death and burial. Her Beloved has now disappeared into the night and her soul is heartbroken in sadness. She realizes he was the only one who mattered in her life.

We all have missed opportunities to love and this should cause us the most distress. Jesus, when he went out in the night to the garden of Gethsemane to pray before his impending death, took with him Peter, James, and John to keep him company in his hour of greatest anguish. He said to them, "I am deeply grieved, even to death; remain here, and stay awake with me" (Mat 26:38). After his impassioned prayer to the Father to let this cup of suffering pass, surrendering his own will to the Father's, he returns to find the three of them sleeping. This happened three times. Jesus needed their support in his distress and found them indifferent, preferring their

---

[3] Arminjon, 243-244.

own comfort. Jesus is then arrested and taken away from them. He disappears into the night like the Bridegroom. He had predicted that the Bridegroom would be taken away, and that then the wedding guests would fast, and perhaps weep and mourn his loss (cf. Lk 5:35).

Now the bride in the Song, regretting her indifference, frantically runs after him, disregarding the cold and darkness of the night, and her own comfort. God disappears, especially when we fail at love, so that our hearts might be pierced with contrition and love, so we might seek him more fervently. Gregory the Great says that "The Bridegroom hides when he is sought, so that, not finding him, the Bride may seek him with a renewed ardor; and the Bride is hampered in her search so that this delay may increase the capacity for God, and that she may find one day more fully what she was seeking."[4] Meanwhile, the watchmen make their rounds and find the bride. They beat and wound her, for no good reason, taking away her cloak. She encounters the coldness and brutality of humanity in the world, and even in the holy city, Jerusalem. As the Psalmist cries: "I see violence and strife in the city. Day and night, they go around it on its walls, and iniquity and trouble are within it; ruin is in its midst; oppression and fraud do not depart from its marketplace" (Ps. 55:9-11). The absence of God is accompanied by the harshness and persecution of human beings, and the bride now finds no peace or comfort. But in her frenzy to find her Bridegroom, she is undeterred by the sufferings she endures. This scene reminds us of Mary, the mother of Jesus, Mary Magdalene, and St. John, who seek Jesus out during his passion and stand steadfast and vigilant at his crucifixion.

Jesus is the one wounded by his love for us. His side is opened, and we are wounded with love by his sacrifice for us. His wound is the one which heals our many wounds. Now overcome with love for the Lord, we can

---

[4] Gregory the Great, *Moralium,* V:6; PL 76.

tend to the wounds of others. Even in our service to the Lord, we aspire to fight without heeding the wounds, unconcerned about ourselves in our desire to tend to the suffering and crucified Lord in the guise of so many hurting people. The French poet Leon Bloy describes the wayfarer following a great explorer who enters into the most difficult part of the journey:

> We are entering into the desert, into solitude. Here are Cold, Darkness, Hunger, Thirst, vast Weariness, dreadful Sadness, the Agony, the Bloody Sweat. The rash traveler looks for his companions. He understands, then, that it is God's good pleasure that he be alone amid torments, and he goes on into the black immensity, bearing his heart before him like a torch![5]

The same Apostles who had fallen asleep during the Lord's agony eventually went out on his behalf to proclaim his love. Like the bride they endured cruel persecution, beatings and even death. James the Greater was executed in Jerusalem by Herod Agrippa in the year 44 AD. During Nero's persecution in Rome, Peter was crucified upside down and Paul was imprisoned and killed. For the others, tradition states that Andrew was crucified on an X-shaped cross by the Roman governor of Patras, Greece. In Hierapolis, Turkey, Philip was crucified after being stoned. In Armenia, Bartholomew was crucified and flayed. Thomas was speared to death in Southern India. Ethiopian authorities burnt Matthew to death. In Egypt, James the Lesser was beaten to death with clubs and stones after being flung from the walls. Jude Thaddeus was nailed to a cross and shot to death by arrows in Syria. In Armenia, Simon the Zealot was sawed to pieces. Most of them had been executed as martyrs before the end of the first

---

[5] Leon Bloy, *The Pilgrim of the Absolute*, transl. John Coleman and Harry Lorin Binsse (London: Eyre and Spottiswoode, 1947), 79.

century. Both the boiling and the poisoning attempts by the Romans failed to kill the Apostle John. He was sent to the Greek prison island of Patmos, where he was made to do hard labor.

The Healing Power of the Cross

Thanks to the blood of the Apostles and Martyrs, Christianity was finally legalized in the Roman Empire. Emperor Constantine's power was extended throughout Europe, North Africa, and the Middle East. Constantine's mother, St. Helen, like the bride in the Song, went on pilgrimage to Palestine, looking for the cross of her beloved Lord. When she arrived in Jerusalem, the local bishop, St. Macarius, helped her dig up the hill of Calvary in an effort to find the exact cross that Jesus was crucified on. (According to tradition, it was interred nearby.) To everyone's astonishment and delight, they discovered not just one, but three crosses, including those of the two criminals who were crucified with Jesus. How to identify which one was the cross of Christ became a challenge. St. Macarius devised a brilliant strategy. He ordered the crosses to be delivered to a woman's house who was in critical condition. In comments reported by the priest Rufinus, he ardently pleaded with God to make known which crucifixion was the real one:

O God, who through your only-begotten Son has inspired the heart of your handmaid [St. Helen] to seek the holy wood upon which our salvation depends, show plainly which cross was identified with the glory of the Lord. Grant that as soon as the health-giving wood touches this woman who is lying half-dead, she may be recalled to life from the gates of death.[6]

Then he sequentially touched the flesh of the dying woman with each of the crosses. With the first two, nothing occurred, but with the third, the woman's eyes opened and she hopped out of bed in excellent health. This demonstrated which Cross truly belonged to Christ. On Calvary, where the precious relic of the genuine cross is enshrined, St. Helena constructed the Church of the Holy Sepulchre.

The power flowing from the cross of Jesus effects healing in our lives. Because of the cross, we know that we are loved unconditionally. Even if we should hate ourselves or one another due to sin, God still loves us and forgives us. Because of the unconditional love of Christ, we can break out of our selfishness and vice, which leads to death, and be open to a new way of life in God. Because of our fallen nature, there is suffering in our growth process which can lead to ever richer growth and maturation on all levels of our human life. The Swiss psychologist Carl Jung, just days before his death, wrote: "To this day God is the name by which I designate all things which cross my willful path violently and recklessly, all things which upset my subjective views, plans and intentions and change the course of my life for better or for worse."[7] He did not believe in meaningless, chance accidents; rather, he sensed those "crosses" that challenged him made him grow into a better person. The poet expresses it eloquently: "If I always

---

[6] Epriest, *Homily Pack, The Feast of the Triumph of the Cross*. Epriest Website, https://epriest.com/homily_packs

[7] Carl Gustave Jung, *Carl Gustave Jung, One of the Founders of Psychiatry, tells: "Why I Believe in God,"* Interview with Frederick Sands, Good Housekeeping Magazine, June 2, 1961. Carl Jung Depth Psychology Website, https://carljung-depthpsychologysite.blog/2022/02/12/dr-carl-gustav-jung-one-of-the-founders-of-psychiatry-tells-why-i-believe-in-god/ #.ZDmCj3bMLIU.

stayed on the mountaintop, and never experienced pain, I would never appreciate God's love, and would be living in vain. I have so much to learn, and my growth is very slow. Sometimes I need the mountain tops, but it's in the valleys I grow."[8] According to psychiatrist Kazimierz Dabrowski, there is a positive kind of disintegration which involves the dissolution of lower-level functions that is necessary to achieve higher-level integration and greater maturity. This may involve turmoil within, feelings of inferiority, experiences of shame and guilt, environmental alienation, and various mental conflicts. We melt-down and die to our lower-level of being and functioning as a preparation for rebirth to a higher-level integration in the more authentic self.[9] When Jesus invites us to take up our cross and follow him, it is an invitation to accept in an enlightened way the tensions and suffering in growing and becoming more whole and perfect. Those who do so find his yoke easy and his burden light (cf. Mt 11:30), thanks to the more enlightened and higher form of existence in Christ.

Meaningful Suffering

Suffering is not meaningless in an unfair world of accidents, but a momentous call to wholeness and perfection. According to Bernard Tyrell,

Sometimes an accident is a summons to renounce some conscious or hidden sinful way of being-in-the-world; sometimes it is a revelation of a new vocation or direction to follow; sometimes an accident is an invitation to grow in loving adoration of the mystery

---

[8] Jane Eggleston, *It's in the Valley's I Grow,* All Worship Website, https://www.allworship.com/valleys-grow/

[9] See Kazimierz Dabrowski, *Mental Growth through Positive Disintegration* (London: Gryf Publications, 1970), 82.

that guides all things lovingly and wisely but often leaves human beings baffled and confused.[10]

Job teaches us that through suffering we come to enlightenment:

> Who is this that hides counsel without knowledge? Therefore, I have uttered what I did not understand, things too wonderful for me, which I did not know. I had heard of you by the hearing of the ear, but now my eye sees you; therefore, I despise myself, and repent in dust and ashes. (Job 42:3, 5-6)

Through his sufferings, Job now knows his Lord better and is filled with wonder at God's mysteries.

Jesus, a fulfillment of the figure of Job, did not perceive his suffering and death as absurd, or as the result of blind fate. He knew it was the Father's will and he chose and accepted it lovingly. As a result, his death on the cross was a triumph, as he proves both by the way he died and by his resurrection to new life. Jesus showed absolute trust in his Father's presence and will in speaking Psalm 22, an expression of confidence and victory. He forgave his persecutors from the cross and brought our redemption to completion: "It is finished" (Jn 19:30). He brought about belief in his divinity by his courage, peace, and joy in his death, so that the witnessing centurion could say "Truly this man was God's Son!" (Mk 15:39). The Greek crucifix which displays Jesus clothed in grandeur expresses well the triumph of the Cross, the triumph of his love, even of his enemies.

Christianity is unique in its command to love one's enemies, even as they inflict torture. Non-believers often find this love incomprehensible.

---

[10] Bernard Tyrell, *Christo-Therapy, Healing through Enlightenment* (New York: Seabury Press, 1975), 114.

Archbishop Van Thuan of Saigon, while he was imprisoned for thirteen years without a trial, told his guard that he loved him. The guard thought it was impossible, but Van Thuan assured him it was true. The guard then asked him if when he was freed, he would send his fellow Christians to burn the guards' homes and kill their families? Von Thran assured him the even if the guards killed him, he would still love them, because Jesus taught him to love even his enemies. The guard was dumbfounded, but admitted it was very beautiful.[11] Jesus taught us to love not only our friends, but our enemies as well, and to pray for those who persecute us (cf. (Mt 5:44).

This loving stance towards even our enemies becomes a witness to Christ and evangelizes our neighbors. When Van Thuan was in isolation, five prison guards took turns so that there were always two watching him. The leaders had told the guards they would replace them every two weeks with another group so that they would not be infected by this dangerous bishop's teaching. Sometime later, the leaders decided not to switch the guards anymore because this bishop might contaminate all the police. Von Thuan relates:

> In the beginning, the guards did not talk to me. They only an-
> swered me with a yes or no. I was terribly sad. I wanted to be kind
> and polite with them, but it was impossible. They avoided speak-
> ing with me. One night a thought came to me: "Francis, you are
> still very rich. You have the love of Christ in your heart: love them
> as Jesus has loved you."
>
> The next day I started to love them even more, to love Jesus in
> them, smiling and exchanging kind words with them. I began to
> tell stories of my trips abroad, of how people live in America, in
> Canada, in Japan, in the Philippines … about economics, about

---

[11] See Van Thuan, *Testimony of Hope*, 70.

freedom, about technology. This stimulated their curiosity and they began asking me many questions. Little by little we became friends. They wanted to learn foreign languages, French, English … and my guards became my students.[12]

Like the bride who is unconcerned about her sufferings and only desires to seek her Beloved, Van Thuan accepted his mean circumstances and chose to focus solely on the love of Jesus. He found joy in the cross and by its power he evangelized his enemies.

Jesus suffered as the righteous one for the sake of the unrighteous. While this might seem to be the ultimate injustice, it gave great joy to Jesus. As Jesus ate the Last Supper, he loved his Apostles to the end, and desired that they would have his joy in them and that their joy would be complete by imitating him in laying down their lives for one another (cf. Jn 15:11). Jesus' only joy and goal was to do the Father's will in accomplishing our salvation. He felt the closeness and intimacy of the Father and communicated it to his Apostles: "Abide in me as I abide in you" (Jn 15:4). Jesus experienced the ecstasy, or "standing outside oneself," of transcending his own humanity by his divinity. He shows himself to be a man concerned for others and zealous for the Father's glory. The love of the Father dominated his mind. Jesus tells his disciples they will experience the same joy in suffering persecution for the sake of his name. "Blessed are you when people revile you and persecute you and utter all kinds of evil against you falsely on my account. Rejoice and be glad, for your reward is great in heaven" (Mt 5:12). When the Apostles were flogged by the Sanhedrin, they left the council and "rejoiced that they were considered worthy to suffer dishonor for the sake of the name. And every day in the temple and at home they did not cease to teach and proclaim Jesus as the Messiah (Acts

---

[12] Ibid., 72.

5:41-42). St. Paul speaks to the Corinthians of his joy in tribulation, "I am filled with consolation; I am overjoyed in all our affliction" (2 Cor 7:4). He writes to the Philippians from prison: "But even if I am being poured out as a libation over the sacrifice and the offering of your faith, I am glad and rejoice with all of you— and in the same way you also must be glad and rejoice with me" (Phil 2:17-18).

It is a great joy as a priest to help relieve people's sufferings, to give them purpose and meaning in Jesus Christ, and to see their transformation. We become transmitters of the healing power of the Divine Physician. Dr. Tom Dooley captured the imagination of the world in the middle of the twentieth-century. After graduating from medical school, Dooley enlisted in the Navy as a doctor. The big day of his life came one hot July afternoon off the coast of Vietnam. That is when his ship rescued 1,000 refugees who were drifting helplessly in an open boat. Many of the refugees were diseased and sick. Given that Dooley was the only doctor on the ship, he had to tackle, single-handedly, the job of giving medical aid to these people. It was backbreaking, but he discovered what a little medicine could do for sick people like this. He said: "Hours later, I stopped a moment to straighten my shoulders and made another discovery— the biggest of my life. I was happy treating these people. ... happier than I had ever been before."[13]

Dooley's experience on that hot July afternoon changed his life forever. When he got out of the Navy, he returned to the jungles of Asia and set up a small hospital to serve the poor and the sick. One of Dooley's favorite Bible passages was the Beatitudes in the Sermon on the Mount. Tom said that his work among the poor gave him a new insight into the meaning of the Beatitudes, especially "Blessed are those who mourn, for they

---

[13] Mark Link, *Illustrated Sunday Homilies, Years A,B,C, Series I,* Year A, Fourth Sunday in Ordinary Time, 55.

shall be comforted" (Mt 5:4). In his own case, Dooley said: "To mourn is to be more aware of the sorrow in the world than of the pleasure. If you're extra sensitive to sorrow," he said, "and you do something, no matter how small, to make it lighter— you can't help but be happy. That's just the way it is."[14]

As priests who constantly encounter suffering, we are more aware of the suffering in the world than the pleasures. As priests we share the full range of peoples' experiences. But perhaps the thing we are most keenly aware of is their suffering. We encounter suffering when we go on sick calls, conduct funerals, help people grieve, and hear of sin and failure in confessions. I remember hearing about a man who became a psychologist and gave up after two years because he could not handle the steady diet of peoples' pain. As priests, we can only endure because we have Christ to support us. We experience the gift of his compassion which literally means "to suffer with." But Jesus does not end simply with empathy, feeling what the other is feeling. He does something to alleviate the suffering. He heals. So too, we as priests are in the work of healing souls, and bodies.

Walter Hooper, advisor to the estate of the great C.S. Lewis, and a Catholic convert, once had the opportunity to meet St. John Paul II. Hooper had recently been diagnosed with cancer, and was in tremendous pain. When he greeted the pope, he kissed the papal ring and immediately felt his pain disappear. At that moment, John Paul winced and momentarily tightened his grip. It seemed the pope had himself assumed the agony of the cancer, healing Hooper of his illness. Walter glanced up at the pope and said, "I'm sorry Holy Father, I didn't realize that would happen." And the pope replied, "No, that's quite alright."[15] And the cancer dis-

---

[14] Ibid.

[15] Jacob Imam, *Obituary for Walter Hooper*, Dec. 7, 2020, New Polity Website, https://newpolity.com/blog/walter-hooper-19312020.

appeared. Often, our ministry of healing as priests comes with a cost, as we extend compassion to people in their painful situations. Like Jesus, we may groan and be deeply moved in spirit and troubled at other people's sufferings.

Ministers of Mercy

Deep down, the healing people need is often more spiritual than physical. Back in the 1990s The American Medical Association polled thousands of general practitioners, asking them what proportion of patients they see each week have needs that their training as doctors qualifies them to handle. The answers to that query were astounding. In response, the medical professionals said that they only felt qualified to handle roughly 10 percent of their patients. When questioned about the other 90 percent, the doctors claimed that the patients experienced genuine pain, but that their issue was psychological rather than biochemical or physical. In other words, it was a "life problem" that could not be resolved with standard medical care. Their illnesses were actually brought on by things like wrath, repressed hostilities, negative emotions, and negative attitudes. These are issues that a typical doctor is ill-prepared or unqualified to address. One researcher made a comment regarding the impact these things have on health: "Our feelings about ourselves and others and the quality of our relationships may have more to do with how often we get sick than our genes, chemistry, diet or environment."[16]

Doctors are quick to admit there is little in their medical training to help patients with these life problems. One doctor told me back in the 1990s that there were fifteen thousand people walking around New Jersey

---

[16] Mark Link, *Illustrated Sunday Homilies, Series 1, Years A,B,C,* Year C, Fourth Sunday of Lent, 25-26.

with undiagnosable illnesses. So, the answer is not just physical, or even psychological, but spiritual. Even Carl Jung admitted that deep down, every psychological problem is a spiritual problem. Problems at the level of the soul radiate out to all levels of the psyche and even the body. The priest, the soul doctor, traces the problem all the way back to its deepest point. A hurting person should be addressed at all levels, but it is the soul doctor who addresses the very deepest level. The soul is just as complicated as the body, and more rich, strange, and puzzling. The true soul doctor is the depth psychologist. In the sacraments of healing (Penance and Anointing) we especially exercise our roles as doctors of spirit.

> By the sacred anointing of the sick and the prayer of the priests the whole Church commends those who are ill to the suffering and glorified Lord, that he may raise them up and save them and indeed, she exhorts them to contribute to the good of the People of God by freely uniting themselves to the Passion and death of Christ.[17]

Again, the Lord heals by the power of his cross through the sacred minister.

Today we hear a lot of emphasis on holistic healing. The Sacrament of Anointing can heal us at every level of our being—body, soul, and spirit. The following is part of a letter from a Vietnam War veteran. He wrote it from a hospital bed, while recuperating from battlefield injuries. He writes:

> From the split second I was hit, I was completely alone. I was hurt bad, real bad; a 4.2 mortar landed about six feet behind me and took off my leg, badly ripped up my left arm, hit me in the back,

---

[17] *Lumen Gentium*, 11.

head, hip, and right heel and ankle. Shock was instantaneous, but I fought it—knowing that if I went out, I'd never wake up again. Three or four medics were hovering over me, all shook up, trying to help me; but all I could do was pray. The trouble was I couldn't think. No one could tell me there wasn't a God at that moment. I knew I would die and fought desperately for ground—every inch, breath of life. I knew I was in the state of serious sin." He made it to the chopper two hours after being hit. When he made it to the first-aid station and was scrubbed up, he continued: "Someone bent over me. I wasn't sure who it was, but it looked like our battalion chaplain. After I saw him, I started to go out—I figured I for the last time. As I was going out, my eyes closed and I heard Father say, "are you sorry for your sins?" With my last breath and all I had, I whispered, "Hell yes!" Then I felt oil on my forehead; all of a sudden, I stopped grasping for every inch of life. I just burst with joy … I felt like I had just got a million cc's of morphine. I was on Cloud Nine. I felt free of body and mind.[18]

He went on to recuperate in a powerful experience of the sacrament of anointing. Some people, like this Vietnam veteran, receive complete or partial bodily healing. Others also go through a mental recovery, which leads to a state of tranquility similar to the soldier's. Others undergo a spiritual transformation that leads to a heart-stirring encounter with God's mercy and love, such as the soldier's forgiveness.

In sickness, people experience their own powerlessness and limitations. Every illness can make us glimpse our own mortality. Sickness can lead to anguish, self-absorption, sometimes even despair and revolt against

---

[18] Mark Link, *Illustrated Sunday Homilies, Series II*, Years A,B,C, Year B, Fifteenth Sunday in Ordinary Time, 81.

God. It can also make people more mature, helping them strip away in their lives what is non-essential so that they can turn toward what is. Very often illness provokes a search for God and a return to him. Through the Sacrament of Anointing, the Holy Spirit renews trust and faith in God and strengthens against the temptations of the enemy to discouragement and anguish in the face of death. Anointing effects a greater union with the passion of Christ.

> By the grace of this sacrament the sick person receives the strength and the gift of uniting himself more closely to Christ's Passion: in a certain way he is consecrated to bear fruit by configuration to the Savior's redemptive Passion. Suffering, a consequence of original sin, acquires a new meaning; it becomes a participation in the saving work of Jesus.[19]

The bride is willing to endure suffering with disregard for her own welfare in her search for her Beloved. St. Paul echoes her attitude of rejoicing at his suffering as he completes in his own flesh what is lacking in Christ's afflictions for the sake of his body, the church (cf. Col 1:24). As priests, we too rejoice because through the burdens of our ministry, we bring healing to those who are suffering.

Questions for Reflection and Discussion

1. How much am I beholden to the expectations of others as a priest? How do I try to be all things to all people while maintaining my own sense of limitation?

---

[19] *Catechism of the Catholic Church,* 1521.

2. Considering the vast array of ministerial duties I perform as a priest, where am I challenged to find God more present in these activities? How do I sense God ordering my days and making me available for all he wants me to do?

3. How much am I aware of the suffering of others? How does it affect me as a minister? Do I perceive Christ present in the weakness of others? How do I experience the mercy of God flowing through me as a minister of the Lord?

4. How has my own experience of weakness or catastrophe been an invitation to accept in an enlightened way the tensions and suffering in growing and becoming more whole and perfect?

5. What is my experience of visiting the sick, offering comfort and healing? Jesus groaned as he healed certain sick people. In what way is my ministry of healing draining and/or life-giving for me?

Prayer Exercises

1. Ponder the Arminjon quote about the Bridegroom standing at the door. Pray with Sg 5:2-8 or Lk 22:39-46 and ask for the grace to see the suffering Christ in others.

2. Reflect on the story of Bishop Macarius and the holy Cross. Pray with Jn 3:13-17 and ask for the grace to know the healing power of the Cross of Jesus.

3. Consider the story of Cardinal Van Thuan in prison. Pray with Sg 5:2-8 or Mt 5:38-48 and ask for the grace to love your enemies and pray for your persecutors.

4. Ponder Dr. Tom Dooley's medical mission in Indochina. Pray with Lk 6:6-19 and ask for the grace to be aware of the suffering in the world, and to bring Christ's healing and solace.

5. Reflect on the Vietnam war veteran's healing through the Sacrament of Anointing. Pray with Jas 5:13-20 and ask for the grace to realize the healing power of Christ the Divine Physician flowing through you as his priest.

Chapter 16

Columns of Strength

What is your beloved more than another beloved,
O fairest among women?
What is your beloved more than another beloved,
that you thus adjure us?
My beloved is all radiant and ruddy,
distinguished among ten thousand.
His head is the finest gold;
his locks are wavy,
black as a raven.
His eyes are like doves
beside springs of water,
bathed in milk,
fitly set.
His cheeks are like beds of spices,
yielding fragrance.
His lips are lilies,
distilling liquid myrrh.
His arms are rounded gold,
set with jewels.
His body is ivory work,
encrusted with sapphires.
His legs are alabaster columns,
set upon bases of gold.
His appearance is like Lebanon,
choice as the cedars.

His speech is most sweet,

and he is altogether desirable.

This is my beloved and this is my friend,

O daughters of Jerusalem.

Whither has your beloved gone,

O fairest among women?

Whither has your beloved turned,

that we may seek him with you?

My beloved has gone down to his garden,

to the beds of spices,

to pasture his flock in the gardens,

and to gather lilies.

I am my beloved's and my beloved is mine;

he pastures his flock among the lilies. (Sg 5:9–6:3)

On my first visit to Jerusalem as a priest in 1997, our group went to pray at the Wailing Wall, the last vestige of the Holy Temple of God. The lower stones of the remaining foundation are massive and visible, each weighing about two tons, making an impression of the enormity of the temple. I was next in line to pray, ready to take my turn, when a rabbi approached me and asked for a donation to the school for children across the terrace. I said, sure, but pointed to the wall and told him it was now my turn to pray and that I would give him a donation afterward. I went forward, covered my head with the hood of my jacket, and began to bob my head back and forth like the Jews. In the rhythm of this prayer, I was thinking of Jesus himself praying this way in the temple. In the profundity of the moment, the *Anima Christi* prayer came to mind, which I pray every day after holy Communion: "Soul of Christ, make me holy, Body of Christ be my salvation …" I felt myself having an intense encounter with Jesus in his sacred humanity. Deep into this moment, I felt a tap on my shoulder. I opened my eyes to see the rabbi with his hand out, asking me again for the donation. Perturbed, I said, "yes, but I'm still praying. I said I would give it to you when I was finished!" He backed off. I tried to get back into the rhythm and depth of my prayer, but with difficulty, so I ended it, and started to walk back in the reverse direction I had come. The rabbi swooped in like a vulture and collected his donation from me. I thought to myself that not much has changed in two thousand years, when Jesus was angry with the moneychangers and animal sellers who disrupted prayer in the Temple.

Jesus cleansed the Temple because zeal for his Father's house consumed him (cf. Jn 2:17). He drove out the buyers and sellers, and overturned the tables of the money changers saying, "It is written, 'My house shall be called a house of prayer;' but you are making it a den of robbers." (Mt 21:13). The sellers were cheating the pilgrims, many of whom were poor, by charging them exorbitant prices for the animals of sacrifice. Many of the Jews were coming from neighboring countries and had to exchange currency. The moneychangers gouged them with a very unfair exchange rate, so it was a terrible injustice, especially to those who were poor. The moneychangers were set up right inside the temple courts. The outermost court was the Court of the Gentiles, reserved for gentiles who might also wish to come and pray during the Passover. The cacophony of the negotiations and animal noises, along with the commotion of the marketplace, must have made it nearly impossible for anyone to pray. Jesus expected the sellers and moneychangers to have reverence for God, and respect for the faithful.

After Jesus turned over their tables, these same Jews then said to him, "What sign can you show us for doing this?" Jesus answered them, "Destroy this temple, and in three days I will raise it up." The Jews then said, "This temple has been under construction for forty-six years, and will you raise it up in three days?" John then tells us: "But he was speaking of the temple of his body" (Jn 2:19-21). Jesus would die and after three days be raised up again in his resurrection. The rejection and crucifixion of Jesus means at the same time the end of this Temple. The era of the Temple is over. A new worship is being introduced, in a Temple not built by human hands. Pope Benedict XVI explains:

> This Temple is his body, the Risen one, who gathers the peoples and unites them in the sacrament of his body and blood. He himself is the new Temple of humanity. The crucifixion of Jesus is at the same time the destruction of the Old Temple. With his Resurrection, a new way of worshipping God begins, no longer on this or that mountain, but 'in spirit and truth' (Jn 4:23).[1]

The Temple of the Body

The Temple prefigured Jesus, and Jesus fulfilled the meaning and purpose of the Temple in his very being. The prayer of the People of God flourished in the shadow of God's dwelling place, first the Ark of the Covenant and later the Temple.

> The Temple was to be the place of their education in prayer: pilgrimages, feasts and sacrifices, the evening offering, the incense, and the bread of the Presence ("shewbread")—all these signs of the holiness and glory of God Most High and Most Near were appeals to and ways of prayer.[2]

---

[1] Pope Benedict XVI, *Jesus of Nazareth, Holy Week, From the Entrance into Jerusalem to the Resurrection* (San Francisco: Ignatius Press, 2011), 21-22.

[2] *Catechism of the Catholic Church*, 1580-81.

But ritualism often encouraged an excessively external worship. The people needed education in faith and conversion of the heart.

The Temple was the sign of God's presence, his nearness, and his care. It was also a symbol of God's transcendence and glory. In Jesus' humanity, God drew close to us and cared for us. "He is able to deal gently with the ignorant and wayward since he himself is subject to weakness" (Heb 5:2). In Jesus' divinity, God transcends us and remains the all-powerful mystery. The precious elements that made up the Temple were meant to instill awe and reverence for God. The Temple was ordered to worship, sacrifice and holiness, through the ministry of the priests. "Every high priest chosen from among mortals is put in charge of things pertaining to God on their behalf, to offer gifts and sacrifices for sins" (Heb 5:1). Christ in his paschal mystery revealed himself to be the priest, the altar, and the sacrifice.[3] He did not offer an external sacrifice of an animal. He instead offered his own body as sacrifice. "Consequently, when Christ came into the world, he said, 'Sacrifices and offerings you have not desired, but a body you have prepared for me; in burnt offerings and sin offerings you have taken no pleasure. Then I said, 'See, God, I have come to do your will, O God'" (Heb 10:5-7).

Jesus assumed human flesh. Let us consider how remarkable a structure the human body is with some amazing facts. The human body consists of some 206 bones which can bear up to twenty-four thousand pounds per square inch, or four times the endurance of steel. Our bones are encompassed by six hundred and fifty different muscles that move with coordinated balance. If all our six hundred and fifty muscles were to pull together in one direction, we could lift twenty-five tons. The small organ of the heart can pump two thousand gallons of blood each day through the sixty thousand miles of arteries and veins that make up our circulatory system.

---

[3] See *Roman Missal*, Preface 5 for Easter Season.

The human brain weighs less than three pounds, yet one brain is composed of more connections and circuitry than the largest computer on earth.[4] Finally, consider the astonishing living cells of the human body. The cell is the smallest functioning unit in the human body. It can be likened to a city so tiny that it is invisible yet having millions of accesses that open and close. The cell possesses a transportation system, libraries of information, manufacturing plants, computers, and much else. Imagine each of these microcities replicating itself in an afternoon.[5] The human body is an amazing work of engineering fashioned by God.

Christ's body became the locus of his sacrifice of his whole being to God. The body is the visible, tangible, and complete self-gift to God joined together with soul and spirit (cf. 1 Thes 5:23). Christ, in his Incarnation, assumed a body to make a complete sacrifice to God. As a mediator between God and man he completely shared both a divine nature and a human, bodily nature. As members of Christ's body, we worship within the Temple of his Body, the Church, in spirit and in truth (cf. Jn 4:24). We no longer offer external animal holocausts, but our own bodies in sacrifice. St. Paul exhorts the Corinthians to chastity: "Do you not know that your body is a temple of the Holy Spirit within you, which you have from God, and that you are not your own? For you were bought with a price; therefore, glorify God in your body" (1 Cor 6:19-20). Our bodies are sacred as God's sanctuary and can also be a place of sacrifice to God. Our bodies are not just part of us, we *are* our bodies, just as we are also soul and spirit. What we do with our bodies symbolizes our entire selves. Jesus offered himself as a complete gift to the Father and to each of us when he said, "This is my body" and "this is my blood." (Mk 15:22, 24).

---

[4] See Carl Koch and Joyce Heil, *Created in God's Image, Meditating on our Body* (Winona, MN: St. Mary's Press, 1991), 56-57.

[5] See *Newsweek*, "Secrets of the Human Cell," August 20, 1979, p. 49.

Through celibate chastity, the priest offers his body as a sacrifice to God in imitation of Jesus, who chose to remain celibate. One's sexual powers for unitive and procreative purposes are among the most precious gifts one can offer as a sacrifice. "I appeal to you therefore, brothers, by the mercies of God, to present your bodies as a living sacrifice, holy and acceptable to God, which is your spiritual worship" (Rom 12:1). God uses such a gift to make us priests spiritually generative of new life in Christ and in his Church. Eusebius, the early Church historian, notes:

> And this explanation of the ancient men of God begetting children cannot be said to apply to the Christians today, when by God's help through our Savior's Gospel teaching we can see with our own eyes many peoples and nations in city and country and field all hastening together, and united in running to learn the godly course of the teaching of the Gospel, for whom I am glad to say we are able to provide teachers and preachers of the word of holiness, free from all ties of life and anxious thoughts. And in our day these men are necessarily devoted to celibacy that they may have leisure for higher things; they have undertaken to bring up not one or two children but a prodigious number, and to educate them in godliness, and to care for their life generally.[6]

The sacrifice of celibacy frees the priest to beget and care for his spiritual children more effectively. "The unmarried man is anxious about the affairs of the Lord, how to please the Lord; but the married man is anxious about

---

[6] Eusebius of Caesarea, *Demonstration of the Gospel*, 1:9, Transl. W.J. Ferrar, Early Church Fathers–Additional Texts Website, Ed. Roger Pearse, http://www.tertullian.org/fathers/eusebius_de_03_book1.htm

the affairs of the world, how to please his wife, and his interests are divided." (1 Cor 7:32b-34a).

Jesus, in the cleansing of the Temple (Mt 21:13) refers to the passage
in Isaiah, "my house shall be called a house of prayer for all peoples" (Isa
56:7) in which Isaiah had prophesied the Christian priests who would remain celibate as foreign "eunuchs" in his house and within his walls in his
house of prayer, his Body, the new Temple.

> Let not the foreigner who has joined himself to the Lord say,
> 'The LORD will surely separate me from his people'; and let not the
> eunuch say, 'Behold, I am a dry tree.' For thus says the LORD: 'To
> the eunuchs who keep my sabbaths, who choose the things that
> please me and hold fast my covenant, I will give in my house and
> within my walls a monument and a name better than sons and
> daughters; I will give them an everlasting name which shall not be
> cut off. And the foreigners who join themselves to the LORD, to
> minister to him, to love the name of the LORD, and to be his serv-
> ants, everyone who keeps the sabbath, and does not profane it, and
> holds fast my covenant— these I will bring to my holy mountain,
> and make them joyful in my house of prayer; their burnt offerings
> and their sacrifices will be accepted on my altar; for my house shall
> be called a house of prayer for all peoples.' (Is 56:3-7).

Scott Hahn notes that

> The Israelites considered Gentiles and eunuchs to be unclean, un-
> worthy to stand in God's presence. Eunuchs were men who had
> been castrated, deprived of the exercise of their sexuality, so that

they could be trusted to guard and serve a king's harem of wives. They were not quite men in the eyes of the world.[7]

Still, Isaiah prophesied a time when foreign eunuchs would come to God's holy Temple and offer priestly sacrifice, faithfully exercising true religion. Jesus invited all men who could accept the invitation to remain celibate to do so: "there are eunuchs who have made themselves eunuchs for the sake of the kingdom of heaven." (Mt 19:12). Hahn concludes: "Though the King of Kings has no harem, he loves his bride, and now calls a new class of celibates to guard his bride the Church."[8] Jesus remained celibate so that he could take the Church as his bride. He brought together Jews and Gentiles in his body, the Church, which is his temple.

In the Song of Songs, the bride describes her Bridegroom using images from the Temple. All the precious materials and symbols refer to Jesus as the Bridegroom who is the Temple. "It is certain that gold and ivory, metals, stones, and very precious woods, especially the cedars of Lebanon, which she evokes one after the other to describe him whom she loves, were indeed materials used in the construction and decoration of the Temple."[9] He is radiant and ruddy, distinguished among ten thousand, meaning that he has no equal. In Hebrew *kadosh*, or holy, means to be rare, exceptional in all creation, distinctly set apart, intricate and exalted. He is the holy one and the only one whom she loves and seeks. So, too, we keep the name of the Lord holy when he is our only love and our sole purpose in life is to seek him. As priests, we must be especially concerned to live holy lives, which means that God is always at the center. Vatican II reminded us that living lives of holiness in charity is the universal call of all Christians,

---

[7] Hahn, *Many are Called*, 128.

[8] Ibid.

[9] Arminjon, 259.

especially priests. "Priests who perform their duties sincerely and indefatigably in the Spirit of Christ arrive at holiness by this very fact."[10]

The Bridegroom's head is the finest gold. The Holy of Holies, where the Lord's presence dwelt, was at the head of the Temple of Jerusalem. Solomon had much gold placed there. "The inner sanctuary was twenty cubits long, twenty wide and twenty high. He overlaid the inside with pure gold, and he also overlaid the altar of cedar" (1 Kgs 6:20). Gold is a symbol of the divinity of Jesus, who was the purest of gold, without sin. Gold is not only beautiful, but it is an excellent conductor of electricity. As priests we conduct the power of God to the people, interceding before the Lord to bring divine gifts to them. We are called to mediate God to them with purity of intention, moral purity, and the pure doctrine of God. Pure gold is malleable and can be hammered into any shape. As priests we are called to be shaped according to God's will and plans for our lives. Finally, pure gold is radiant and reflects light gloriously. Our priestly lives are meant to purely reflect Jesus to others. Saint Gregory Nazianzen exclaims:

> We must begin by purifying ourselves before purifying others; we must be instructed to be able to instruct, become light to illuminate, draw close to God to bring him close to others, be sanctified to sanctify, lead by the hand and counsel prudently. I know whose ministers we are, where we find ourselves and to where we strive. I know God's greatness and man's weakness, but also his potential. Who then is the priest? He is the defender of truth, who stands with angels, gives glory with archangels, causes sacrifices to rise to the altar on high, shares Christ's priesthood, refashions creation,

---

[10] *Presbyterorum Ordinis*, 13.

restores it in God's image, recreates it for the world on high and, even greater, is divinized and divinizes.[11]

The locks of the Bridegroom's hair resemble the palm fronds decorating the gates of the Holy of Holies. His hair is black as a raven's, which symbolizes Christ's eternal youthfulness, as well as the strength and attractiveness of a young man in the prime of his life. With the strength provided by the Holy Spirit, we can vigorously perform the works of the Lord: "But those who wait for the Lord shall renew their strength, they shall mount up with wings like eagles, they shall run and not be weary, they shall walk and not faint" (Is 40:31). The Holy Spirit given to us at our ordination keeps us young in heart and gives us the energy to continue to lead his faithful people. Black also symbolizes the invisibility and incomprehensibility of God. The priest is the mysterious one who leads people into the transcendent mystery of God. "O the depth of the riches and wisdom and knowledge of God! How unsearchable are his judgments and how inscrutable his ways!" (Rom 11:33).

The Bridegroom's eyes are doves at a pool of water. Doves were an important decoration in the Temple. There was also the water basin of pools that made up the bronze sea of the Temple. The dove is a symbol of peace that can be seen in the serene eyes of the Prince of Peace. As priests, our eyes should convey peace to others and help instill the peaceful gaze of Christ in the hearts of others. The depths of water suggest the infinite depths of the inscrutable matters of the Spirit, which can only be probed by the Spirit. As priests, the Holy Spirit enables us to probe spiritual truths to convey them to others:

---

[11] St. Gregory Nazianzen, *Oratio* 2, 71, 74, 73: PG 35, 480-481.

These things God has revealed to us through the Spirit; for the Spirit searches everything, even the depths of God. For what human being knows what is truly human except the human spirit that is within? So also no one comprehends what is truly God's except the Spirit of God. Now we have received not the spirit of the world, but the Spirit that is from God, so that we may understand the gifts bestowed on us by God. And we speak of these things in words not taught by human wisdom but taught by the Spirit, interpreting spiritual things to those who are spiritual (1 Cor 2:10-13).

Sharing Christ's Mediatorial Role

The Bridegroom's cheeks are compared to the sweetly scented beds of spices that attract all who smell his fragrance. His lips are lilies that drip pure myrrh. The lips of Christ speak with flaming love the words of everlasting life. His lips breathe the Holy Spirit upon us who enters the innermost depths of our souls to recreate us. As we speak sincerely as priests sent from God and standing in his presence, "we are the aroma of Christ to God among those who are being saved and among those who are perishing" (2 Cor 2:15). The Bridegroom's hands are golden and set with jewels of Tarshish. Christ's hands extended his inner divinity to us by his actions. In his humanity he touches and embraces us. His hands were wounded by the nails on the cross. He hands us the bread of life which is his body. His hands are set with rare jewels from Tarshish, including the beryl stone which was set in gold on the high priest's breastplate when he acted as mediator on behalf of Israel (cf. Ex 28:20). Moses extended his arms in priestly intercessory prayer to enable the Israelites to win the battle against the Amalekites. So too, Christ our high priest extends his hands to the Father to forever intercede for us. "For there is one God; there is also one mediator between God and humankind, Christ Jesus, himself human, who gave himself as a ransom for all" (1 Tm 2: 5-6). In the very same passage, Paul exhorts us as priests to share in Christ's mediatorial role, "lifting up holy hands" (1 Tim. 2:8), urging that

> supplications, prayers, intercessions, and thanksgivings be made for everyone, for kings and all who are in high positions, so that we may lead a quiet and peaceable life in all godliness and dignity. This is right and is acceptable in the sight of God our Savior, who desires everyone to be saved and to come to the knowledge of the truth. (2 Tm 2:1-4)

The Bridegroom's belly is compared to the ivory columns that flank the gate of the Holy of Holies. "Bright ivory, a symbol of purity and innocence, suggests that his humanity had to undergo much suffering to be polished, so as to glisten with a spotlessly clean and pure love for all. Jesus's compassion came from his bowels of compassion."[12] As he wept at the death of his dear friend Lazarus, he was moved at the depths of his being. As priests we are filled with the compassion of Jesus which comes from his passion and death. We pray in the *Anima Christi*, "Passion of Christ, strengthen me." We are strengthened by Christ to be columns of strength, to be his compassionate heart to his people, fortifying them through the sacraments. The blue sapphires that cover the ivory body of the Bridegroom are the azure color of heaven, reflecting Christ's heavenly and perfect virtues, which we seek to imitate. [13] Finally, the Bridegroom's legs are alabaster columns set in sockets of pure gold. Christ's humanity, like legs strong as alabaster columns, is set into his divinity in sockets of pure gold.

---

[12] Maloney, 112.
[13] See Ibid.

Beloved Lover: The Priesthood in the Song of Songs

The humanity of Christ is the instrumental cause of our salvation because he is divine. St. Paul writes: "For in him the whole fullness of deity dwells bodily, and you have come to fullness in him, who is the head of every ruler and authority" (Col 2:9-10). According to St. Gregory Nazianzen, the priesthood far exceeds royal dignity as the soul exceeds the body. Even though the priesthood is practiced on earth, it belongs to the realm of the heavens. The emperor is more likely to go to the priest than the priest to the emperor when he needs any good thing from above. King and priest spheres of authority are distinct. The king's role is to exercise temporal power; the priest's authority derives from heaven, and everything the priest performs on earth is confirmed in heaven. The priest utilizes spiritual weapons, while the king uses physical ones. The head of the king is placed under the hand of the priest because the priest has greater power than the kings.[14]

Often throughout history, civil authorities have tried to usurp the authority of the Church's ministers and suppress her worship as the Body and Temple of Christ. Bishop Karol Wojtyla, in the face of communist repression, responded courageously in freedom to extend religious liberty. The Polish government established the first new communist city, Nowa Huta to be populated by industrial workers. No church was allowed to be built in the city or its environs, and Nowa Huta was to be a model of official atheism. In the face of such restrictive laws, Karol Wojtyla held outdoor masses in an open field, to which thousands flocked in all kinds of weather. In this, it became more evident that the Church was composed of persons and did not depend on mere bricks and mortar. His action was highly risky as Wojtyla could have easily been arrested and imprisoned for defying the

---

[14] See Gregory Nazianzen, "Julian the Emperor," Oration 4, *First Invective against Julian*, trans. C. W. King (London: Convent Garden, 1988), The Tertullian Project Website, https://www.tertullian.org/fathers/gregory_nazianzen_2_oration4.htm

authorities. He was always encouraging others to take calculated risks to further freedom, gradually pushing the government.

Two decades later he proposed to have the Ark Church built in Nowa Huta, symbolic of Mary, the Ark of the Covenant, through whom God was saving his people. The Church was built over ten years with all volunteer labor. It contains a stone from St. Peter's tomb at the foundation which was donated by St. Paul VI. Its exterior is decorated with 2 million small, polished stones from the riverbeds of Poland. The interior is dominated by a great steel figure of the crucified Christ forged by the workers at Nowa Huta's Lenin Steelworks. Austria donated a tabernacle shaped as a model of the solar system. The Church's decoration includes a piece of moon rock, given to St. Paul VI by an American astronaut. The Dutch donated the Church bells. It was Cardinal Wojtyla who in 1977 led the building campaign to its triumphant conclusion. When the church was finally built, he told the congregation of fifty thousand pilgrims from all over world who attended its consecration:

> This city of Nowa Huta was built as a city without God. But the will of God and the workers here have prevailed. Let us all take the lesson to heart. This is not just a building—these are living stones! ... This is not a city of people who belong to no one, of people to whom one may do whatever one wants, who may be manipulated according to the laws or rules of production and consumption. This is a city of the children of God ... This temple was necessary so that this could be expressed, that it could be emphasized.[15]

---

[15] Karol Wojtoya, in Adam Boniecki, "1977", in *The Making of the Pope of the Millenium, Kalendarium of the Life of Karol Wojtoya* (Stockbridge, MA: Marian press, 1977).

Wojtoya led the Church with authority in the name of Christ. He demonstrated the true freedom of the sons and daughters of God, how to live for God, to be abandoned to him, and to be led in his ways, no matter what the consequences.

Christ is unrivaled as the one who towers above all human persons, like the cedars of Lebanon (Sg 5:15). "He has Lebanon's incomparable splendor, incomparable in the eyes of the Jews, especially because of the high regal cedars covering the mountains, towering above all the other trees."[16] The priest leads people to the transcendence of the grace of Christ, to the things of eternity, which are incorruptible, as symbolized by cedar wood. "So, if you have been raised with Christ, seek the things that are above, where Christ is, seated at the right hand of God. ... When Christ who is your life is revealed, then you also will be revealed with him in glory" (Col 3:1, 4). The Bridegroom's speech is most sweet, and different from the ordinary words of men (cf. Sg 5:16). "Never has anyone spoken like this!" (Jn 7:46). The Lord's speeches speak to the bride's interior heart, at times sweetly and tenderly. As priests we communicate the speech of Christ. We prefer spiritual conversation, imbued with the values of Christ, to ordinary conversation. We desire to make Christ loved by all. "He is altogether desirable" (Sg 5:16) exclaims the bride. The priest's human personality becomes a bridge and not an obstacle for others to meet Jesus Christ as their Redeemer, and reveal his supremely loveable person:

> It is necessary that, following the example of Jesus who 'knew what was in humanity' (Jn 2:25; cf. Jn 8:3-11), the priest should be able to know the depths of the human heart, to perceive difficulties and

---

[16] Arminjon, 264.

problems, to make meeting and dialogue easy, to create trust and cooperation, to express serene and objective judgments.[17]

Beyond the Temple Walls

The bride, having contemplated in detail her Bridegroom's magnificent beauty, summarizes her discourse by saying that he is altogether loveable. Such is her Beloved, such is her friend (cf. Sg 5:16-17). She has described him to the best of her ability, but her words fall far short of his grandeur and transcendence. The Lord is the unutterable and unknowable, which no word can express. As many words try to express who he is, they are inadequate. The daughters of Jerusalem ask the bride where her Beloved has gone, that they too may seek him. She replies that he has gone down to his garden to pasture his flock there and to gather lilies. The verb *to go down* is often employed by the Hebrews to describe going down from the Temple in Jerusalem to the Holy Land. As transcendent and glorious as the Lord is in his temple, he stoops to seek out his beloved in her humble garden. As present as God is in the Temple, he will also be present in his bride's soul. When we celebrate the Holy Eucharist, we assist this entrance of God into the soul of his beloved bride. John Chrysostom instructs us:

> Would you also learn from another miracle the exceeding sanctity of this office? Picture Elijah and the vast multitude standing around him, and the sacrifice laid upon the altar of stones, and all the rest of the people hushed into a deep silence while the prophet alone offers up prayer: then the sudden rush of fire from Heaven upon the sacrifice: these are marvelous things, charged with terror. Now then pass from this scene to the rites which are celebrated in

---

[17] St. John Paul II, *Pastores Dabo Vobis*, 43.

the present day; they are not only marvelous to behold, but transcendent in terror. There stands the priest, not bringing down fire from Heaven, but the Holy Spirit: and he makes prolonged supplication, not that some flame sent down from on high may consume the offerings, but that grace descending on the sacrifice may thereby enlighten the souls of all and render them more refulgent than silver purified by fire. ... Do you not know that no human soul could have endured that fire in the sacrifice, but all would have been utterly consumed, had not the assistance of God's grace been great?[18]

This amazing, all-consuming mystery of the Lord's presence in the soul leads to an experience of union and mutual possession. The bride exclaims, "I am my beloved's and my beloved is mine" (Sg 6:3). In the book of Revelation, the city of God, the New Jerusalem, comes down from heaven like a bride prepared for her husband (cf. Rv 21:2). There is no longer a Temple, for the people of God, the Body of Christ are in Jesus Christ, the new Temple.

I saw no temple in the city, for its temple is the Lord God the Almighty and the Lamb. And the city has no need of sun or moon to shine on it, for the glory of God is its light, and its lamp is the Lamb. The nations will walk by its light, and the kings of the earth will bring their glory into it. Its gates will never be shut by day— and there will be no night there. (Rv 21:22-25)

---

[18] John Chrysostom, *Treatise concerning the Christian Priesthood*. In P. Schaff (Ed.), W. R. W. Stephens (Trans.), Saint Chrysostom: *On the Priesthood, Ascetic Treatises, Select Homilies and Letters, Homilies on the Statues* (Vol. 9, p. 47). (New York: Christian Literature Company, 1889).

The dimensions of the city measure evenly in length, height, and breadth to make a perfect cubic structure, recalling the Holy of Holies, which was an even cube in shape. The holiness of God in Jesus Christ is no longer confined to the physical structure of the Temple, or the Holy of Holies. Holiness is extended to wherever there are Christians, to the entire Church, the Body of Christ, the new Temple. Here, as priests we are invited to "worship the Lord in holy splendor" (Ps 29:2) with all God's holy people.

Questions for Reflection and Discussion

1. To what degree do I appreciate the goodness, dignity, and wonder of the temple of my human body? How well do I care for it and use it to glorify God? In what ways do I feel my body to be a drag on my humanity and a cross of suffering to bear?

2. In what way do I experience celibacy as a pleasing sacrifice to God of my body and sexuality that unites me more closely to Christ and frees me to proclaim the gospel more effectively? What is my experience of God's power of spiritual generativity working in and through me?

3. How well do I keep the name of the Lord holy as my only love and seeking him as my sole purpose in life? Do I realize that when I perform my duties sincerely, charitably, and untiringly in the Spirit of Christ I arrive at holiness?

4. Do I recognize in the priesthood a power greater than the royal power of kings or governors? How does this realization help me to be more courageous in speaking truth to power, especially in the face of cultural opposition?

5. How do I experience the Mass as calling down the fire of the Holy Spirit as an all-consuming mystery of the Lord's presence in the soul leading to an experience of union and mutual possession?

Prayer Exercises

1. Ponder the physical wonders of the human body. Pray with Heb 10:5-7 and ask for the grace to better appreciate the Word made flesh in the Incarnation.

2. Reflect on the Eusebius quote. Pray with 1 Cor 6:19-20 and Rom 12:1 and ask for the grace to offer yourself more fully to the Lord through the charism of celibacy.

3. Consider the symbolism of the temple—the gold, the palms, the doves, and the ivory—and their relation to the priesthood. Pray with Sg 5:9-6:3 and ask for the grace to appreciate the virtues of Christ's priesthood in your life.

4. Ponder the John Chrysostom quote about priestly dominion and the story of St. John Paul II at Nowa Huta. Pray with Col. 2:9-10 and ask for the grace to be courageous in speaking prophetically in our culture.

5. Reflect on John Chrysostom's quote about calling down the consuming fire of the Holy Spirit in the Mass. Pray with Rv 21:22-24 and Sg 6:3 and ask for the grace to be more receptive to the all-consuming mystery of the Lord's presence in the soul leading to union and mutual possession.

Chapter 17

Spiritual Accompaniment

You are beautiful as Tirzah, my love,
comely as Jerusalem,
terrible as an army with banners.
Turn away your eyes from me,
for they disturb me—
Your hair is like a flock of goats,
moving down the slopes of Gilead.
Your teeth are like a flock of ewes,
that have come up from the washing,
all of them bear twins,
not one among them is bereaved.
Your cheeks are like halves of a pomegranate
behind your veil.
There are sixty queens and eighty concubines,
and maidens without number.
My dove, my perfect one, is only one,
the darling of her mother,
flawless to her that bore her.
The maidens saw her and called her happy;
the queens and concubines also, and they praised her.
"Who is this that looks forth like the dawn,
fair as the moon, bright as the sun,
terrible as an army with banners?"
I went down to the nut orchard,
to look at the blossoms of the valley,

to see whether the vines had budded,

whether the pomegranates were in bloom.

Before I was aware, my fancy set me

in a chariot beside my prince.

Return, return, O Shu'lammite,

return, return, that we may look upon you.

Why should you look upon the Shu'lammite,

as upon a dance before two armies? (Sg 6:4-12)

Back in 1990, I was making my retreat at the National Shrine of Our Lady of Fatima in Washington, New Jersey before my first profession of vows as an Oblate of the Virgin Mary. I was praying with the Song of Songs for the first time, using a spiritual commentary. I began to pray with Chapter One, verse fourteen, where the Bridegroom calls his bride beautiful. I was struck with the fact that as human beings, God calls us beautiful. God creates us good and beautiful. Though disfigured by sin, we retain our essential beauty, which is restored by his redeeming us. He wishes us to know how beautiful we have become, especially interiorly by his grace of inner transformation. He desires us to surrender ourselves to his loving presence and his purification. This beauty begins to flow outward to others whom we meet. This was the crowning moment of my novitiate year, which had been so challenging for me, not only to grow, but to surrender to God's workings in me. After this prayer experience, I went to my Oblate retreat director and openly expressed everything that had happened, wondering what his reaction would be. Would he think I was foolish and deceived, entertaining romantic nonsense? No, he was perfectly affirming of my experience, understanding immediately what I had felt. He asked questions to draw out my experience and the implications of the grace received. I asked him what I should do with the experience. He simply encouraged me to linger with the grace, to soak in it, and let the Lord continue to lead me. He also urged me to make a gift of myself to God in some fashion. Having been affirmed by my retreat director, I continued to draw fruit praying with that scripture passage.

Transformation Through Spiritual Direction

Such is the gift of spiritual direction, which is one Christian helping another pay attention to God's personal communication, to respond to God, to grow in intimacy with God, and to live out the consequences of the relationship in greater freedom and commitment.[1] My director focused me on what God was saying to me, helped me deepen my union with Him, and assisted my response of surrender to Him. According to Trappist Monk Thomas Merton,

> The whole purpose of spiritual direction is to penetrate beneath the surface of a person's life, to get behind the façade of conventional gestures and attitudes which one presents to the world, and to bring out one's inner spiritual freedom, one's inmost truth, which is what [Christians] call the likeness of Christ in one's soul. This is an entirely supernatural (spiritual) thing, for the work of rescuing the inner person from automatism belongs first of all to the Holy Spirit.[2]

God breaks through our own egoism and opens us to a deeper immersion into the life of Christ within us. God's grace leads to greater peace and self-acceptance. He gives us the freedom to respond to his invitation to greater

---

[1] See William A. Barry, SJ and William J. Connolly, SJ, *The Practice of Spiritual Direction* (New York: HarperOne, 1986), 16.

[2] Thomas Merton, *Spiritual Direction and Meditation* (Collegeville, Liturgical Press, 1960), 16.

life, light, and love. We are better able to know God's presence in every situation. Spiritual direction is at the service of the Spirit in this transformational process.

The bride in the Song is undergoing a transformation, which is reflected in her awesome beauty, recognized by the Bridegroom.

> Now he describes her beauty after the many purifications that have led her not only to a deeper union with him, but also to a new harmony and integration within herself. ... Christ not only rejoices to see his image reflected in the Christian contemplative, but he eagerly wishes to receive the bride's beauty as a new love, a personal gift of herself to him.[3]

The Bridegroom is so enraptured by his bride's eyes gazing upon him that he entreats her to turn her eyes away because they hold him captive, and literally assault him (cf. Sg 6:5). She has ravished his heart with her beauty, and it seems too much to take. Marie of the Incarnation dares to say to the Lord, who caused her anguish by his seeming absence, "You enjoy tormenting me; I must have my revenge by inflicting on you the same wounds you gave me. ... Oh yes, I must have my revenge!"[4] He knows she will not turn away, and they are forever united as lovers. Yet he seems to have an ever-new appreciation of her beauty, which is ever-increasing. "Love always begets a new release of beauty. What the bridegroom earlier saw of beauty in his bride he now sees as more fully visible and more easily witnessed by his beloved."[5] She is much stronger in her increased perfection, like the fortified cities of Tirzah and Jerusalem, striking terror in her ene-

---

[3] Maloney, 120.

[4] Marie of the Incarnation, in Arminjon, 288.

[5] Arminjon, 121.

mies who are loath to attack her (cf. Sg 6:4). She now emerges terrible as an army in battle array. Her teeth are paired with one another, able to chew, eat and digest the word of God (cf. Sg 6:6). She chews and is nourished by the flesh of the Son of God in his Body and Blood of the Eucharist, and his word in the Scriptures. Her cheeks, like pomegranate halves, remain beautiful beneath her veil (cf. Sg 6:7). The red pomegranates suggest the passion and death of Christ, which is the source of her beauty. The bride in her hidden, veiled self (cf. Sg 6:7) remains hidden in the wounds of Christ: "For you have died, and your life is hidden with Christ in God. When Christ who is your life is revealed, then you also will be revealed with him in glory" (Col 3:3). She has put to death all that is not of God, and entered Christ's sufferings, dying to self, and living for God.

The bride symbolizes the Christian who wants to grow closer in union with God through spiritual direction, and the increase toward perfection that results. Priests, because of the dignity of their calling to be ministerial representatives of Christ, are especially called to a high degree of sanctity. The Angelic Doctor explains that the priest requires a great inner holiness to ascend to divine things, for "by holy orders a man is appointed to the most august ministry of serving Christ Himself in the sacrament of the altar."[6] And, "The worthy exercise of Orders requires not any kind of goodness but excellent goodness ... when they receive Orders they are given a yet greater gift of grace, whereby they are rendered apt for greater things."[7] They are regularly called to renew that gift of priestly grace given to them at their ordination: "I remind you to rekindle the gift of God that is within you through the laying on of my hands; for God did not give us a spirit of cowardice, but rather a spirit of power and of love and of self-discipline" (2 Tim 1:6). The Rite of Ordination exhorts the priest to

---

[6] *ST* II-IIae, 184, 8.

[7] *ST*, Supplement, 35, 1, ad 3.

meditate on God's word, to believe what he reads, to teach what he believes, and to practice what he teaches.[8] The priest must draw disciples to Christ by his words and actions and so edify the Church. The priest must interiorize and appropriate the mystery he celebrates on the sacrificial altar by deeply penetrating the mystery of Christ through contemplative prayer. The priest will then radiate Christ to others and draw them to seek holiness of life.

Why We Need Spiritual Direction

The priest has so much to juggle in his life. He must balance prayer and action. His life is ordered to evangelization, but he must also attend to his own sanctification. He must have an intimate knowledge of God's word and sacred theology, while also having a grasp of our contemporary culture, to dialogue with society. The priest maintains a multitude of pastoral and social relationships, and at the same time must tend to the "parish" of his own soul in solitude. While entering the sorrows of his people with heartfelt compassion, he cannot let himself over-identify with their sufferings. Spiritual direction will help him maintain proper balance in his life, giving each situation its due attention. Having a daily prayer schedule will open his soul to God's power to accomplish all that is necessary. He will be led by the Spirit. I find that when I as a priest am disciplined in my life of prayer, God orders my day. I am more open to the Spirit's promptings and able to spontaneously respond more generously. If I do not pray, my day seems more chaotic, and I feel more disconnected to God and his plan for my life.

The priest who receives spiritual direction is better prepared to offer it

---

[8] See *Rite of Ordination of Priests* (Washington D.C.: United States Conference of Catholic Bishops), 62.

to others. There is such a great need for direction in our Church today. Pope Benedict XVI wholeheartedly recommended the practice of spiritual direction to those who wish to follow the Lord closely, indeed to every Christian who wishes to live conscientiously one's baptism and the new life in Christ. He says: "Everyone, in fact, and in a particular way all those who have received the divine call to a closer following, needs to be supported personally by a sure guide in doctrine and expert in the things of God."[9] The Holy Father notes how a spiritual guide helps ward off subjectivist interpretations of religious experiences as well as providing the counseled with the guide's own reservoir of knowledge and experiences in following Jesus. This avoids the pitfalls of a solitary appraisal and a peculiar individuality. Benedict compares spiritual direction to the "personal relationship that the Lord had with his disciples, that special bond with which he led them, following him, to embrace the will of the Father (cf. Lk 22:42), that is, to embrace the cross."[10] God has ordained that we as Christians walk the spiritual journey together, not as autonomous, isolated individuals. We are a Church of communion and God's grace is often mediated to us through one another.

Spiritual direction has always been my favorite ministry. What can be more rewarding than helping someone draw closer to Christ on a sustained basis? In spiritual direction, there is a profound intimacy that develops among God, the directee, and the director. I am privileged as a director to see deeply into the soul of another, at that most profound place of encounter between the person and God. It offers me an opportunity to contemplate God and his workings in his beloved people throughout my day. God reveals his truth to the directee, not only for the directee's benefit,

---

[9] Pope Benedict XVI, *Address to the Pontifical Theological Faculty Teresianum*, May 19, 2011, Zenit Website, https://catholicismpure.wordpress.com/2011/05/20/pope-recommends-spiritual-direction-to-everyone/

[10] Ibid.

but for my own benefit as well. I am constantly nourished with spiritual food as I receive insights about God and his relationship with us. For me it offers endless fascination with the wisdom of the divine. The preacher and storyteller John Shea once helped a spiritual directee when her dear doctor died, his death leaving her wondering how she would get through the upcoming funeral. She called at a most inconvenient time on a Sunday morning at 7:00 a.m. After processing her experience with him, she apologized for her timing as she was leaving. He said it was no problem, that he was up early anyway. Afterwards, he thought to himself:

> I wanted to tell her there was no inconvenience, only feast. I wanted to tell her that I would rather be here than any place on earth. I wanted to tell her that when the hardened terrors of her mind relented and the subtle Spirit emerged with its meek unyielding strength, I shared her aliveness and drank from her well. I wanted to tell her that in the world of the Spirit, giving and receiving turn mutual and the "sower and reaper may rejoice together" (Jn 4:36). I wanted to tell her that when she opened her soul, it was the Grand Canyon to me.[11]

Christian perfection is a challenging art, and the guidance of the human soul is a delicate project. It would be presumptuous to expect great spiritual growth and perfection without a master to guide the soul. According to theologian Segundo Galilea,

> The way of prayer is full of insecurities, illusions, subtle temptation, deceptions, and confusion. Prayer has criteria, certain prin-

---

[11] John Shea, *On Earth as It Is in Heaven* (Collegeville, MN, Liturgical Press, 2004), 181.

ciples and "laws," confirmed by the spiritual tradition of the church, bringing to mind the saying that "no one is judge of his or her own case." For that reason, it is an axiom of Christian spirituality that pray-ers, above all in the long period of their training, need the guidance of another person who is competent and experienced. The counselor (advisor, spiritual director, confessor—the name does not matter) is of primary importance for education and progress in prayer.[12]

We are not meant to walk the spiritual journey alone, which would be an expedition fraught with peril. St. Bernard wrote: "Let those listen who without a guide and without a teacher dare to enter upon the ways of life playing both the teacher and the pupil in the art of the spirit. ... How many are they who have thus been found to have most dangerously abandoned the right path!"[13] John of the Cross warned: "He who insists on being left to himself, without a director to guide him, is like an unowned tree by the wayside; however fruitful it may be, then travelers pick its fruits and none of it ripens." Spiritual direction is especially important for those who are leaders in the Church. Those who lead others should submit themselves to others in order that they might behave better and more prudently. The benefits of direction are noticeable and beneficial to both pastors and other church leaders. We often offer spiritual direction through the Lanteri Center for Ignatian Spirituality to parish staff members. One woman, a married mother of three children, testified that growing in her relationship with God through spiritual direction enabled her to become a more effective disciple of Jesus. She said: "It has helped me to be more present to

---

[12] Segundo Galilea, *Temptation and Discernment* (Washington, D.C,: ICS Publications, 1996), 76.

[13] St. Bernard of Clairvaux, *Sermons on the Song of Songs*, 77, 6.

people at the parish and to listen to them better. It has helped me teach catechesis and lead OCIA [Order of Christian Initiation] in a deeper and more profound way."

Priests, by virtue of their ordination, are qualified to give spiritual direction. "By virtue of his office he is a director: it is for him to guide the religious and the simple faithful alike in the ways of perfection."[14] However, priests must develop the gift. Often it remains as an unopened gift because some priests have no clue about how to proceed in one-on-one spiritual guidance. It will help if they have a good experience of receiving spiritual direction, a director who models good technique. Being serious about one's own spiritual growth is a prerequisite to leading others in Christian perfection. As priests, we can offer this precious gift to others. As Pope Benedict XVI said, "The faithful expect only one thing from priests: that they be specialists in promoting the encounter between man and God. The priest is not asked to be an expert in economics, construction, or politics. He is expected to be an expert in the spiritual life."[15]

Developing the skill of spiritual direction is helped by reading books on the subject and perhaps even enroll in one of the many training programs where principles and practices can be learned. Role-playing in practica is an excellent way to hone one's skills in these courses. At the Lanteri Center, we teach a receptive, contemplative method of spiritual direction. The director is primarily a listener who encourages the directee to tell his or her story. The director listens with compassion, fully attentive and alert to key motions of the spirit. The director reflects to the person what he or she has said to help one clarify experiences of who God is and what He is

---

[14] Marmion, 69.

[15] Pope Benedict XVI, *Address to the Clergy*, Warsaw Cathedral, May 25, 2006, Libreria Editrice Vaticana, Vatican Website, http://www.vatican.va/content/benedict-xvi/en/speeches/2006/may/documents/hf_ben-xvi_spe_ 20060525_poland-clergy.html

asking. There may be moments where we do offer our insights based upon our own experience and wisdom of walking the Christian journey, but spiritual direction is less about us imparting our knowledge to the directee.. Sometimes people have gaps in their understanding of faith, prayer, and the spiritual life. As directors, we do not go into a session thinking we have all the answers. We are very receptive to learning new insights about the spiritual life based on the directee's experience of God. It is often difficult at first for a directee to articulate one's experience of God. One feels clumsy in finding the language to describe it. Nevertheless, as a directee expresses oneself, he or she usually arrives at greater clarity. As directors we act as a kind of sounding board to help a person understand God more clearly. When sound bounces off a literal sounding board, not only does it reach more people, but it also comes across more clearly. Likewise, *bouncing* ideas off another person can lend clarity to one's thought processes. If someone comes to another and says, "How does this sound?" and leaves with his or her mind made up (whether or not the listener ventured a word), the listener has served as a very effective sounding board. Through direction, a person arrives at greater reflective awareness of God's presence and activity in one's life.

Spiritual direction will foster growth in holiness when there is accountability, specificity, and realistic expectation.[16] It should be acknowledged from the outset that there will be an expectation that the directee will engage in some daily contemplative prayer with Sacred Scripture and some other religious practices. Meeting regularly with a director is an occasion to reckon with oneself about one's prayer discipline and to summarize what has been happening and where one is finding God in prayer and in daily life. It is also a stimulus to pray when a person knows one must

---

[16] See Robert Morneau, *Spiritual Direction, Principles and Practices* (New York: Crossroad, 1992), 92.

report one's progress or regress to one's director. Goals should be reasonable and achievable. A person should not try to do too much too soon. Using the analogy of physical fitness, we do not introduce extreme workouts when a person is just beginning to get into shape; rather, we gradually introduce more as the person becomes more spiritually fit and ready.

Discernment Through Spiritual Direction

There is room for gentle confrontation in direction, always with loving care to keep a person honest and unmask illusions that can be deceiving. One director challenged a directee who was caught up in busyness and was falling away from faithfulness to a grace received. He asked her what had been happening:

> Jean: Prayer's been one round of distractions, really; home, work, the church—they all just crowd in. And I'm just so busy; there's no time really.
>
> Joe: You know, it might be a good idea if we could take a look together at just what has been happening the last couple of months while you've been seeing me.
>
> Jean: That could be a good idea.
>
> Joe: How do you see it, Jean? I know you enjoy our exchanges, but there's more to it than that, isn't there?
>
> Jean: Well, I wanted a deeper, closer relationship with the Lord and I'm seeing that in a wider context of the family, the church, and work, bringing him into all those areas. That's what's been happening.
>
> Joe: I think I see it in a somewhat more detailed way. I was very moved a couple of months ago when you shared your experience of

hearing the Lord say to you, "My daughter." Do you remember that? You were going to go back to that, and you were going to talk to the Lord about your relationship with your own father. That intention seemed to fade, though. Then there was your experience of Jesus as a friend. That was very strong. After that, time with the Lord seemed to get crowded out. You were going to pray over the choices you felt you were faced with and you talked about your own riches and following the Lord. Some of these have been pretty important issues for you, but you've never followed through with any of them.

Jean: That's very true.

Joe: What stops you, Jean?

Jean: I'm scared, really, afraid I might find out I'm not the sort of person I'd like to be. I'm really afraid.

Joe: What's the worst that might happen?

Jean: I'd find out I'm pretty worthless and incompetent and I'd run away.

Joe: How would you feel if you did?

Jean: I don't know; pretty ashamed, I guess.

Joe: How do you think the Lord would feel?

Jean: Oh, I just need to hear him say "My daughter, your sins are forgiven."[17]

In this exchange, Joe questions why Jean has forgotten about the grace she received to be a spiritual daughter of the Father. By gently questioning her, he can help her to return to a realization of God's unconditional, merciful love.

One major goal of spiritual direction is discernment of the will of God,

---

[17] Barry and Connolly, 93-94.

which is recognizing what God is asking of us and responding to the concrete life situations we encounter in following our calling. The spiritual director helps a person discover one's giftedness. One comes to identify, develop, and use one's gifts, which might be concealed beneath a poor self-image. Realizing and affirming one's gifts makes a person come alive interiorly. We help a person to self-knowledge, leading to self-acceptance, which in turn moves a person to self-gift in love. The spiritual director helps directees to discern God's will, which is an art that relies more on God-inspired intuition than observable signs. St. Ignatius of Loyola offers principles and techniques for discerning God's will that primarily involves both paying attention to God's Spirit moving our hearts and a supernatural prudence that evaluates choices based on positive and negative reasons.

A woman named Karen describes how a priest helped her discern God's will for her life:

> I had a good job, but I wasn't happy with the environment at work. I was also working with young adults at the parish and that was fulfilling. I wasn't sure what God wanted. Should I continue in my job? Go on for my PhD.? Was it time to think more seriously about religious life? I just didn't know. I had no spiritual director, so I phoned a priest I knew and we talked. He gave me the name of another priest who did spiritual direction, and I met with that priest. We've been meeting since then. It wasn't easy at first. I didn't know what spiritual direction was, and I wasn't yet ready to trust. But it has helped me a lot as I continue to discern. The director helped me to bring God into things, to become aware of God's presence throughout the day. I talk to God and he talks to me; sometimes I don't listen. It took me awhile to see how God speaks, and I'm still learning a lot. I write things down so that I

can look back over them.[18]

The spiritual director offers encouragement along one's spiritual journey, which is often marked with many trials. There are temptations to quit, and we need perseverance and supernatural fortitude. According to the Catechism:

> Our battle has to confront what we experience as failure in prayer: discouragement during periods of dryness; sadness that, because we have "great possessions," we have not given all to the Lord; disappointment over not being heard according to our own will; wounded pride, stiffened by the indignity that is ours as sinners; our resistance to the idea that prayer is a free and unmerited gift; and so forth. The conclusion is always the same: what good does it do to pray? To overcome these obstacles, we must battle to gain humility, trust, and perseverance.[19]

Acedia or "sloth" is a distaste for spiritual things that can afflict us and lead to sadness and discouragement. It is helpful to have a knowledge of St. Ignatius' teaching on discernment of spirts to understand the origin of certain spiritual movements, to accept those from God and to reject those from the enemy spirit—the world, the flesh, and the devil. "Resist the devil and he will flee from you" (Jas 4:7). The director helps a person guard and react against spiritual discouragement. The devil will also try to distract us from our fundamental identity and mission by giving deceptive consolations that are based on subtleties and false reasonings.[20] For instance, St.

---

[18] Timothy Gallagher, *Discerning God's Will* (New York: Crossroad, 2009), 60.

[19] *Catechism of the Catholic Church*, 2728.

[20] See St. Ignatius of Loyola, *Spiritual Exercises*, par. 329.

John Vianney was tempted to flee from his parish duties and join a monastery. He fell prey to the temptation not once, not twice, but three actual times! He was summoned to return each time either by the bishop or the people who came to retrieve him. As time went on, he realized that the enemy proposed monastic life as a subtle deception to distract him from his true identity and calling.

There are many aspects of reality and experiences that we need to integrate in our spiritual life. Some of these phenomena are seemingly contrary and need to be balanced in a wholistic spirituality. Prayer, which is more passive, receptive, and unifying, must be integrated with apostolate, which is more active, assertive, and dispersive (of attention and energy). Leisure is more about rest, wonder, and celebration, while work is more about expending effort, remaining more narrowly focused on tasks and production. Jesus taught Martha and Mary that work and prayer, though different, were two "parts" of an integrated life. There is also the *kataphatic* experience of God through images, concepts, and real knowledge which must be balanced with the opposite *apophatic* experience of God without images and concepts, respecting God as being far beyond human knowledge and categories. One may alternate between experiences of light and darkness at different stages of the Christian journey. God is immanent, nearer than my nearest, closer to me than I am to myself; by contrast, God is also transcendent, higher than my highest being or thought. Obedience to the Law of God ironically leads to greater freedom in the Spirit. I am called to a mature, responsible faith while at the same time I need to become childlike in dependence on God. I must hold these contrary realities in tension. God can be experienced primarily in my thinking or more as a deeply felt reality. I should pay attention to both thoughts and feelings about God. There is the truth of my own spiritual poverty and weakness to be understood within the opposite context of God's strength. A spiritual director can help me realize that there are times when I feel I might be regressing in the spiritual life when, John of the Cross tells us, I may actually be making progress. God might be leading me to a new stage of simplified prayer, or a new level of dependence on him.

When I do receive a grace or inspiration from the Holy Spirit, I must integrate that truth into my daily life and way of thinking. This is not always easy and takes time. When Paul became aware of Jesus Christ's presence on the road to Damascus, he was blinded. He needed the help of another, Ananias to regain his sight. He consulted with Apostles and teachers of the faith. It took him about eight years to integrate his Christian faith with all that he had known as a devout Hebrew before he was ready to go on missionary journeys and begin to establish churches. It takes time, energy, and attention to develop the mind of Christ by the power of the Holy Spirit.

A spiritual director can greatly facilitate the process of integration. One directee received the grace to become a child of God, but continually resisted it. His director asked him what was difficult?"

> Directee: Being a child of God. I mean you have to really give yourself; you have to sacrifice so much. It's worth it if you get that wonderful feeling of joy, but when nothing comes in return for it …
>
> Director: Did it seem like a sacrifice when you were feeling good about everything?
>
> Directee: No, I felt like I was giving—no, it was more like God was giving Himself through me to others. No, it didn't seem like I was doing anything special … well, I did start giving at some point. I remember I was thinking "This is wonderful … I can express God's love so fully. … I can do for others, be for others, a symbol of God's love." I suppose I started to *do* it more.

Director: Did it get to be too much? For a while you felt so close to God, and all that love was just coming through you, and then after a while maybe you started trying to do it yourself. Then perhaps it was a little less God and a little more you? Maybe it was too much not to be *doing* anything for *yourself*. It's possible that that's where the real sacrifice was, that you weren't doing it yourself.

Directee: That sounds right. I can feel myself relaxing as you talk. But it's crazy. There didn't seem to be any distress until I started trying to do it myself. Before that everything just flowed. I just flowed, the world just flowed, God just flowed through it all. It was so delicious. … It's crazy that I'd pull away from that. Yes, but I know I've always pulled away. That's the story of my life; I keep pulling away just when things start seeming perfect. That's the same old thing. I know what I need to do. I need to take a deep breath and relax again. … Oh, I don't have to do it all.[21]

The spiritual director assists the Holy Spirit, who is the true director. "The spiritual director is not making the spiritual journey; he follows it by assisting the person he is directing in his concrete life. The Holy Spirit is the one who directs souls and therefore the spiritual director should always support the action of the Holy Spirit."[22] The direction given by the Holy Spirit emerges from within the directee. God lovingly works specifically in and through each person to purify and transform. As directors, we should

---

[21] Gerald May, *Care of Mind/Care of Spirit* (San Francisco: HarperCollins, 1992), 57-58.

[22] *The Priest, Minister of Mercy*, par. 103, Congregation for the Clergy (Vatican City, Libreria Editrice Vaticana, 2011), Clerus Website, https://www.clerus.org/clerus/dati/2011-08/08-13/sussidio_per_confessori_en.pdf.

never impose or coerce our own spirituality on the directee, because God might be leading us in a different way than our directees. We cannot fit people into a mold or categorize them according to a class of persons. Rather we guide them according to the way the Spirit is already leading. It is our goal so perceive the spirit at work and help the person notice the presence and action of the Spirit. According to St. John of the Cross:

> The whole concern of the director should be not to accommodate souls to his own way or to what suits him. Rather he ought to see if he can discern the particular way along which God is leading them. If he cannot discern the way proper to each, he should leave them alone and not disturb them.[23]

The Need for Flexibility in Spiritual Direction

While we keep in mind certain principles of spiritual growth, we cannot engage directees with fixed plans and predetermined answers to their problems. Within the one way that is Christ Jesus, there are as many ways to God as there are individuals.[24] What is suitable for one person may not be applicable for another. According to the promptings of the Spirit, we spontaneously take people where they are, not where we expect them to be. The Spirit uses us in many different ways to lead people, sometimes challenging people with firmness and confrontation, and at other times encouraging them with gentleness and affirmation, and always with love.

The director helps a person to accept oneself in one's existential circumstances in relation to God, as God strips away the barriers that stifle

---

[23] St. John of the Cross, *Living Flame of Love*, 3, 46, in *The Collected Works of John of the Cross.*

[24] See Joseph Ratzinger, *Salt of the Earth, The Church at the End of the Millenium, An Interview with Peter Seewald* (San Francisco, Ignatius Press, 1997), 32.

the action of the Holy Spirit within. One woman describes her encounter with an Oblate priest who is her spiritual director:

> It has so much to do with the soul because you're trying to articulate intangible movements of the heart. It's unbelievably intimate. There's an amazing grace and amazing reverence. They're totally at the Lord's service, stewards, trying to help figure out what this person is trying to say. You won't realize the power of the relationship until you have an experience of God in the midst of direction that reveals God working in your heart. They have such a reverence, gentleness, tenderness of a spiritual father—not out of curiosity. You're allowing them to hold your soul in a way that no one else can. They know their sacred and holy responsibility. They hold your soul so reverently. … As priests they're ultimately stewarding the soul to Jesus. There's something about the safety and protection of it. I feel completely safe in their hands and hearts. They're defending your soul from evil too. There's a protection they have on your soul. I've entrusted them with this responsibility too by coming to them for this service. A spiritual father helps me "become me" in the Lord. … There was a place in myself that needed a spiritual father at the time to affirm me.[25]

We as directors help people to become *alter Christus*, "other Christs." Christ's image in their soul becomes more pronounced and recognizable through the process of spiritual direction.

The bride at this later stage in the Song resembles the Bridegroom, becoming more and more an *alter Christus*. He is seen to be terrible in his glory, surrounded by warriors, instilling fear in his enemies (cf. Sg 3:6-8).

---

[25] Cabrini Pak, *Men of Mercy, Sons of Mary*, 37.

She shines forth in glory, surrounded by queens and concubines, fair as the moon, bright as the sun and terrible as an army (cf. Sg 6:8-10). Enemies dare not attack her. She is even called the Bridegroom's perfect one, the only one, the flawless one (cf. Sg 5:6). Just as she resembles her Bridegroom, we are called to increasingly resemble Christ in his beauty and virtue. Christ is perfect and sinless. Though we always struggle with sin, we are called to overcome mediocrity and strive for perfection by the power of the Holy Spirit. St. Therese of Lisieux realized:

> Later on when perfection was set before me, I understood that to become a saint one had to suffer much, seek out always the most perfect thing to do, and forget self. I understood, too, there were many degrees of perfection and each soul was free to respond to the advances of the Lord, to do little or much for Him, in a word, to choose among the sacrifices He was asking.[26]

The bride finds herself lifted and set upon the chariot next to her prince. Through prayer and spiritual direction as means to holiness of life, we will draw close to Christ on his chariot, more closely resemble him, and move more swiftly in his ways toward our destination of eternal life.

Questions for Reflection and Discussion

1. What has been my experience of receiving spiritual direction in the past? How much of it was merely friendly conversation? To what extent was it helping me pay attention to God's personal

---

[26] St. Therese of Lisiesux, *The Story of a Soul: The Autobiography of St. Therese of Lisieux,* trans. John Clarke, O.C.D. (Washington, D.C:, ICS Publications, 1975), 27.

communication, to respond to God, to grow in intimacy with him, and to live out the consequences of the relationship in greater freedom and commitment?

2. How do I see spiritual direction as essentially different from counseling, teaching, confession, or mentoring?

3. Do I feel qualified as a priest to give spiritual direction? Do I value it as a ministry? In what ways am I equipped to offer direction? In what ways do I feel lacking and need to develop the gift?

4. How well do I as a priest achieve a balance of life between prayer and so much ministry? Am I comfortable integrating seemingly opposite experiences in prayer, such as contemplation/action, light/darkness in prayer, thinking/feeling about God, law/freedom, God's transcendence/immanence, willpower/reliance on grace, mature responsibility/childlike abandonment, etc.?

5. To what degree do I accept people where they are spiritually and help to guide them as the Spirit is already leading them? Do I realize there are as many ways to God as there are individuals and that I should not seek to conform souls to my own way, but help discern the way proper to each person?

Prayer Exercises

1. Reflect on the Merton quote about spiritual direction. Pray with Mt 3:13-17 and ask for the grace to know your identity in Christ.

2. Consider the description of the bride's transformation. Pray with Lk 9:38-46 and ask for the grace to experience growth in perfection by God's grace.

3. Ponder the priest's balancing act in life and ministry. Pray with Mk 1:32-39 and ask for the grace that the Lord order your day through prayer.

4. Reflect on John Shea's experience of the beauty of the soul in offering spiritual direction. Pray with Sg 6:4-12 and ask for the grace to see the goodness and beauty in people.

5. Consider the description of the Oblate priest and spiritual director. Pray with 1 Pt 5:1-11 and ask for the grace to exercise care of souls with love, compassion, and gentleness.

Chapter 18

Communion of Saints—and Sinners

Return, return, O Shu'lammite,
return, return, that we may look upon you.
Why should you look upon the Shu'lammite,
as upon a dance before two armies?
How graceful are your feet in sandals,
O queenly maiden!
Your rounded thighs are like jewels,
the work of a master hand.
Your navel is a rounded bowl
that never lacks mixed wine.
Your belly is a heap of wheat,
encircled with lilies.
Your two breasts are like two fawns,
twins of a gazelle.
Your neck is like an ivory tower.
Your eyes are pools in Heshbon,
by the gate of Bath-rab'bim.
Your nose is like a tower of Lebanon,
overlooking Damascus.
Your head crowns you like Carmel,
and your flowing locks are like purple;
a king is held captive in the tresses.
How fair and pleasant you are,
O loved one, delectable maiden!
You are stately as a palm tree,

and your breasts are like its clusters.

I say I will climb the palm tree

and lay hold of its branches.

Oh, may your breasts be like clusters of the vine,

and the scent of your breath like apples,

and your kisses like the best wine

that goes down smoothly,

gliding over lips and teeth.

I am my beloved's,

and his desire is for me. (Sg 6:13–7:10)

I once went on a pilgrimage through Greece in the footsteps of St. Paul and was exposed to Greek culture at its finest. The Greeks have a special dance called "perichoresis" that is meant to be performed by three dancers. The dancers begin to move in circular motion, looping in and out in a lovely pattern. As they continue to move in perfect rhythm and time with one another, they begin to move faster. They eventually become indistinguishable as they dance so swiftly and with such ease. Each of their unique selves is a component in a greater dance. The early Church Fathers observed the perichoresis dance and were impressed with it as an amazing representation of the Holy Trinity. In the Trinity there is reciprocal giving and receiving in a loving, harmonious relationship. The dance of love in the Holy Trinity serves as the inspiration for this perichoresis. The Trinity's three persons accommodate one another. They engage in reciprocal indwelling and solidarity through their dancing around and alongside one another. Perichoresis is the union of three equal individuals who are fully encompassed by one another in love and harmony, displaying an intimacy that is beyond human understanding. According to John 3:16, the Father sends the Son, and according to John 15:26, the Son sends the Spirit, a revelation of the perichoresis which graces God's people.

A Unifying Dance of Ecstasy

All three Persons of the Godhead glorify one another as a result of their bonds of love within the Trinity. Nothing divides the three individuals of the Trinity or halts the perichoresis's unfathomable exchange. A grand dance of love is in motion. Theological tradition had long ago interpreted the Trinitarian indwelling as communion in the first century. The notion of the perichoresis was developed in part by John of Damascus, who defined it as a "cleaving together." The Father, Son, and Spirit not only embrace one other, but they also enter into one another, permeate one another, and dwell inside each other in perfect communion. They are one in existence and are always one in the closeness of their communion. We interact with one another as humans in the movement of life here on earth. Our human dance is modeled after the three members of the Trinity and their dynamic, communicative, loving, and serving interactions.

Christ entices His wife, the Church, into this passionate "dance." Our destiny and dignity are to be drawn into the magnificent dance of the Trinity's love one day. Heaven is not a distant, frozen view of God; rather, it is a beatific vision, a dynamic experience of love, a dance of ecstasy. In the Song of Songs, the Bridegroom now asks the maidens why they are mesmerized by the dance of the Shulamite bride between two armies? (Sg 6:14) Her dance unites the two camps that had been divided, just as Jeremiah had imagined the unification of the two kingdoms of Israel and Judah after the Babylonian exile:

> Again I will build you, and you shall be built, O virgin Israel! Again, you shall take your tambourines, and go forth in the dance of the merrymakers. ... Then shall the young women rejoice in the dance, and the young men and the old shall be merry. I will turn

their mourning into joy, I will comfort them, and give them gladness for sorrow. (Jer 31:4, 13)

This unification is fulfilled in the Holy Catholic Church, the bride, and
Body of Christ, in whom all are united: "There is no longer Jew or Greek,
there is no longer slave or free, there is no longer male and female; for all
of you are one in Christ Jesus" (Gal 3:28). All peoples and nations are one
in Christ and in his Church: "After this I looked, and there was a great
multitude that no one could count, from every nation, from all tribes and
peoples and languages, standing before the throne and before the Lamb,
robed in white, with palm branches in their hands" (Rv 7:9). They are especially united in worship. The reciprocal dynamism of the dance between
God and God's creatures is found in the liturgical action of sacrament, celebrating the sacred mysteries in Eucharistic communion, described in
terms of continuity and apostolic unity.

The bride's dance suggests harmony and a flowing together in unity.
"Strong joints that fit the legs to the body and allow the athlete to run with
speed and coordination here aptly describe the bride's integration in perfect obedience to move under Christ's commands."[1] St. Paul aptly explains
how the Church as a body moves together in synchronicity in Christ: "we
must grow up in every way into him who is the head, into Christ, from
whom the whole body, joined and knit together by every ligament with
which it is equipped, as each part is working properly, promotes the body's
growth in building itself up in love" (Eph 4:15-16). Paul is concerned that
we are "making every effort to maintain the unity of the Spirit in the bond
of peace. There is one body and one Spirit, just as you were called to the
one hope of your calling, one Lord, one faith, one baptism, one God and
Father of all, who is above all and through all and in all" (Eph 4:3-6).

---

[1] Maloney, 132.

Horizontal Communion in the Body of Christ

The priest is called to be a man of communion, according to Jesus' intention "that they may all be one" (Jn 17:21). Of course, we begin with communion in the Holy Trinity, going to the Father, through the Son, in the Holy Spirit. We must abide in Christ as he abides in us, for without him we can do nothing. He calls us friends and we should cultivate that friendship in unceasing prayer. We are called to unity with our bishop who is the special presence of Christ in the diocese.

It is fitting, therefore, that you should be in agreement with the mind of the bishop as in fact you are. Your excellent presbyters, who are a credit to God, are as suited to the bishop as strings to a harp. So, in your harmony of mind and heart the song you sing is Jesus Christ. Every one of you should form a choir, so that, in harmony of sound through harmony of hearts, and in unity taking the note from God, you may sing with one voice through Jesus Christ to the Father. If you do this, he will listen to you and see from your good works that you are members of his Son. It is then an advantage to you to live in perfect unity, so that at all times you may share in God.[2]

Priests form a brotherhood, a true family and fraternity that emerges from ordination. They experience a special bonding when they go through an adventure together, especially one that is difficult and dangerous. Men who fight a battle in the trenches are willing to die for one another and

---

[2] St. Ignatius of Antioch, *Letter to the Ephesians*, Ch. 4, Crossroads Initiative Website, https://www.crossroadsinitiative.com/media/articles/unity-with-the-bishop/

develop a deep mutual admiration as a band of brothers. According to St. John Paul II:

> This grace takes up and elevates the human and psychological bonds of affection and friendship, as well as the spiritual bonds which exist between priests. It is a grace that grows ever greater and finds expression in the most varied forms of mutual assistance, spiritual and material as well. Priestly fraternity excludes no one. However, it can and should have its preferences, those of the Gospel, reserved for those who have greatest need of help and encouragement.[3]

When a fellow soldier goes down, wounded, he cannot be left stranded. All efforts must be made to save him. I have helped many priests in crisis through retreat ministry and spiritual direction. I find it rewarding to help bring healing to those most in need and help to preserve their priestly vocation. In some cases, priests have been on the verge of resigning their parish assignment or leaving the priesthood together. They have come with anger, bitterness, hurt, and discouragement in search of healing. God's grace working through spiritual direction and psychological counseling has rehabilitated them. We can never leave them behind.

Horizontal communion in the body of Christ only happens through vertical communion with the Lord. Our communion with the Lord is continually nourished through the Holy Eucharist, which makes the Church Christ's body. We ask in the Eucharistic Prayer that we who are fed by Christ's body and blood be filled with his Holy Spirit to become one in body and spirit in Christ. It is during the Mass that we experience the deepest level of communion with God and one another. Through his sacrifice,

---

[3] St. John Paul II, *Pastores Dabo Vobis*, 74.

the Lord brings about a communion that we could never achieve simply based on our goodwill or friendship. We often find that relationship happens through the Eucharist because it is already there in Christ.

The Bridegroom describes his union with the bride with Eucharistic overtones. Her belly is a heap of wheat, and her kisses are like fine wine that goes down smoothly, gliding over lips and teeth (cf. Sg 7:2-3). The mystical bride of Christ is beautiful because spiritually she is nourished by Christ's indwelling presence who comes to her in the fullest symbol of bread and wine, body and blood, fully God and fully man. That place of harvest of mystical union between bride and Christ is surrounded with lilies, which symbolize purity. The bride enters union with Christ only in the purity of heart where she lives totally and completely for Christ. She is intoxicated by his love and sees all reality in the light of his loving presence. Her love in return is likened to wine flowing over his lips and teeth.

The bride's belly is a "heap of wheat" (Sg 7:2). In the Church, the Body of Christ, the stomach must be considered a vital organ. As the saying goes, "an army marches on its stomach." An old African fable illustrates the stomach's importance. Once upon a time, various parts of the body began complaining against the stomach. "Look at me," says the hand, "I till the soil to plant the seeds, I harvest the crops, I prepare the food. All that the stomach ever does is lie there waiting to be fed. This is unfair."

The feet agreed, "Me, too, I carry the heavy stomach around all day, I carry him to the farm to get food, I carry him to the river to get water, I even carry him up the palm tree to get palm wine, and all the stomach ever does is lie there and expect to get his ration of food, water and wine whenever he needs them. This is unfair." The head, too, complained how he carries all the heavy load from the farm and from the river, all to feed the stomach that does nothing to help. The parts of the body decided that this injustice had to stop. To force the issue, they decided to embark on a protest action. They agreed to stop working and feeding the lazy stomach until the stomach learned to be a responsible citizen of the body. A whole day went by, and the stomach was not given any food or water or wine. All that the stomach did was groan from time to time while the others taunted him. By the second day of starving the stomach, the head said that he was beginning to feel dizzy. By the third day, the hands reported that they were feeling weak, and the feet were wobbly and could not stand straight. Then it dawned on them that, much as they were visibly supporting the stomach, the stomach was also supporting them in a less obvious but equally important way. It dawned on them that by feeding the stomach they were feeding themselves without knowing it. So, they called off their strike action and went back to work to feed the stomach. Their strength returned and together with their stomach they lived in harmony together from that day on.

The story makes the point that everybody in the community is making a vital contribution, even those who appear to do nothing but consume what others produce. The priest depends upon the entire Christian community for his support and livelihood. Yet he is the most necessary member of the body for its survival and flourishing. Of course, the priest labors tirelessly for the good of the Body of Christ: "Let the elders who rule well be considered worthy of double honor, especially those who labor in preaching and teaching; for the scripture says, … 'The laborer deserves to be paid'" (2 Tm 5:17-18). St. Paul reminds us:

> The eye cannot say to the hand, "I have no need of you," nor again the head to the feet, "I have no need of you." On the contrary, the members of the body that seem to be weaker are indispensable, and those members of the body that we think less honorable we clothe with greater honor, and our less respectable members are treated with greater respect … that there may be no dissension within the body, but the members may have the same care for one

another. If one member suffers, all suffer together with it; if one member is honored, all rejoice together with it. (1 Cor 12:21-24, 25-26)

When I was Associate Pastor at St. Andrew's parish in Avenel, New Jersey, we catechized the seemingly most useless members of the Body of Christ—the physically and mentally handicapped residents of the Developmental Center in our neighborhood. It was a team ministry begun by a laywoman who had a handicapped child. We would teach the residents on the most basic level that they were special, and that Jesus loved them. Our time spent with them was very interactive, and we often played games as simple as rolling a ball from one person to the next around the table. Every so often, we would hold a mass in the big hall for the residents. It was especially in the Holy Eucharist that the Spirit revealed to me the dignity of each of these children of God. The Eucharist was the hope for the restoration of their minds and bodies in eternity. I realized Jesus had come especially for such as these. Though by worldly standards they could do nothing of significance to contribute to society, they made a definite and profound gift of self to us as a Church. Christ, in his desire to give and receive love, shone through their hearts and faces.

Priests are called to deep communion with the people in their local church. He is not just a shepherd and father, but he is one of them as a brother, sharing in the same life of Christ by Baptism. Of course, we priests cannot be close friends with everyone, and the pastoral relationship takes precedence, but the brotherhood with all Christians is real. Priests need to experience fellowship not just as leaders in front of the people, but as brothers within the body of Christ. I have experienced this fellowship throughout my own priesthood. I rub elbows with the laity in setting up the church hall, cooking meals for the poor, or spending time with their sick relatives. In the ministry of retreats, spiritual direction, and teaching,

I collaborate with laypeople. I often pray with the faithful for their needs and my own. I love spending time in leisure activities with lay faithful and colleagues enjoying a nice meal, attending a jazz concert, skiing the mountains, or playing golf. We laugh at the divine intervention at work when my tee shot bounces off a tree and lands in the middle of a fairway. My friends must watch their tongue for profanities when they skull a golf shot, and so do I! Sometimes, I wince with pain as I genuflect at the consecration while celebrating mass together after skiing moguls all day. I enjoy cooking a meal for my brothers and sisters in the faith, then lingering into the evening in fellowship on the rectory patio. Sometimes, the conversation is light and fun; other times it goes deep into theological and spiritual questioning. God is remarkably present in those moments, and I feel deep communion with Christ and my brothers and sisters in the faith.

Priests are called to extend this communion with God and one another to all peoples, not just the members of our fold. Priests are not just pastors of Catholics in their parish, but to all people in their sphere of influence. Experiencing the joy of this communion we are impelled with desire to share this gift with everyone. St. John Paul II explains:

> Precisely because within the Church's life the priest is a man of communion, in his relations with all people he must be a man of mission and dialogue. Deeply rooted in the truth and charity of Christ and impelled by the desire and imperative to proclaim Christ's salvation to all, the priest is called to witness in all his relationships to fraternity, service, and a common quest for the truth, as well as a concern for the promotion of justice and peace. This is the case above all with the brethren of other churches and Christian denominations, but it also extends to the followers of other religions, to people of good will and in particular to the poor and the defenseless, and to all who yearn—even if they do not

know it or cannot express it—for the truth and the salvation of Christ, in accordance with the words of Jesus who said: "Those who are well have no need of a physician, but those who are sick; I came not to call the righteous, but sinners. (Mk 2:17).[4]

Archbishop Von Thuan of Saigon was first arrested in 1974 and sent to various prisons while traveling toward North Vietnam alongside a member of the parliament known for his traditional Buddhist beliefs. However, Von Thuan's sharing the same dire circumstance with the parliamentary official moved them both on a deep level. Von Thuan had the chance to interact with a wide range of persons at the rehabilitation camp, including leaders, lawmakers from parliament, prominent governmental and military representatives, as well as religious leaders from the Cao Dai, Hoa Hao, Buddhists, Brahmanists, Muslims, and other Christians, including Methodists and Baptists. The archbishop was chosen by his fellow inmates to serve as bursar of the camp, which included distributing food, getting hot water, and lugging the coal on his back to keep everyone warm at night. All of this because the inmates trusted him as a man. Upon leaving Saigon, Jesus, who was executed beyond the boundaries of Jerusalem, made Von Thuan realize that he had to undertake an innovative method of mission.

> I no longer acted as a bishop within a diocese, but *extra muros*; as a missionary *ad extra, ad vitam, ad summum*—going outside, for all my life, to the very limits of my capacity to love and give of myself. Now, yet another dimension opened itself, *ad omnes*, for all. In the obscurity of faith, in service and in humiliation, the light of hope had changed my vision. I understood that at this point, on

---

[4] Ibid., 18.

this ship, in this prison, was my most beautiful cathedral, and that these prisoners, without exception, were the people of God entrusted to my pastoral care. My prison was divine providence. It was the will of God. I spoke of all of this to the other Catholic prisoners and there was born among us a profound communion, a new commitment. We were called to be together witnesses of hope for all people. … The Good news of God who is close can be manifested only if we make ourselves close to all people.[5]

True Unity and Its Threats

There are challenges to unity in the Body of Christ. In my priesthood, I have discovered that people who are zealous in the Lord's service will come into conflict with one another over vison and strategy. Such conflict is healthy and can only happen when there are relationships based on trust and security. A Church family or team often attempts to avoid conflict because it feels negative and counter-productive, causing us to over-compensate by dodging disagreements altogether. While group harmony is a noble aim, true unity comes when team members trust each other enough to discuss (even debate!) issues fully. When members of the team feel secure enough to express opposing opinions, a firm foundation of trust results. On the contrary, if people don't feel safe enough to disagree, trust in the team and its decisions will diminish. Digging for conflict ensures that all voices will be heard. Team members need to make each other feel safe enough to share differing opinions and alternative approaches, even if it feels risky. With more ideas, opinions, and viewpoints, the team will have more to work with. This includes the surfacing of more potential problems which are better to know early on. When conflict is suppressed and people

---

[5] Von Thuan, *Testimony of Hope*, 79.

feel they have not been heard, commitment to action items will be superficial. To get true commitment and an "all in" investment from one another, it's imperative that everyone's voice be heard and that everyone's ideas be considered by the group. With full discussion and debate, a closer look at all the ideas and inputs, and the resulting commitment, our church families will make better decisions.

There are strong forces at work trying to sabotage this unity, namely, the world, the flesh, and the devil—the three sources of temptation in our Christian life. These forces may cause division within our very selves:

> The truth is that the imbalances under which the modern world labors are linked with that more basic imbalance which is rooted in the heart of man. For in man himself many elements wrestle with one another. Thus, on the one hand, as a creature he experiences his limitations in a multitude of ways; on the other he feels himself to be boundless in his desires and summoned to a higher life. Pulled by manifold attractions he is constantly forced to choose among them and renounce some. Indeed, as a weak and sinful being, he often does what he would not, and fails to do what he would. Hence, he suffers from internal divisions, and from these flow so many and such great discords in society.[6]

St. Paul struggled and sometimes failed to avoid the evil he did not want to do and to do the good he wanted to do (cf. Rom 7:15-20). We are often tempted to be someone we are not, split from our authentic identity, and need to be wholly converted. For instance, St. Augustine left his home because of his love for a mistress, and, having subdued his love, returned; then one day meeting his old favorite and not speaking to her, she, being

---

[6] *Gaudium et Spes*, 10.

surprised and supposing that he had not recognized her, said, when they met again, "It is I."

"But," was his answer, "I am not the former I."[7]

To resist temptation, we must know who we are and remain firmly rooted in our true identity and integrity as priests.

There is no end to the unhealthy conflicts and division that can upset the unity desired by Christ for his Church. From the time of the Tower of Babel, human pride has caused confusion and discord. St. Paul warns against the works of the flesh such as enmities, strife, jealousy, anger, quarrels, dissensions, factions, and envy (cf. Gal 5:19-21). He faced rivalries and factions in many of the churches he founded: "For it has been reported to me by Chloe's people that there are quarrels among you, my brothers and sisters. What I mean is that each of you says, "I belong to Paul," or "I belong to Apollos," or "I belong to Cephas," or "I belong to Christ." Has Christ been divided?" (1 Cor 1:11-13). It is easy to fall into factionalism in the Church. Avery Dulles, who was named a Cardinal by St. John Paul II, wrote:

> The conflict between the liberal and conservative wings has markedly politicized the Church. Both sides are tempted to subordinate an even-handed concern for truth to the demands of a party spirit in which every action and statement is evaluated according to whether it supports one cause or the other. The Church as a universal communion is severely wounded by such partisanship. ... The opposed parties seek to discredit their opponents, often by acrimonious attacks that are uncharitable and even unjust. ... In spite of the agitation from both extremes, the Catholic Church

---

[7] See St. Ambrose, *Concerning Repentance*, Book II, Ch 10, par. 96, New Advent Website, https://www.newadvent.org/fathers/ 34062.htm

remains a communion of tradition and authority, open to dialogue and progress. Thanks to its deposit of faith, it has the resources to cope with the modern crisis of truth.[8]

We all have opinions and should respect and listen to the opinions of others in a climate of trust and mutual dialogue. We should try to understand the other person's perspective without judgment of his or her intentions. St. Ignatius counseled patience and clarification:

> Let it be presupposed that every good Christian is to be more ready to save his neighbor's proposition than to condemn it. If he cannot save it, let him inquire how he means it; and if he means it badly, let him correct him with charity. If that is not enough, let him seek all the suitable means to bring him to mean it well, and save himself.[9]

When the priest tries to be respectful of others' opinions and not fall into a faction, he might be rejected and even vilified by either a so-called "traditionalist" or so-called "progressive" camp. The Capuchin priest Benedict Groeschel quips:

> In my own life I have been at one time or another styled as a liberal or a conservative, a radical or a traditionalist—just to mention the respectable positions. I have also been, in some people's estimation, a rat fink, a yellow rat, a pink, a leftist, a rightist, and an undercover agent for the Swiss Guard. I blissfully hid from myself

---

[8] Avery Dulles, S.J., *A Testimonial to Grace and Reflections on a Theological Journey*, fiftieth anniversary edition (Kansas City: Sheed and Ward, 1996), 133-135.

[9] St. Ignatius of Loyola, *Spiritual Exercises*, par. 21.

behind these rather meaningless designations. All the time I was really just a poor sinner.[10]

It is also easy to color our own positions as virtuous and demean the other side, when, in actuality, each of us is in need of conversion. We should also not feel too smug about being neutral or "moderate" on every issue when we are called to take a stand and testify to the truth. But we should always speak the truth with charity and humility (cf. Eph 4:15).

As Christians we should first repent in our own hearts before we re-form others. Jesus spoke of removing the log in our own eyes before taking it upon ourselves to remove the splinter in our neighbor's eyes. A teacher once opened his Bible to Jesus' parable of the weeds and the wheat and read to his class "Gather the weeds ... to be burned, but gather the wheat into my barn." (Mt 13:30). He mused, "Wouldn't it be wonderful if we could weed out the Church?" as he put the Bible away and sat back in his chair. "Wouldn't it be wonderful if we could get rid of all the half-hearted Christians from it? Imagine the effect the Church might have on the world if it only had devoted members! Twenty-five million half-hearted Christians would not compare to one million dedicated Christians as a witness for Jesus." Right away, the students got it. They started to nod in unison. "I concur with what you say," a girl in the back of the room stated as she raised her hand. "But who would decide who should be kept and who should be weeded out?" Lots of hands shot up. "I think nearly anyone could decide that," one boy stated. "I have a list of names I can provide you straight away!"[11]

Would it be beneficial to occasionally purge the Church? Would it be

---

[10] Benedict Groeschel, C.F.R., *The Reform of Renewal* (San Francisco: Ignatius Press, 1990), 201.

[11] Mark Link, *Illustrated Sunday Homilies, Year A,B,C, Series II,* Sixteenth Week in Ordinary Time, Year A, 83.

beneficial to everyone, even lukewarm Christians? Would it jolt individuals into motion and strengthen their resolve to be exemplars and catalysts
for the world? Jesus used the story of the wheat and weeds to address this
very topic. The darnel weed looked like real wheat until harvest, when the
grains would appear on the wheat. It would be easy to mistake the wheat
for weeds and pull up the good with the bad. Similarly, we might weed out
good Christians in seeking to get rid of the bad or lukewarm ones. In addition, by condemning the poor Christians, we might deny them the
chance to repent and become wholehearted Christians. Only God can
judge peoples' hearts and we should judge no person as beyond God's
mercy. It is better to engage others and try to influence them with Christian charity and truth. Paul said,

> I am not aware of anything against myself, but I am not thereby
> acquitted. It is the Lord who judges me. Therefore, do not pro-
> nounce judgment before the time, before the Lord comes, who will
> bring to light the things now hidden in darkness and will disclose
> the purposes of the heart. Then each one will receive commenda-
> tion from God. (1 Cor 4:5)

We should not judge others, nor even ourselves, but leave judgment
to God. Otherwise, we risk condemning others and ourselves. A retired lay
missionary and his wife once lived on a small farm, living out their last
days. The pair put forth great effort raising chickens and vegetables. Because they were unable to consume everything they produced, they sold
what was left to the villagers. The townspeople eventually started speaking
ill of the former missionary and his wife about how miserly they
were. "They weigh every vegetable, and they count every egg twice," commented one local. "If their life depended on it, they wouldn't give you an
additional potato or egg," another said. "I wonder what sort of evangelists

they were?"

The missionary's wife eventually passed away. The truth finally surfaced. Every penny the couple made from selling their eggs and produce went to two elderly widows who were solely dependent on them.[12] The townspeople who had gossiped about the couple were stung with remorse for having misjudged them. Often, we speak ill of others and are quick to judge them because we do not have all the facts.

We must be accepting of the fact that sinners and saints coexist in both the world and the church. Saints have their sinfulness and sinners have the potential to become saints. The Church is more a hospital for sinners than a museum for saints. As Henry Ward Beecher put it: "The Church is not a gallery for the exhibition of eminent Christians, but a school for the education of imperfect ones."[13] Or as Charles Clayton Morrison put it: "The Christian Church is a society of sinners. It is the only society in the world in which membership is based on the single qualification that the candidate be unworthy of membership."[14] The Donatists were sectarian figures from antiquity who provided a straightforward solution to the problem. On the one hand, the world was filled with children of the evil one who had no chance of being saved, while on the other, the Church (of the Donatists) was made up entirely and completely of the perfect. They were disputed by St. Augustine, who argued that the Church as well as the world constitute the field of Christ's parable. In the Church, there is space for sinners alongside saints to mature and experience conversion. "The evildoers," he said, "exist in this way either so that they will be converted, or

---

[12] Ibid., 84.

[13] Henry Ward Beecher, Brainyquote Website, https://www.brainyquote.com/quotes/henry_ward_beecher_150010

[14] Charles Clayton Morrison, AZquotes Webpage, https://www.azquotes.com/quote/922469

because through them the good exercise patience."[15] In the sixteenth century, Luther reproached Erasmus of Rotterdam for remaining in the morally corrupt Catholic Church. Erasmus replied: "I support this Church in the hope that she will become better, because she is also constrained to bear with me in the hope that I will become better."[16] God's might is revealed in the form of patience, mercy, and the intention to redeem us.

Complete Union with the Church

As priests we are about the Spirit's work of reconciliation through the forgiveness of sins. We seek to forgive and be forgiven and strive to lead others to reconciliation. Marriage is a great sign of unity and struggle to remain faithful in the face of difficulties. When a couple renews vows after twenty-five or fifty years of marriage, it is a tremendous testimony to the grace of God and forgiveness. Married couples must constantly forgive one another, "Seventy times seven times" (Mt 18:22). They are called to unconditionally love one another especially on their worst days.

A man said to a counsellor: "My wife and I just don't have the same feelings for each other we used to have. I guess I just don't love her anymore and she doesn't love me anymore. What can I do?"

The counsellor asked, "The feeling isn't there anymore?"

"That's right." He affirmed. "And we have three children we are really concerned about. What do you suggest?"

"Love her," the counsellor replied.

---

[15] St. Augustine, in Raniero Cantalamessa's *Of Weeds and Seeds*, Gospel Commentary for the 16th Sunday in Ordinary Time, July 20, 2008, Zenit, www.zenit.org, Pierced Hearts Website, https://www.piercedhearts.org/scriptures/commentaries_sunday/cantalamessa/sunday_homilies/ordinary_time_a_16sunday_2008.htm

[16] Erasmus of Rotterdam, in Ibid.

"I told you the feeling just isn't there anymore."

"Love her."

"You don't understand. The feeling of love just isn't there."

"Then love her. If the feeling isn't there, that's a good reason to love her."

"But how do you love when you don't feel love?"

"My friend, love is a verb. Love—the feeling—is the fruit of love, the verb. So, love her. Serve her. Sacrifice. Listen to her. Empathize. Appreciate. Affirm her. Are you willing to do that?"[17]

Often when couples make the decision to love regardless of feeling, the chemistry between them is re-created. As priests, we are called to unconditionally love our bride, the Church, sacrificing everything to purify her and ourselves. We are to listen compassionately to her, appreciate and affirm her, even when she seems difficult to love.

The Bridegroom sees only the good in his bride and affirms her. He has sacrificed everything for her to make her a pure and spotless bride (cf. Eph 5:25-27). The Bridegroom is mesmerized by her beautiful dance that brings about unity between the rival camps. He then extols her beauty and fruitfulness that have resulted from his union with her. According to George Maloney, Christian commentators saw the breasts of the bride, the Church as one in mind with Christ, as symbolic of love of God and of neighbor. These two breasts of the bride "are two fawns, twins of a gazelle" (Sg 7:4). The bride's neck is an ivory tower, suggesting her inner strength as a participation in Christ who is her whole strength. In total obedience to Christ, her beloved, she purely and simply trusts that she can do all things in his power (cf. Phil 4:13). Her neck is what gracefully attaches her completely to Christ, her head. Her eyes are compared to the lovely, limpid

---

[17] Harold Buetow, *Ode to Joy, Homily Reflections for Sundays and Holy Days,* Sixth Sunday of Easter, Year A (Staten Island, NY: Alba House, 1995), 126.

pools of Heshbon, an ancient Amorite royal city famous for its reservoirs of fresh, pure water. The bride's pure commitment to Christ is reflected in her eyes which see with his vision in all her relationships with others. The beauty of the bride's nose is compared to a tower of Lebanon, a protective sentinel facing Israel's enemy, Damascus. The palm tree is a symbol of Jesus Christ, who lifted high on the cross has won the palm of victory. The bride is like the palm tree because she is one with him and stands straight and tall, mature as Christ.[18] Like the bride we are called to be built up into the Body of Christ, "until all of us come to the unity of the faith and of the knowledge of the Son of God, to maturity, to the measure of the full stature of Christ" (Eph 4:13).

The bride shares in the Bridegroom's royalty through their union. The bride's head and hair are rich and luxuriant, symbolizing her higher faculties of knowing and loving her spouse. Its tresses are dark as purple, the color of royalty and divinity. The bride has truly been wedded by Christ and, therefore, reigns with him. The king is held captive in her tresses, which applies to each of us. George Maloney reflects:

> It is as if he, your bridegroom, contemplating your inner beauty, your virtues, your degree of passionate surrender to his guidance, sees in you as in a mirror his own beauty and perfections. You have been made according to his image and likeness. He is really the mirror in whom you see reflected your true, beautiful self in your transforming oneness with him: 'They are the ones he chose specially long ago and intended to become true images of his Son' (cf. Rom 8:29).[19]

---

[18] See Maloney, 134-135.
[19] Ibid., 137.

She concludes by saying "I am my beloved's, and his desire is for me" (Sg 7:10). She knows based on his praise of her that she belongs entirely to him and that he ardently desires her. According to St. John of the Cross:

> He makes her entirely His own and empties her of all she possesses other than Him. Hence, not only in her will but also in her works she is really and totally given to God, without keeping anything back, just as God has freely given Himself entirely to her. This union is so effected that the two wills are mutually paid, surrendered, and satisfied (so that neither fails the other in anything) with the fidelity and stability of an espousal.[20]

Such is the complete union experienced by the bride the Church, with her Bridegroom. The priest is the mediator of that union, himself united with Christ as a bride, while also espousing himself in the person of Christ to his bride, the Church. These espousals happen especially through the power of Christ in the Eucharist, the heap of wheat and the wine flowing over the tongue (Sg 7:2-3), which expands the unitive experience: "In receiving Holy Communion, the bonds of union in Christ are drawn tighter; the desire to unite people to him grows in its expanse; the gratitude for the gifts that are ours in Christ impels us to share them universally."[21]

---

[20] St. John of the Cross: *Spiritual Canticle*, Stanza 27, 6, 518-519.

[21] Cardinal Francis George, O.M.I., "Universal Communion," in Stephen Rosetti, Ed., *Born of the Eucharist, A Spirituality for Priests* (Notre Dame, IN: Ave Maria, 2009), 45.

Questions for Reflection and Discussion

1. How does the image of the perichoresis dance help me to understand my participation in the life of the holy Trinity? How do the dynamic, interactive, loving, and serving relationships among the three Persons of the Trinity form the model for our human dance steps in the Church?

2. What is my experience of unity in the hierarchy with my bishop and with my fellow priests in the priestly fraternity? Have I ever reached out to priests who are most in need of God's mercy?

3. Are there any members of the Church whom I tend to disregard or consider less important? How can I help to acknowledge and affirm them in their gifts?

4. How does my ministry extend beyond the boundaries of membership in the Church to the wider community? How is this enriching to me and them?

5. What are the tensions I experience in my life and ministry within the presbyterate, my parish staff, and my parish community? How open am I to many and various points of view and disagreement? What are some polarizing forces that I need to overcome?

6. Have I ever felt tempted to write off half-hearted Catholics in my parish or other ministries? When have I felt called to love the Church unconditionally as bride?

Prayer Exercises

1. Ponder the Greek perichoresis dance. Pray with Jn 14:15-24 and ask for the grace to enter more fully the unity of the holy Trinity.

2. Reflect on the St. Ignatius quote on unity among priests and

bishop, and St. John Paul II's quote on priestly fraternity. Pray with Jn 17:20-26 and ask for the grace to realize greater unity within the presbyterate.

3. Consider the story of the stomach among members of the body. Pray with 1 Cor 12:12-31 and ask for the grace to realize the importance of every member of the Church, especially the neediest.

4. Ponder the need to allow for differing, even opposing opinions in the Church, as well as the threats to unity. Pray with 1 Cor 11:17-26, or Sg 6:13–7:10 and ask for the grace to bring about peace and unity, especially through the Holy Eucharist.

5. Reflect on the story of the teacher suggesting purging the Church of lukewarm members. Pray with Mt 13:24-30 and ask for the grace to be patient, merciful, and encouraging toward lukewarm members of the Church.

6. Consider the advice of the counselor to the married man. Pray with Sg 6:13-7:10, or Eph 5:25-27 and ask for the grace to love the Church unconditionally as bride.

Chapter 19

Jesus, the Way

Come, my beloved,
let us go forth into the fields,
and lodge in the villages;
let us go out early to the vineyards,
and see whether the vines have budded,
whether the grape blossoms have opened
and the pomegranates are in bloom.
There I will give you my love.
The mandrakes give forth fragrance,
and over our doors are all choice fruits,
new as well as old,
which I have laid up for you, O my beloved. (Sg 7:11-13).

A missionary who had spent time evangelizing in Africa's countryside made a brief trip back to England. Once back home, he unexpectedly came upon an exquisite sundial. He got to thinking, "that sundial would be perfect for my African villagers, they could learn to tell time with it." The missionary purchased the sundial, packed it in a container, and shipped it to Africa. He presented it to the local chief who was impressed upon seeing it. The chief ordered that it be placed in the town center. The townspeople were equally impressed with the sundial. They had never in their lives witnessed anything so exquisite. When they discovered how it functioned, they became even more ecstatic. The missionary was thrilled at the way his sundial was received by everyone. Consequently, he was completely caught off guard by what ensued a few days later. The residents of the village banded together and erected a roof over the sundial to shield it from the sun and rain.[1]

Sometimes, we do a similar thing as those villagers with our faith. Doctrine is important, but sometimes we so enshrine it that it becomes like a museum piece to be admired, rather than a reality to be lived. The doctrine of the Trinity as three persons in one God is amazing and wonderful, while remaining incomprehensible to a large degree. We cannot build a fence around the doctrine to protect it, but we can realize it is a dynamic force of God in our lives. The Father sends the Son to reveal God to us and to save us. The Father and Son send the Spirit so that God may dwell within us and sanctify us, reproducing Christ in us. Both the Son and the Spirit are sent as Apostles to bring us into their communion of life. When Jesus concludes his mission, he sends forth the Apostles to complete his mission, promising he will remain with them always, until the end of time. The Spirit accompanies us and helps us go before the Lord to bear fruit for the Kingdom. Now we are not merely admirers of Christ and his teaching, but true disciples.

Admirers and Followers of Jesus

We should internalize Jesus' teaching so that it becomes part of us and transforms us. We cannot remain content to merely know what Jesus teaches and observe it externally; His teaching must penetrate our hearts. Only then will we be able to set people's hearts on fire for Christ. We could distinguish between the admirer of Jesus and the follower of Jesus, who

---

[1] See Mark Link, *Illustrated Sunday Homilies, Years A,B,C, Series I,* Year B, Trinity Sunday, 65.

both stand in the crowd and listen to him speak. [2] The admirer of Jesus lets the words of Jesus influence his conduct. The follower of Jesus lets the words of the Lord influence his life and burn like a consuming fire in his heart. The admirer agrees with Jesus that the world is a sinful place. The follower grieves because of his own sinfulness and accepts God's forgiveness. The admirer goes home enthusiastic about Jesus' teaching. The follower invites Jesus to come to his home and have dinner with him. The admirer eats bread and thanks God for his food. The follower becomes bread broken for the life of the world. The admirer drinks wine and enjoys good friends. The follower enjoys good friendship and becomes wine poured out for her friends. The admirer goes out among the crowd along the way of the cross. The follower walks in Jesus' footsteps carrying the cross. The admirer knows he is a creature made by God, an earthen vessel, beautiful and intact, inviolable, and safe. The follower is an earthen vessel, vulnerable, broken for others, revealing Christ within. The admirer has a good life but is not fully alive. The follower has the gift of an abundant life and lives it to the fullest. Before we evangelize, we must be evangelized by putting on Christ, sharing his desires, attitudes, and values. As we become one with him in discipleship, we follow him into ministry.

The bride now is the one who invites her beloved spouse to go out into the country wherever they can be of service to others. She is of only one mind, to do what he always desires, which is to go and bear plentiful fruit so that others may partake of his abundant life. She does all this only in union with her beloved:

Now she has entered into a synthesis of the contemplative and the

---

[2] See Soren Kierkegaard and Charles E. Moore, *Provocations, The Spiritual Writings of Soren Kierkegaard* (Walden, NY: Plough Publishing House, 2002), 83-87.

active life with no separation, for she is always not only in the presence of Christ, but she is worshipping the Father and loving his entire creation as she works with Christ to this end. Before, she experienced Christ working in her, but now he works with her. She lives in a synergy, a working with him, in and for him. Everything she does is prayer. As she rests in the oneness with her beloved that no one can take away from her, she is able to move out into the world of great multiplicity and diversity and never lose the inner "grounding" in him. And yet she is able with Christ to give herself completely to the moment and the work at hand as most important in building up the body of Christ.[3]

The bride is now happy to be anywhere in the world, if she is with her Beloved and working with and for him. She speaks of spending the night in the villages, which indicates she no longer has any fixed abode she can call home. She is a pilgrim with Christ, detached from all securities, ready to pass the nights in any village throughout the world to share their communion.

As priests, we are called to leave everything to follow him who had no home: "Foxes have holes, and birds of the air have nests; but the Son of Man has nowhere to lay his head" (Mt 8:20). We leave everything behind to follow Christ, and our reward is to be with him in all we do and for all eternity. St. Ignatius of Loyola, in his meditation on the call of the king, invites us to share in Jesus' lifestyle, to share in his labors, that sharing in his sufferings, we might also share in his glory.[4] Jesus' invitation is not to be workers under him, like a boss to an employee, but to be co-workers with him in a spousal relationship. An employee seeks orders and a job to

---

[3] Maloney, 145.

[4] See *Spiritual Exercises,* pars. 91-100.

do and goes and does it on his own. Spouses are "yoked" together and share life and activity with one another in a mutual project of communion and love. As priests we are yoked alongside Christ and he is pulling the plow along with us, so to speak. His yoke is easy and his burden light because we do it in union with him (Mt 11:30). He is the one who brings fruit from our activities. "I planted, Apollos watered, but God gave the growth" (1 Cor 3:6). Jesus said: "The kingdom of God is as if someone would scatter seed on the ground, and would sleep and rise night and day, and the seed would sprout and grow, he does not know how." (Mk 4:26-27). We are simply called to be obedient to God's command to plant seeds and nurture the plant, while marveling at God's power to make things grow.

There will be times of seeming failure when we are called to be patient and wait for God in trust and hope. Jesus' own life appeared to be a failure, as captured in the poem "One Solitary Life":

> He was born in an obscure village, the child of a peasant. He grew up in another village, where he worked in a carpenter shop until he was thirty. Then, for three years, he was an itinerant preacher. He never wrote a book. He never held an office. He never had a family or owned a home. He didn't go to college. He never lived in a big city. He never traveled two hundred miles from the place where he was born. He did none of the things that usually accompany greatness. He had no credentials but himself. He was only thirty-three when the tide of public opinion turned against him. His friends ran away. One of them denied him. He was turned over to his enemies and went through the mockery of a trial. He was nailed to a cross between two thieves. While he was dying, his executioners gambled for his garments, the only property he had on earth. When he died, he was laid in a borrowed grave, through the pity of a friend. Twenty centuries have come and gone, and

today he is the central figure of the human race. I am well within the mark when I say that all the armies that ever marched, all the navies that ever sailed, all the parliaments that ever sat, all the kings that ever reigned—put together—have not affected the life of man on this earth as much as that one, solitary life.[5]

The disciples experienced that seeming failure early after the Resurrection of Jesus. Peter and the other Apostles were fishing all night without catching anything. Tired, frustrated, and hungry, they approached the shore at dawn. Jesus appeared to them on the beach and told them to cast their net on the right side of the boat, and they caught one hundred and fifty fish, representing all the nations of the known world at the time. Later, by the Spirit's power, they would baptize three thousand new converts on Pentecost. All Jesus needs is our contribution, which might not seem like much, but by his power it becomes much. The boy who contributed five loaves and two fish might not have thought he was making a big difference, but it was enough for Jesus to multiply and feed the five thousand.

After twenty years of laboring to convert the pagan Irish, St. Patrick had a dream that showed him his work would continue to bear fruit. He stood in a field and could see lights burning in the shadows. Jesus stood in front of him, quietly motioning to follow him. Jesus led him up a high mountain surveying the valley where the Lord pointed to the shadows below. "Look," he said. Patrick stared below and saw, at dusk, a great number of burning fires which illuminated the open fields, which comforted him. He realized they represented the Christian faith he had planted, the faith that had progressed and now spread across the island country. He glanced at Jesus and grinned. But Jesus wasn't grinning. He pointed down the

---

[5] Rev. James Allan Francis, "One Solitary Life," originally published in *The Real Jesus and Other Sermons* (Philadelphia, Judson Press, 1926), 123-124.

valley and said once more, "Look." Patrick stared. Sadly, he looked as gradually, the fires were extinguished, leaving only wafting smoke. In the shadows of dusk, the old and tired bishop turned back at Jesus with tears in his eyes. "Oh, let me know," he exclaimed, "Master, let me know, that Ireland will never lose the Faith!" And as he hung his head in tears and despair, he felt a mighty arm lifting him up and a tender hand pointing his face down again to the valley beneath. There upon the knoll in the shadows was a solitary light flaming, a small fire that had remained from the start, though Patrick had not noticed it before. Suddenly, as before, another fire seemed to emerge from that fire, and another from that one; and one more and again, until the fires ignited all over the open country, and the fire of faith blazed than any other time in recent memory.[6] Christ our King is the unconquerable light of the world. He came to kindle the fire of his Spirit in our hearts. Even when all seemed lost, St. Patrick experienced that burning flame of the Spirit which the Lord used to enkindle the Christian faith in the hearts of the Irish people.

How We Measure Success

There is a difference between worldly success and spiritual fruitfulness. Our society is obsessed with worldly success. There are times when we cannot believe that our economy, banks, and major industries are failing. Our favorite American sports, once defined by character and fair play, have been tainted by steroid abuse and other scandals. Everyone tries to get ahead of one another at all costs, even one's health. This attitude creeps into our churches. Success is defined by numbers of conversions or attendance at mass. Sometimes it is the bottom-line financial success of our

---

[6] Epriest, *Homily Pack, Pentecost Sunday, Year B,* Epriest Website, https://epriest.com/homily_packs

churches or schools that becomes our focus. In the first diocese where I
was ordained, it seemed as though status was conferred on you if you were
financially successful at your parish. Statistics are helpful benchmarks of
success. If they are good, we feel good about ourselves; if they are bad, we
feel lousy. We might be tempted to compare ourselves to other pastors and
feel like failures—perhaps we have a smaller parish, or one that is shrink-
ing in size or influence. It may be impossible to improve things even with
the best of efforts. A negative mood about ourselves and our work could
then take over. Our egos start to dominate.

When Samuel was looking for the man God would choose to succeed
Saul as King of Israel, he was led to the house of Jesse. Here Samuel thought
that God would surely choose Jesse's older and impressive son Eliab as the
future king, and not the youthful David. But when Samuel questioned God
about Eliab, God replied, "Take no notice of his appearance or his height
for I have rejected him; God does not see as man sees; man looks at appearances, but the Lord looks at the heart" (1 Sm 16:7). God is interested
in individual people transformed into His sons and daughters and not in
how many people are in the group. Henri Nouwen reminds us that success
in worldly terms is different from fruitfulness in God.

> Success comes from strength, control, and respectability. A suc-
> cessful person has the energy to create something, to keep control
> over its development, and to make it available in large quantities.
> Success brings many rewards and often fame. Fruits, however,
> come from weakness and vulnerability. And fruits are unique. A
> child is the fruit conceived in vulnerability, community is the fruit
> born through shared brokenness, and intimacy is the fruit that
> grows through touching one another's wounds. Let's remind one

another that what brings us true joy is not successfulness but fruit-fulness.[7]

We are better off focusing on the few and not the many, for it is the gifted, mature, godly person who transforms the world. When I left my first parish assignment to work in seminary formation, I was leaving a large mass of people to focus on a few who would be leaders. Though I was giving up an enriching experience of ministry, I was gaining a greater one which would in the long run have more impact. I had to let go of some of the satisfactions of ministry to receive new and different experiences, such as living a more intense community life, and offering a more intense formation. Jesus at a certain point in his ministry seems to have focused less on the crowds and more on forming the Twelve, realizing they would go forth and extend his ministry.

When a priest first arrives at a parish, especially in today's mega-parishes, he is often overwhelmed by the sheer number of people and their needs. St. John Vianney, the Curé of Ars, had that experience. He developed a pastoral plan that helped him concentrate his energies as a parish priest. Vianney first focused on the families that were already strong in their faith and had resisted the waves of worldliness and indifference. This approach may seem counter intuitive. Why expend energy on people he already had? His answer is that they would become the fiery coals, which would dry out the damp the wood of the rest of the parish and help set it ablaze. His work had a ripple effect expanding outward from these initial families to more and more of the village and surrounding area. His efforts to galvanize the faithful, strong families also met a deep human need in the holy Curé: the need for support. He did not simply depend on himself, but

---

[7] Henri Nouwen, *Bread for the Journey, A Daybook of Wisdom and Faith* (New York: HarperCollins, 1997).

he needed people who would assist him in his efforts to convert the village, especially because his initial efforts elicited ridicule and criticism. These families would be there for him, speak well of him and begin setting the example for the rest of the parish to follow. This support was not a "cult of personality" around Vianney or because they were best friends; rather, their support came from the fact that he was their Curé and they both shared the Church's vision for the parish.[8] I am always impressed by pastors who seek to form and evangelize their lay parish leaders. It opens space for the Holy Spirit to operate and creates a common vision and bond in the parish ministry.

Experiencing Intimacy of Life Through Christ

The pastor has the important role of affirming and drawing out the gifts of the faithful. We exercise our ministry in heartfelt communion with the lay faithful. Collaborative ministry assumes an awareness and admiration of the various charisms, of the assorted vocations and assignments entrusted by the Spirit to the lay faithful. Cooperation with the laity

> demands a living and precise consciousness of one's own identity in the Church and of the identity of others. It demands mutual trust, patience, gentleness, and the capacity for understanding and expectation. It finds its roots above all in a love for the Church that is deeper than love for self and the group or groups one may belong to.[9]

---

[8] See Fr. John Cihak, S.T.D. St. John Vianney's Pastoral Plan, Ignatius Insight Website, http://www.ignatiusinsight.com/features2009/print2009/jcihak_ stvianneyhpr_june09.html

[9] St. John Paul II, *Pastores Dabo Vobis*, 59.

Vatican Council II says of priests: "They should be willing to listen to lay people, give brotherly consideration to their wishes and recognize their experience and competence in the different fields of human activity. In this way they will be able to recognize with them the signs of the times."[10] The priest shows pastoral solicitude for the laity teaching and supporting them in their vocation to be present in and to transform the world with the light of the Gospel.[11] I often recommend people take an inventory of their charisms of the Holy Spirit.[12] We then prayerfully consider how each charism has been operative in their lives, and how they might exercise it more intentionally in concrete ways. Usually, people experience great joy when they become aware of the charisms and begin to use them. They often experience great fulfillment in bringing joy to other peoples' lives through these gifts. Recently I helped one of my spiritual directees discover her charism of teaching and encouraged her to consider how she might put it into practice. She came back the next month glowing after beginning not one, but two bible studies on the internet.

Ministry itself becomes intimacy with the Father and the Risen Lord, in the communion of the Holy Spirit. I often feel most at one with Christ when I am ministering in his name. I feel that he is leading me carefully and intimately in all my endeavors. Amid offering an intense retreat from sunrise until late into the evening, while giving four conferences and a homily per day, while meeting retreatants individually in every free moment in between talks, I experience the Lord's burning love in my heart. He is interested in and involved in everything that takes place, delighting in all that is virtuous, holy, and beautiful in the experience. He rejoices with me in the accomplishments and delights in me as I delight in him.

---

[10] *Presbyterorum Ordinis*, 9.

[11] See Saint John Paul II, *Pastores Dabo Vobis*, 59.

[12] A good resource is the Catherine of Siena Institute *Called and Gifted Workshop*, which includes a spiritual gifts inventory.

Sharing in my sorrows and sufferings, Jesus strengthens me under the strain. He shares my life in its smallest and most personal specifics, illuminating my mind and strengthening my will. He gives us the insight and courage to reveal his presence and to lead the community.

In his risen nature Jesus retains his compassionate human personality which becomes one with our own, such that we have the mind of Christ. According to spiritual author David Hassel:

> Each time Christ, the divine teacher, illumines the mind or pulses the imagination or strengthens the will of a particular human person, he would share in any human insight generated by the illumination, in any inventive leap of the human imagination, in any strong decision bettering the community of this same person. At this point, the sacraments would become peak experiences of friendship between Christ, this person, and his community. For Christ would be sharing deeply with this person in new birth, apostolic endeavor, repentance for sin and healing of sorrow, marriage or priesthood, health, and life. Of course, all these experiences would be summed up, even daily, in the mutually intimate moment of the Eucharist.[13]

The Song of Songs shows us that in their joint mission, the bride experiences this intimacy of life with her Bridegroom as she constantly gives her love to him. Because he is one with her, she can always remain united in mind and heart with him. She no longer seeks so much to withdraw from activity to discover her lover. Her apostolic works take her more into his presence. George Maloney proclaims:

---

[13] David Hassel, S.J., *Radical Prayer* (Ramsey, NJ: Paulist Press, 1983), 121.

The Spirit of love flows over her at all times. She is on fire with love for Christ. The more she loves the more she burns to love. As she discovers her union with Christ to increase through the very activities done out of love for him, she dares to do more, to pray more for the entire world, to be more available to all who come to her. She becomes compassion, like a universal mother to the entire suffering world.[14]

Shaped By God

We are not sure where the Lord will take us in our ministry and we must be prepared for anything. Saint John Paul II asserts that the priest

should be open and available to all the possibilities offered today for the proclamation of the Gospel, not forgetting the valuable service which can and should be given by the media. He should prepare himself for a ministry which may mean in practice that his readiness to follow the indications of the Holy Spirit and of his bishop will lead him to be sent to preach the Gospel even beyond the frontiers of his own country.[15]

We might be afraid that God is calling us beyond our comfort zone. In my own vocation, I know that I sometimes cringe when our provincial superior makes his annual visit, especially when I know there is a position to be filled for which I may be under consideration. It forces me to pray for the grace to surrender to God's will and to be less attached to the comfort of my current assignment. We need to take one step at a time in our

---

[14] Maloney, 148.
[15] St. John Paul II, *Pastores Dabo Vobis*, 186.

service of the Lord and be open to whatever he asks.

Back in 2012, I felt like I was in a rut. I had been assistant director at our spirituality center for six years and the routine was starting to wear on me. I needed something fresh and renewing. I noticed one of my fellow Oblates who had been ordained after me was taking a six-month sabbatical. It's rare that any of us Oblates even take a sabbatical, which we are allowed every ten years. I had been ordained seventeen years and I thought, "now is the time!" It took some time for the sabbatical to be approved by our provincial council. When it was approved, I didn't have much of a plan of where to stay or what to do. When praying with the Song of Songs I had always noticed themes of the *Spiritual Exercises of St. Ignatius* in the text. So, I decided to pursue the connections and compose some retreat talks. I found some friends and family members to stay with and set to work. I had no idea where the project would take me, but the Holy Spirit was definitely at work. I received inspiration each time I looked at the scripture text and was able to connect it with the Spiritual Exercises. At the end of each chapter of composition, I had no idea how the next chapter would come about. After several of these instances, I realized I could depend on the Spirit for inspiration every time I began a new section. It took five years for my work to eventually become the book *Awakening Love* and though I had no idea of how to write, edit, or seek publication, the Lord guided every step of the process. I learned to surrender to him in every moment and at every step along the way. As a result, my ministry was revived and given a new direction.

We do not need to see the whole picture of where God is leading us, only the next step to take. There is a charming tale about a young farm boy who was dreadfully scared of the dark. One evening, his father instructed him to go outside and feed the horses in the barn. The young boy appeared pale and shuddered at the command. After lighting a lantern, his father led his son outside and stepped onto the porch. Whereupon he asked his son,

"How far can you see?"

"I can see halfway to the barn," the boy said.

"Bring this halfway to the barn," the father instructed his son as he handed him the lamp.

After the youngster had gone halfway, the father cried out, "How far can you see now?"

"I can see the barn and the barn door," the boy yelled while holding up the lantern.

The father commanded, "Walk to the barn door." When the youngster yelled back that he had arrived at the barn door, the father said, "Now open the door and tell me what you see."

"I can see inside the barn," the boy yelled back as he opened the door. "The horses are there!"

"Great!" his father exclaimed. "Now, feed 'em!"[16]

The boy stopped being afraid of the dark that night. More significantly, he advanced considerably in maturity. He discovered that not everything could be accomplished at once in life. Things must be carried out gradually. The boy was unable to see the barn when the father first held up the lantern. He could only see half the distance. But that was sufficient to motivate him to travel as far as he could visualize. The boy could not see the horses inside the barn when he reached the midway point and held up the lamp once more. The barn was all he could see. However, it was enough to inspire him and empower him to move toward the barn door. He couldn't see the horses or feed them until he reached the door.

God does not reveal his plan for our lives all at once. It is constantly unfolding and often changing. We need to be flexible to conform to the Lord's plans and not become hardened in our own mindset. St. John Henry

---

[16] Mark Link, *Illustrated Sunday Homilies, Years A,B,C, Series II*, Fourth Sunday of Lent, Year B, 25.

Newman, apprehensive about his future, could only see one step of the Lord's plan at a time, as expressed in his poem:

> Lead, kindly Light, amid the encircling gloom,
> Lead Thou me on!
> The night is dark, and I am far from home—
> Lead Thou me on!
> Keep Thou my feet; I do not ask to see
> The distant scene—one step enough for me.
> I was not ever thus, nor prayed that Thou
> Shouldst lead me on.
> I loved to choose and see my path; but now,
> Lead Thou me on!
> I loved the garish day, and, spite of fears,
> Pride ruled my will: remember not past years.[17]

Newman articulates his absolute reliance on God, surrendering his footsteps and his way forward, going along without hesitation.

Madeleine Debrel was a French mystic devoted to caring for the poor and evangelizing culture. She mused that the imperative to spread the Gospel mixes God's walking pace with our own which often gives us the gait of someone who is crippled or half-blind. We try with all our heart, mind, soul, and strength to put God's program into practice, but we have a very dim understanding of the plan. Even if we accomplish all the goals of a particular day, we have no idea of how the Lord will use it. If we blunder through our day, we have even less an idea of what he will do with it. We

---

[17] St. John Henry Newman, *Lead Kindly Light*. Journey with Jesus Website, https://www.journeywithjesus.net/poemsandprayers/658-john-henry-newman

only know that God will never lose anything that we give to him.[18] St. Irenaeus reminds us that it is not we who shape God, but God who shapes us. "If you are the work of God, await the hand of the artist who does all things in due season. Offer God your heart, soft and tractable, and keep the form in which the artist has fashioned you. Let your clay be moist, lest you grow hard and lose the imprint of God's fingers."[19] Our wills must be open and malleable to conform to the Lord's will for us.

The Lanteri Center for Ignatian Spirituality, which is committed to providing one-on-one spiritual direction, retreats, and spiritual director training, has been under my guidance since 2014. We were down to one priest instead of two and three lay staff members when our founder and prior director relocated to Boston. Along with the intimidating prospect of taking over from the founder and director, I also felt an obligation to continue to expand our ministry. I had the same reaction as the Israelites when the Egyptians expected them to make more bricks without straw (Ex 5:7ff.). I prayed during my customary holy hour every morning, feeling inadequate as a leader, asking for the courage and inspiration to carry out any tasks that God might assign to me. He did inspire me, and as a result, I was motivated to launch a new initiative to introduce Ignatian spirituality to parishes. I had the urge to provide mission-style parish retreats on prayer and discernment so that a much larger audience could benefit from the Ignatian practice. I was apprehensive when I thought about this undertaking. I questioned how I would manage to achieve this while attending to all of our other activities and my new administrative responsibilities. I shared the idea with my spiritual director, the staff, and graduates of our program. We forged ahead despite

---

[18] See Madeleine Delbrel, *We, the Ordinary People of the Streets* (Grand Rapids, MI: Eerdman's Publishing, 2000), 72.

[19] Attributed to St. Irenaeus.

concerns from everyone that I could be pushing myself to the limit. Within the first two months, we had five requests for missions, which confirmed this was something parishes were looking for. Powerful spiritual encounters in prayer and discernment started to occur frequently and still do. The Lord decided to carry out his plan when I was at my most uncertain and burdened.

The Lord invites us to offer our lives as a holocaust for Christ by laboring for his kingdom, remaining available for whatever he is asking of us. We cannot remain mere admirers of Christ; we must involve ourselves as true disciples by carrying our crosses with Jesus. When we join with Christ and his mission, the Lord gives us the inspiration and we labor with the perspiration, the sweat, blood, and tears it will entail to follow him. We overcome our self-indulgent tendencies, roll up our sleeves, and get to work in serving Christ. Like the bride of the Song of Songs, we are called to accompany the Lord, going into the fields, villages, and vineyards, bearing fruit in our work for his kingdom. Together, the Bridegroom and bride look to see if the pomegranates are in bloom. The red pomegranates symbolize the redemptive act of Christ dying on the cross and shedding his blood for the life of the world. Christ's passion, death, and resurrection are the source of any fruit that is born. The bride no more considers her own fruit or work within the Church, but views all works done for Christ. She desires to do her part to help him bring forth fruit everywhere in the world, in every soul.

When we experience the life of Jesus within ourselves, we feel compelled to share it with others. Our gratitude for all the Lord has done for us should overflow in love for God and one another. Others in turn will spread that love to others and bring others into the fold. A man with cataracts was treated by a missionary physician in China at the turn of the twentieth century. The individual was nearly blind prior to surgery, but he was able to see very well afterwards. The man was overjoyed. He openly shared his delight with other patients at the tiny mission clinic, and it seemed as though his thankfulness to the doctor knew no bounds. The man made his way back to the far-off village where he lived after leaving the clinic. He didn't linger in the village for very long, though. Instead, he took a tour of the nearby towns then returned three months later to the tiny mission clinic where his sight had been restored. The missionary doctor was astounded to see outside his window the man, and forty-eight other people, firmly grasping onto a rope. The man had led them through the countryside to take them to the location where he was healed. The only other thing they had in common, besides the rope, was that they were all blind. The appreciative man offered to lead them to the location where he regained his vision and introduced them to the missionary doctor so that they too might be healed.[20] Having received so much grace from the Lord, we are moved to seek out others in need of mercy and healing.

Questions for Reflection and Discussion

1. Have I ever fallen into the trap of so enshrining doctrine (such as the Holy Trinity) at an intellectual level that I neglect to live the doctrine spiritually and practically? Do I notice this tendency in any of God's people?

2. In what ways do I feel like more of an admirer of Jesus Christ than a disciple who shares his desires, attitudes, and values, seeking to imitate him? Where in my life am I challenged to become more of a follower?

3. Have I ever felt in my ministry a synthesis of the contemplative

---

[20] See Tim Perkins, "Leading Others to Jesus," *Across the Preacher's Desk*, October 3, 2019, Shelby County Today Website, https://scttx.com/articles/across-preacher%E2%80%99s-desk-%E2%80%9Cleading-others-jesus%E2%80%9D

and the active life with no separation? In what ways have I experienced Christ working with me, a living in synergy, a working with him, in and for him, wherein everything is prayer?

4. How do I measure success in my life and ministry? How am I tempted to gauge success by worldly standards? How can I be better concerned with spiritual fruitfulness, and more patient in waiting for it?

5. To what degree do I like to see God's plan for my life all at once? How patient am I in waiting for it to unfold? How flexible am I in conforming to the Lord's plan versus being hardened in my own mindset? Can I rely more on God and surrender more to his plan with less hesitation?

Prayer Exercises

1. Ponder the differences between the admirer and follower of Jesus. Pray with Jn 13:1-17 and ask for the grace to imitate Jesus in his life and actions.

2. Consider Henri Nouwen's distinction between worldly success and spiritual fruitfulness. Pray with Jn 15:1-11 and ask for the grace to abide in Christ in order to bear lasting fruit.

3. Reflect on St. John Vianney's pastoral plan. Pray with Sg 7:11-13 and ask for the grace of greater availability to the people of God.

4. Ponder David Hassel's quote and the author's experiences of intimacy in ministry. Pray with Sg 7:11-13 or Mt 28:16-20 and ask for the grace to experience greater intimacy with Christ in your apostolic work.

5. Consider the author's sabbatical experience and the story of the boy feeding the horses. Pray with Jn 14:1-14 and ask the grace to trust the Lord even in darkness.

Chapter 20

Disciple and Teacher

O that you were like a brother to me,
that nursed at my mother's breast!
If I met you outside, I would kiss you,
and none would despise me.
I would lead you and bring you
into the house of my mother,
and into the chamber of her that conceived me.
I would give you spiced wine to drink,
the juice of my pomegranates.
O that his left hand were under my head,
and that his right hand embraced me!
I adjure you, O daughters of Jerusalem,
that you stir not up nor awaken love
until it please. (Sg 8:1-4)

During the 1800s in Turin, Italy, children were the chief victims of the Industrial Revolution. There were hundreds of boys living on the streets without care or supervision. God sent them a man with unfaltering faith, a knack for storytelling, a heart full of laughter, and an extraordinary love for children. God sent them St. John Bosco. Bosco was born in northwest Italy, the son of a peasant farmer. His father died when he was two years old, and the family was left in poverty. At an early age, he felt a strong desire to teach others the Catholic Faith. The first hint of his vocation came in a dream. He found himself in a crowd of children who were swearing and fighting. He tried using his fists to calm the children down. Then, Jesus appeared and told him he could help the boys only by being kind, leading them, and teaching them to hate sin and love purity. Without a male role model, Bosco sought out a father-figure who would be a spiritual mentor. He chose St. Francis de Sales, who lived two hundred years prior. Francis de Sales had been the bishop of Geneva, Switzerland, during the Protestant Reformation—a time when many Catholics left the Church. Through his diligence, patience, and gentleness, St. Francis guided sixty thousand fallen away Catholics back to the Faith. Later, he wrote *Introduction to the Devout Life*, which St. John Bosco read again and again, receiving the needed guidance and formation from this spiritual father.

Teaching is an Act of Love

Bosco was eventually ordained a priest and was known as Don Bosco. One day, when preparing to celebrate Mass, a boy was rudely ejected by the sacristan when he balked at serving for Mass. Overhearing, Don Bosco had the boy brought back, spoke kindly to him, and invited him to return the next Sunday with his friends. Nine boys came. Before long, the number rose to more than one hundred youths who came for Sunday Mass, instruction, and play. The number of boys eventually grew to eight hundred. Don Bosco developed a "Preventative System" that relied on reasonableness, religion, and loving kindness. He guided many young people to Jesus, resulting in young saints such as St. Dominic Savio. In training his teachers, Don Bosco insisted on kindness and a familiar presence—spiritually accompanying young people by forming their wills and character. The teachers were to earn the student's trust and give a clear Christian witness of intimacy with God in their own life. He also believed that good music greatly assisted in the growth of young minds, helping to awaken the spiritual part of human nature. Don Bosco was always mindful of young people's need for joy, fun and laughter.

Don Bosco's last letter to his Salesians sketched the place of friendship, relationship, and recreation in his "preventative" approach. He made it a priority:

> That the boys should not only be loved but realize that they are loved. ... That they be loved in the things which they themselves like by a sharing in their youthful interests; in this way they will learn to see your love in matters which naturally speaking are not very pleasing to them, as is the case with study, discipline, and self-denial: in this way they will learn to do these things also with love. When a person knows he is loved, he will love in return, and when a person is loved he can get anything, especially from boys. This confidence sets up an electric current between boys and superiors. Hearts are opened, needs and weaknesses are made known. This love enables superiors to bear with weariness, annoyance, ingratitude, or the troubles, failings, and neglect of the boys. Our Lord did not break the bruised reed nor quench the smoking flax. He is your model.[1]

Though most of us as priests are not full-time teachers like Don Bosco, we can learn a lot from his approach. The most important thing people need to know when they are taught is that they are loved. Teaching is an act of love. The bride invitingly suggests to her beloved that he come to her mother's house and that he teach her (Sg 8:2)[2]. Jerusalem was mother and teacher for the Jews, prefiguring the bride's mother, the Church, wherein

---

[1] St. John Bosco, *An Exhortation to Educators*, Rome, May 10, 1884. Available in the informal education archives: https://infed.org/mobi/an-exhortation-to-educators/

[2] The footnote for Sg 8:2 RSVCE shows that other ancient manuscripts add the words "you will teach me."

she was born to new life from above by water and the Spirit. It is in the Church where she wishes Christ to teach her his personal love for her and for all humanity. Christ is known as *Hagia Sophia*, "Holy Wisdom," in the Eastern Church. He invites all who wish to learn his teaching: "Come, eat of my bread and drink of the wine I have mixed. Leave simpleness, and live, and walk in the way of insight" (Prv 9:5-6). Now that the bride in the Song of Songs is becoming more intimately united with her Bridegroom, she wishes to be fully enlightened by him (cf. Sg 8:2). Christ's enlightenment transforms her into a mature lover.

In the Old Testament, the Lord is the first teacher, who teaches Moses his *torah*, which literally means "instruction." His instruction is his statutes and judgments—his ways. The tradition of teaching is then established, transmitted, and applied by the priests whose office includes teaching the revealed truth. The Lord's teaching is addressed to the entire person, not just to the intellect. The listener's acceptance of the teaching is the acceptance of the Lord revealing himself as the Lord and savior of Israel. This acceptance demands a total surrender of life. For the Greeks, who influenced Old Testament wisdom literature, the teacher is more than a revealer; it is his role to awaken the disciple's aptitudes by the presentation of problems, and to cultivate the students use of his powers by demanding that he exercise them.

In the New Testament, Jesus comes as a teacher, the title given him most frequently. He is a teacher of the Law who teaches the way of God truthfully. As a teacher he was a familiar and acceptable figure in the Jewish community. It was his originality of the form and content of his teaching and his departures from the rigid pattern of rabbinical teaching which aroused hostility. He was not a mere expounder of traditional teaching; he taught his own positive doctrine and based it upon his personal authority. In the exposition of the Scriptures his teaching was a demonstration that the kingdom of God had arrived and was fulfilled in Him. Jesus' teaching caused admiration and astonishment because it was an exhibition of power and authority. "Never has anyone spoken like this!" (Jn 7:46) And "They were astounded at his teaching, for he taught them as one having authority, and not as the scribes" (Mk 1:22). Other teachers, according to rabbinical standards, had to cite at least two sources of other rabbis to support their opinions. Jesus never cited any other rabbi, but only cited his own divine authority. He only spoke what he heard from his Father: "For I have not spoken on my own, but the Father who sent me has himself given me a commandment about what to say and what to speak" (Jn 12:49).

When we further compare and contrast the teaching of Jesus with that of the scribes, we notice three distinguishing qualities: First, Jesus taught from the heart, not just the head. He taught with absolute conviction in his message because he knew that his message was in accordance with the mind of God. As he says in the Gospel of John when trying to persuade his unbelieving audience, "Very truly, I tell you, we speak of what we know and testify to what we have seen; yet you do not receive our testimony" (Jn 3:11). His preaching was a personal testimony of his intimate relationship with God his Father. The scribes, on the other hand, got their knowledge not from their personal communion with God but from their long and intricate study of commentaries on the Law. As a result, most of their teaching was from the head and not from the heart, as they tried to recall the portions of the commentaries that applied to the situation at hand.

A second difference between the teaching of Jesus and that of the scribes lies in the content of the message. Whereas the scribes sought to apply the prescription of the Law to the letter, Jesus went deeper to find out the spirit, the original intent of the law. Consequently, Jesus was able to discover the positive value that the Law seeks to protect, whereas the scribes busied themselves with words and their minutest applications. Take, for example, the law of Sabbath observance. The scribes would busy themselves trying to determine precisely when the Sabbath began and ended, and what constituted work and what didn't. Jesus sought the mind of God who gave the law to His people as an expression of His fatherly care and love. His conclusion: the Sabbath is a day we keep away from our work in order to serve God and do God's work (Jn 5:17). Because of this positive emphasis of his message, people perceived the teaching of Jesus as liberating good news in contrast to that of the scribes which they perceived as a heavy burden.

The final difference between the teaching of Jesus and that of the scribes we shall consider is that Jesus' teaching was intended to bring about a positive change of heart in the people, not just to make the people feel bad. Whereas the scribes taught whatever made sense in terms of their understanding of the Law and traditions, Jesus taught that which made a positive difference. Presented with a man blind from birth the scribes sought to explain why he was blind—whether it was he who sinned or his parents. Jesus, on the other hand was only interested in curing the blindness. For this reason, Jesus performed healings and exorcisms together with his teaching, to show that his primary concern was to change the human situation not just to explain it.

Jesus used parables, "stories" to convey the most original parts of his teaching. In the parables there is a touch of the Socratic method. Jesus leaves the listeners with questions to which he has given an answer, but the listeners must form the answers for themselves. In our training program for spiritual directors at the *Lanteri Center for Ignatian Spirituality* in Denver, Colorado, we teach both principles and practice of spiritual direction. We employ more of an "andragogical" method of instruction, where a student takes responsibility for one's learning. Adult learning is based upon comprehension, organization, and synthesis of knowledge, rather than filling the mind with information. Whenever we teach concepts, we show the practical application of the thought, then invite discussion and feedback from the learner. Our students feel the need to learn and to contribute to what, why, and how they learn. What is to be learned relates to the individual's current life situation and tasks. All the content and processes of our program have some meaningful relationship to the student's past experiences, which are used as a learning resource. For instance, some of our candidates have a background in psychological counseling, which can be an asset in the one-to-one helping relationship of spiritual direction. Psychologists have a great understanding of human nature. However, the starting point, context, focus of content, and goal of spiritual direction is different from counseling. There is also a difference in the kind of relationship established between the two people involved. So, the expertise of the psychologist must be radically re-oriented to the spiritual focus of the individual's relationship to God, religious experience, and prayer life. Still, their proficiency is a valuable learning resource. As a teacher, I most enjoy drawing out the learner's response to the material I present based on their understanding and capabilities. I ultimately learn more about the art and science of spiritual direction from the feedback of the students.

Maturity of Faith and Life Through Discipline

Christ the teacher does not merely impart information; he transforms souls. He is the one who leads us out of darkness, ignorance, sin, and death, and carries us from mortality to eternal life. He fulfills the role of the educator: the Latin word "e-ducere" means *educate* or to lead out of darkness. Paideia, the Greek term from which we derive pedagogy, indicates bringing children through education from childhood to mature adult life. The purpose of education is to develop the full person—spirit, intellect, and body—and help them to maturity. Paideia aims to actively mold the young, encouraging them to pursue excellence in virtue while recognizing and embracing the true, the good, and the beautiful. Educator John Ruskin wrote: "the entire object of true education is to make people not merely do the right things but to enjoy them; not merely industrious; but to love industry; not merely learned; but to love knowledge; not merely pure, but to love purity; not merely just, but to hunger and thirst after justice."[3]

Clement of Alexandria referred to Christ the Educator who brings us to fullness of life and maturity in our faith. Jesus gathers disciples, whom he calls children, and leads them to maturity in the truth and imitation of his life. Salvation includes education of the soul leading to maturity. Jesus himself was made perfect through suffering and became the source of eternal salvation to all who obey him (cf. Heb 5:8-9). St. Paul uses the term "discipline" in describing the education and training of the person to maturity of faith and life:

And you have forgotten the exhortation that addresses you as children— "My child, do not regard lightly the discipline of the Lord, or lose heart when you are punished by him; for the Lord disciplines those whom he loves, and chastises every child whom he accepts." Endure trials for the sake of discipline. God is treating you as children; for what child is there whom a parent does not discipline? If you do not have that discipline in which all children share, then you are illegitimate and not his children. Moreover, we had human parents to discipline us, and we respected them. Should we not be even more willing to be subject to the Father of spirits and live? For they disciplined us for a short time as seemed best to them, but he disciplines us for our good, in order that we may share his holiness. Now, discipline always seems painful rather than pleasant at the time, but later it yields the peaceful fruit

---

[3] John Ruskin, *Unto This Last and Other Writings*, ed. Clive Wilmer (London, Penguin Classics, 1985), 137.

of righteousness to those who have been trained by it. (Heb 12:5-11).

Discipline in the Christian faith involves attending to the individual with a fatherly and motherly care to convey the presence of Christ and his merciful gaze. A parent disciplines his or her child with gentle care and enlightenment toward the good, explaining from experience the meaning of life. Pope Francis notes:

> The Church will have to initiate everyone—priests, religious and laity—into this 'art of accompaniment' which teaches us to remove our sandals before the sacred ground of the other (cf. Ex 3:5). The pace of this accompaniment must be steady and reassuring, reflecting our closeness and our compassionate gaze which also heals, liberates, and encourages growth in the Christian life.[4]

To make disciples we must invest in people and be available to them in companionship.

Jesus invested himself completely in his Apostles as his companions. He then commissioned his Apostles to make disciples of all the nations, and to teach them all he commanded them (cf. Mt 28:19-20). The Apostles developed a body of teaching about Jesus based on the Scriptures. Teachers appeared as an office in the Church. Sound doctrine and the apostolic traditions were thus preserved and explained. For those who had accepted the faith an explanation of their belief was necessary. From the moment of

---

[4] Pope Francis, *Evangelii Gaudium*, 169 (Libreria Editrice Vaticana, 2013), Vatican Website, https://www.vatican.va/content/ francesco/en/apost_exhortations/documents/papa-francesco_esortazione-ap_20131124_evangelii-gaudium.html

Pentecost, the Apostles are inspired to teach the faith with passion. Scott Hahn describes their efforts:

> In the Acts of the Apostles, we find them training others in basic prayer and worship. We find them delivering lessons in history. We find them guiding advanced disciples, like Apollos, still deeper in their knowledge of Christian theology and sacraments (see Acts 18:24-25). To make their points, the apostles are willing to be dramatic—to rend their garments and strike the standard poses of orators. They've studied broadly in secular culture, and they're able to draw from popular poetry and philosophy. They refer to current events. They draw analogies and comparisons—to sports, family life, the trades, and the military—in order to make themselves understood. Most remarkably, they're able to range familiarly through all the Scriptures, calling witnesses from Israel's law, prophets, psalms, and chronicles. They were consummate teachers.[5]

The Apostles were convincing in the first place because of the witness of their lives. They were willing to leave all they had to follow Christ, and to lay down their lives in service to him. If Christ had not truly risen from the dead, would they have been willing to endure all kinds of torture and suffering? Their martyrdom was their greatest witness. Paul VI taught us that the first means of evangelization is the witness of an authentically Christian life, given to God in an abiding communion while given to one's neighbor with limitless zeal: "Modern man listens more willingly to witnesses than to teachers, and if he does listen to teachers, it is because they

---

[5] Hahn, *Many Are Called*, 80.

are witnesses."[6] In order to be a witness to the truth, a teacher must embody what he teaches. Disciples will remain unmoved by a teacher if they think he does not care for them or show interest in them. They will not accept what that teacher is offering. Education expressed through love will free the mind and inspire the soul.

When we train spiritual directors at the Lanteri Center, we personally accompany each student with individual supervisory meetings throughout the course. Initially, we teach them the content material, engage them in discussion, and observe them in practicum sessions. All that instruction is valuable, but more is required. We also help the students process their experience of giving actual spiritual direction for their own personal and spiritual growth. While directing, the student may have a wide range of reactions to their directees. They may feel joy at the Lord's work in the directees and be moved to spiritual consolation. Even in failures as a director, one might be given the grace to surrender everything to God and feel great peace. One may feel resistance to a directee expressing anger or vulnerability, which might distance the director from the directee. There may be areas of unfreedom, blind spots, unresolved issues, and other life experiences that color one's experience of giving direction, perhaps even leading to spiritual desolations. Supervision is an opportunity to help students to discover and be affirmed in their gifts as directors. It also gives me great joy as a supervisor to see our students grow in greater interior freedom and self-awareness to become better directors through challenging situations. We are companions and co-discerners with our students on their journey, which ultimately engenders greater commitment to our ministry and greater effectiveness.

---

[6] St. Paul VI, *Evangelium Nuntiandi*, 21 (Vatican City, Libreria Editrice Vaticana, 1965), Vatican Website, https://www.vatican.va/content/paul-vi/en/apost_exhortations/documents/hf_p-vi_exh_19751208_evangelii-nunti-andi.html

Teaching also impacts us as we teach. We delight in helping others to enlightenment and are also challenged to ongoing personal growth. According to American teacher and author Parker Palmer:

> Teaching, like any truly human activity, emerges from one's inwardness, for better or worse. As I teach, I project the condition of my soul onto my students, my subject, and our way of being together. The entanglements I experience in the classroom are often no more or less than the convolutions of my inner life. Viewed from this angle, teaching holds a mirror to the soul. If I am willing to look in that mirror and not run from what I see, I have a chance to gain self-knowledge, and knowing myself is as crucial to good teaching as knowing my students and my subject.[7]

Teaching the Truth

Jesus had a unique way of teaching. He did not confine his teaching to the synagogues at particular times for instruction. He went about teaching everywhere, on the seashore or on the Mount of Beatitudes, in peoples' homes, or walking along a path. Jesus was also able to use the language of the people to connect with their own experience of life. Jesus used repetition of sounds and words, rhythm, rhyme, and language structure as effective instructional means. When Jesus criticizes the Pharisees for straining a gnat and swallowing a camel, he says, in Aramaic, "You strain a *galma*, but swallow a *gamia!*" (cf. Mat 23: 24). Not only is the imagery striking, but the wording is catchy and memorable. Jesus did not use the technical or scholarly language of rabbis who would engage in lengthy disputations

---

[7] Parker J. Palmer, Megan Scribner, *The Courage to Teach Guide for Reflection and Renewal* (Hoboken, NJ, John Wiley & Sons, 2007), 102.

over the interpretation of the Law. He instead used the common language of the people of the day, their figures of speech and ordinary discourse. He borrowed from the agrarian culture using down-to-earth imagery about seeds and planting, growth, and harvest to make his points. Jesus commonly used simple and clear stories close to the life experience of the people that would challenge people to re-imagine God and his kingdom.

Pope Francis suggests we need a new language of parables to convey the faith in our contemporary culture:

> We must be bold enough to discover new signs and new symbols, new flesh to embody and communicate the word, and different forms of beauty which are valued in different cultural settings, including those unconventional modes of beauty which may mean little to the evangelizers, yet prove particularly attractive for others.[8]

Storytelling, drama and movement are artistic processes that can enhance religious education.

> Stories help us get beyond established defenses, slow down the established defenses, slow down the processes of judgment, and cultivate alternative perspectives. They pull hidden memories to the surface, encourage self-examination without condemnation, suggest levels of selfhood the dentist never sees, and document the detours that develop between intention and action.[9]

---

[8] Pope Francis, *Evangelii Gaudium*, 167.

[9] John Shea, *Gospel Light, Jesus Stories for Spiritual Consciousness* (New York: Crossroad, 1998), 45.

Stories make learning new insights a delightful experience. St. Gregory of Nyssa warned that "concepts create idols; only wonder comprehends anything."[10] Experience engages the whole person—mind, emotion, will, memory, imagination, and body—and takes us in unpredictable directions. Our conscious minds are only the tip of the iceberg in our overall knowing. Gloria Durka maintains:

> There is an immense amount of evidence suggesting that unconscious processes make up by far the greater portion of mental activity. These include intuition, creative imagination, spiritual awareness, and dreams, to mention a few. This shows that the power of attitudes, beliefs, suggestions, expectation and imagining greatly influence perception, behavior, and health. Unconscious knowing has been demonstrated to be a more pervasive aspect of human experience than we had thought. Biofeedback, hypnotic suggestion, and holistic healing continue to inform our theories of knowledge. Individual and cultural beliefs about potentialities greatly affect actual human potential. Human potentiality is far greater than is ordinarily realized. Studies of aware-ness, imagination, empathic understanding, creativity, altruistic love, for example, support this statement.[11]

When we pray about the truths of our faith, God engages our whole being, and we come to greater conviction in our belief. We can appropriate truths at a deeper level as God is speaking into our life experience.

---

[10] Gregory of Nyssa, Goodreads Website, https://www.goodreads.com/quotes/485600-concepts-create-idols-only-wonder-comprehends-anything

[11] Gloria Durka, *The Teacher's Calling, A Spirituality for Those Who Teach* (Mahwah, NJ, Paulist Press, 2002), 42.

Here, another book is opened: the book of life. We pass from thoughts to reality. To the extent that we are humble and faithful, we discover in meditation the movements that stir the heart, and we are able to discern them. It is a question of acting truthfully in order to come into the light: "Lord, what do you want me to do?"[12]

St. Ignatius of Loyola continued to teach catechism until the end of his life. Part of his teaching method was to assign prayer exercises based on the content of his class so that the student would learn to integrate that truth into his life. His goal was to help the person construct a spiritual vision, to respond in faith, and come to a firm conviction regarding supernatural truth. He also knew that acts of love would be aroused in the will if presented by the intellect. According to St. Thomas Aquinas, "The Son in turn is the Word; not, however, just any word, but the Word breathing love. ... Consequently, not just any enhancing of the mind indicates being sent, but only that sort of enlightening that bursts forth into love."[13] Praying about the truths of our faith is a preparation for the arousal of love. In giving prayer exercises, Ignatius always insisted that the student observe interior reactions that occur under the influence of the good and evil spirit, which helped a person to rudimentary discernment of spirits. He also used the method of dialogue and there developed an exchange of ideas and sentiments between himself and the learner. Ignatius could thus follow the reactions of the student and respond to the difficulties that arose in him. The fruits of meditation on doctrine were great and often surpassed that of simple conversions. One observer spoke of "loud conversions." Ignatius himself explains: "He [Ignatius] gave Spiritual Exercises and explained Christian doctrine. And in so doing, he brought forth fruit for the glory of

---

[12] *Catechism of the Catholic Church*, 2706.
[13] *ST* I, 43, 5, ad 2.

God. There were many persons who came to a full knowledge and delight in spiritual things."[14]

Knowledge of the love of the Lord is meant to lead to union with him. In the Song of Songs, the bride offers her Bridegroom the juice of her pomegranates. What she has come to know of her beloved has led her to deeper love and fruitfulness to offer him in return. Saint John of the Cross explains:

> The pomegranates stand for the mysteries of Christ, the judgments of the wisdom of God, and the virtues and attributes uncovered in the knowledge of these innumerable mysteries and judgments. Just as the pomegranates have many little seeds, formed and sustained within the circular shell, so each of the attributes, mysteries, judgements and virtues of God, like a round shell of power and mystery, holds and sustains a multitude of marvelous decrees and wondrous effects.[15]

Through the Holy Spirit she has drunk of the many attributes of Christ's personality, his divinity and humanity, of all that is written about his beauty and love in the gospels.

Faith and the Intellectual Life

The priest should be a disciple before he becomes a teacher. In few professions is there as extensive a training as for the priesthood, with our long and wide-ranging seminary formation. Still, we know there is much for

---

[14] St. Ignatius of Loyola, *The Autobiography of St. Ignatius*, par. 57, trans. Joseph O'Conner (New York: Benzinger Brothers, 1900).

[15] St. John of the Cross, *Spiritual Canticle*, Stanza 37, 7, p. 552.

which the seminary did not prepare us. Some of us priests found seminary studies to be intellectually stimulating; others found them to be stifling and oppressive. Some theology students couldn't wait to burst out of the seminary to do pastoral work. Even if we didn't enjoy our studies, we still need to be growing intellectually in order to grow in charity and effective service. There is so much we can easily forget from our initial formation that we need to re-appropriate at a deeper level—in the way of being more authentically human, growing in faith, hope and love, and being configured more fully to Christ. St. John Paul II notes that study is not just for the sake of knowledge:

> To be pastorally effective, intellectual formation is to be integrated with a spirituality marked by a personal experience of God. In this way a purely abstract approach to knowledge is overcome in favor of that intelligence of heart which knows how 'to look beyond,' and then is in a position to communicate the mystery of God to the people. If our faith truly welcomes the word of God, it will lead to a radical "yes" on the part of the believer to Jesus Christ, who is the full and definitive Word of God to the world (cf. Heb 1:1ff.). As a result, theological reflection is centered on adherence to Jesus Christ, the wisdom of God: Mature reflection has to be described as a sharing in the "thinking" of Christ (cf. 1 Cor 2:16) in the human form of a science (*scientia fidei*).[16]

There is so much new to learn in so many fields in order to dialogue with our culture: Priests should study in the fields of science, philosophy, history, psychology, sociology, literature, and the arts, in order to address people in contemporary society and show them the relevance of the

---

[16] St. John Paul II, *Pastores Dabo Vobis*, 51, 53.

Gospel.[17] In my own life I have not taken this imperative seriously enough due to interior obstacles and exterior distractions. My usual excuse is that I am too busy with pastoral work to take time to read. I am addicted to accomplishing things and staying on top of my work. There is always more work to be done. Taking time to study seems fruitless—there is no immediate payoff. Other times I have the attitude that "there is nothing new under the sun" (cf. Eccl 1:9), that I have already studied every field of theology in the seminary and there will be nothing novel in reading something more about the faith. If I do not have a particular enthusiasm for a topic, or need to do research for a conference, then I am just not interested. It is always easier to be entertained with a television show or news. There is also the continuous distraction of social media and tangential topics to explore on YouTube. I have never played video games, but I know the younger generation of priests can easily get hooked.

It is also possible to get sidetracked by our own pet projects and interests to the point where we lose our focus on cultivating expertise in our priestly ministry. Saint Jerome had such an experience. He was born in Dalmatia (Croatia) in 347 AD. After being educated by his father, he was sent to Rome where he studied classical literature and rhetoric. While there, he was baptized by Pope Liberius in 366. While in Rome, he eagerly studied Greek, Latin, history, and philosophy. He built his own library diligently copying most of the works he read. Being versatile, he also enjoyed games and spectacles, and travelled widely. His pagan classics were his treasures. As a scholar, he found the writing style of the biblical authors rough and crude in comparison to the smooth and sophisticated texts of Cicero and Plautus. Jerome was in Antioch with a group of affable Christian friends who considered vocations to monastic life, when he became sick and had a dream, which he describes:

---

[17] See *Gaudium et Spes*, 62.

Suddenly, I was caught up in the Spirit and dragged before the Judgement Seat. The light was so bright there, and those standing around the Seat were so radiant, that I threw myself to the ground and dared not to look up.

A voice asked me who and what I was.

"I am a Christian," I replied

"You are lying," said the Judge. "You are a follower of Cicero, not of Christ. For where your treasure is, there also is your heart."

I began to cry and wail, "Have mercy on me, O Lord, have mercy on me."

At last, the bystanders fell down at the knees of the Judge and asked him to have pity on my youth, and give me a chance to repent. ...

Accordingly, I swore an oath calling upon God's name. "Lord, if ever again I possess worldly books, or if ever again I read such, I have denied you!"

On taking this oath I was dismissed.

I returned to the upper world, and when I opened my eyes, they were drenched with tears. Everyone was surprised. My distress convinced them all. ... I call to witness the Judgment seat before which I lay and the fearful judgment which was held over me—that this experience was no mere sleep or idle dream, such as those by which we are often mocked. After that I read the books of God with a greater zeal than I had been giving to the books of men.[18]

---

[18] St. Jerome, *Letter XXIII, to Eustochium,* 30, New Advent Website, https://www.newadvent.org/fathers/3001022.htm

Soon after this important dream, Jerome set off to become a hermit in the desert of Chalcis in the hopes of finding inner peace. A few years later he moved to Constantinople and was tutored by Gregory of Nazianzen. He became a great Bible scholar, was called to Rome by Pope Damasus, and was urged to undertake the monumental task of translating the entire Bible into Latin, the language of the empire. At the time, there were few scholars like Jerome, well-versed in Greek and Hebrew.

Where would Scripture scholarship be in the Church without St. Jerome? Had he not renounced his vain and excessive pursuits of classical philosophy and poetry, he would never had been prepared to undertake the herculean task of translating the entire Bible. The great Dominican scholar Antonin Sertillanges asks:

> Do you want to have a humble share in perpetuating wisdom among men, in gathering up the inheritance of the ages, in formulating the rules of the mind for the present time, in discovering facts and causes, in turning men's wandering eyes towards first causes and their hearts towards supreme ends, in reviving if necessary, some dying flame, in organizing the propaganda of truth and goodness? That is the lot reserved for you. It is surely worth a little extra sacrifice; it is worth steadily pursuing with jealous passion.[19]

We can begin by cultivating silence in our lives, retiring from the world and media to our rooms or libraries to collect ourselves in the Lord and his truth. We need the will to renunciation and detachment which disposes us to the intellectual life. We also need to clear practical and

---

[19] Antonin Sertillanges, *The Intellectual Life: Its Spirit, Conditions, Methods* (Washington D.C.: Catholic University Press, 1987), 15.

administrative matters as best we can in advance. It is best to start small, with perhaps one half-hour of study each day and to gradually increase our time. We do not need to read much, and we should focus more on formational reading of less text than informational reading of too much text. "For it is not knowing much, but realizing and relishing things interiorly, that contents and satisfies the soul."[20] We can reflect on what we are reading, assimilating the text, making it our own. Truth comes from the reality and the light of God within us. We might even consider writing to form our thoughts, especially when we are directing our reflections toward preaching or teaching a conference.

Our study should lead to conversion of our minds. In some cases, we are affirmed in what we believe and how we conceive of ourselves in relationship with God. At other times we will be challenged to new insights that lead to our growth in faith, hope and love and greater self-awareness. To be human is to change and to flourish. These can be enigmatic moments in which God is illuminating us with new insights. T. S. Eliot counsels:

> To arrive where you are, to get from where you are not,
> You must go by a way wherein there is no ecstasy.
> In order to arrive at what you do not know
> You must go by a way which is the way of ignorance.
> In order to possess what you do not possess
> You must go by the way of dispossession.
> In order to arrive at what you are not
> You must go through the way in which you are not.
> And what you do not know is the only thing you know

---

[20] St. Ignatius of Loyola, *Spiritual Exercises*, par. 2.

> And what you own is what you do not own
> And where you are is where you are not.[21]

In coming to truth, we are often led to a journey of amazement beyond our natural knowing. "Love … sees what remains inaccessible to reason. Love goes beyond reason, sees more, and enters more profoundly into the mystery of God. … All this is not anti-intellectual: it implies the way of reason but transcends it in the love of the crucified Christ."[22]

The bride prays for the fullest wisdom and personal awareness of God's love for her in the person of Jesus Christ. She exclaims: "I would give you spiced wine to drink, the juice of my pomegranates." (Sg 8:2). George Maloney declares:

> She has received this intoxicating, sweet smelling wine from her Savior through his Spirit. She has drunk deeply of this wine and has come now to know the mysteries of God's tender and passionate love for her in giving her his Son, Jesus Christ. Through his teaching she has come to a transforming knowledge. She has been lifted up to be an exhilarating, intoxicating love to Christ, and now she is offering to give herself completely to him as he has given himself to her.[23]

---

[21] T.S. Eliot, *East Coker*, III, *The Four Quartets*, In *Collected Poems*, 1909-1962 (New York: Harcourt, Brace and World, 1963), 187.

[22] Pope Benedict XVI, *St. Bonaventure (3)*, General Audience, March 17, 2010 (Libreria Editrice Vaticana), Vatican Website, https://www.vatican.va/content/benedict-xvi/en/audiences/2010/documents/hf_ben-xvi_aud_20100317.html

[23] Maloney, 153.

Through her knowledge of and participation in the mysteries of Christ the Bridegroom, the bride is reinvigorated by his love and led to a more complete self-offering to him.

Questions for Reflection and Discussion

1. When I teach, am I able to convey love to the faithful? Am I able to show interest in their activities? How does this love help to open their hearts and share their needs and weaknesses?

2. What is my teaching style and how effective is it? Have I ever experienced being taught through the "andragogical" method, drawing on the student's knowledge and experience? Was it helpful and could I incorporate it into my pedagogy?

3. How well do I use images, analogies, and anecdotes in my teaching? Have I been impressed by Jesus' use of metaphor and analogy from everyday life in his teaching? How can I use new signs, symbols, and artistic beauty to teach and evangelize in our culture?

4. How did I experience seminary studies, as intellectually stimulating, or as too conceptual? How do I view ongoing study and intellectual enrichment? Am I drawn to study, or do I lack interest? What are the distractions that keep me from studying more?

5. To what degree have I been transformed intellectually and in my whole being by new insights into the mystery of God? Am I willing to surrender to this way of conversion of heart?

Prayer Exercises

1. Ponder St. John Bosco's story and quote on teaching. Pray with Mt 11:25-30 and ask for the grace of meekness and humility of heart in approaching Christ's faithful.

2. Consider Jesus' attitude toward teaching in contrast to that of the Pharisees. Pray with Mk 1:21-28 and ask for the grace to teach from your own experience of Christ's presence and authority in your life.

3. Reflect on Scott Hahn's quote about the Apostles' teaching. Pray with Eph 4:11-16 and ask for the grace to lead the faithful to mature understanding and living of the Christian faith.

4. Ponder St. Jerome's dream about judgment. Pray with Mt 28:16-20 and ask for the grace to make the study and transmission of the faith your primary concern.

5. Consider T.S. Elliot's quote from the Four Quartets. Pray with Sg 8:1-4 and ask for the grace to be transformed more into the likeness of Christ by his mysteries.

Chapter 21

The Heart of Christ

Who is that coming up from the wilderness,
leaning upon her beloved?
Under the apple tree I awakened you.
There your mother was in travail with you,
there she who bore you was in travail.
Set me as a seal upon your heart,
as a seal upon your arm;
for love is strong as death,
jealousy is cruel as the grave.
Its flashes are flashes of fire,
a most vehement flame.
Many waters cannot quench love,
neither can floods drown it. (Sg 8:5-7a)

Back in 2005, I watched an English movie called *Heartless* about a vain barrister named Harry Holland who lives an immoral life. When he has a sudden heart attack, his life is saved by an emergency heart donor. As he recovers, Harry thinks he will carry on with life as usual; but he notices changes in his personality. He finds himself more caring and sensitive, desiring to love other people. Now, he is driven to figure out who the person is who donated his heart. He travels to a remote Scottish town and befriends the widow, Amanda, of the man whose heart saved his life. From there, he starts to learn about love and the important things of life. He falls in love with Amanda and marries her. Amanda naturally loves him in return because he bears the heart and character of her beloved husband.

A Change of Heart

The movie spoke to me about my own priesthood. Jesus is the one who died to save me and to give me his own heart. A priest receives a kind of heart transplant, a character transformation. He becomes a new creation, beyond the change that began in baptism and confirmation. Through the character change, ordination fashions a new being. We see this symbolized in the gospel when Jesus confers a mission upon Simon and gives him a new name, Peter. According to theologian Jean Galot, "since the Hebrew mind equates the name with the reality named, to impose a new name on a person means somehow to bring to being a new personality."[1] A priest retains his own basic personality—the dynamic and organized set of characteristics that uniquely influences thoughts, interests, desires, and behaviors in various situations. However, the priest is changed ontologically, at the level of his being. This fundamental change within is like a heart transplant and it affects one's personality and especially one's character.

> It is ontological because the priestly character affects personal being thoroughly by bringing itself to bear upon the person's deepest feelings. It seeks to surrender to God not only deeds, but the very source from which springs the doing of deeds, the human being itself with all its capacities and possibilities.[2]

The character of ministerial priesthood affects our deepest feelings. We assimilate Christ's opinions, values, attitudes, and inclinations to virtue at a profound level. Returning to our analogy of a heart transplant,

---

[1] Jean Galot, *Theology of the Priesthood* (San Francisco: Ignatius Press, 2014), 202.

[2] Ibid.

researchers surmise that the behaviors and emotions acquired by the recipient from the original donor are due to the combined memories stored in the neurons of the organ donated. Heart transplants are said to be the most susceptible to cell memory where organ transplant recipients experienced a change of heart. In 1994, Neuro-cardiology pioneer Dr. Armour developed the idea of a functional "heart brain." His research showed that the heart has its own intrinsic neurological system, which contains about forty thousand sensory neurons. The autonomic nervous system enables the heart to communicate meaningful signals on its own, acting independently of the brain. It's probable that the memory transmission is caused by this recently found center of intelligence.[3] For instance, a seventeen-year-old black male student's heart was transplanted into the body of a forty-year-old white foundry worker who later discovered he had an interest in classical music. He reasoned, stereotypically, that since his donor would have chosen "rap" music, his newly discovered love of classical music could not possibly be related to his new heart. It turns out that the donor adored classical music and passed away while riding his bicycle with his violin case to a music lesson. Another instance included a retired catering manager with subpar sketching abilities who, following a heart transplant, unexpectedly displayed artistic flair. He was shocked to learn that the man who gave him his new heart had a passion for painting.[4] The heart of Jesus will change the ordained minister at the deepest level of his being to make him one with His eternal ministerial priesthood and to exercise that priesthood in action. In his heart, Jesus gives us the memory of all that he said and did, especially his passion, death, and resurrection.

---

[3] See Armour, J.A., Ardell, J.L., eds. *Neuro-cardiology.* (New York: Oxford University Press, 1994).

[4] See Sandeep Joshi, *NAMAH, Journal of New Approaches to Medicine and Health,* Vol. 19, Issue 1, April 24, 2011, http://www.namahjournal.com/doc/Actual/Memory-transference-in-organ-transplant-recipients-vol-19-iss-1.html

Through the Holy Spirit, his heart memory is operative in bringing his be-ing to bear upon our entire life and activity. We no longer perceive things only through our own eyes or with our own heart, but also through the eyes of his heart.

By giving us his heart, Jesus takes ownership of our entire being. He wants to gain possession of the whole person, and not only of the superfi-cial level of function. If the priest is to be capable of doing God's work, he must belong to God with his whole self. It is not in vain that he is called not merely God's messenger, but the "man of God." Grasped by God in his whole being, he can radiate and communicate God by everything he is. According to Andre Manaranche:

> His being as a baptized person receives an indelible ministerial de-termination by reason of which he will no longer be able to truly realize himself apart from the task entrusted to him to engender mankind into the Body of the Lord. Jesus does not entrust to a man a mission of this kind without engaging him in an existence which is irreversible. This means that he does not employ him for a time, by the job, as it were, as a journeyman or a seasonal worker at harvest time. He does not employ him; he consecrates him to himself.[5]

Sealed With the Mark of Christ

In the Song of Songs, the bride requests to be inscribed as a seal on the arm and heart of her husband. She desires to embody her beloved as a seal. The signet ring that served as the source of the seal was hung around the

---

[5] Andre Manaranche, *Pretres a la manière des Apotres pour les hommes de demain*, Paris, 1967, 51-52, in Galot, Ch. 10, footnote 24, 214-215.

wearer's neck. It gave the user the authority to enter contracts in the family's name. When the seal was intact, the recipient knew the container's contents were authentic. Because it featured a person's official signature and credentials, the seal also served as ownership proof. To enable Joseph to serve as his royal representative, Pharaoh gave him his signet ring (cf. Gn 41:42). Zerubbabel was designated by the Lord to be his signet ring (Hg 2:23). Every action and statement made by Israel would represent and convey God. The bride in the Song of Songs expresses her wish to become so totally ingrained in her husband that she is transformed into his very imprint and symbol of his being.

> Her place will now always be on the very heart of her beloved. And thus, he will never be able to cease thinking about her. Not only will she not be absent from his memory, but she will always and everywhere be with him, accompanying him everywhere, and at all times. And who could take her place away from her?[6]

The priest will always remain at the heart of Jesus as his character seal. Wherever the priest goes he will be the sign of Christ's presence and action. St. Paul knew that God had reconciled the world to himself through Jesus Christ, who entrusted the message of reconciliation to his Apostles: "So we are ambassadors for Christ, since God is making his appeal through us" (2 Cor 5:20).

Jesus is the one who is sealed by the Holy Spirit (Jn 6:27) and is the perfect image of the Father. The seal of the Holy Spirit adds God's certification to all that Jesus does. As the Eternal Son, Jesus reveals the Father in all that he is and does. He is "the exact imprint of God's very being" (Heb. 1:3), which means the express character—the very stamp, mark, and

---

[6] Arminjon, 344-345.

impression—the very reproduction of God. Jesus Christ is the perfect imprint and very image of God's nature. The word "image" (Greek *hypostasis*) means "substance." Not only is Jesus Christ's God's spokesman, but He is also God Himself—the full revelation and complete embodiment of God. The eternal engendering of the Son is seen to consist, then, in the impression of a character. St. Cyril of Alexandria discovers in this character mark the first source of the sacramental character: "The Father affirms his own self somehow wholly and impresses on him as a seal what he himself is because of his own substance."[7] This is why Jesus can say: "Whoever has seen me has seen the Father." (Jn 14:9).

Priestly character is the Father's imprint on the Son which makes the man Jesus the supreme shepherd. The express character of Christ's priesthood is impressed upon all those who participate in his eternal ministerial priesthood:

> The Father who 'inscribes his own self' on the Son inscribes that same self on priests in a very special way. What Jesus was in his own priesthood, as Word become flesh, namely, the Father's inscription and signature on human life—an inscription that 'recounts' the ineffable (Jn 1:18) and renders visible the one no one has ever seen—this is what priests are called to be in their turn by virtue of the priestly character. Their mission as heralds of the Word rests upon the same foundation, upon the Father's self-revelation imprinted upon their own human selves.[8]

The priest, like the bride, will bear the mark of Christ in all that he is and

---

[7] St. Cyril of Alexandria, *Commentary on Second Corinthians,* 2 Cor 1:21-22, PG 74, 924 AB.

[8] Galot, 204.

does. Arminjon declares: "And because she will be his seal, all that he will do in the world and history of men she will also do with him. She will participate in all his works. Without her, he will not do anything anymore. They can work only together. They can be committed only together."[9] The priest will not only represent Christ, but everything also he does will be through him, with him and in him. As emissaries of Christ to bring his presence and teaching to the world, the priest is totally dependent on Jesus and his Spirit in accomplishing the work of evangelization. The Song of Songs illustrates this dependence as the bride is now seen "coming up from the wilderness, leaning on her beloved" (Sg 8:5). According to a literal translation of the Hebrew, the bride is leaning on the bridegroom's very heart,[10] suggesting her utter dependence, complete union, and total abandonment to her beloved. The priest must remain in union with Christ as a branch on the vine, depending totally upon him. Jesus reminds us, "Apart from me you can do nothing" (Jn 15:5). Apart from the abiding presence of Christ, the priest will remain ineffectual. Only through, with, and in Christ will we bear much fruit.

A Life of Service in the Spirit

I am filled with awe and humility when I consider what God does in ordaining a priest. Often, the congregation at a priestly ordination is most impressed by the moment when the candidate for holy orders prostrates himself. I remember the moment well at my own ordination. As I was called forward by my provincial rector before the bishop, I was examined and asked a series of questions, culminating with "Are you resolved to

---

[9] Arminjon, 345.

[10] See Origen, *The Song of Songs, Commentary and Homilies*, Homily 1, trans. R.P. Lawson, Ancient Christian Writers Series (New York: The Newman Press, 1956), 276.

consecrate your life to God for the salvation of his people, and to unite yourself more closely every day to Christ the High Priest, who offered himself for us to the Father as a perfect sacrifice?" I answered, "I am, with the help of God." After the homily, I prostrated myself as the congregation sang the Litany of the Saints, imploring their intercession. The saints were inspiring to me in that, conscious of their own weakness, they relied completely on God's grace to become holy and reach eternal life. As I lay prostrate, I was in awe of what God was doing for me and for his people. He was calling me to share in the priesthood of the bishops and to be molded into the likeness of Christ, the supreme and eternal Priest. By consecration he was making me a true priest of the New Testament, to preach the Gospel, to sustain God's people and to celebrate the liturgy—above all, the Lord's sacrifice. My ministry would perfect the spiritual sacrifice of the faithful by uniting it to Christ's sacrifice, which is offered sacramentally through my hands. I was being called to imitate the mystery I would celebrate. In that moment, I surrendered myself to his plan for my life. I surrendered my life into his. I no longer belonged to myself, but was completely his, totally at his disposal.

My prostration before the altar symbolized my unworthiness for the office I was assuming. I was acknowledging my complete dependence upon God and the prayers of the Christian community. When the Lord appeared to Abraham and asked him to walk blamelessly, Abraham fell on his face, considering himself unworthy to face the Lord (cf. Gn 17:1-22). Priests are "clay vessels" called into the priesthood of Jesus Christ. The task before them is enormous, and so, like Moses and Aaron they prostrate before God for help (cf. Nm 20:2-8). They ask for mercy and purification like the leper who prostrated himself before the Lord (Lk 5:12). They surrender to the will of God in imitation of the Master, Jesus, who prostrated himself before the Father and surrendered to his will (Mt 26:39). Prostration is an act of humility which recognizes that the priest is a self-effacing servant of

God. He knows it is only by the call and power of God that he ministers. To minister means to serve. That is why Christ left us an example of service at the Last Supper. He told his apostles "If I your Lord and Master wash your feet, you must also do the same for others." The priest shares in a special way in the priesthood of Christ, who offered sacrifices on behalf of mankind with tears and loud supplications and was heard because of his obedience. Saint Augustine explains that God did not bestow the priesthood on angels, pure and sinless though they be. God bestowed it rather on men, so that, mindful of their own weakness, they might show compassion to others.[11] Priests share in people's broken humanity with compassion and prayer and act in a special way as mediators between God and man, just as Jesus shared our humanity and became our mediator with God. A priest offers the holy sacrifice of the people to God and brings down God's grace to human beings through the sacraments. God provides for his people through the priest and through the sacraments.

The priest is God's special possession. He is also conformed to Christ and inscribed with his likeness. He should bear a resemblance to Christ who influences all his actions. All the priest's actions should be conformed to Christ, which involves surrender and transformation. The priest should surrender his entire being to the Lord, as modeled by the prayer of St. Ignatius: "Take, Lord, and receive all my liberty, my memory, my intellect, and all my will—all that I have and possess. Thou gavest it to me: to Thee, Lord, I return it! All is Thine, dispose of it according to all Thy will. Give me Thy love and grace, for this is enough for me."[12]

Priests are also intended to undergo internal character transformation within the heart of Jesus. If the priest is ready and eager to carry out God's will rather than his own, he will accomplish this. Priests must completely

---

[11] Attributed to St. Augustine.

[12] St. Ignatius of Loyola, *Spiritual Exercises*, par. 234.

dedicate themselves to serving others, ministering in the Spirit and in righteousness, while dying to sin within themselves. The holy priest can carry out a more effective ministry. In his grace, the Lord could employ less holy pastors to complete his salvific work. However, God favors those who are more receptive to the influence and guidance of the Holy Spirit. Due to their close union with Christ and their holiness of life these more potent tools are more effective. They could say with St. Paul: "And yet I am alive; or rather, not I; it is Christ who lives in me" (Gal 2:20). The priest will adopt Christ's inclinations and virtue by paying attention to God's word while praying. Christ, through his own character of heart, will manifest his face through the face of the priest.

Saint Pope John Paul II was one who not only ministered fruitfully but radiated the genuine traits of the Savior. During the Cold War of the 1980s between the U. S. and former Soviet Union, John Paul played a key role in upending Communism. Biographer George Weigel tells the story of Yelena Bonner, the tenacious wife of Soviet nuclear physicist and human-rights activist Andrei Sakharov. Sakharov went on a hunger strike while under house arrest to press Soviet authorities to let his wife leave the country for life-saving medical care. The authorities finally agreed, but Sakharov was dependent on Bonner's good behavior abroad. For her, that meant no meeting with world leaders or the press. An Italian ambassador named Irina Alberti thought it would be beneficial if Bonner met John Paul and arranged a covert meeting. Bonner was emotionally hardened by decades of fighting the KGB, and not given to sentimentality. Nor was she religious. Yet a two-hour, one-on-one conversation with John Paul left her sobbing. She gushed to Alberti afterward: "He's the most incredible man I've ever met. He's all light. He is a source of light!"[13] Weigel submits that John Paul

---

[13] George Weigel, *Witness to Hope, The Biography of Pope John Paul II* (New York: Harper, 1999), 570.

touched the minds and hearts of even hardened atheists because he was a radically converted disciple. He was "a man of probing intelligence, an experienced pastor, a polyglot, and a shrewd operator on the world stage."[14] Over the course of his tenures as the archbishop of Krakow and the pope, he repeatedly demonstrated his dedication to fundamental human rights, regardless of religious conviction or lack thereof.

John Paul paid the price of that advocacy with his own blood, surviving an assassination attempt that he certainly suspected had been initiated in Moscow. In his last years, wracked by Parkinson's disease, he could still draw vast crowds and lift the spirits of the suffering. He was a source of light because he spent his life allowing what he had experienced as divine light to shine through him. The priestly character of Christ was impressed upon his heart, and he spent his life living up to it by imitating the Good Shepherd. John Paul powerfully demonstrated the Catholic priesthood's impact on culture:

> Passing entirely over the supernatural blessings derived by mankind from the prayers of the priesthood, the celebration of the Holy Sacrifice, and the administration of the sacraments, we shall confine ourselves to the secular civilization, which, through the Catholic priesthood, has spread to all nations and brought into full bloom religion, morality, science, art, and industry. If religion in general is the mother of all culture, Christianity must be acknowledged as the source measure, and nursery of all true civilization. The Church, the oldest and most successful teacher of mankind, has in each century done pioneer service in all departments of culture. Through her organs, the priests and especially the members

---

[14] See George Weigel, "Pope John Paul's Soviet Spy," *Wall Street Journal*, May 14, 2020.

of the religious orders, she carried the light of faith to all lands, banished the darkness of paganism, and with the Gospel brought the blessings of Christian morality and education.[15]

Another name for the pope is "pontifex maximus," which means "great bridge builder." Bishops are also called pontifex or *pontiff* for short, and so are priests, by extension of the bishop's priesthood. The clergy are a bridge to unite God and man, and a bridge among people, communities, and nations. To fulfill the beatitude, "blessed are the peacemakers," the priest builds bridges to bring about reconciliation within culture, just as Jesus reconciled us to God and one another. The following example illustrates this point.

Two brothers who once resided on neighboring farms got into a fight. It was their first significant disagreement in forty years of cooperative farming, equipment sharing, and seamless labor and product trades. As a result, the lengthy partnership broke down. It had started off as a minor disagreement, developed into a significant controversy, and finally erupted into an angry trading of insults, followed by several weeks of silence. Early one morning someone knocked at Jimmy's door. When he opened it, he saw a man standing there carrying a carpenter's toolbox.

"I'm interested in a few days' work," he declared. "Perhaps you could use some help with a few little things around here? Can I be of service?"

---

[15] J. Prohle, Priesthood, *Catholic Encyclopedia* (New York: Robert Appleton Company, 1912), Catholic Online Website, https://www.catholic.org/encyclopedia/view.php?id=9625

"Yes," the older brother replied. "I have something for you to work on. Take a look at that farm across the creek. Actually, that's my neighbor, my younger brother. When he used his bulldozer to clear the river breakwater last week, there was a field between us instead of a stream. He did this to get even with me, but I'll beat him by one. Look at the stack of wood next to the barn. I want you to construct me an eight-foot fence so that I won't have to go to his house or see him again."

"I guess I understand your predicament" the carpenter said. "I'll be able to complete the work to your satisfaction if you just show me the nails and the post hole digger."

The older brother assisted the carpenter in getting the supplies ready before leaving for the day because he had to go into town. That entire day, the carpenter put in long hours measuring, sawing, and hammering. When the farmer came back at dusk, the carpenter had just finished his work. The farmer's chin dropped and his eyes widened. There was absolutely no fencing. It was a bridge, spanning the creek from one side to the other! A beautiful construction project with handrails and everything. His younger brother, the neighbor, approached and stretched out his hand, saying, "After everything I've said and done, you are quite a fellow to build this bridge." The two brothers had been standing at opposite ends of the bridge before they came together in the center and shook hands. The moment they turned around, they saw the carpenter lift his toolbox onto his shoulder. "No, hold on! Spend some time here," The older brother remarked, "I have lots of other projects for you. The carpenter responded, "I'd love to stay longer, but I have lots more bridges to build."

Like the carpenter, priests help to bring about reconciliation among people, especially in the confessional. The priest's presence usually helps people let go of their resentments and judgments against one another, just as a father's presence will quell children's rivalries. Sometimes, a priest will be called upon to engage in conflict resolution in families or communities. St. Augustine was once, by the force of his personality and words, able to quell a riot in the city of Ceasarea Mauretanesis. He resolved disputes between business and local government. Augustine outlined a new way to understand human society, setting up the "City of God" over the "City of Man." Rome was dethroned in favor of the heavenly Jerusalem, the true home and source of citizenship for all Christians. The City of Man was doomed to disarray. Wise men would keep their passports in order as citizens of the City of God above, living in this world as pilgrims longing to return home. The priest, sharing in the work of Christ as Head and Shepherd of the Church, seeks to bring the faithful together into a unified family and lead them effectively, through Christ and the Holy Spirit, to God the Father.

As I have journeyed through my life as a priest, I have grown more into the heart of the Shepherd. My priesthood remains fundamentally the same, even as outward circumstances change, especially in a society that values faith less than in years past. I am still called to preach the Gospel in season and out of season. Every day I must commit my life to God as a priest. Each day I begin anew and seek to realize the gift of my calling and the grace of Christ's ministerial priesthood. My feelings go up and down, but my commitment to the Lord is strengthened with every act of fidelity to his heart. Sometimes I feel like Phil Connors in the movie Groundhog Day, who wakes to find he is living the same day of his life over and over. He grows out of his selfishness and arrogance to use each moment of the day to become a better person, living for others. There may be varying degrees of passion felt in what we do as priests, but what is important is our firm and constant will to serve. Augustine wrote:

> Love is a temporary madness. It erupts like an earthquake and then subsides. And when it subsides you have to make a decision. You have to work out whether your roots have become so entwined together that it is inconceivable that you should ever part. Because this is what love is. Love is not breathlessness, it is not excitement, it is not the promulgation of promises of eternal passion. That is just being in love which any of us can convince ourselves we are. Love itself is what is left over when being in love has burned away, and this is both an art and a fortunate accident.[16]

Our roots, the source of our being as priests, grow so together with those of Jesus in the depths of our hearts, that we are forever one with him. We cannot imagine life other than as ministerial priests of Jesus Christ.

Inextinguishable Love

After the bride sings of their union in love, setting herself as a seal upon her beloved's heart, she extols their everlasting union.

> Because she is his seal, they will thus have the same mark, the same identity, the same name. Your name will be my name. As I belong to you, you belong to me. Thus, does the bride want to mark with her own seal the one of whom St. John says that the Father had marked him with his seal (Jn 6:27). Double seal indeed since it is divine and human at the same time, inscribed in the humanity of

---

[16] Attributed to St. Augustine.

Jesus.[17]

Nothing can destroy their union, not even death, "for love is strong as death, passion fierce as the grave. Its flashes are flashes of fire, a raging flame. Many waters cannot quench love, neither can floods drown it" (Sg 8:5-6). Not even death itself will come between them. Love will overcome death: "Death has been swallowed up in victory. Where, O death, is your victory? Where, O death, is your sting?" (1 Cor 15: 54-55). Arminjon elaborates:

> She contemplates all that is in the world threatens her love, all that cannot be resisted by men, all the powers of disaster and evil, with this distinction between the floods and the torrents: the floods represent above all the great abyss, the sojourn of the monsters, the bestial Leviathan and the 'tortuous' of Job. Behemoth, in other words, the locus of the infernal powers, while the torrents symbolize above all the anxieties and distresses to which the soul is exposed in this life.[18]

The bride passionately exclaims that absolutely nothing could end their love, not even death itself. This is the first mention of death, and it is vanquished by love. St. Augustine exclaims,

> Love is as strong as death. Brothers, who resists death? Listen to me: one resists flames, waves, the sword. One resists tyrants and kings. But when death comes, who resists? Nothing is stronger. Only love can be as strong. One can say that love is strong as

---

[17] Arminjon, 345.
[18] Ibid., 348.

death.[19]

By the power of Christ we overcome death and share everlasting life in union with him. Christ is the bridge through death to everlasting life. Through the priest he gives us food for our pilgrimage to the promised land of eternity. The priest, acting in the name of Jesus, protects his chosen people along their journey.

The eighteenth chapter of Wisdom describes the inescapable death of the Egyptian first-born on the night of Passover, as well as the plague that befell Israel when the people grumbled against Moses and Aaron in the wilderness. God's people, unlike the Egyptians, were spared death because of their priests:

> The experience of death touched also the righteous, and a plague came upon the multitude in the desert, but the wrath did not long continue. For a blameless man was quick to act as their champion; he brought forward the shield of his ministry, prayer, and propitiation by incense; he withstood the anger and put an end to the disaster, showing that he was your servant. He conquered the wrath not by strength of body, not by force of arms, but by his word he subdued the avenger, appealing to the oaths and covenants given to our ancestors. For when the dead had already fallen on one another in heaps, he intervened and held back the wrath, and cut off its way to the living. For on his long robe the whole world was depicted, and the glories of the ancestors were engraved on the four rows of stones, and your majesty was on the diadem upon his head. To these the destroyer yielded, these he feared; for merely to test the wrath was enough. (Ws 18:20-25)

---

[19] St. Augustine, *Sermons on the Psalms*, 121:12, PL 37, 12, C. 1628.

It is a staggering witness to the might of the priesthood that not even the angel of wrath sent by God would dare to cross outside the lines established by God's priests. The priesthood in the Catholic church possesses the same authority but in a more comprehensive way since Christ is the fulfillment of these kinds. While Aaron represents the priesthood of Jesus Christ, Catholic priests also participate in it and carry out their duties *in persona Christi*. Additionally, the Catholic priest has ultimate control over spiritual life, whereas Aaron only was able to stop physical death: "Whatever you bind on earth shall be bound in heaven; whatever you loose on earth shall be loosed in heaven" (Mt 16:19; 18:18). While no heavenly angel would oppose the priest's good works, the fallen angels are forced to surrender to the priest. We have a wonderful gem that we have yet to fully comprehend. Priests need to be continuously mindful of their position of honor and power, remaining confident that when they order evil spirits, they speak with Christ's authority, "you are powerless in this situation." In the presence of the priest's words and sacraments, evil has no choice but to instantly cease causing injury. Through his priests, Christ has the power to protect his people and lead them to everlasting salvation.

The bride remarks that love is like a blazing fire, with bursts of flame. All that might approach or hurt her is annihilated and devoured by the living flame of her bridegroom. As the object of the bridegroom's love, she is surrounded by a ring of fire. In all theophanies of Horeb and Carmel, as well as Pentecost later, fire is the sign of the Lord. His fire, the blazing Holy Spirit, is the flame of love. The bride is aware that nothing will ever be able to put out this roaring blaze. The priest is inflamed with the burning abyss of love of the Sacred Heart of Jesus, transplanted into the priest, which animates all that he does. Priestly character is imprinted on personal being and impacts his entire existence. It expands the personal capacity for existence and imparts the capacity required to bring to life whatever is implied in the mission of the shepherd carried out in the name of Christ. The imprint that etches the traits of Christ the Shepherd onto the depths of our being is animated by dynamic power and is a blueprint by which to live. It strives to mobilize all personal resources and powers for the sake of pastoral existence. We should see in that mark an energy meant to burst, the energy of Christ the Shepherd that seizes one's entire being to grasp one's activity and confer upon it the much wider dimensions of Christ's own mission. Thus, priestly power engages all the vital powers of a human being to raise them to a higher level.

The flood waters of the Song of Songs, far from extinguishing love, paradoxically stoke it. St. Francis de Sales writes:

> The waters and tribulations and the floods of persecution cannot drown out love. Moreover, not only does it not die, but love grows richer in poverty. It grows in abjection and humility. It rejoices amid tears. It is strengthened when abandoned by justice and deprived of its help, when, if it claims it, nobody gives it. It is recreated amid compassion and empathy when it is surrounded by miserable and suffering people. It is delighted to give up all kinds of sensual and worldly delights to obtain purity and clarity of heart. It is courageous when it puts an end to wars, quarrels, and dissents, and has only contempt for temporal grandeurs and reputations. It is strengthened by all kinds of suffering. And it knows that its true life is to die for the Bridegroom.[20]

The priesthood becomes a vision of the world burning with the universal fire of love, through the Lord who said, "I came to bring fire to the earth, and how I wish it were already kindled!" (Lk 12:49).

---

[20] St. Francis de Sales, *Treatise on the Love of God*, Book XII, ch. XII..

Nothing will ever end the love of the Bridegroom for his bride. The priesthood itself is eternal and shall never pass away. The union of the priest with Christ the eternal high priest lasts forever. Scott Hahn elaborates:

> They're called to be priests forever. They're called to something permanent—more permanent than marriage, which lasts only as long as both spouses are living. Priesthood is more permanent than the Pyramids of Giza and the Colosseum, more permanent, in fact, than the Himalayas. Long after the mountains are worn to dust, Peter and Paul, Ignatius and Cyprian, and your local pastor will still be priests.[21]

In his funeral oration for the death of his dear friend and priest, Gregory Nazianzus proclaimed that Basil, would eternally be a priest in heaven: "And now he is in heaven, where, if I mistake not, he is offering sacrifices for us, and praying for the people, for though he has left us, he has not entirely left us."[22] Saint Therese, patroness of priests, wanted to spend her heaven doing good for people on earth. As priests, we will forever be exercising our priesthood in union with Christ, the great High Priest, on behalf of God's holy people. The Indian poet Rabindranath Tagore expresses well our aspirations:

> Let Your love play upon my voice and rest on my silence.
> Let it pass through my heart into all my movements.

---

[21] Hahn, *Many Are Called*, 148-149.
[22] Gregory of Nazianzus, *Orations*, 43, 80, *Funeral Oration on St. Basil the Great*, New Advent Website, https://www.newadvent.org/fathers/310243.htm

Let Your love, like stars, shine in the darkness of my sleep and dawn
in my awakening.

Let it burn in the flame of my desires and flow in all currents of my
own love.

Let me carry Your love in my life as a harp does its music,

And give it back to You at last with my life.[23]

Questions for Reflection and Discussion

1. How does the character transformation of ministerial priesthood affect your deepest feelings? To what degree do you assimilate Christ's opinions, values, attitudes, and inclinations to virtue at a profound level. How aware are you of this phenomenon?

2. In what way do you experience utter dependence, complete union, and total abandonment to God in your priesthood? How does prostrating yourself express humility before God in your broken humanity and unworthiness to serve the Lord? How do you rely on the call and power of God to ministers?

3. Where do you see the priesthood impacting not only the Church, but wider culture? Do you ever conceive of your role as a peace-maker and a bridge-builder in the Church and in society? In what way do you perceive a connection between greater holiness and more fruitful ministry?

4. In what way have you experienced love in your priesthood as a "temporary madness" or passion like St. Augustine? How have you experienced love in your priesthood as a quiet and subtle com-mitment to serve the Lord regardless of feeling?

---

[23] Rabindranath Tagore, *The English writings of Rabindranath Tagore*, Part 1, Poems, #55, ed. Sisir Kumar Das, New Dehli, India, Sshitya Akademi, 2004), 233.

5. How is your love as a priest fueled in the face of persecution, poverty, abjection, humility, and tears? In what way is your love strengthened when abandoned by justice and deprived of its help? How is it re-created amid compassion and empathy when it is surrounded by miserable and suffering people?

Prayer Exercises

1. Ponder the Galot quotation on character change and the accounts of the heart transplant recipients. Pray with Sg 8:5-7a and ask for the grace to be the character seal of Christ.
2. Consider the author's experience of lying prostrate at ordination and ponder the moment you were ordained a priest. Pray with Nm 20:2-8 or Gn 17:1-22 and ask for the grace of humility and awe at God's call to you as a priest.
3. Reflect on the Proehle quote about the cultural impact of the Catholic priesthood and the story of the carpenter. Pray with Eph 2:11-21 and ask for the grace to be a peacemaker after the heart of Jesus.
4. Ponder the quote from Augustine about love being strong as death. Pray with Ws 18:20-25 or Sg 8:5-7 and ask for the grace to overcome the forces of death with your priestly authority.
5. Ponder the St. Francis de Sales quote about love growing in the face of trials and persecution. Pray with Sg 8:5-7 and ask for the grace to conquer evil through love.